AT THE CROSSROADS

AT THE CROSSROADS

An Astrologer Looks at these Turbulent Times

Jessica Murray

Jessica Murray MotherSky Press
San Francicso

For information about special discounts for bulk purchases for educational, business, or sales promotional use, contact MotherSkyPress@gmail.com.

First Jessica Murray MotherSky Press printing, June 24, 2012

Library of Congress Control Number: 2012911178

Cover design by Dee Turman
Author Photograph by Jason Langer

ISBN-13: 978-0-9814875-1-9
ISBN-10: 0-9814875-1-3

Printed in the United States of America on acid-free paper
10 9 8 7 6 5 4 3 2

Acknowledgment

Portions of this book first appeared, in altered form, in
The Mountain Astrologer Magazine,
MotherSky.com, and
DayKeeperJournal.com

ABOUT THE AUTHOR

Jessica Murray has been writing cultural commentary and practicing astrology since 1975. After graduating from Brown University in psychology, fine arts and linguistics, Jessica toured with a political theatre group before moving to San Francisco where a study of Jung led her to astrology.

Her first book was *Soul-Sick Nation: An Astrologer's View of America* (Jessica Murray, MotherSky Press, 2008). Jessica offers a lecture series, a monthly *Skywatch* column and a blog on her website, MotherSky.com. She also writes commentary for *DayKeeperJournal.com* and articles for *The Mountain Astrologer Magazine* and other publications.

She offers a full range of astrological readings, by phone or in office, in a professional, comfortable setting complete with a pot of fine tea.

CONTENTS

FOREWORD

What a task we face *at the crossroads*.

Jessica Murray's new book is a phenomenal work. It leads us through a sequence of scenarios in world events and human consciousness month-by-month, event by event. Objectively, but also very personally, she writes of the things that have brought us to global and spiritual emergency. One of which has been building, cycle by cycle, over centuries. But in this most unusual diary, we see each piece as a whole and how we got here from there. As Murray states in every way – practical, political, psychological and spiritual – the *real* revolution now is occurring in the brain, in the mind, in the psyche and soul of each of us, individually. Now the power for change truly does lie in "the people."

In her introduction, Murray says, "Uranus' pressure upon Pluto suggests the will of the citizenry to throw off its passivity and become boldly proactive." And: "We cannot control the agencies either in our personal or collective reality . . . but we can and we must remain *in charge of them*." She indicates we *can* steward our futures by attending to the present.

She clarifies through events, parables, imagery and astrological symbolism the circumstances that we have not only been in the grips of, but also are undergoing – both as a global awareness and an individual experience. We must be *"empowered or devoured by the transits,"* as she says in her first chapter. Throughout the book, it becomes increasingly clear that now we might actually do that very thing. We have reached a turning point in technical ability (Uranus) to take positive action and control within our environment and within our own selves . . . they *must* work hand in hand. And, in that work to employ Pluto, the guardian of Gaia's resources, to achieve that end over the next five years of the Uranus/Pluto squares. Step by step, thought by thought, act by act.

The underlying intent of the book – indeed, the obvious intent – is to encourage each one of us to come to a non-fearful and empowered relationship with our times.

It is now obvious we are agents of planetary evolution: at this moment it is in our hands, and within our ability, to act in accord with the crucial message at this juncture. *At the Crossroads* is a call to attention to those of us who are in the privileged position to think, act and be in the light of the moment. We are mandated not to bow to the catabolic elements, but to see them as a crucible for transformation and transmutation. We need to work with the enlightenment of the heavenly cycles – that is, with the overarching vision of (Ouranos/Uranus) and within the deep, all knowing powers at the core of our planet (Hades/Pluto). In this book, we see the evolution of a cycle that historically has been the prime motivator of massive, if lumbering, social and global revolution.

In "Mastery from Chaos," from 2009, Murray writes: "I believe we all come equipped with cellular memory of our antecedents. All the agonies and ecstasies of our karmic past are stored in some deep basement of our psyches." Indeed.

Cycles are prescient. They contain within their symbolism an archetypal foundation that is individuated through cultures, religions, races, and ideologies and thence, people. This phenomenon is predicated on growth patterns, which lie within the archetypal *imago* - the knowledge of all time. There is a continuum of unfolding. Events irrupt through the membrane between the collective unconscious into the individual consciousness, and revolutions happen. Throughout Murray's book, we find times of calm and times of hope identified by date and place, as well as times of catastrophe (literally, *an overturning*) and times for action.

The first intimations of activism, and the precursor to our current crossroads, were in the mid nineteen sixties, with the titanic battle between Saturn and the "new order," the new mythology.

It was an uprising of youth and the intelligentsia; Uranus in conjunction with the "power to the people" planet, Pluto. Both opposed by the old guard, the fearful Kronos/Saturn, mythic swallower of his own children. Saturn refers to the past: history and previous generations (who did things right). Uranus refers to change, individuation, collective ethics, as well as revolution and a 'correction' – what Jung called *enantiodromia*: a condition, psychic or worldly, which reaches absolute imbalance, will switch to its opposite.

It is necessary for each successive generation to overthrow the previous; such is the nature of progressive movement. Saturn always devours his children and Jupiter always liberates them, creating a new mythology. The global grip of the nineteen-sixties lived out the collective planets' archetypal intent, and has led to the world becoming disenchanted, as cultrural historian Morris Berman has said.

Shall we continue to adulate and elevate this shadow? Will Pluto remain above his domain, or will he return to his proper place, as guardian of Gaia's wealth, natural assets and reserves? As for reserves, there are few left. The up-side of this bifurcation, this nature/culture polarity, is the brilliance of culture in the form of science, which is trying to find ways to do this very thing: to save Gaia's nature and find repair. The once philosophical divide of nature and culture has become a vast rent in the fabric of our collective consciousness.

Pluto entered Capricorn on November 28, 2008, just a few months before Jessica Murray began her re-minding with this memoir of current history. Her chronicle details the events that particularly express the Zeitgeist foreshadowing a major configuration that will inaugurate a massive reorganization of heaven and earth.

On August 1, 2010 there was a T-square in Cardinal signs. Pluto had moved to 3° Capricorn retrograde, Uranus had entered Aries at 0° while Saturn was at 0° Libra (bolstered by Mars at 1° Libra, and Jupiter at 3° Aries). On August 3, 2010, Murray wrote, "Transits this powerful have one main purpose: to shake us out of our lethargy." She speaks of telluric events, earthquakes and volcanoes and obvious changes, but primarily notes: "For those who are awake to them these transits are psychological earthquakes . . ."

The three outer planets are shamanistic in that they elect the time to lead us, the tribe, slowly and with great solemnity, to the edge of existence as it is known, and initiate us into something we have never seen before. *At the Crossroads* does this same thing: it takes us to the threshold of change.

The Uranus/Pluto square which forms, recedes, reforms again, slowly over five years (2010 – 15) will take us to a place in which we must find a nucleus of our own, while all the time engaging in a massive conversation, becoming intimate with the immensity of the universe, within and without. Working on what you can do and offering up your own unique skills, will not go unrewarded. The events of this time, the world in this moment, provide the crucible for refinement and transmutation. Each of us, you and I, must enter this alembic with a fierce intentionality.

Erin Sullivan
Santa Fe, NM
June 24, 2012

Introduction

Maintaining Perspective

There's a lot of buzz to this era of ours. Both personally and globally, people are aware of an extraordinary intensity in the air. Many of us feel overwhelmed by the chaos, so we tune out. This is understandable, but shutting down a part of our consciousness is not a good plan for meaning-seekers. The healthier option is to find a way of understanding what's going on that allows us to stay sane and grounded. The intention of this book is to encourage this understanding.

One of the currents running through the mass mind right now is apocalyptic anxiety. Groups as different from one another as environmentalists and religious fundamentalists are framing what's going on in terms of breakdown and termination, to which their followers are reacting with panic and dread.

Another current is that of a luminous new beginning. A remarkable number of ancient traditions, among them the Mayan calendar and the Hindu scriptures, have identified our epoch as a definitive threshold. Channeled material has recently come forth[1] that explains these turbulent times as the darkness before the dawn. Many Western astrologers believe we are straddling the cusp of the World Ages, clearing out the toxic features of the old world to make way for the new.

This book considers our epoch from an astrological perspective, though not the kind you see in the Sun-sign columns. I do touch on personal astrology in this book, but mostly I use the movement of the planets (transits) to map vast, overarching macro-cycles, as the earliest astrologers did. To look at our world this way is to see things from a very big picture. It allows us to consider the fraught times we live in as a phase: a chapter in the long story of humanity's spiritual evolution.

Wisdom Paths

I have found astrology very useful as a lens through which to look at our

---

[1] For example, channel Tom Kenyon's reports from The Hathors (http://tomkenyon.com).

confused, tormented world. It can also be used to identify our unique place in this world, for each one of us has a creative part to play.

But any system that encourages us to see the long view is useful. Any language that allows us to step back from the personal way of looking at things, and even from the societal way of looking at things, stretching our viewpoint to the cosmic way of looking at things, is going to help us. All true wisdom paths offer essentially the same teachings about the purposefulness of every individual life, and about the need to identify with the present moment.

At this point in Earth's evolution it is urgently necessary that we cultivate a new approach to learning, a new way of deriving meaning about ourselves and the world. The trove of knowledge humanity has accumulated at this point in history is nothing if not impressive, both mechanically and technologically. But we have some catching up to do where right-brain understanding is concerned.

The hard sciences have sent us careening into the modern era, but they're not much use in the soul department. Ours is a dis-ensouled age, as Richard Tarnas puts it.[2] It isn't just knowledge we need right now, but wisdom. It's going to take spiritual maturity to heal the Earth and the beings upon it, starting with ourselves.

Mass Events

The essays in this book consider the symbolic meaning of certain hot-button current events, the underlying premise being that the ascendancy of a movie star, or the election of the first mixed-race president, or a debt crisis in the cradle of Western civilization are symbolic of something the whole group is going through. Mass events bubble up from the collective mind as part of a growth process by which humanity becomes aware of itself.

Astrological archetypes work as an interpretive schema because "real life," just like dream life, is a flow of symbols. An angry dog barking at you on the day of a Mars transit is a symbol. So are big collective happenings, like political movements, oil spills and tsunamis. Astrology provides a marvelously precise and subtle vocabulary with which to talk about the meaning of these things.

But you don't have to speak the language of astrology – certainly you don't have to "believe" in it – in order to benefit from the distance it provides. Like all symbolic languages, including those of folk tales, parables and dreams, astrology helps us stand back from our literal world and find meaning on multiple levels.

---

[2] See Rick Tarnas, *The Passion of the Western Mind*, Harmony Books, 1991, and Cosmos and Psyche: Intimations of a New World, Viking Press, 2006.

Responding Creatively

Observing life from this kind of distance is not a luxury but a necessity in an era like this one. Amidst the cacophony of our information-saturated modern lives, it is perhaps harder than at any other time in history to achieve clarity of mind. Every society on Earth right now is struggling. Old structures are falling apart everywhere in preparation for more life-affirming replacements.

First and foremost, we need to maintain a compassionate detachment from the day-to-day dramas and the media-generated nonsense that passes for reality. Those who meditate or pray know how much easier a stressful day can become after copping just a few minutes of psycho-spiritual distance. This kind of distance, however we get it, allows us to see meaning in the apparent chaos. We start to feel we are part of our environment for a reason.

With enough perspective we can not only understand, but appropriately respond to these intense times, rather than merely react to them. I believe that each of us chose, on a soul level, to incarnate into this epoch. For me it's a given that we each have all the resources we need to respond creatively to whatever arises.

But to do so we need a worldview that confers meaning on global traumas, as well as on our own. Thus equipped, we not only avoid going insane in the face of insanity in our environment, but we can find our soul-appointed role within them.

The essays in this book are an attempt to help us find the method in the madness.

Preface

Prophecy and Symbolism

During the several years leading up to the year 2012, there were swarms of prophecies buzzing around. We can learn a lot from them; not about 2012 so much as about the human mind. They show us how the popular imagination reacts to the underlying currents from which history is created.

There was a common thread between all the different 2012 scenarios posted on the internet, reported on TV and written about in books. They all described a preternatural cataclysm that would happen all at once, like the chimes of a grandfather clock when its hands reach the midnight hour.

The mass rapture that was predicted by certain religionists, the extraterrestrial visitations anticipated by UFO enthusiasts, the telluric disasters and meteor collisions warned of by apocalypse trackers – all of these featured sudden, cinematic dramas taking place in the external realm.

Coded Pictures

The existence of these fevered pictures leaves no doubt that the public is well aware of the convulsive growth spurt that has been associated with our epoch by any number of spiritual traditions. And they show us how the mass consciousness deals with such convulsions: they get interpreted as big, splashy, literal events. But in many ways these interpretations are too simple. Like the brightly colored illustrations in children's picture books, such images are clear and eye-catching, but they fail to address our need for meaning.

In the same way that pictures of God as a bearded old white man strike many spiritual thinkers as risibly reductive, the idea that a world-altering transit can only express itself as a meteor hitting the Earth, or something equally cinematic, feels similarly unsatisfying. Like caricatures, these images fit the bill for their quick, evocative power, and as such they are good metaphors for the energies upon us. But if they are taken literally rather than metaphorically, they lead us astray.

Throughout history, seers and sages who wanted to express important, complicated ideas have used the language of metaphor. In legends and scriptures worldwide, prognosticators have explained their visions in symbolic code. When the Buddha wanted to talk about the attainment of impeccable wisdom, he told a story about the discovery of a priceless gem. When Jesus wanted to evoke innocence, he told a story about a lamb.

Granted, there have always been believers who took these things literally. There were and are Christians, for example, who believe that evil is personified – not allegorically, but actually – by a red-skinned man with horns, hoofs and a goatee. And there are traffickers in astrological predictions who find plausible the idea of Earth being taken over by aliens, or of humanity being enlightened in one fell swoop by a New Age bolt of lightning.

Endings and Beginnings

We modern thinkers are capable of more subtlety of thought than this. Certainly we are brought up to see ourselves as more advanced than, for example, the medieval philosophers who saw the world as flat. "How could they be so silly as to believe that if a ship were to sail out to the horizon, it would fall off into nothingness?" we ask ourselves. But that's not very far removed from the belief that, after December 21st 2012, the world will end.

I am not even sure what "the world will end" means. I wonder what it looks like in the imaginations of those to whom it is imaginable, for something to simply cease to exist. The closest approximation I can visualize would be an animated cartoon, or a CGI-enhanced movie, where the picture was there, and then – poof – it wasn't.

I think we can be sure that the ancient Mayan seers, from whom the year 2012 derives so much of its currency, did not see endings this way. For them and for other ancient peoples, death didn't exist in a vacuum. It was a precursor to rebirth. They saw the period we are in right now as an organic clearing of the decks, in preparation for the cycle to come.

Not that it takes an ancient sage to see that endings and new beginnings are flip sides of the same coin. The notion of anything in the universe abruptly stopping – period – would be hard to entertain for a farmer, or anyone else who's ever lived intimately among the animals and vegetable kingdoms; or who has witnessed winter turning into spring, or who has looked up at the night sky over a few weeks' time and observed the Moon segue from waning to waxing and back again.

Metaphorical vs. Literal

It isn't difficult to see why astrology came to be associated with the prediction of literal events exclusively. Even in the psychologically oriented schools of astrology, we often describe transits in terms of events in the physical world, because it's the quickest and clearest way to get a point across. Sometimes, in the process of trying to explain the abstract energy of a planetary transit, we astrologers choose a metaphor that exactly matches what will soon be announced in the headlines as a fact.

This is because in astrological symbolism there is no absolute boundary of meaning between literal and figurative. It is quite true that the planet Uranus, for example, is associated with actual earthquakes, and, in combination with Pluto in Capricorn, with literal stock market plunges and the collapse of governments. But the reason these symbols are said to "govern" these things is because of the energy patterns that underlie the events.

Those patterns are where the cosmic teaching lies. A literal prediction may offer the what, the where and the when of the transit, but not the why. We can collect probable answers to "What will the future bring?" till the cows come home, but they will do nothing to enhance our spiritual maturity.

Granted, there isn't much buzz in forecasting that the world will experience... well, pretty much *more of the same*. Not a very sexy prediction. But in our hearts, each of us knows quite well that, barring radical intervention, the trajectory humanity is on will indeed bring us tomorrow what we have today – only more so.

The big news about these epochal transits isn't about the outside world at all. It's about what happens inside of us.

CHAPTER 1

HUMANITY AT THE CROSSROADS

What a time to be alive.

Mystical traditions old and new have singled out the first few decades of the 21st century as being an exceptional period. Whether they chalk it up to the end of the Mayan calendar or the Kali Yuga, to peak oil or the orbit of Nibiru, there are people all over the world who are identifying this point in time as a crossroads for planet Earth. From the point of view of Western astrology, the buzz around these years derives from the complex configurations being formed in the sky, anchored by the relationship between a couple of distant planets.

Each of the planetary cycles in the modern astrological alphabet carries a distinct archetypal symbolism. By decoding the geometrical relationships between the planets (*aspects*), we infer shifts of mass consciousness. The more rare the aspect, the greater the potential leap of consciousness.

Lessons for Humanity

In the kind of astrology I practice, humanistic astrology, the planets in their various signs represent cosmic lessons for humanity. Right now a number of these lessons are becoming available in an explosive rush.

The following essays describe the great dramas of our age in terms of two main astrological themes. These themes are showing up in the form of geometrical patterns made by the planets in the sky; patterns that appear, in successive variations, throughout this turbulent period.

To understand these themes, we need to get a bead on two key planetary archetypes:

1. **Pluto** symbolizes the most profound kind of transformation there is: the process of birth turning into death turning into rebirth. Natural Law mandates that all things must submit to breakdown in order to evolve. Whatever is no

longer viable must die. Our identities, our society and our world must eliminate whatever is toxic and outdated in order to grow into something new.

2. **Uranus** is the planet of revolution and liberation. It represents the force of the new slamming up against the old. Its disruptions and inspirations usher in social and personal changes that derive from the needs of the present moment. It is not our comfort zone that dictates these changes, nor our self-image, nor our ego-based beliefs. These changes are dictated by the universe's need to keep things moving.

The teachings represented by these planetary archetypes are being presented to humanity right now with unprecedented power, and showing up as global issues of corresponding intensity. The more subtly we can refine our understanding of the lessons being taught, the better we'll be able to negotiate the years ahead.

With this goal in mind, let's take a closer look at Pluto and Uranus, the major players. These two outer planets have laid the backdrop for most of the important scenarios afoot, and it is to them that Western astrologers chalk up the enormous shifts we are going through individually, and as a world. Neptune, Saturn and Chiron are also playing key roles.

Pluto: Breakdown/ Renewal

As planetary symbols go, Pluto is easily misunderstood. It is known as the planet of death; but more precisely, it governs breakdown: a natural cycle by which obsolete matter is purged or rots away. Pluto's key role in the transits of this era indicates that we all need to wrap our minds around the inevitability of this process. Things fall apart in order to make way for the new. Living things all decompose; physical structures crumble with time. Whole societies, and the attitudes of the people within them, must submit to decay.

We tend to accept this process easily and magnanimously when it comes to leaves turning lovely colors and falling from their branches in the autumn. But we resist it tooth and nail when we see it playing itself out in terms of human systems. According to astrological law, however, it's the same cosmic principle at work; and the choice before us is to understand it, as a value-neutral and necessary part of Life, or shut down to it and flail around in fear and futile resistance – an especially bad idea under skies like these.

The essays in this book discuss some of the breakdowns we see occurring all around us. Pluto's transits to the Sibly chart of the USA[1], in particular, indicate a dramatic transformation in America's group values. The collective attitudes towards money, for example, are going through an immense shift. How did industrialized societies become so focused on money in the first place? What does it mean that the monetary systems of the world are going belly up, and how do we avoid getting swept up in the deprivation anxiety polluting the psychic atmosphere?

Pluto is also associated with raw power. When misused by human agencies, it manifests as the dominance-and-control type of power that drives corrupt governments and profit-hungry corporations. Its destructive potential has sprouted a plethora of peculiarly modern wars, including one against "terror," one against drugs, and one against the Earth's environment.

When misapplied, Plutonian energy is so ghastly that most of the subjects under its rule make us uncomfortable to even think about. The planet is said to preside over taboos (sex), secrets (cover-ups) and classified information (the Wikileaks documents).

The essays in this book invite the reader to understand this dark energy from the distance provided by a metaphysical perspective. We have to back away from Pluto to get a good look at it; it will certainly not work to ignore it. In its pure form, Pluto represents the sublime force that will usher us into a new world age.

Pluto in Capricorn

In 2008, Pluto entered the sign of Capricorn. As the governor of death and rebirth, Pluto is now culling the dead wood from any and all institutions governed by Capricorn. As was the case with religion when Pluto was in Sagittarius (1995-2008), the ultimate point of the Pluto in Capricorn transit (2008-24) is to revive an aspect of human experience that has developed pockets of unsustainable decay. Governments, corporations and all other patriarchal hierarchies are currently being screened assiduously by Pluto to ascertain their viability.

Capricorn's governance of *governance* suggests the exposure of corruption in persons and agencies that play the role of the authority figure, whether expressed

---

[1] The Sibly chart is the most commonly used birth chart for the group soul of the USA. It is based on the most likely moment of the signing of the Declaration of Independence: July 4th 1776 at 5:10 pm, in Philadelphia.

on the family level (fathers), the village level (mayors, tribal elders), the company level (CEOs), the national level (presidents, kings, prime ministers) or the deific level (patriarchal gods such as Allah, Yahwe and Jehovah).

As the paternal archetype is being purged, we are seeing a sea change in the global acceptance of women in positions of leadership. In addition, the whole notion of federalism is being shaken to its core, while regionalism and local authority are enjoying a new ascendancy (clues of this trend have been in the air for a while: consider the flurry of state challenges to Washington's environmental policies, and the emphasis placed by sustainable agriculture upon edibles being locally grown).

To understand this sixteen-year transit in big-picture terms is to see that Plutonian change is neither about punishment nor about demonstrating right-and-wrong thinking. All Pluto cares about is ridding the global organism of toxins in a certain arena, so that the world body as a whole can survive.

Uranus: Revolution

Uranus is the planet of explosions. It is famously associated with earthquakes, sudden storms and other freak telluric activity. There has definitely been an uptick, globally, in these events, as well as more forest fires and floods. But if our intention is to pick out patterns of meaning from the flow of events, it is the cultural explosions that deserve our particular attention.

The technological changes taking place right now, for example, are inciting a veritable revolution of consciousness. Uranus, the planet of advanced machines, is triggering social and intellectual shifts that historians of the future will see as having defined this era.

Uranus has also played a role in the financial shocks resulting from the lending industry's gambling spree. The following essays suggest that there are ways to use even economic disruption creatively. When we view urgent situations like these in a non-evaluative way – as neither bad nor good, just intense – real genius is unleashed.

Uranus rules the concept of freedom in general and democracy in particular. Since the planet's entry into Aries (activism, anger) in the spring of 2010 we have seen a significant upsurge of ideological defiance worldwide, and an astounding number of breakaway movements, one after the other. The essays below look at the populist impulse that has been exploding since the Uranus in Aries transit series began and which will only get stronger still.

Uranus is not operating alone. Its tense angles with Saturn and Pluto have been giving it a particular punch. It is in combination that these planets augur world-altering scenarios. The complex patterns that result have their own unfolding cycle; a developmental arc that helps us understand what's going on at ground level. For example, we can better understand the implications of the WikiLeaks revelations of late 2010, which took place when Saturn and Uranus were opposed in the sky, by making note of an earlier political bombshell that took place on the day the opposition began. That was on November 4th, 2008, the day Barack Obama was elected president of the USA.

Another theme in the following essays is Uranus's challenge to our psychological and spiritual complacency. Uranus despises the stale and lifeless, and doesn't think much of the familiar. Its transits are pushing us to question society's notions of what constitutes normalcy. It is daring us to question our own personal status quo, to embrace the possibility of something more exciting.

Pluto-Uranus Square

During the pivotal years 2010-16, Pluto and Uranus are significantly configuring in what is known as a *square*, which means that the two planets are a quarter of the sky away from each other. Planets in square aspect are equally weighted but incompatible. The sense of tension between them derives from the confrontation between an archetypally masculine element, like fire, and an archetypally feminine one, like earth (Pluto is now in Capricorn, an earth sign, and Uranus is now in a fire sign, Aries).

The most enduring and most potent of the assembled forces, the Uranus-Pluto square forms the backdrop of all the other transits of our era. This tense planetary relationship functions as a main plot does in a well-told story, anchoring the meaning of the subplots that surround it.

As described above, Uranus represents the unstoppable force of ideas whose time has come, and Pluto represents the raw power and inevitability of breakdown and renewal. Together they force consciousness changes in the collective that are – relatively speaking — explosively sudden. Already we can see the accelerated speed that is characterizing this new phase of human evolution. When we consider the normally snail-like pace of changes in entrenched collective consciousness, it is nothing short of astonishing that a massive shift in popular awareness about, for example, global warming has happened in no more than a couple of years' time – thanks not just to Al Gore, but to the Saturn-Neptune opposition (2006-07) and the square between Jupiter (social reform) and Uranus (revelation) (2010-11).

The Dark Mysteries Revolutionized

If we agree that Uranus' job is to revolutionize whatever it touches, then its function here must be to drastically change the meaning of everything under Plutonian governance. In this confrontation between the planet of science and the planet of secrets, even death will face the Uranian challenge.

We have seen that the notion of physical death began to shift dramatically when the Uranus square yanked Pluto into the 21st century. Experimental life-extension technologies are pushing and pulling at mass assumptions about this most dreaded of human experiences, with existential quandaries and ethical questions coming along for the ride.

The square is certainly jacking up the tension that already exists in the human mind between the role of human intelligence (Uranus) and those Dark Mysteries which ordinary intelligence alone cannot fathom (Pluto). The secular societies of the West are not known for their acceptance of the role of mortality in the human condition; on the contrary, a fear-driven stagnation in the collective unconscious has stymied our understanding of death and shrouded the subject in denial.[2]

The blaring klieg light of Uranus has been stimulating a new curiosity in the mass mind about this and other cultural taboos. Through the elegant balance of a perfect ninety-degree angle, Pluto — which represents scenarios that are often so viscerally disturbing that they are difficult to even think about clearly, let alone act upon — has been confronted by a planet that is, especially in warrior-like Aries, fearless in the face of taboo.

Another opportunity for breakthrough that the transit has brought not a moment too soon is a revolution (Uranus) in the world's approach to recycling detritus and waste (Pluto), still being generated at breakneck speed by the consumer cultures of the world — China being the latest contender for this sorry award. Radioactive waste in particular (Pluto) is one of those issues that is so troubling that most of us try to avoid thinking about it, unless, that is, a toxic dump were being proposed for our own neighborhood.[3]

---

[2] For a historical overview on how the phenomenon of death changed in meaning over the millennia in the Western world, see "The Big Death Scam" in the article archives of my website, MotherSky.com.

[3] It is in the Third World that tens of millions of toxic consumer items have been piling up in dumps, where they are picked apart for reusable parts by, in many cases, the tiny fingers of children (see Giles Slade, *Made to Break: Technology and Obsolescence in America*, Harvard University Press, 2006).

Uranus, associated with ingenuity and pristine clarity of mind, is the antidote to mass unconsciousness around this Plutonian subject. Again, in Aries, the Great Awakener is expressing itself through actions, not merely words and ideas.

The Sixties: Harbinger of the Pluto-Square Years

Many of the essays in this book make reference to the 1960s as a point of comparison for what's going on right now. During 1965-66, Uranus and Pluto were conjunct in the sky; now, they're ninety-degrees of zodiacal arc apart.

In the mid-1960s, Uranus and Pluto occupied the same location in the zodiac for a few mind-blowing years, a period that those who lived through them will never forget. This was the transit that made the sixties "The Sixties": Uranus, governor of revolution, and Pluto, governor of social decay, conjoined in the sky while opposing Saturn: status quo thinking — and KABOOM: the counter-culture was born.

Taboo-busting cultural ideas raced around the globe like an uncontained wildfire, changing the mores of the generations extant and the ones not yet born. The babies who drew their first breath under that epochal conjunction – which was in Virgo when it occurred: the sign of health, work and service – are in their prime productive years now. We have seen some of the members of this intense generation create subcultures of skateboarder punk and nihilism, and others use their Virgoan genius to remodel health movements both personal (natural nutrition, alternative medicine) and global (radical ecology, sustainable agriculture).

In 2010, Uranus and Pluto began taking the next big step in their relationship. The heady revelations of the hippies and yippies are ready for post-millennial application. The winsome flower-child vision has developed into a set of responses – or reactions, depending on the level of consciousness involved – to the crises the globe is facing at present. To cite the most obvious example, the precedent of the Nixon presidency, a casualty of the massive social dissent accompanying the mid-60s transit, found its parallel in the elections of November of 2008, which expressed the same *change vs. status quo* narrative.

Now with Uranus and Pluto squaring, it's like the other shoe dropping. If we think of the sixties as the New Moon, the period we're in now is the First Quarter: the next phase of the cycle, when whatever was begun encounters resistance, and the ante is upped.

But the stakes are higher this time. Since the sixties we have been through the sexual revolution, the discrediting of the Church of Rome, and the tech revolution. We're awake to what's happening to the rain forests, we know about the decline of animal species, and we're aware of the state of the atmosphere and the oceans.

Our understanding of societal dysfunctions and corruptions has become far more sophisticated over the past fifty years. Blind patriotism has ceded to a more informed critique of governments and of militarism. Income inequality has been opened up to public discussion. No longer naïve about the financial cartels that control the world economy, people all over the world are filling the streets in an explosion of genuine populism. We are ready to embrace our responsibilities to a planet in peril, and wake up to a new era bursting with the potential for freedom and change.

Oil: Black Gold

The operative principle that we must envision here is that of Uranus waking Pluto up to its regenerative power, shocking it into dropping its lethal, outmoded manifestations. To have faith in the ultimate benefit of this shake-up is to remember that, by Natural Law, it will not destroy anything except that which has grown toxic.

Another Plutonian arena that has become fatally distorted is the world's relationship with oil. Tem Tarriktar's prescient articles in *The Mountain Astrologer* magazine[4] linking the peak oil years with the Uranus-Pluto square, anticipated what now seems to be a general consensus in the industrialized West: that our dependence upon fossil fuels is untenable. The pairing of the words "addiction" (Pluto) and "oil" has become a commonplace in American parlance. More and more of us have come to understand that the USA has ignored its manufacturing base – as well as any serious search for clean energy solutions – like a drunk who has forgotten to eat. The oil-drunk First World has been in the driver's seat of the globe for some time now. Uranus is coming along to slap that drunk sober before he drives us all over the cliff.

With every passing month, the meaning of oil in the collective consciousness – due to the geo-military patterns that have grown up around it and the ecological side effects of its use – segues into a new and complex transitional meaning, encompassing the hybrid symbolism of wealth and war, power and destruction.

---

[4] Among them, the editorial "Saturn-Pluto and Peace" in the April/May 2003 issue and "The Neptune-Pluto Cycle and the Next Seven Year" from the June/July 2004 issue.

Oil is undergoing an iconic status change.

Uranus' job is to jolt humanity into alertness, jettisoning stale material like a wet dog shaking its fur. The petro-politics of foreign policy, the grotesque profit disparities that accrue to the fossil fuel business and all the other aspects of what oil represents no longer remain the privileged information of political observers, but are being pushed into the domain of received wisdom among the populace. The squaring-off between common knowledge, i.e., that of The People (Uranus) and the clandestine knowledge held by elite power groups (Pluto) is a running theme during this peak oil period.

Uranus Plutonized

Uranus in Aries (2010-17) signifies a new phase in technology that is fast and furious. While the Pluto square is active, science (Uranus) is being forced to confront Nature and its laws (Pluto) – among them, decay and renewal. This suggests that the tech industry is to come to grips with the pattern of planned obsolescence for which it is notorious.[5] Pluto eliminates excess, and has no patience for flash and superfluity, qualities that characterize the current tech-gadgetry boom.

Uranian genius is being forced to apply itself to pursuits that match the needs of the times; e.g., the new engineering techniques that will become increasingly necessary to deal with the results of climate change. The way the world uses its technology and medicine (Uranus) is being rapidly updated as civilization turns to science to save itself.

Popular Dissent

Uranus in Aries is giving the world a seven-year lesson in new ways to challenge authority, and its square with Pluto can be expected to raise this defiance to a fever pitch. Right on schedule, the political uprisings against autocratic rule in the Middle East, Africa and Asia, and the Occupy movement in the USA have expressed the symbolism of the transit with uncanny precision.

Pluto pushes whatever planet it touches to extremes, and pumps it full of power. This presents a disturbing picture of social unrest unless we consider the

---

[5] It is estimated that at least 90% of the 315 million still-functional personal computers discarded in North America in 2004 were trashed; along with, the following year, 200,000 tons of cell phones (see Slade, *op cit*).

powerful creative change that comes of spiritually informed dissent. Our work as conscious creators of the world must involve visualizing a fiery Uranus worth empowering.

When we imagine the sign Aries at its highest – not the ego-driven warmonger, but the fearless pioneer – we have an appropriate archetype with which to characterize Uranus' new model of leadership. This kind of leadership is not just irascible, but mindfully iconoclastic. Uranus has been linked with the myth of Prometheus, the divine outlaw who broke rank in order to bring fire to humanity.

Optimally used, Uranus in Aries provides the people of the world with the courage to shake off whatever political, economic and social circumstances that have grown oppressive. Many are feeling the impulse to assert (Aries) their vision of democracy (Uranus) rather than sit around and argue about it. Pluto is providing the life-or-death circumstances that make this a requirement.

Pluto's pressure upon Uranus suggests the will of the citizenry to throw off its passivity and to become boldly pro-active. Forward-looking Uranian individuals are being prompted to perform from the core of their beings. The adolescent infighting that afflicts so many progressive movements has the chance, now, to change relatively suddenly, and be replaced by coalitions of mature and responsible social reformers.

Ultimately, the puerile arrogance of contemporary humanity itself – that aspect of the modern personality that imagines it should dominate Nature simply because it can – is getting a dose of Pluto's cold, dark comeuppance now that the square has become activated.

The Cardinal Cross

Off and on, during the years 2010-15, the Uranus-Pluto square is being filled out by other planets, so as to form a more complex geometrical picture: a full Grand Cross. This is the name astrologers give to a configuration made up of four or more planets juxtaposed just so, to form a box pattern in the sky. We have the relationship between Uranus and Pluto anchoring the Cross, while other, more quickly-moving planets join in several times over the course of the period, to complete the picture.

So the Cross of 2009-14 (sometimes referred to as the "Cardinal Cross" because the main planetary players are in Cardinal signs) is really a series of transits, a powerful ongoing, shifting configuration. All of its several constituent parts have been inspiring a torrent of astrological speculation. One of the period's highlights, called by some astrologers the Cardinal Climax, took place off and on during 2010. Around the Summer solstice, no less than seven planets came together to form a square in the sky: the more quickly-moving planets clicked into place with the perfectly aligned slower-moving planets, each augmenting the force of the whole.

The essays in this book address the various aspects of the Cross as they get pushed to the fore by fleeting transits (as happened during the Cardinal Climax), as well as by lunations (phases of the Moon) and stations (the apparent directional shift of a planet along its zodiacal course, relative to Earth).

Our goal should be to gradually cultivate an approach to this riff of years, feeling our way into the transit as it builds; getting to know it intuitively, while, out of respect for the mystery of free will, avoiding the temptation to second-guess the energies afoot. There is already plenty of fear in the air, and we should avoid it like the plague.

With transits this intense, we need to ward against two all-too-human forms of self-protection: the tendency to deny what is happening around us, and the urge to control our immediate environment. Both are very bad ideas with outer-planet transits in general, and with multiple outer-planet transits in particular.

We cannot control the urgencies afoot, either in our personal world or in the collective reality (which is nothing more or less than the compendium of all-of-our personal worlds), but we can and we must remain in charge of them. This is where Saturn's energy comes in. Taking responsibility (Saturn) for the radical nature of these times, both individually and *en masse*, begins by looking at our attitudes. To be energized, even transformed, by these years, entities and individuals must develop a conscious attitude. A stance informed by spiritual perspective is the only approach that makes sense.

Empowered or Devoured by the Transits

Each of us is going through a series of unique initiations during the period upon us. Some may be experiencing revelations; some may be feeling that they've been waiting many lifetimes to be alive right now. Those with Cardinal planets in their natal chart that are being hit by the Uranus-Pluto square may experience a burgeoning of long-dormant potential. All of us should try to locate within our beings the soul intelligence that chose this time to incarnate. Inchoate though this awareness may be, the very act of looking for it will help to get it conscious.

Group entities are faring magnificently or miserably, depending on how well they are able to match their resources to the evolutionary forces now cranking up to high gear. We are seeing certain companies, institutions and governments flourish: those that are loosening up their structures, both physical and ideological, and are able to flex with the changes. Many of these may surprise us. We may hear about someone or something that seemed stuffy and old suddenly transformed into a progressive leader.

The greatest deed that can be done by those alive now is to open up and try to channel the urgency of the era in the most respectful ways possible to meet the demands upon us. Is a drought threatening your area? Inform yourself about how it has come about. Is the price of gas keeping you from your annual vacation? Consider the forces at work in the fuel industry. Is your supermarket pulling unsafe foods off the shelves? Check out the information becoming available about GMOs and the way agri-business works. Connect the dots.

Only big-picture thinking will profit us during these years, and revealing the big picture is just what astrology does. Decoding the meaning of an epoch via celestial patterns gives us a road map with which to turn frightening and chaotic energies into power that we can use: that is, it shows us how to channel the energy of the times rather than be devoured by it.

Our Mission if We Choose to Accept it

When using astrology to look at the future, it must be remembered that we are accessing a mystical language that works not with specifics but with symbols – which must be decoded, like a dream. This astrologer's view is that events are not immutably "written in the stars" or fated to happen in a precise form. Though the great themes of a given epoch are laid out in the sky, the particulars of the future are written with every moment. This is what makes our attitudes towards the current transits so important.

In the monthly *Skywatch* essays included in this book, I look at the themes being expressed by the planets in a given month, and explore their impact personally, socially & globally. Also included are essays from my *Daykeeper Journal* column, "America in Transition," which deals primarily with the US (Sibly) chart from a political and spiritual perspective. Others of the essays are from my blog on MotherSky.com, where I write about current events that match up especially precisely with the transits under which they happen, or provide a compelling teaching point.

I suggest that a spiritually oriented approach to the times we're in is one that deliberately cultivates a viewpoint that goes beyond fear. Neither is passive incredulity an appropriate response at this point: none of the global challenges being heatedly discussed right now – by the U.N., by the media, by concerned citizens amongst themselves – is new or surprising to anyone who has been paying attention. We are seeing conditions long in the making rendered obvious for the sake of wrenching the collective into a new consciousness. Our goal must be to get in touch, on a gut level, with the fact that the breakdowns we see around us are signals of incipient breakthrough.

The modern Western mind itself, with its machines and weapons and power games, has grown so out-of-whack as to be needful of tough-love intervention, like a self-harming child. The transits we are experiencing are no more or less dramatic than they have to be, in order to apply the appropriate restorative treatment. And when our hearts are open to the task, we may find ourselves not only able but eager to engage in the healing, as if a part of our being knew all along that we were born to the task.

As meaning-seekers regarding these intimidating transits, we walk a fine line. We must neither lapse into unrealism about their severity, nor forget that although the trends they suggest are immutable, their specific manifestations are not. The spiritually informed response to the current transits is to name, confront and transform – as a collective, and as individuals each blessed with different gifts and proclivities – the transits' potentials at as high a level of expression as possible.

This is fundamentally what is meant by the much-touted truism "We create our own reality," the corollary of which is that we each decided, on a soul level, to be right here, in this particular place, at this particular time.

CHAPTER 2

COSMIC MELTDOWN
2009

2009 was the year the planets starting taking their positions, getting ready for the rare configurations that make our era unique. The year before, Pluto, the most powerful of all the planetary archetypes, had moved into Capricorn for the first time in roughly 250 years; setting the stage for its long-awaited confrontation with Uranus. Meanwhile, a series of highly stressful angles (transits) were forming between Pluto and key planets in the US (Sibly) chart.

For its part, Uranus spent 2009 in a tug-of-war with Saturn. This created a doubly combustible situation, given that the meanings of these two planets are already opposed: Uranus represents radical change, and Saturn represents the status quo. Saturn moved into Libra in October of 2009, getting ready for the square pattern it would form with Uranus and Pluto over the months to come.[1] Also during 2009, Neptune and Chiron were orbiting neck and neck, getting ready to overlap with Jupiter in another unusual celestial event that astrologers dubbed the Super Conjunction.

The symbolism described by the planets in the sky during this calendar year was matched so exactly by events on the ground that it seemed the stuff of fiction. It was in the sign of advanced technology – Aquarius – that Neptune (universalism) and Jupiter (internationalism) made their rare conjunction in 2009, the year computers made the leap *en masse* from desktops to pockets for cutting-edge users all over the world.

Also during 2009, Pluto (plutocracy) was opposing Venus (finances) and Jupiter (excess) in the US (Sibly) chart, an arrangement that coincided with a public uproar over the Wall Street bailouts. And in a mind-blowing synchronicity, the opposition in the sky of Uranus (the challenge of the new), and Saturn (the pull of the old) was exact to the degree of zodiacal arc on the very day Barack Obama was elected the first mixed-race president of the USA.

---

[1] Astrologers call this geometrical configuration a T-square. This particular T-square was striking enough to warrant its own special moniker: the Cardinal Climax.

During a year that saw the planets Neptune (oceans, flooding), Chiron (wounds) and Jupiter (extension of knowledge) coming together in the sky, the international conversation about global warming experienced an abrupt shift. It morphed from being marginalized, speculative and conceptual to deadly serious and urgent.

It wasn't just polar ice caps that were dissolving in 2009. Astrologers who study the US (Sibly) chart were watching like a hawk as the US Moon (home, real estate) was pinpointed by Neptune, the planet of dreams. At home and abroad, America-watchers began to sense the ebbing away of a key chunk of collective mythology: that vague but heavily freighted set of longings evoked by the phrase "the American Dream."

THE DREAM THAT FADES UPON WAKING

(originally published in *Skywatch*,
January 2009)

Now that Pluto is in Capricorn to stay (until 2023) and approaching an exact opposition with the US Venus and Jupiter, it makes sense that Americans are obsessing (Pluto) about their values (Venus). This most materialistic of nations is facing ugly truths that would be much less distressing to a culture that didn't care quite so much about money.

The transit upon us is making America look at its mania for possessions, especially those that have acquired iconographic status. What is it that leads us to bestow upon certain valuables (Venus) a preternatural power (Pluto)? How is it that the prosaic desire to own real estate, for example – referenced with starry-eyed yearning in the phrase "the American Dream" – has acquired such driving force in this country that it has become tantamount to a spiritual quest?

Houses

The astrology of America's birth chart provides our first clue. Pluto is placed in the second house of the US (Sibly) chart. This is the house of our physical attachments, usually expressed through the act of ownership. In America's mass mind, the material world – associated in astrology with the earth element – gets so much more attention than the other worlds (those of air, fire and water) that it has set itself apart as the only "real" world.

The consummate example of a big, expensive possession that has captured the national imagination is the *house*. The ownership of a physical house (2nd house), as opposed to the cultivation of emotional connectedness via family or community (4th house), has become so central to the idea of the American Dream that it has become the deal-breaker for many people's sense of life-purpose.

The housing bust at the beginning of 2008 took place when Pluto (breakdown) was provoked by Mars in Cancer (home and shelter).

Cars

Similarly, when we look at cars as objects, and then consider the symbolic freight involved in the possession (or not) of these objects, it helps us understand why the automaker bailout was initially getting so much more attention than the bailouts to the lending industry moguls. People need a nice concrete icon to wrap their minds around, and a car is a lot more concrete than a credit default swap.

As the Uranus-Saturn opposition starts to shatter everything the status quo holds dear,[1] Americans are waxing ambivalent about big ol' American cars, and the traffic and pollution that comes with them. Amidst this sea change in group values the tide is turning towards hybrids and light-rail trains. The preferences (Venus) of an entire country are being transformed (Pluto). The USA seems to be getting ready for a huge perception shift: that of seeing a gas-guzzling Hummer as a dinosaur going extinct.

And taxpayers are taking umbrage at the idea of throwing their money at the industry that created these clunkers. Thus were the Detroit titans recently raked over the coals by indignant congressmen who, a couple of months earlier, had simply sat there in mute bewilderment as far more gargantuan sums were being authoritatively demanded by the patrician crooks of Wall Street.

Pluto's current transits to the US (Sibly) chart's Venus and Jupiter are leading us towards the Pluto Return of 2022, of which we are now on the on-ramp. A profound change to the American system is inevitable, one that will prove way more far-reaching than simply a change of administrations. The self-image of the USA will be gutted and overhauled. Neptune's conjunction with the US Moon, now also in orb and reaching its initial peak in spring 2009, portends a massive blow to the nation's feelings about itself.[2]

Removing the Mask

A gaping chasm exists between the romantic ideal of the American Dream and the facts of people's actual material lives. Although this has been so for some time, the configurations gathering in the sky right now indicate a meltdown of this "dream" on myriad levels of meaning.

---

[1] Uranus represents the introduction of disruptive, unfamiliar influences; Saturn represents *the way things used to be*. The 44-year Saturn-Uranus cycle came to a series of five peaks when they opposed to the minute of arc between November 4, 2008 and July 26, 2010.

[2] Jupiter and Chiron will also be players in this conjunction.

First of all, the populace is starting to let a big, unsavory truth sink in: that the country's economic gains have merely been trickling to the top. As news of the automaker bail-out blares out of their TVs day in and day out, Americans are being forced to listen to the facts; e.g., that the CEO of General Motors makes seven to eight million dollars a year, whereas the incomes of workers adjusted for inflation are lower today than in 2000.[3]

For several decades now, this disparity has been masked. People didn't notice it because they were living beyond their paychecks (more working mothers, more workaholism,[4] and over-mortgaging the house[5]). But the transits upon us are removing this mask. Realities long ignored are now disarmingly visible.

Group Healing

One does not have to be an economist to see that the government bailouts have not worked. After investing four trillion dollars in an attempt to lubricate the wheels of lending, the only result is the enrichment of the wildly reckless speculators who caused the crisis in the first place. From a metaphysical point of view the economic crisis is a purgative, an unpleasant but necessary precursor to healing.

As the transit of Neptune (spiritual yearning) to the US Moon suggests, beneath America's panic about the economy is a malaise that has nothing to do with the material world. Clients who visit an astrologer these days and insist that all they want to talk about are "practical" issues like their 401ks are missing the point. As distressing as the financial facts are, the deeper issue is that of psycho-spiritual health.

The abyss of difference between the stories American-dreamers tell themselves and the statistical realities of their economic lives is reaching the point where there will be either an unprecedented mass revelation or a mass psychotic breakdown. *[Editor's note: Just such a mass revelation occurred in the form of Occupy Wall Street, a little less than two years after this essay was written.]*

---

[3] The last time there was a disparity like this was in 1928. Justice and morality aside, even on a baldly pragmatic level the skewing of GDP towards the rich is bad news because the very rich don't buy things as often as they invest.

[4] Americans have overtaken even the Japanese in numbers of hours worked per week.

[5] The literal meaning of mortgage, "a pledge unto death" (Pluto), offers us clues as to its cosmic meaning. It is an obligation that could either become as a chain around the neck to one's dying day, or a means to transform oneself.

The cosmos is using this *recession* (the act of receding or withdrawing) to force us to reassess the role played by material issues in human experience. How much does matter *matter*?

Up against The Man

It was not just astrologers who saw the meltdown coming. Many economic theorists predicted exactly this kind of market failure, back when Clinton was killing off the last of the post-Depression-era protections. The smart number-crunchers said then that the answer was not tax breaks for big business but investment in small business; and in working people in general, through good schools, health insurance and rebuilt infrastructure. It seems that only now has the moment arrived for the concept to crystallize within the public's consciousness that money might actually be spent for people (Uranus), not for corporations (Saturn).

What would America look like, if its businessmen were pledged to confine their profit making to the creation of products that were beneficial to society? What a concept. What would happen if the billions now being demanded by failing monster companies went instead into mass transit, solar panels, organic farms and health care? The crisis is inspiring an outpouring of eager Uranian voices, asking once-heretical questions. Instead of transferring our wealth to another corporate boardroom, why not try giving it to the employees directly?

One pole of the opposition in the sky right now invites recoiling in fear (Saturn). The other invites a rupture in the bonds of conventional thinking (Uranus). We know from history, both collective and personal, that crisis inspires invention. Crises usher in new ways of living. When a container (Saturn; in this case, the economic system) sustains cracks and fissures (Uranus), it starts to let in light.

Yes, We Can

Many Americans who took to heart the 2008 rallying cry "Yes, We Can" are thinking outside the box in ways that go beyond the political. An example is the daring suggestion that for a few more billion than the auto industry is asking for, the federal government could give all 600,000 employees of GM, Ford and Chrysler a $75,000 personal-survival buyout each. Some have had the audacity to propose that the government could then take out the whole industry and rebuild it, as the Japanese did after WWII, with great success. What a refreshing change it would make, if American automakers were to emulate that success rather than begrudging it!

A heartening example of this New Thinking spontaneously arose (Uranus) in December 2008 in Chicago, when 240 union members took over the windows-and-doors plant that the bailout-rich bank had shut down (Saturn).

But lest we astrologers fall into the same sort of stereotyping that culture warriors fall into with their opposing points of view, let us remember that planets are neither bad nor good. It is a misreading of Natural Law to view Uranus as the valiant knight on the white charger galloping forth to vanquish the evils of bad old Saturn.

Unions

Consider the role of the unions (Saturn in Virgo) in this period. For decades the government-corporate alliance that controls the American system has been trying to eliminate this last gasping remnant of the industrial labor movement. But only now, in the anything-goes atmosphere of the post-meltdown economy, have the powers-that-be actually had a shot at doing so. It makes sense astrologically that it would take an outer planet like Uranus to destabilize Detroit's entrenched labor machine, the last of its kind in the country.

Clearly the rhetoric being used by bailout advocates is intended to frighten labor into thinking that they'd be better off holding on to their jobs at any cost. (It has been suggested that the reason Gov. Blogojevich of Illinois got into so much more hot water than his many equally corrupt colleagues is that, under his watch, the SEIU had gotten too strong[6].)

Who wears which hat?

This contest is not like a football game, where one side achieves a decisive victory over the other and then everybody goes home. Like the dizzying stock market swings that started with the Uranus-Saturn opposition in September 2008, sending the Dow soaring to record-breaking heights only to plummet the next day, this latest round of the Uranus-Saturn dance is just a warm-up.

There will be plenty more radical ups and downs before this part of the transit configuration is over, after which we should be sufficiently loosened up to handle the series of Cardinal Crosses. Humanity will experience Uranian triumphs sharply followed by those of Saturn, only to be followed by yet another jaw-dropping reversal.

---

[6] Twenty thousand home healthcare workers were enrolled under his watch.

Why do you suppose Universal Intelligence putting humanity through all this? Certainly not for the sake of declaring one side or the other the "winner." It's about waking us up. Uranus, as the higher octave of Mercury, is a mental planet. It destabilizes us in order to make us think. And to think, not merely in terms of gathering old information, but to think in outlandish new ways.

Uranus wants to shake things up and allow change in. Saturn wants to make the process productive.

HIGHER GROUND

(originally published in *The Mountain
Astrologer Magazine* August/September
2009)

Upon the inauguration of America's new president, millions of people felt something marvelous happen; something that went beyond a victory party. It felt to many as if a flood of inspiration was unleashed – not just in the USA, but, remarkably, all over the world – whose power astrologers chalk up not to a man winning an election, but to the epochal transits upon us. The fact that Americans selected their candidate on the very day of the opposition between Saturn (the past) and Uranus (the future) is only one piece of the story.

Much has been written about the world-altering configurations overlapping in the sky between 2008 and 2023. In order to tease out their meaning, this article will present the period in terms of two overriding themes: that of Neptunian meltdown and Plutonian transformation.

Meltdown

As a starting place, let us consider the Aquarius transits upon us in these last years of the first decade of the millennium, of which Neptune is the star of the show. The conjunction of Neptune (melting) and Chiron (wounding) that will happen February-November of 2010 is being introduced by their triple conjunction with Jupiter (increase), peaking between May and December, 2009. Astrologers have been calling this stunning collection of energies the Super Conjunction. It has a particularly poignant relevance for the USA: it is on top of the Moon in the US (Sibly) chart.

The Moon in a national chart can be read as the collective inner child: that collection of needs and vulnerabilities shared by a whole culture. As we know from studying its role in an individual chart, the Moon shows us our instinctive self, a layer of our being that reaches far deeper than theories and rationalizations. The multiple transits hitting the US Moon throughout 2009 (with a tail through 2011) are showing us the tender feelings of a whole populace undergoing a mass meltdown.

Since the late 90s Neptune, the planet of dissolution, has been in Aquarius, the sign of humanity as an intelligent collective. Under this transit we were hit with the bombshell of global warming, a learning curve that is demanding a unique flexibility – a flexibility on physical, intellectual and spiritual levels – from the peoples of the world. The fact that the US Moon is involved suggests that something far more primal is taking place here than merely an increase of geological-meteorological information. It is America's emotional body that is getting hit. Our feelings about our planetary home are changing, and will never be the same.

Unmooring the Cradle

Perhaps the closest historical antecedent was the blow delivered by Copernicus, whose astronomical discoveries wrenched humanity out of its Earth-centered complacency by proposing that our planet was just one of many, revolving around our home star, the Sun. Similarly, the news of global warming has, in a scant few years, ruptured a set of associations that had been lodged in the mass mind since the dawn of time: the perception of the physical Earth as the ultimate solid mass, the epitome of security and stability.

Age-old assumptions about polar ice, permanent and immutable, are being undermined daily. Consider the quiet distress felt by American parents reading their children the Christmas stories they listened to when they themselves were young, and having it dawn on them that, by the time these children read the same stories to their children, Santa's home, the North Pole, may have become open ocean.

As the collective inner child, the US's Moon is undergoing what in an actual child would feel like a visceral threat to its relationship to its mother; more than enough to justify many future hours on a psychoanalyst's couch. Here the maternal relationship is between ourselves and Mother Earth. Neptune is unmooring our collective cradle, and we are feeling it drift out to sea.

The Great Flood

To the world at large, the central mythopoeic image behind climate change is that of a Great Flood washing clean a polluted world. Legends have been discovered all over the globe that describe some sort of deluge (Neptune) whose purpose was to destroy a corrupted, irremediably wounded (Chiron) human race, for the sake of giving it a brand new start.

The 1970s version featured a retelling of the ancient tale of Atlantis, a technologically sophisticated civilization whose hubris caused it to vanish beneath the sea; with the popular codicil that many of the drowned would reincarnate, lessons learned, to usher in a New Age. Global warming is the latest iteration of this theme, including the watery backlash. The Earth's industrial societies have set in motion a chaos of breaking levees, rising seas and animal species seeking higher ground,[1] as they did in the story of Noah's ark.

From this perspective we see that the power of climate meltdown derives from the fact that, somewhere in our collective psyche, we've always known about it. It isn't news at all: the tale has existed since the beginning of time. The role of the Neptune/Jupiter/Chiron transit is to raise this apocalyptic imagery to the surface, a necessity if humanity is to evolve beyond its current state. We are being reminded that, among the myriad potential futures we could create for ourselves, we could choose this one.

When we look at the astrological symbols involved, we can easily understand the peculiar disquiet the issue is provoking for Americans. The Moon represents our need to feel safe, and here it is being broadsided by a planet that obliterates stability (Neptune). Jupiter is supplementing these gut feelings with the requisite scientific knowledge (Aquarius) to support our understanding, while simultaneously stretching our perspective to an international scope hitherto unfamiliar to many Americans.

Meanwhile, Chiron is rubbing salt into the wound. The Centaur has been linked to the universal human memory of being excluded, rendered separate – through the act of incarnation – from the All-That-Is (or, more precisely, separated from our inner knowing that we are *not* separate).[2] For all humans on Earth, Chiron's involvement symbolizes an anguished reminder of our aboriginal untethering from Source.

Global Warming

The phrase "global warming" was quickly enlisted in the culture wars when it first came into currency, and became associated with a parsing of physical events and debates about scientific evidence. In the Western world, we are brought up to

---

[1] Including the human animal. Refugees from drought-stricken and war-ravaged African states are making their way *en masse* to the more temperate and still-governmentally-functional countries of northern Europe. In Equatorial South America, warming temperatures are disallowing age-old farming methods and also compelling a migration north, to the US and Canada.

[2] See Adam Gainsburg, *Chiron: The Wisdom of a Deeply Open Heart*, SoulSign, 2006.

see facts as more "real" than symbols. By contrast, for the metaphysically inclined, the reverse is true: the archetypal meaning, not the statistics, is where the teaching lies.

In this view, climate change is a collective psychic trauma. In the language of psychology, it is a global cry for help. But unlike in the psychotherapeutic model, in this case no external agency can come in and fix us. There are no therapists or family members to stage an intervention. The patient itself, the human race, must do its own healing.

Yet the external realm does provide a kind of help, for astrologers. Just as a patient gets perspective from a wise caregiver, sky watchers can get perspective from the planets, decoding their configurations to reveal the themes we are experiencing down here on Earth. This allows us to respond not merely with fear, natural though such a response may be, but with a curiosity about the larger meaning of the crisis.

We cannot do this unless we loosen our allegiance to the literal significations of the archetypes. Indeed, many astrologers see the literal level of events as being merely the universe's ploy of last resort: the means by which the cosmos gets its point across when the recalcitrant human mind fails to comprehend it in any other way.

For those who believe that everything in life is a symbol, even catastrophic events can be seen as invitations into an unprecedented state of possibility. To view global warming and its attendant Earth changes this way is to see that an infinite number of potential scenarios are at our disposal. The years ahead start to look not like an ending, but a beginning: a *tabula rasa*.

Affirmation

If we base our observations on the premise that a benign universe is behind everything that happens, what clues might we glean from the transits about how to meet this challenge? What would it look like to use the energies of Chiron and Neptune in the highest possible way? To answer these questions we need to return to the planets' raw meaning, and commit ourselves to absorbing, embodying, and actually working with the lessons they represent.

Those who have worked therapeutically with visualization and other meditative techniques on an individual level can attest to the fact that they can elicit results that can only be described as magical. We are suggesting that affirmation works in the same way on the collective level. Many spiritual groups will convene during the years ahead to create such visions together (Aquarius); and many single individuals around the world will explore similar imagery alone, the better to pool it psychically.

We are not talking about pie-in-the-sky prayers for protection, of the type that dismisses the peril the Earth is in, trying to wish it away as would a frightened child. We are talking about aligning our imagery with the forces these transits represent; accepting and honoring them from a place of spiritual maturity.

An example of such an affirmation might be to imagine a baby being rocked to sleep in its mother's arms, to the strains of a lullaby about drifting off to sea in a boat. Rather than reacting against the terror of the idea of being swept away and lost, the overriding feeling might be one of being watched over by a benevolent force far greater than a human caregiver. The image here is one of being released by gentle waves into an infinite dream, as if being welcomed back into the universal *amnios*; not backward, into the womb, but forward, into a state of recognition that the cosmos itself is our ultimate womb.

Our intellects may scoff at meditations like these, confusing them with escapism or denial of the literal facts. But we are not calling upon the intellect here. We are calling on the inner child (Moon) and the image-making capacity of the human mind (Neptune). Actual children are capable of terrible fears, but are also capable of seeing beyond the mundane to the numinous. When we were very young we understood the power of our imaginations. Remembering this power now is an appropriate response to the transit upon us.

Religion and Mysticism

A more-all-embracing willingness to believe, and to work with belief as a consciousness tool, is in the air. When we consider Jupiter's association with philosophy and Neptune's with mysticism – the most *yin* of worldviews – we see augured a subtle but profound change in humanity's construction of faith. In particular, the ideological climate in America (conjunction to the US Moon) is experiencing a sea change. As in my example above, where the child in the meditation segued from its human nurturer to a divine one, those seekers (Jupiter) who are alive to the transpersonal promptings of Neptune may find their yearned-for safety in the shift from mother to Mother.

And what of the father-gods humanity has worshipped for the past several millennia? It would seem that the patriarchal religions of the world have not been very helpful lately in the world-healing department. Jehovah, Allah and Yahwe spent the past thirteen years of Pluto in Sagittarius slugging it out on center stage, exhibiting their ugliest faces. The current transit gives us a hint about a different kind of religious vision.

If we are to tackle severe problems of international proportions such as global warming and a worldwide financial crisis, humanity will need an unprecedented ecumenicalism of vision: precisely the kind of vision symbolized by this Aquarius conjunction. Used optimally, Jupiter (theology) and Neptune (universality) suggest a spiritual approach that will defy religious categories already extant. Rigid ideologues will not feel comfortable under these skies. Traditional frameworks of belief are likely to leak out of their previous confines, becoming broader (Jupiter) and less defined (Neptune).

There are those who will be inspired by the Neptune/Jupiter/Chiron transit to move beyond intolerance into tolerance. And there are those who will move even further: beyond mere tolerance into the vision of a profound mutual understanding among the peoples of the world.

Trans-nationalism

Such a shift will come in handy when we consider the changes afoot in Americans' sense of their homeland (Moon). The Neptune cluster is about redefining our emotional identification with the outworn hearth-and-home imagery of a former era. Though Normal Rockwell still sells well, his Thanksgiving dinner scene looks less and less like that of a post-millennial American family.

Neptune can be expected to confuse our provincial allegiances and loosen our isolationist tendencies. The global scope of climate change and the financial crisis has already forced America to drop a good deal of its notorious insularity. The limitations of old-fashioned flag-waving are already apparent, by virtue of Pluto (breakdown) having moved into Capricorn (national boundaries). Though resistance is strong among those segments of the population who would build walls to keep out the diaspora, the truth is that human beings will not stop hitting the road to destinations that they believe offer them a chance at survival.

Indeed, the old way of constructing this human movement – "immigration" – is anachronistic. These are not immigrants; they are refugees. Globalization and global warming have hit the Third World hard; and chaos, poverty and violence make for porous borders. The Neptune cluster on the US Moon is our heads-up that realities like these are forcing a reconsideration of what many Americans think of as patriotism. The world is moving in a trans-national direction. All over the globe, exclusionary chauvinisms will prove to be increasingly problematic.

Urge to Merge

For those sensitive souls who are receptive to it, the Aquarian line-up is provoking an existential sense of psychic restlessness, even claustrophobia. Among the several planets that are associated with fear (Saturn with fear of loss, Mars with fear of threat, Pluto with fear of annihilation), the fears Neptune and Chiron trigger are perhaps the hardest to conceptualize.

Chiron activates our fear of being broken-off from the Whole. Neptune activates our fear of being trapped in an unreal world. Their conjunction is creating a wellspring of yearning in the human spirit, a craving to reach a realm of higher truth. When this yearning isn't understood for what it is, it manifests as a desire to merge blindly with whatever's handy. In Aquarius, this means whichever organization offers ready membership. From high school cliques to political parties, groups are seducing us to join them.

Aquarius' association with technology is playing a key role in this process. Neptune (interconnectedness) in Aquarius (advanced machinery) has utterly transformed what people think of as normal human interaction. Thanks to the internet we can sit on a chair in the comfort of our own home and dive headfirst into the universal waters of the group mind.

Heralded by the Uranus-Neptune conjunction of 1993, the speed with which personal computers have changed humanity is so extreme, historically speaking, that we have yet to get our breath. From farmers in rural China to guerilla fighters in the Amazon, everyone has a mobile phone. It will be centuries before sociologists fully grasp the immense implications to human functioning of the incessant communication that digital messaging has made possible.

When channeled creatively, this pooling (Neptune) of ideas (Aquarius) is not only healthy but revolutionary. The capacity for citizens to share opinions over the web has broken through government censorship here and abroad. Free downloading is allowing musicians and filmmakers to get around the corporate entertainment moguls. And the role played by web networking in the Obama victory has changed the face of politics. The generation credited with putting their candidate over the top is sending its brightest nerds to Washington to wire the White House. As an apt symbol of 21st century democracy, the new president carries a Blackberry everywhere he goes.

In an immature state, Neptune's urge to merge expresses as a desire to conform as a plan of least resistance. We identify with what we imagine "everyone" is thinking; we release our personal data into the infinite space of Facebook; we run out and buy the same dress we saw the starlet wearing in the movie. Purveyors of fashions and cosmetics make a lot of money off of Neptune.

But an even more insidious – because more subtle – form of Neptunian fantasy is the self-loss that accompanies the process of idolization. Similar to *falling in love* (as opposed to *loving*), infatuation is an expression of Neptune, whether on an individual level or on a collective level – as when we fall in love *en masse* with a rock star or a glamorous new president.

When the essentially spiritual impulse behind such yearnings is understood, a torrent of creativity is released. What starts out as a nagging psychological restlessness becomes the inspiration to pour ourselves into something larger than ourselves – something bigger and more meaningful than our little lives. Immense freedom comes of making contact with the timeless soul that lies behind our time-bound lifetimes. The mundane world then becomes not a prison, but a playground.

Culture Cons

As American cultural observers, we can learn much from what happened during the Neptune-in-Aquarius years (1998-2011), the better to understand Neptune, Jupiter and Chiron's conjunction with the US Moon. In an epochal shift that spanned several American political administrations, the concept of fraudulence (Neptune) has changed meaning in the public mind. Official con games at the highest levels have been grudgingly accepted as normative. Lying has lost its ability to shock.

The lending industry meltdown involves of sums of money so staggering (Jupiter) as to be beyond an ordinary person's conception. And what layperson can fathom the arcane investment bundles with which the brokers played their shell games? With the whittling down of the Glass-Steagall Act, the financial instruments created by Wall Street have become so bizarrely abstract that even their inventors have no idea how to track them. The whole crisis has an aura of surrealism (Neptune).

No More Rules

Neptune's entry into Aquarius coincided with the Clinton impeachment scandal, a paltry sex fraud that displaced all the other truly impactful frauds that were going on at the time. The gargantuan rip-offs perpetrated on the public by Enron and WorldCom passed right over the heads of many news-viewers who were riveted instead on a stained blue dress.

From the point of view of the economic crisis then building, the transit's most significant expression was the dismantling under Clinton of Depression-era protections in the financial industry. It was during these years that outright fraud by big-time lending institutions was handily legalized via deftly rewritten laws. (It is more than noteworthy that several of the masterminds of this chicanery, e.g., Larry Summers, Robert Rubin and Tim Geithner, have been appointed by the new administration to watch over what's left of the federal treasury.[3]) The disastrous legacy of these Wall Street shenanigans was deregulation, the product of an unbalanced Neptune. This is the planet that loosens strictures, blurs definition, makes amorphous that which was once explicit. Misused Neptune undermines rules and governance, creating disorder where there was order before.

With foreclosures reaching epidemic proportions, evicted families (US Moon) personify the deeply personal pain (Chiron) behind the numbers. When Jupiter (runaway growth) entered Aquarius at the beginning of 2009, Americans started to realize that the economic crisis was bigger than the partisan divides that had riveted the nation's attention for the previous several years.

The theme here is out-of-control expansion, and it echoes a theme that resides deep within the national psyche. The Sun is conjunct Jupiter (excess) in the US (Sibly) chart,[4] a natal warning that the transit has brought home. The giddy exorbitance of an American Dream predicated upon the credit card is over.[5] The country's self-image (US Moon) is struggling to reconfigure itself at a higher level of awareness.

Transformation

At the same time as the Aquarius cluster melts down the US Moon, Pluto and Uranus are making a T-square to the US Venus and Jupiter. The Uranus-Pluto square, which reaches exactitude seven times between 2012 and 2015, will have many subplots. At this writing, the strongest of these is Pluto's opposition to Venus, peaking at the Pluto station in April 2009.

---

[3] See Robert Scheer, "Wall Street Robber Barons Ride Again:" http://www.truthdig.com/report/item/20090113_wall_street_robber_barons_ride_again/

[4] For a discussion of this and other aspects of the country's karma, see *Soul-Sick Nation: An Astrologer's View of America*, Jessica Murray, MotherSky Press, 2008.

[5] How telling it is that the word "credit" derives from the Latin for "believe." The forces that propelled the housing and dot-com booms in the US included a distortion of faith (Neptune) to which Americans, with natal Neptune in the 9th house, are peculiarly prone. It is a suspension of disbelief by which we imagine that what goes up need never go down.

Pluto (makeovers) opposite the US Jupiter and Venus (values) is compelling a radical reexamination of America's spending patterns. The global financial crisis has brought to the fore a host of unsavory features upon which the nation's middle-class lifestyle has been based; including an addiction to cheap money, cheap gas and cheap Chinese imports manufactured through inhumanely cheap labor. As Americans listen to the air hissing out of the economic balloon, many astrologers are seeing this as a preview of the nation's Pluto Return in the house of money, peaking in 2022.

The second house refers to our physical attachments, usually expressed through the act of ownership. This natal signature hints that the USA is fated go through radical ruptures in the financial arena, regardless of which economic theories happen to be in fashion, and regardless of what political faction happens to be in power. Pluto demands so thorough an overhaul of the arena signified by the resident house that the experience feels like a death, after which the only option is rebirth.

American Purge

Uranus (sudden awakening) and Pluto (cover-ups) on the US Venus/Jupiter are using the economic crisis as a purgative. Pluto's regurgitant function is perhaps the most unpleasant of all the planetary healing techniques, but an appreciation of the whole transit sequence allows us to see its rigors as just another step in the process of transformation. As distressing as the financial facts are, the deeper issue is that of collective psycho-spiritual health.

The cosmos is using the Great Recession to force us to reassess the role of physical resources in our lives. As we wend our way towards the US Pluto Return of 2022 (at which point transiting Pluto will come back to the position it was in when the country was born) we can see that profound change to the American system is inevitable. If the republic is to survive as an integral entity, a whole new economy will have to be created.

The question that arises at this point is "What would this new economy look like?" and, as astrologers are forever telling their clients, this we cannot know. A certain surrender is required with outer-planets transits, for countries as well as for individuals. All we know for sure is that there can be no renaissance without rupture. The new economic model will rise out of the ashes of the old.

When one acknowledges the organic logic of this idea, one does start to get a sense of some of the qualities the new approach would necessarily possess. We can infer already that if the USA survives its Pluto Return intact, its new financial philosophy would need to be based not simply upon maximizing shareholder profits for a relatively small number of wealthy Americans, but upon prioritizing the health of an Earth now in geological, as well as financial, peril.

The Uranus-Saturn opposition (2008-10) has already begun this process by ushering in a veritable storm of innovative technology. Ingenious scientific and visionary thinkers (Uranus) are coming out of the woodwork, offering up new technologies to replace our old environmentally damaging infrastructure (Saturn). Consider the $18 billion in venture capital money that flowed into California in 2008 alone, some of it funding such efforts as turning algae into jet fuel and developing carbon-negative cement.

Big money could be made on these sane, planet-healing ventures. If there is sufficient consciousness in the collective, the forces of invention and implementation will feed each other rather than polarize against each other. Allowing these two planets to work together would mean that wild-and-crazy ideas (Uranus) such as these would turn out to be actually good for business (Saturn).

A Good President

As Pluto moving into Capricorn would suggest, a popular attention bordering on the obsessive has been focused in recent months upon the changes in our political power structure. But the transits overhead signify mass awareness shifts; their demands will not be quieted with election results. The planets do not care who wins these contests, no matter how high the office or how much cooler the new guy is compared to his predecessor. As conscious citizens in a new era, our work is cut out for us: we are to hold our leaders accountable (Saturn) for the change (Uranus) we have been inspired to envision. We, not Mr. Obama, are responsible for what he does next.

It is not that there was no cosmic meaning in the thunderous political excitement accompanying America's recent regime change. It's just that the real news was the astounding influx and degree of engagement of those millions of voters who had been disengaged before. The new president, with his exquisite intellect and seemingly solid character, is clearly the man of the hour. But after all is said and done, he is just a man.

It will become increasingly clear to even his most adoring fans that the citizenry must embody the change augured by Obama's victory. The People (Uranus) must inspire the government (Saturn) and not the other way around. As journalistTim

Redmund has said, "Electing a good president is necessary but not sufficient."[6]

Death and Taxes

Two venerable old taboos are making a showing under Pluto's opposition to America's Venus and Jupiter. One of them is taxes, a hot button in our national discourse before the country was even born.
It is not for nothing that the rallying cry "No taxation without representation," reiterated in every American history book, strikes a deep chord of moral outrage (Jupiter) in the country's sense of itself. The house associated by astrologers with taxes is the 8th, where America's Mercury resides, and it is opposed to natal Pluto. Here is a case where the pairing up in the vernacular of "death" and "taxes" makes perfect sense; and predictably, both send frissons down America's collective spine. (So taboo has the idea of taxes become that a euphemism had to be devised: *revenue enhancement*.)

During the 2008 Vice Presidential debate, Joe Biden was said to have shot himself in the foot by suggesting that paying taxes was patriotic. Surely this must be so, given that it's illegal not to pay them.[7]. But politicians risk campaign death by pointing it out. Traditionally, the inspirational model of choice in the USA has been that of singular self-advancement — not through public service, but through private business. This ideal, unchecked and unbalanced, has led to the current era of massive privatization. Now, as everything from public schools and hospitals to fire houses and the military is taken over by for-profit corporations, many Americans are remembering wistfully what taxes are supposed to be for.[8]

Neptune's transit over the US Moon is also challenging America's entrenched anti-tax bias. One of the key visions of Neptune in Aquarius is that of individuals

---

[6] *The San Francisco Bay Guardian*, 11/19/08

[7] That is, it is illegal in theory. Hardly a secret, though rarely expressed in public debate (unless the opposition party wants to block a presidential appointment), is the fact that those who could most easily fill the nation's coffers do not pay taxes. They pay instead for the politicians who allow them to keep their money. America's mega-companies have vast legal teams and lobbyists in Washington; its wealthy private citizens have Cayman Islands bank accounts.

[8] Most historians and economists agree that what ended the Great Depression was massive public spending: huge investments in infrastructure and jobs for the working class. Tax cuts played no part in the New Deal, nor did government layoffs. FDR did the opposite: he taxed and he spent, big-time. And all that tax money was scrupulously channeled into huge public programs, not showered upon incompetent, felonious business titans via the bailouts that Obama's predecessor proposed and Obama himself supports.

34

pooling their resources so that the common weal may thrive.[9]

Money for Death

The other taboo deriving from America's natal 8th house- 2nd house opposition expresses Pluto at its most Plutonian, and as such it is almost never mentioned in public discourse: the money the country spends on war. Something very deep in the American mind keeps politicians and pundits from questioning the percentage of federal budget priorities that goes to the military, a tax dollar-swallowing death pit (Pluto) with a lobby in Washington so powerful that it occupies a category unto itself.

What is especially remarkable is that this immunity to challenge exists even now, when all sorts of heretofore unheard-of cost-cutting proposals are on the table. Financial emergency notwithstanding, policymakers would rather gut school funding, close libraries and defund health care than propose withholding a penny from the Pentagon and the CIA.

This gentlemen's agreement to keep mum about the military budget seems to extend to the mainstream media, from whom one hears fulsome rants about pork barrel spending (e.g., re-sodding the National Mall) in reference to every other issue but this one. Meanwhile the Pentagon continues to outspend the next fifteen largest militaries in the world. Its every pet project is green lighted by a small clique of defense contractors who design state-of-the-art munitions whose use-value is either hypothetical (nuclear weapons that are, thank Goddess, never deployed) or ludicrously cost-inefficient (manufactured without oversight and rendered obsolete every few years).

For a debt-crippled nation with a tanking GDP to allow these expenditures makes so little sense that we must look for its rationale somewhere other than common sense or reason. The fact that the subject provokes so little curiosity or outrage among the hard-pressed citizens who pay for it, and upon whose karma all this destruction devolves, calls to mind Pluto's association with the experience of horror: certain things are just too gut-wrenching to look at.

A related subject similarly absent from the economic debate is the USA's recession-proof arms-brokering industry, equally unperturbed by the vicissitudes of party politics. By far the biggest munitions maker in the world, America manufactures, trades and sells state-of-the-art weaponry to other countries. Fifteen billion dollars annually goes to Israel alone.

---

[9] Astrology gives Neptune governance over socialism, along with other economic models that seek to vest in the community as a whole both the control and the benefit of a group's resources.

Morality aside (made-in-the-USA munitions are in frequent contravention of UN mandates), this immense chunk of the economy might as well be black market – as some of it literally is; Iran-Contra, for example – for all the consideration it gets in discussions of financial reform. But Pluto is the planet that flushes corruption out of hiding. Its overhaul of the American economy cannot be counted on to honor these traditions or the codes of silence around them.

A Deeper Humanity

As psychologists know, the energy it takes to keep secrets under wraps builds dangerously until there is either a breakdown or a breakthrough. The current opposition to US Venus and Jupiter and the financial ruptures associated with them are offering the USA the chance to purge flaws at a deep-structure level, and to come up with radically new economic principles. But it is an opportunity, not a guarantee.

Which course will the USA take? What will the nation do with its first-ever Pluto Return? When interpreted wisely, planetary configurations give us the right questions. Answers, however, are determined only by our level of awareness. As with Neptunian meltdown, Plutonian transformation makes use of the image-making capacity of the mind to nudge us towards awareness. We can, if we engage it, use this power to align ourselves with the transits upon us rather than buying into the illusion that we are the cosmos' helpless pawns. The extraordinary era into which we have incarnated is offering just the right energies for both self-destruction and complete renaissance.

It would be foolish to expect stability from the years between now and 2022. That would be barking up the wrong tree. But it is clear that what these transits disallow in terms of stability they more than compensate for in terms of enhanced collective wisdom. All things considered, it could be argued that stability is overrated.

This idea may make us recoil. But to at least consider it as a hypothesis could come in handy right now; because the transits afoot are about something other than security as we usually think of it. They are about rupturing the bonds that have held us back from cultivating our deeper humanity.

Consciousness seekers will have a lot of material to work with during the years ahead. Healers of every stripe will be busy. Light workers will come into their own.

MASTERY FROM CHAOS

(originally published in *Skywatch*,
May 2009)

Congratulate yourselves, fellow travelers. You have incarnated into one of the least boring epochs in human history.

Astrologers are paying special attention to the window between 2012 and 2015, with another spike at the US Pluto Return in 2022. The world is in for quite a ride. To approach the Cardinal Cross years with our eyes open would be a very useful prayer to incorporate into our spiritual practice right now. We are dealing with big energies here, and we need to draw on the highest parts of ourselves.

My first recommendation for how to approach the next few years with a maximum of grace and a minimum of fear is to remember that, on some level, we chose to be here. (Granted, not everybody believes that they have an immortal soul that selects what dimension they want to incarnate into, and where on the Earth they want to live it out. But if one does profess to such a belief, now is a good time to consider its implications.)

Such consideration is not merely an abstract exercise. It's a rush. When we get in touch with the part of ourselves that "remembers" why we incarnated here and now – instead of, say, 12th-century France, or prehistoric China – something in us explodes open.

Soul Intention

I believe we all come equipped with cellular memory of our antecedents. All the agonies and ecstasies of our karmic past are stored in some deep basement of our psyche. When we access this part of our knowing, something in our awareness that was disconnected before is suddenly connected, igniting a new state of aliveness. We *get it*, on a visceral level: that we and the world around us are part of the same system. At this point we start looking at our birth chart with new eyes. We start to see in it the skill set our higher selves gave us to deal with the years ahead. And not just to *cope* with the years ahead, but to come into mastery through them.

The fact that the human race has experienced previous End-Time scenarios is well documented by historians. There have been plenty of tsunamis, plagues, floods and other mass extinctions over the many millennia of humanity's existence. Through weather, warfare or tectonic shifts, the Earth has shuddered like a dog – with human beings, like so many fleas, getting radically disrupted or picked off entirely.

For those of us who presume that human lives recycle, as everything else in the universe does, it follows that many of us were around during these past crises. We may now feel these earlier incarnations breaking through the surface of consciousness. Whether or not we are aware of them *per se*, we all have a vast reservoir we are drawing on – with a pointed emphasis, right now, on lifetimes that featured some world-altering crossroads. These soul memories number among the important resources we came in with.

I believe that on some level we are each fully aware that we've been waiting all our lives for the years upon us right now. There was even a public announcement of this idea, at the Harmonic Convergence in 1987, when the spiritual anthropologist Jose Arguelles gave us a preview by turning us on to the Mayan Calendar, and the significance it gave to 2012.

So here is my second recommendation: Remember that there is no lack of information flowing in, and no lack of support. Teachers, embodied and otherwise, are everywhere. Global visionaries and ancient wisdom models, like astrology, are more easily accessible than ever before.

It is axiomatic in metaphysical law that people hungry for consciousness will attract into their lives any number of teachings with just the right subtlety and intelligence to resonate perfectly with what's happening to their world at a given moment. This is the Universe doing its part of the bargain. Our part is to exercise quality control in terms of what we let in. In order to link into these higher ways of seeing, we need to detach from many of the information streams we've been conditioned to see as normal.

Bringing us to recommendation #3: Turn off the TV.

Picking through the Rubble

Throughout the spring of 2009, Pluto (breakdown) continues transiting in opposition to Venus in the US (Sibly) chart. The fact that Venus is the planetary ruler of money should come as no surprise. Pluto, the most powerful planet in the sky, is slowly creeping backwards in the USA first house (self-image), flushing out new revelations with every week that passes. The Dark God is unburying America's financial myths, opening up for inspection the crypts that held our family jewels. What is being exhumed here are not merely the toxic (Pluto) financial instruments that were cobbled together, Frankenstein-like, by those greed-crazed Wall Street traders. On a symbolic level what is being laid bare are America's core values (Venus).

America's stories about itself are being shattered (Uranus-Saturn T-squaring the US Mars-Neptune). Our illusions about what was going on for the past thirty years are going up in smoke. We are in the midst of a national trauma. And as those who have gone through trauma on a personal level know only too well, it takes a while to assimilate. Pluto is retrograde right now (spring 2009), giving us time to do this.

The retrograde periods that occur during long-running Pluto transits are analogous to the resting time we get between contractions during childbirth. Every year we get several months' worth of these, to review and assimilate whatever difficult psychological material Pluto has been dredging up. It's a chance to stand back from recent events and take stock. Pluto, the God of the Underworld, is doing a mid-year inventory – good accounting being a virtue even in Hell.

So what the hell just happened?

False Security

America has just had the biggest credit bubble in history burst in its collective face. This blowup exposed the raw truth about our ethos of consumerism: a worldview that was envied, despised and imitated throughout the world.

Only now that it is all coming undone can we ask the question: How is it that American consumerism became the Holy Grail of modern life? Surely social historians of the future will look back and marvel at the fact that, during the post-WWII years in the West, humanity's ultimate yearnings found their focus in something so altogether unremarkable: the prosaic experience of *buying things*.

This cult of materialism has come to be known throughout the world by its mantra "the American Dream," a phrase that has remained blissfully undefined. Did it refer to the American citizen's entitlement to spend to his heart's content? Or to an impoverished immigrant's right to someday live like a king? Whatever it meant, it has now given up the ghost. This calendar year, 2009, with Neptune on the US Moon, is the year of its wake.

The planet of illusions (Neptune) is asking Americans to reconsider everything we thought we needed to feel secure (Moon). Insecurity is shimmering through the group mind. Collective values and assumptions are being subjected to deeply unsettling questions. Did an upsurge of hedge-fund millionaires make America feel as secure as having a food bank in every neighborhood? Did the chance to strike it rich with a condo deal in an inflated real estate market make the buyer as secure as free hospital care would have? For a generation, Americans acted as if this were the case.

The general belief seemed to be that the availability of illusory financial gambles was worth crippling the programs that supported people's basic needs. The idea prevailed that it was acceptable to funnel the government's resources to the wealthy through tax cuts, and to allow self-appointed "conservatives" to loot government coffers the way gangsters loot legitimate businesses. As part of their campaign to cut social funding to shreds, politicians were applauded when they proposed "to shrink the government to the size where you can drown it in a bathtub."[1]

But of course these big talkers didn't shrink the government at all. They enlarged it, and made sure its revenues trickled upwards. John Kenneth Galbraith's prediction of "socialism for the rich" morphed from a wry figure of speech to the actual game plan in the USA.

Change vs. "Change"

As Pluto scans the territory we have just been over, we are being given the chance to consider the implications of the November election and of a newly engaged citizenry. We must also factor in the collateral damage that can be expected when old dinosaurs thrash around in protest of their own extinction.

As discussed in an earlier essay, Obama has given vast policymaking power to a pair of gentlemen who, more than perhaps any other pair, have the wet blood of the wrecked economy on their hands: Larry Summers and Tim Geithner. These appointments were early signs that the new president's pledge to fill the ranks with new voices must be taken with a grain of salt.

Even the moderates among the American intelligentsia are now calling on the government to nationalize insolvent banks, suspend payroll taxes and offer every homeowner in the country a cheap mortgage. The White House knows that

---

[1] These are the words of anti-tax crusader Grover Norquist.

gestures such as these, as obviously appropriate as they are, would induce an apoplectic fit in the old guard. Those with ill-gotten gains are not known for ceding their power voluntarily. But if our new president wants to be like FDR, as he claims, he's going to have to express not just with his words but with his actions that he understands what Pluto has now revealed: that the American financial establishment is corrupt to the bone, and that placating the dinosaurs is a losing strategy.

With men like Geithner and Summers in charge of policy while genuine visionaries are shut out of his cabinet, will Obama be able to overhaul the economy? This raises the rhetorical question: Can a problem be solved using the same mindset that caused the problem?

It is not from the bowels of the political establishment that we will get change deep enough to satisfy Pluto. Whether the forces of evolution can happen within the political structure at all depends upon whether the system can be dismantled and rebuilt so radically that it would be all but unrecognizable from what we have known.[2]

Health Care Reform

Neptune (drugs, hospitals) goes retrograde at the end of this month, in Aquarius (medicine). This station represents the peak of the most powerful conjunction of 2009: that of Neptune (universality) with Chiron (wounds) and Jupiter (social reform). The symbolism is about as clear as it could be. There's no way the explosive issue of universal health care can be put off any longer. It was fated to go public in a new way this year, 2009.[3]

What does it mean that this transit is hitting the US Moon? The Moon is the collective inner child. The reason this issue is so emotionally charged is that it evokes our most poignant need: that of being cared for when vulnerable.

Moreover, when we factor in the opposition between transiting Pluto (raw power) and transiting Mars (ego) that kicked off this calendar year, we can better understand the implications of the political power plays involved in health care

---

[2] For this change to happen outside the political structure, the American public would have to recognize and do something about the way the corporate media co-opts popular dissent and incipient rebellion. Thus the Goliath that needs to be slain first is a two-headed giant: the telecommunications-industry/government alliance.

[3] The conjunction of Neptune and Chiron, which will continue beyond Jupiter's involvement, peaks for the first time in February 2010 and for the last time in November 2010.

reform.[4] Forces intent on total control are circling this issue like dark clouds announcing a storm. Any challenge at all to the entrenched American insurance industry constitutes the premier David-and-Goliath battle in a year that is being defined by such battles.

Locked Out of the Debate

One of the gravest disappointments Obama has dealt his supporters so far is his "taking off the table" the eminently rational system of single-payer health care. The reason for its removal from public debate is clear: it would eliminate private insurance companies.

Under the plan Obama removed from discussion, the public would still get their choice of doctors and hospitals, but the exorbitant administrative costs and obscene profits that insurance companies add to the health-care bill would be eliminated. This is how it works in much of Europe, where health care does *not* number among life's worries. Is it any wonder that the powers-that-be don't want us to think about it? For Americans to spend any time at all imagining how their lives might feel without the constant threat of falling ill and going bankrupt might make the for-profit system we have now seem too absurd to tolerate for one more day.

Its cost-effectiveness, fairness and workability make the idea of single-payer health care one of the most dangerous threats that exist to the current plutocratic system. It is for this reason that the media almost never mentions it.[5] The only mainstream context in which it comes up is when grossly ill-informed or deliberately dissembling pundits and politicians allude to it indirectly, in their bizarre rants against "European-style socialism."

Guerilla Theatre

Also in play is the other major influence of this period: the ongoing opposition of Saturn and Uranus, whose essential message is this: If real change is to occur, it will not be through established channels. It will be through ordinary citizens

---

[4] See "Put Single Payer on the Table" at
www.truthdig.com/report/item/20090310_put_single_payer_on_the_table/

[5] According to Amy Goodman, a study released by Fairness and Accuracy in Reporting found that in the week before Obama's health-care summit, of the hundreds of stories that appeared in major newspapers and on the networks, only five included the views of advocates of single-payer – none of which appeared on television.

thinking creatively and acting surprisingly.

Russell Mokhiber, editor of the *Corporate Crime Reporter*, is an example of the Uranian archetype in action. Mokhiber plans to station himself outside the American Health Insurance Plans convention and burn his insurance bills. He and his cohorts are carrying forward the torch of the Vietnam War protesters a generation ago, who went in front of TV cameras and lit their draft cards on fire when conventional means of arguing against the war hit a brick wall of establishment corruption and popular apathy.

Guerilla theatre is Uranus' cup of tea. And as Grand Cross watchers know, the Great Trickster is moving into Aries, the sign of sparking and igniting. What is happening to the popular mood will feel familiar to those of us who danced in the streets a generation ago. There is a clear astrological parallel between the creative disruption we will now be seeing and the wild antics of the 1960s.

Let the games begin.

KNOWLEDGE AND KNOWING

(originally published on *Skywatch*,
July 2009)

"I have such a feeling of solidarity with everything alive that it doesn't seem
important to know where the individual ends or begins."
—Albert Einstein

Like the scientists, mystical thinkers honor Einstein as uniquely inspiring, but
from a somewhat different point of view. For us, the wispy-haired old fellow
with the unforgettable eyes exudes a wisdom that trumps intellectual smarts.

In fact he was prodigious on both scores: that of mental acuity (Aquarius) and
spiritual understanding (Pisces).[1] I can't think of another scientist whose face has
been reproduced on postcards, lapel buttons and tote bags. Though Western
culture tends to reserve the word *genius* for people gifted in conceptual thinking,
those of us who hung posters of Einstein on our dorm room walls did so for other
reasons. I, for one, was enchanted by the rumor that he didn't wear socks.

It's an appropriate time to consider why we are so drawn to Einstein. Right now
in particular, humanity is hungry for his embodiment of both knowledge and
knowing: a combination symbolized in astrology by Neptune in Aquarius, the
key player in the Super Conjunction that dominates the skies this calendar year,
2009.

This unusual grouping of planets is introducing the obdurate mass mind to a new
kind of subtlety. Chiron is trying to teach us how to use our pain to achieve true
humanness. Jupiter, whose role in the transit diminishes after December 2009, is
pushing us beyond our provincialisms, stretching our grasp of what's going on in
the wide world beyond our normal frames of reference. And Neptune, star of the
show, is blurring the boundaries between the ego-defined self and the rest of

---

[1] Einstein's chart features a Midheaven Sun in Pisces (ruled by Neptune) and an Aquarius Jupiter
opposite the planetary ruler of Aquarius (Uranus).

Creation.

Just as we might hang a mandala on the wall to focus upon during meditation, we could gaze at a picture of dear old Albert. His eyes reflect the mysteries the universe is inviting us to understand.

Cardinal Cross

The Aquarius cluster (group membership) is welcoming us into the world-altering years between 2012 and 2015, during which our identification with certain groups over others will mean more than ever before. Right now we are doing nothing less than determining the future of planet Earth, and the Aquarius transit is asking us to choose our allies accordingly. Who will best bear the standard for humanity's forward movement? The years surrounding 2012 will blow out of the water our conventional assumptions about leadership.[2]

Leadership is signified in astrology by the Cardinal signs, all four of which will be part of the great configurations in the sky. It will be a time of asking who we want our leaders to be, and what we'll do with them once we've chosen them. It won't be enough to show up at the ballot box and then go home and go back to sleep.[3]

Pluto in Capricorn (2008-23) is the first member of the Cardinal Cross to establish itself. The planet of breakdown in the sign of authority has already gotten to work, aiming its wrecking ball at the mightiest and sturdiest of national governments.

This is not to say that the planet *caused* this state of affairs. Pluto does not create decay; it merely reveals it. All over the world patriarchal systems are crumbling under their own weight. Among the big players are China (Pluto square natal Sun), whose corrupt old boys' network is cracking with the strain of world attention (focused upon, for example, its internet censorship, its relationship to Tibet, human rights, pollution and out-of-control urbanization); England (Pluto conjunct natal Sun), whose ruling party is coming apart at the seams; and in the

---

[2] The period 2008-23 is dominated by the square between Uranus in Aries and Pluto in Capricorn, which is exact seven times between 2012 and 2015.

[3] Leadership lessons will be taught on a personal level as well as a group level. Readers should check their charts for planets occupying the early degrees of Aries, Cancer, Libra and Capricorn, and make note of the houses these degrees fall in. This will show us the parts of ourselves where we may be inspired to demonstrate initiative with family, in one-to-one relationships or on a societal stage.

USA, Pluto opposed to natal Sun).

Many traditions besides Western astrology have called attention to the age we're in right now, characterizing it as a time when false leaders would be exposed. The seers of ancient India referred to our era as the Kali Yuga, which translates as the Dark Time (in this usage the Sanskrit word *kali* means discord and strife), They declared that in our era those in power would become a danger to the world.[4]

Moral Meltdown

Aquarius is the only one of the twelve signs that singles out the human species: it symbolizes the qualities that separate us from other creatures. What this transit is doing is raising questions about the essential nature of human society, such as: What is the point is of having these extraordinary minds, unique in the animal kingdom? What benefits does planet Earth draw from what we call *civilization*? What makes a human group civilized, and what makes it uncivilized?

This is the question underneath all the other questions in the debate about torture.

Growing up in the USA, most of us were conditioned to believe that our country not only did not torture its enemies, but would never do so, *could* never do so. This made us special. This belief was so integral a part of the national self-image that, only a generation ago, most Americans would have found it unimaginable that they would one day be debating the issue. One didn't debate the unthinkable. But as soon as Pluto (taboos) started opposing the Sun cluster (self-definition) in the US (Sibly) chart in 2008, that's exactly what we started to do.

When we remember the core meaning of Pluto aspects, it is easier to make sense of the crossroads at which the USA finds itself. Such transits constitute a profound threat to an entity's sense of self. Historically, the American public's conviction that their country would never engage in torture both established a point of moral pride and underlay a geopolitical sense of entitlement. That is, so long as they believed their system to be superior – morally, politically, economically — to every other, Americans felt justified in acting like kings of the world. But this fundamental belief has been shattered.

---

[4] Some scholars say the *yuga* that's now ending started in 3102 BC (very near the date of the beginning of the Mayan Calendar: around 3100 BC). The Kali Yuga also predicted unseasonable weather conditions and the estrangement of human beings from the gods.

Abu Ghraib

Against the backdrop of the Pluto opposition to the US Sun cluster, the Super
Conjunction began to form. Neptune (fog, obscurity) started to cloud issues once
deemed utterly clear.[5] Over the last three years, the closer Chiron (wounding) got
to Neptune, the more distressingly blurred societal certitudes became.

During Chiron's opposition to transiting Saturn, torture hit the headlines. When
the Abu Ghraib photos were released on 2/15/06, visible proof was thrust in our
faces to disprove the lie (Neptune) at the country's righteous core (Jupiter). A
blood-curdling visual icon – that unforgettable hooded figure with arms
outstretched – was introduced into the vocabulary of the American imagination,
dealing the deadliest blow yet to the country's sense of self.

For the American conscience, the publication of those photos marked the end of
the era of deniability. By the time Jupiter (ethics) ingressed (entered into a new
sign) into Aquarius in January of 2009 the issue had become the centerpiece of
America's moral meltdown.[6] Anti-war activists had long argued that the Bush
regime tortured its captives in order to coerce false testimony that linked Saddam
Hussein to the September 11th attacks — testimony that would have provided an
alibi for the invasion of Iraq and handily avoided the Nuremberg definition of a
war crime. This scenario is no longer merely the opinion of a fringe minority.
That which had remained unadmitted by the majority of the population has
broken through the crust of collective awareness.

American schoolchildren reading their history books may find themselves
making comparisons that would never have crossed their parents' minds. Such
as, how was the CIA's treatment of Saddam Hussein's chauffeur any different
from the treatment meted out by the royal interrogators of Tudor London, who
routinely postponed sending their victims to the gallows in hopes of getting them
to implicate others while strapped to the rack?

The torture issue is the most visceral of several violations to America's self-

---

[5] The Neptune conjunction to the US Moon (popular feeling) began in 2008 and remains strong
through 2011.

[6] The election of President Obama has not lessened America's quandary. Congress has backpedaled
on its vow to close Guantanamo, whose prisoners have been identified by federal lawyers as being
"not persons" – thus torturing them is supposedly legal. And after blasting military commissions as
"an enormous failure" on the campaign trail, Obama has revived them; a move Amnesty
International has called "a disastrous misstep." The president's national intelligence director, Adm.
Dennis Blair, has declared he believes that torture works; another senior official has been accused
of covering up the torture of an American nun in Guatemala; still another is an apologist for the late
war criminal Pinochet.

image that have corresponded with Pluto's opposition to the US Venus-Jupiter conjunction (ethical values). To a hugely increased percentage of the US public, the old assertion that *We are good and our enemies are evil* has started to ring hollow. As a consequence, the simplistic tropes of American foreign policy are no longer going to fly. From now on Washington's justifications of its imperial assertions will strain the public's credulity like never before.

Slapped in the Face

It has taken a dramatic economic downturn to expose the American populace to the runaway corruption (Pluto) inherent in the government-business hybrid that runs the country. The downturn is a mass trauma, as Pluto teachings always are.

Thousands upon thousands of small economic injustices, together with a handful of enormous high-profile injustices, are painting a picture whose contrast is stark enough to shake up the multitudes. Americans are seeing their favorite mom-and-pop stores go out of business after serving their neighborhoods for decades, while bloated, bailed-out bankers are not only still in business but getting richer than ever by hoarding their TARP funds. Citizens who never before considered themselves "political" are fuming. Their sense of decency has been flouted.

In this climate a wide swath of Americans are realizing things about their country that the international community has known for a long time. Such as the fact that a larger proportion of the American population lives in destitution and in prison than is true in any other industrialized nation, even as the country maintains its status as the wealthiest and most militarily powerful on Earth. It is a slap in the face to the average American-Dreamer to consider, for example, that income disparities in his country are equivalent to those in the Third World. But such realities can no longer be refuted.

These transits are about rupturing complacency. They constitute a profoundly effective cosmic teaching tool. With Uranus, the Great Awakener, moving into orb of its square with Pluto in 2010, the American consciousness will receive a succession of rousing blows.

As individuals, our wisest move would be to purposefully wake ourselves up before the transits are forced to do it for us. Our goal should be to deliver — metaphorically or, better yet, ritualistically — a bracing splash of cold water to our faces every morning, as a reminder to stay alert to the world moment.

New Template

The election of Barack Obama provided a powerful example of the country's craving to change from the inside out, which is the only kind of change that will satisfy Pluto. Obama rose upon the crest of this deep craving in the collective soul. It is not just that we got a new president. Indeed, policy-wise, not much is new at all. It is the template of leadership that is different now. As a singular leader Obama is less significant than as a rallying icon. It is for this evolutionary role that history will remember him, and it is this perspective that will serve us best as we observe his ongoing travails.[7]

The Saturn-Uranus opposition that ushered Obama November 2008 offers us clues about this new template. It told us that people's expectations of government (Saturn) were radically changing (Uranus), a situation that is both healthy and deeply destabilizing. Meanwhile, the status quo is holding tight to its stale old ideas, as exemplified by the Republican Party's endless invocations of the virtues of Ronald Reagan. But Uranus is shattering the old clichés, as the transit has shattered the GOP. The frenzied culture wars we are seeing at the moment mask a desperate yearning on the part of many to believe in the old lies. With the Super conjunction on top of the US Moon, the force of unconscious Neptune (hypnosis; self-deception) is immensely strong in the USA.

When Neptune was stationary in late May 2009 a small event took place that spoke volumes about the mythmaking that underlies our political stagecraft. California Republicans passed a bill to get rid of a statue in the Capitol Rotunda of Thomas Starr King, a Unitarian abolitionist who was known as "the orator who saved the nation", and replace it with one of Ronald Reagan, a mediocre actor-*cum*-corporate shill-*cum*-Teflon president.

That the right wing would choose this guy to canonize is astoundingly ironic, given the catastrophic results all over the world right now of his notorious "trickle-down economics." The fact that the GOP would substitute a statue of old Bonzo for that of a spiritual giant like Thomas Starr King betrays a lack of historical and moral perspective of bewildering proportions.

We can take fair warning from this incident about the foggy underbelly of the Neptune transit. There will be a lot of mass denial to slog through in the years ahead.

---

[7] Obama, who originally 'unequivocally' opposed that recent notorious $87 billion war appropriation, later supported four separate war appropriations to the tune of $300 billion. He voted against a proposal to remove most of the combat troops from Iraq by July 2009, and supported the GOP resolution to keep military funding flowing there. He's now saying that up to 50,000 troops will be left in Iraq indefinitely.

Hearts and Minds

Since this series of transits began, the pace of developments on Earth has been fast and furious for the world and for each of us individually. It's only natural to feel overwhelmed. Those who don't shut themselves down by means of the ubiquitous escape mechanisms available cannot help but feel inundated by the intensity pulsating in the atmosphere.

This is why the Goddess invented the retrograde cycle. Whenever planets move backwards through the zodiac, it gives us breathing room; time to review and take stock. We are supposed to be turning inwards, opening our beings to what has been happening.

To absorb the deepest levels of meaning that we can from the years ahead, we'll need to keep our wits sharp and our hearts open. Our guide in this is the Aquarius conjunction, which has arrived right on cue to help us make sense of these times. Jupiter is reminding us to stay informed; Neptune and Chiron are reminding us to stay connected to our souls.

And we are not alone. Each of us is surrounded by groups and individuals who are perfectly situated to model knowledge and knowing, and to support us in our work. Brilliant young thinkers, wise elders and finger-on-the-pulse visionaries are everywhere. We just have to notice them.

We will know them by the energy that comes out of their eyes, as we know Einstein.

THE OTHER SIDE OF LETTING GO

(originally published in *Skywatch*,
August 2009)

What begins when the Moon is New comes to a head when it is Full.

This is the core idea of the lunar cycle, and it is a very primal one. Transit-trackers have used it to interpret the sky's messages since the beginning of time. When the New and Full Moons in question are eclipses, the cycle reaches deeper and further in its significance; but it does not depart from this basic formula.

Super Conjunction Summer

How do these lunations fit in with the Super Conjunction in Aquarius? Though Jupiter has moved ahead in the zodiac, Neptune and Chiron are still traveling together, making life confusing at best and incomprehensible at worst for every one of us. Doing your best to gracefully manage the chaos that is your life is a major feat right now. Don't think there's something wrong with you if you feel like you're barely treading water. Give yourself credit for not drowning.

2009 is about letting go. It's about forgiving ourselves for not knowing what we can't know, allowing for frequent mood shifts, and it's about holding plans — if we must make them — with the lightness with which we would hold a bird in our open palm.

And that's just on the personal level. What is the human family as a whole being asked to let go of?

The fact that a lot of prominent people are flipping out is telling. It may not mean what the pundits say it means, but it does convey something about the energy afoot. The erratic behavior of public figures this summer is symptomatic of a worldwide destabilization process. Sarah Palin's surprise resignation of her governorship as the Capricorn eclipse (leadership) was building epitomized the mood in the air: confused and taken-off-guard. Societal (Jupiter) uncertainty (Neptune) is the name of the game.

What We Know

Have you noticed that most of the lead news stories lately are about illusion and fraud (Neptune)? From the adultery of public figures (Berlusconi, Gov. Sanford et al.)[1] to allegations of rigged elections (Zimbabwe, Iran[2] et al.), cultural signposts that once stood tall are careening giddily. As their economies collapse, governments all over the world are foundering, trying to patch together policies that all but the most credulous of their citizens wearily perceive to be made of smoke and mirrors.

More fundamentally, as global warming undermines the very topography of the planet, the Neptune/ Chiron/ Jupiter conjunction is perpetrating a parallel undermining of the psychological grounding of the collective mind. We are being given no choice but to relinquish our 19th- and 20th-century ideas about being masters of Mother Earth.

The material realm has a different meaning than it has ever had before. It is not solid at the moment. It is fluctuating, unpredictable and elusive, like the ever-shifting sea. And if we suspend, even fleetingly, our fears about what's happening, and our good/bad judgments about it all, we may be inspired to understand this period we are living through from a whole new vantage point: from the other side of letting go.

The radical changes the Earth is going through right now are obvious to every sentient being. Even people who do not follow current events in a sociopolitical or intellectual way are hip to the reality of what's happening. We know it

---

[1] The prime minister of Italy had bribery charges added to his legal problems in February of 2009. As for South Carolina Governor Mark Sanford, in June 2009 he suffered a blitz of media interest in his bizarre Lost Weekend. It turned out the Governor had been in Argentina with his mistress. Here's a guy whose utterly human drives burst out from behind his twee Southern-family-man exterior, making mincemeat out of the tightly wound persona that had packaged him. He heard that siren call, and instead of stuffing his ears with wax, as Ulysses did, he jumped right in. He chose the Neptune option.

[2] Although the US media is portraying the situation in Iran this summer as a clear-cut case of The People rising up against an autocracy — a story many progressives are swallowing hook, line and sinker — the scenario becomes a good bit more complicated when we factor in the shenanigans of the CIA over the past year (and well before, of course. Washington has been trying to undermine every Iranian government since the 1978 revolution; not to mention the Anglo-American collusion in 1953 to take back control of the Iranian oil industry via the coup that installed the Shah.). From their concerted disinformation campaign to their financial support of pro-Western factions in Tehran, Washington policymakers have been doing their best to orchestrate regime change in Iran in a way that they hope won't cause them as much trouble as the one they orchestrated in Iraq.

because we are animals (a fact the proud human mind denies): we are blessed with sub-rational animal knowing. And we know it because are all connected to the Earth's fate through super-rational knowing, too: a type of knowing the Aquarius conjunction is trying to deepen.

Many conscious individuals all over the Earth are struggling right now with the question of what to do with what we know. The answer to this conundrum sounds complex, at first blush – even self-contradicting – yet it is fundamentally as simple as pie. If we let go, in the way the Neptune conjunction is guiding us to do, we will be able to detach enough to tolerate the truths that we must absorb if the planet is to survive.

This use of the term *detachment* does not mean *uncaring* or *unemotional*. Quite the opposite. It refers to a state of distanced compassion, in which the heart is fully and vitally engaged. Detachment like this makes us strong enough to face how serious the situation is. Then we can go one step further, and acknowledge that we know what we know. Each little acknowledgment becomes a creative act. By contrast, playing dumb hurts the soul.

Infofest

Since Uranus (cyber technology) and Neptune (universality) conjoined in the early 1990s, the Earth has been transformed into a buzzing ball of continuous information-connectedness. From the symbolism of the transits then and since, we see that the plethora of facts and figures that call out to be acknowledged by us every day are not just some random background condition of modern life but a key characteristic of this era, and a very definite part of the cosmic plan.

Contrast this situation with the almost quaint standard of naïveté that characterized Western societies in the 1950s. We cannot hide behind that kind of informational vacuity any more, or anything like it.

There is more accurate information available now to the average person than there has ever been in the history of the world.

Here are some examples of facts that are pretty universally accessible: Despite the collapsing global economy, roughly $129,000,000 per minute is being spent internationally on "defense."[3] More money is spent on militarism in six hours

---

[3] The term "defense" as used in the American vernacular is one of the most insidious euphemisms of our age. At an earlier point in American history the US Defense Department was called the Department of War, but our militarists grew too psychologically savvy to allow such bald accuracy. This is a shame, because if the American public wanted to know what was really going on

than has been spent on the environment in the last two decades.

We must let this information in. As intelligent beings in alarming times, we need to become open and stay open to lucid, relevant data. Another bit of news that would seem highly pertinent for the taxpaying public: In April 2009, American senators from both parties[4] fought hard for the construction of seven obsolete fighter planes at a cost of $1.75 billion. The Pentagon doesn't want them, but the contractors who build them do. So they pay lobbyists to sell them to congressmen who then justify the project by bloviating about *jobs* (political code for "Vote for me or you'll be in the poorhouse").

Stripped of the nonsense with which politicians and newscasters dress them up, these facts are stark, astounding and appalling. But one thing they are not is secret. Information like this is no longer classified, nor the province of specialists.

One doesn't have to be a biologist to know that a third of amphibians and a quarter of mammals are in danger of extinction because of global pollution. One can turn on the radio and hear it.

Statistics like these are not opinions but realities, and they are so indefensible that the only way to not be repulsed by them is to stonewall them.

Clarity in the Fog

The mass media in its current state, and the vacuous pop culture of which it is a part, are examples of Neptune in its unconscious form. But the transits are simply presenting us with both sides of this archetype, as transits always do. And misused Neptune is no match for consciously used Neptune.

There can be no fence-straddling now. People will either align with fear and denial, or they will truly respond to the urgent realities upon us. This latter

---

geopolitically it would be very useful to go back to the agency's old moniker - the better to distinguish between offensive militarism and the truly defensive kind. Whatever one calls this astoundingly profligate agency, it is the world's costliest military enterprise at $102 billion a year. Under the Obama administration it is becoming even more expensive.

[4] Those who presume substantial differences between the two dominant political parties in the US might consider that Democrats Edward Kennedy and John Kerry were part of the campaign to build these mass-murdering boondoggles.

approach constitutes *living through the chart.*[5] Those who choose it will quite naturally find their place the New Age being born. All we need to do is pour ourselves into the moment, and let go to what wants to happen.

---

[5] By this I mean aligning with the highest expression of who we are. To live through your chart is to draw fully upon the unlimited potential you were born with. And that no one else was born with. They have their own resources, but they're not like yours.

THE POWER OF PONDERING

(originally published in *Daykeeper
Journal,* November 2009)

Did you feel that >click<? On October 29, 2009 there was an energetic shift. Like a telephone jack snapping into the wall socket, Saturn entered Libra, and became a major player in the long-building Cardinal Cross. The ante has just been upped.

Uranus and Pluto are ripening into their much-heralded square, the central drama of the period between 2008 and 2023. The Saturn ingress into the configuration takes us one step closer to a T-square between all three.

Clarity of Mind

The greatest danger to the USA right now is neither socialism nor swine flu. It is fear, a madness as infectious as wildfire. The Saturn transit suggests that the best antidote to this fear is the distancing mechanism of thought. Clarity of thought will now be easier to achieve.

The Libra ingress adds to the mix the detachment of air, in which the mental processes are at their sharpest. Of the four, air is the peculiarly human element. These marvelous brains of ours allow us to go places other creatures can't go. We don't take advantage of this sophisticated feature as much as we could. But in these times, wasting any of our resources, especially our intelligence, is a really dumb idea.

Saturn in Libra impels us to get focused and realistic in our decision-making. Debates (Libra) are subjected to more scrutiny (Saturn) than they were under Saturn in Virgo. The intellectual integrity of an argument counts for more. This should be heartening for observers of America's culture wars, which seem to have reached a new low in terms of their cringe-worthy lack of rationality.

Genius

Moreover, a conceptual boost of another order is coming from Uranus (genius), considered the *higher octave* of Mercury (mental processing). Uranus, whose influence is growing stronger by the week, breaks us out of our shells by knocking down cognitive barriers. At this writing, late 2009, it is getting ready to enter Aries, the most courageous sign in the zodiac.

Then there is the fact that Jupiter is in Aquarius (January 2009 – January 2010), one of the triad of the Super-Conjunction (discussed above, in *The Other Side of Letting Go*). Do you know anybody with natal Jupiter in Aquarius? When these folks are using the blessing they were born with, they personify the idea of "thinking outside of the box." Even if an idea is unfamiliar or uncomfortable to them, they will dive into it and follow it to its furthest reaches. No matter what our charts look like, we all have better access now to the inventive capacity of the human mind. These transits are calls to use the faculty of reason (Libra) more responsibly (Saturn), and to dare (Aries) to break through the prejudices that fetter our thinking (Uranus).

When over-indulged, emotions lead to agitation and anxiety. The risk of emotional over-reactivity will be high during the years ahead, and the universe is fortifying our powers of observation and consideration to negotiate our way through them.
Yet even as we burnish our intellectual capacities we must keep acknowledging our feelings. It is not an *either/or* situation. The mind cannot provide wisdom alone. Our hearts must be engaged.

Sci-Fi Thinking

What would it feel like to apply true mental detachment to our consideration of the current state of planet Earth? It would mean stretching our minds to encompass, without fear or ideological prejudice, imagery that would otherwise repel us.

Science fiction writers achieve this distance, which is why they are able to invent previously unimagined scenarios. Have you read Ursula Le Guin's stories? What a mind (her chart features Venus and Mercury opposite Uranus)! It is the kind of mind that refuses to allow value judgment or fear of the unknown to fetter the imagination.

Denial

Our first step in finding solutions to the immense problems the world faces right now is breaking through our denial. Denial kicks in when we feel ourselves to be under threat. It is a human protection mechanism, and there is no reason to fault ourselves for harboring it.

But right now denial itself is under threat. The countries of the world are no longer able to ignore the issue of environmental degradation. Even in the denial-crippled USA, for years the Earth's primary offender (though we are neck-and-neck with China now in terms of carbon emissions), the news is full of statistics that undermine denial.

The fact that a plastic bag takes hundreds of years for to decompose was not known when I was a child. That is, it was doubtless known in scientific and academic enclaves, but it was not part of the national conversation. Even if ordinary folks had heard such a statistic, they wouldn't have known how to put it into context.
But now a fact like this is common knowledge. The amount and the detail of such information mounts by the week. Americans can pick up a newspaper and read about how the plastic bags they get in stores are made from twelve million barrels of oil each year, and how the average use time for is twelve minutes. An awareness of humanity's impact upon the Earth is burgeoning in the collective mind, crowding out centuries' worth of ignorance.

More and more people are coming to understand the implications of the planet's rising temperatures, and the increased pressure on water, food and land that will ensue unless radical steps are taken. We hear daily about the great poverty afflicting fragile states in Africa and elsewhere, about governments falling, about the waves of refugees searching for safe quarter. No longer seen as Chicken Little fantasies, these scenarios were validated from the lectern of the recent climate change summit by the Secretary General of the U.N. They are here and now, and our denial of them is no longer an option.

Action vs. Thought

Our first response in discussions like these tends to be "But what can we do?" This reaction arises from the premise, especially strong in the Western world, that *action* is the be-all and end-all, the triumphant apex of human capability. Thought and emotion come in a distant second and third.

But if action is launched prematurely, it will be fraught with reactivity and desperation. The question "What can I do?" cannot lead to an inspired answer when it carries this energy. It only leads to paralysis.

Doing must be anticipated by imagining. Action is predicated upon thought, not the other way around. Before we worry about behavioral responses we must conceptualize. With the current air transits to embolden us, we are free in a new way to ponder the meaning of the state of the world. When enough people use their minds imaginatively, the power of thought reaches a kind of spontaneous tipping point. Then action becomes appropriate and arises naturally.

Such a phenomenon occurred on the first Earth Day in the USA. A quorum of individuals amassed a sufficient body of knowledge and had their consciousnesses raised accordingly, and 20 million of them took to the streets riled up for action. This is the kind of explosive, exponential burst of power that changes the world almost overnight.

It is preceded by thinking, learning and pondering.

Thinking Up the Future

The modern linear worldview is that there exists a singular future, sitting there waiting for us to come to it. Time is conceived as a train heading along a straight track towards a station. Since the future is thought to be already in place, the game becomes knowing what it is, so we can prepare for it. No wonder people are always asking astrologers, economists and senior analysts "what will happen."

But humanistic astrology holds that there is no one future. Rather, there is an infinitude of potential futures. So there can be no predictions.[1] The future is a living, breathing, mutating sea of possibilities, whose specific manifestations are created anew at every moment from the raw ingredients of consciousness.

It is the quality of this consciousness that makes all the difference.

This is why the integrity of our thinking – its boldness and creativity – is so important. Once we stop being intimidated by fear, denial falls away and we can open ourselves up to the transits' invitation to muse. (Consider the meaning of *muse* as a noun: a divine spirit, guiding us to a place of inspiration.)

The time is right for us to deliberately challenge our philosophical comfort zones. As with a pre-stretched sweater, the more we stretch our minds to embrace the portent of the years ahead, the better we will fit into them.

---

[1] That is, to paraphrase Rick Tarnas, there can be no predictions of literal events, only of archetypal events.

Gaia

The world is full of people who are blossoming into the recognition that Mother Earth is an interconnected living organism. We can take comfort in the fact that the visionaries of the world are now in the ascendancy.

We all know in our bones that the Earth is alive. Our hearts understand that everything on this planet is linked to every other thing: that the butterfly in the jungle has an impact on the permafrost in Siberia. We are aware on a cellular level that every particle of every one of Earth's systems knows what every other particle is doing.

Those who don't know it, or who have forgotten that they know it – the old – school scientists still preaching mechanistic materialism, and advocates of the hierarchical dominance model that has defined reality in the "civilized" world for the past five thousand years – represent the paradigm of the past. The ecological crossroads upon which humanity finds itself depends upon our rejecting the old paradigm and pledging allegiance to the new one; which is also, of course, utterly ancient.

What would it feel like to embrace the Gaia Theory as not just a theory? What would happen if large numbers of people refused to identify with the false worldview they grew up with, and lived instead in accordance with the rhythms and laws of Life?

Accessing the Transits

When we fully access the detachment of mind now available to us, we start to feel the old ways of thinking as heavy and oppressive. Personal attachments (ideas and behaviors that we cling to just because they are familiar) and cultural limitations (such as nationalism[2] and other ideological creeds) start to feel like ropes holding down a helium balloon that is straining to be free.

Opening up to the long view might lead us to the idea that "saving the world" is not the same thing as "saving humanity." In *The Vanishing of Gaia: A Final Warning,* James Lovelock goes the distance. His perspective on how humans fit in to the big scheme of things is compassionate yet quite unattached to things as

---

[2] The construct of nationalism is breaking down for all sorts of reasons, some of them less spiritually driven than others. Wealthy American expats have been renouncing their citizenship in record numbers since a crackdown on tax evasion in 2008.

they are, the better to see farsightedly. "We are…intelligent social animals," he says, "with the possibility of evolving to become a wiser more intelligent animal, one that might have a greater potential as a partner for the rest of life on Earth. Our goal now is to survive and to live in a way that gives evolution *beyond us* the best chance [italics mine]." Lovelock dares to propose that harm to the Earth system is ultimately more serious than harm to humanity.[3]

Such imaginings can easily turn unproductive if they are entered into out of fear, or in the hope of predicting scenarios. By contrast, the transits are encouraging us to play with ideas without attachment to outcome. In this spirit, the bigger the idea, the healthier it will make us. Daring to entertain the idea of an Earth *without* humans allows us to see what it would take for Earth to flourish *with* humans.

---

[3] The idea of an Earth *sans* people is not just difficult for a lot of us to imagine, but morally repugnant. For most of us it feels blasphemous to even consider it, as if to even wrap one's mind around the idea were tantamount to giving up - to signing off on our ecocidal trajectory. Perhaps counterintuitively, for me it is a peaceful idea, promoting a feeling of safety.

TALKING HEADS

(originally published in *Daykeeper
Journal*, December 2009)

In the previous essay, we discussed the fledgling transit of Saturn in Libra. We talked about the significance of the air element (ideas), and about how the addition of Libra to the celestial mix could provide America's public discourse with a clear-headedness that has been sorely lacking.

We also mentioned the Aquarius conjunction (Jupiter, Chiron and Neptune on the US Moon), which, if we make it through our collective identity crisis, promises a more spiritualized use of the mass mind. This transit, the Super Conjunction, peaks for the third time at the winter solstice 2009. In the process of trying to transform, our national self-image (Moon) is in meltdown mode (Neptune): wounded (Chiron), yet wildly expansive (Jupiter).

Growing up

The American mind is in desperate need of boundaries. Our collective intelligence has become degraded by the anything-goes media circus that has come to be called, with perverse appropriateness, the culture wars. There is a crying need for advocates of differing opinions to define their terms and to get more structured in their expression of them. Mercifully, this is exactly what Saturn in Libra is equipped to provide.

The transits overhead are singling out the USA in another way, as well. The horoscope of the entity born 7/4/1776 in Philadelphia itself features Saturn in Libra. This means the country will be having a Saturn Return, exact in 2011. As those who have experienced Saturn Returns in their own charts know only too well, this is a transit of maturity. It is a call to get practical, to start acting like a grownup. In Libra, it signals the need to organize the workings of the mind and put them to use.

Appointed Messengers

We denizens of the First World, as the beneficiaries (or victims, depending on your point of view) of the Information Age, find ourselves deluged with data day in and day out. How do we organize this mental onslaught, and what meaning do we give to it?

Each of us, to one extent or another, will have to answer to Saturn in Libra (October 2009-October 2012). Depending on where the transit falls in our charts, we will be asked to examine the contents of our thoughts, discard those that are no longer useful, and categorize the rest into a workable order. We will be called upon to take responsibility for our opinions. Where do our opinions come from? For the USA this question will be increasingly pressing. Whose voices run through the American mind?

Every culture has its storytellers: persons appointed to convey the narratives the group uses to generate its reality. Ancient tribes appointed gifted messengers who, it was believed, traveled between the worlds and came back to deliver the news. Some cultures have shamans and oracles who translate the words of the gods. Throughout history societies have primarily sought such guidance from religion and art.

As to the former, there has been a mass discrediting of theological authority since the millennium. As to the latter, in this post-literary age, the secular West is perhaps less inclined than it has ever been to look to its artists as exponents of the great truths.
To whom do we appeal these days? Whom have we chosen to explain the vagaries of our chaotic world? We have given this job to the pundits.

Public Mood

When we consider the societal need filled by our talking heads, it starts to make more sense why America has given them so much power. These are the guys we have assigned to interpret our reality.

The reason our celebrity opinion-mongers attract such ardent fans is certainly not because they exude any particular benevolence of spirit. On the contrary, it almost seems as if the outsized popularity of men like radio personality Michael Savage stands in inverse relation to their capacity to embrace their fellow human beings. Yet as we have seen, they serve a need for which human groups are hardwired.

According to Jungian thinking, our cultural reality is an aggregate of its participants' individual realities.[1] In this view, America's inflammatory pundits

---

[1] See the work of Paul Levy at awakeninthedream.com.

reflect the current state of the national psyche. The USA is in extreme financial, social and psychospiritual disarray, with many of its citizens operating from the most primitive parts of themselves. Thus we get the incendiary battle cries of the Fox News commentators, obligingly offering up the kind of negative cheerleading that the public is already juiced up to hear.

But as consciousness seekers we cannot afford to take on these energies. To be responsible members of the here and now, we must take notice when what we are hearing on TV or the radio is skewed to the point of harmful. To negotiate these critical times we must take a hard look at the pundit phenomenon.
Saturn in Libra, whose goal is to clear the decks of unreason, could be profoundly helpful here if we use it well. This transit bestows a renewed respect for the integrity of conceptual thought. When pressed into service to critique sloppy and manipulative thinking, Saturn is the perfect antidote for the epidemic of raucous verbal irresponsibility that now pollutes the national conversation.

Infotainment

Libra is about the initiation (Cardinality) of ideas (air). In this regard the transit's first lesson may be to expose these dudes as being fakes. That is, although mouth-offs like Sean Hannity, Bill O'Reilly and Glenn Beck are billed as idea men, the issues they espouse are rarely their own.

When the bald realities of the infotainment industry are factored in, we see that these men seldom choose what to get incensed about. They are entertainers, whose boorish adamancy is crafted by their producer-employers. These bosses are, in turn, told what should be raged about by the corporate media powers above them, and so on.[2]

The pose assumed by the Lou Dobbses of this world – that of fierce individualists "telling it like it is" – is particularly contemptible when we consider the degree to which their talking points derive from pollsters and marketing firms. These agencies, ideologically neutral in the sense that they are profit-driven, supply the pundits' bosses with statistics about what would be likely to strike a chord with audiences.

---

[2] Consider the fact that Rupert Murdoch, head of the world's biggest media empire, openly meets with international heads of state. Murdoch, who is known to give his journalists lists of what topics they should report on and which subjects they aren't to mention, is only the most obvious exemplifier of a system that purports to be about information-dispensing but is really about worldview-molding.

At the same time, I do believe that a solipsist like Rush Limbaugh probably does come to believe his own rants. I can visualize the process: he confers with his managers over a list of suitable topics; his eyes start to twinkle as he imagines summoning up the bile necessary to do the job. Once he's behind the mike, he rises to the occasion, finding within his reservoir of personal grievances the vitriol required to finesse a rant on the show.

Both his bosses and his personal delusions are served in the process.

Naked Emperors

The pundits have coalesced into a kind of para-political class in our media-driven age. Obama himself gave a reluctant nod to their newfound credibility a few months back, in autumn 2009, when he referred to Rush Limbaugh as a formidable force among Republicans. I propose it is time to help Saturn in Libra disrobe Rush and his fellow emperors by taking a closer look at their job description.

The *raison-d'être* of these bullies of the airwaves is to pump up ratings by appealing not to ideas but visceral feelings, the arousal of which makes people easy to manipulate. Limbaugh is a brilliant performer, but he and his ilk are pretending to be something else. They are pretending to be ideologues. Though the word has acquired a pejorative meaning, an ideologue is first and foremost a person with ideas.

Let us use this transit to refine our own clear-mindedness, so that we may be judged by our ideas and assess our leaders by theirs.

THE COLOR OF MONEY

(originally published in *Skywatch*,
October 2009)

The years ahead are going to challenge our old ways on just about every front. But human nature being what it is, some issues are going to throw us for more of a loop than others. In groups as in individuals, certain topics are connected to powerful unconscious feelings. These provoke intense reactivity unless or until they are brought to awareness and resolved.

Money is one of the hottest of these hot buttons. In the USA, it is even hotter than death and sex, which come in a close second and third.[1]

The Fear Monster

The Saturn-Uranus opposition, still in orb at this writing (late 2009), is our invitation to practice freedom (Uranus) from fear (Saturn). And with transiting Pluto (breakdown) still opposed to the US (Sibly) chart's Venus (finances), for many Americans it is money that pushes the fear button.

Astrologers are not the only observers who have associated the years ahead with the end of the dollar as a world currency,[2] the breakdown of the US Federal Reserve, and resource depletion on a global scale. Even making a hypothetical reference to such scenarios is enough to freak out a lot of people. And this is part of our reality; the state of the collective mind is part of the terrain of these years. I'm not proposing that we deny the freaking out that's happening all around us. But for the consciousness seeker, freaking out is contraindicated for several reasons.

---

[1] Pluto, the planet of raw power, is in the second house of money in the US (Sibly) chart.

[2] While the US public's attention is riveted on perverse political spectacles like the health care "debate," the rest of the world is watching the financial centers in newly ascendant powers like China, Russia, India, Pakistan and Iran, who are gaining the leverage to rid Eurasia of America's military control trips and government debt. Those Asian countries that have so far accepted US dollars – money everybody knows has no chance of being repaid — are unlikely to keep funding America's military aggression against them.

First of all, it's unhealthful. It would be far better for our bodies, minds and spirits if we were to back up, take a breath, and consider with clear-eyed dispassion events as they arise. Secondly, to let fear dominate us is a waste of the energy at our disposal. Fear is not the most interesting thing about what's happening. It distracts us from the wisdom we could be learning from this extraordinary historical moment.

If one believes that there is a cosmic plan behind this period of global distress, isn't this plan worthier of our interest than the fear it arouses?

The Practice

To tease out what the plan is, we have to look at the situation energetically. We need to begin by separating the subject matter from the charge emanating from it. The subject matter here – that which is being reacted to – is a perceived loss of material security. Or, more precisely, the idea that our financial status quo is going to change in some way. Consider that the charge emanating from these ideas is not the same thing as the ideas themselves.

The emanating charge is an energy pattern with its own unique quality, texture and force. To notice this distinction is our first step towards freedom: the freedom from being sucked in by fear. Imagine being chased by a monster in a nightmare, and, instead of focusing on how scared you are, you focus instead on the color of the monster's fur.

This approach could teach us some useful truths about fear in general. Ancient tradition links panic to the first and second chakras of the human body, the ones linked to physical survival. (If you are someone who can read auras, you might see a lot of people flashing red and yellow right now from their coccyx and groin.)

When we observe reactive energy with detached curiosity, the most salient feature we notice is its sheer power.

Which leads us to the pivotal question: If all that power wasn't going into fear, where might it go instead?

The World of Matter

So how did money and possessions acquire all this psychological power? Why has modern Western culture put so much emphasis on material things? We have suggested that Pluto in the US house of money is our first clue. At this point in history, America's love-hate relationship with the material realm has cranked itself up to a mad fever, and much of the rest of the world has caught the bug.

Esoteric law can also help us understand how this came about. Money is a symbol of the plane of matter (which is why financial issues are described with the adjective *material*). In the modern mind, money represents the material plane concentrated down to its essence. Our distorted relationship with money is a function of our distorted relationship with the material plane.

The human mind craves, fears, and obsesses over that which it has separated itself from. Americans, and those cultures that have followed America's materialist lead, have done this with matter.[3]

Richard Tarnas has chronicled in eloquent detail the tortured journey by which the post-Cartesian mind has estranged itself from the physical.[4] Our ecocidal ways bear witness to the fact that we seem to have forgotten we are children of planet Earth. So does our ambivalent dis-identification with our physical bodies – a strange ontological split that has resulted in sexual urges being seen not as natural but as untrustworthy and dangerous. Another example of this split is the way we interpret physical illness as evidence that the body is the enemy. We speak of a patient "courageously battling" a disease, as if their bodies were war zones within which their mind was the protagonist-soldier.

Humanity seems to have made a collective decision a few centuries ago to approach the material dimension in a completely different way than we approach the other dimensions of existence.
Contrast the way we view the emotional, the spiritual and mental realms. We still see them more or less the way the ancients did: they are part of us, they permeate us, their creations originate within us. But we no longer see the world of matter this way.

The Earth plane is seen as exclusively external, as if it were made of different stuff. Its operations must be tackled and wrestled to the ground. If we are smart or lucky, the material world may be mastered, but not because it's on our side. We are taught to maneuver the world of practical details, logistics, of business and money as if it were hostile terrain.

---

[3] The US (Sibly) chart helps us understand how America's consumer values became exported to the rest of the world over the century that has just ended. See *Soul-Sick Nation,* op. cit. p 30.

[4] See especially *The Passion of the Western Mind* (1991).

This approach minimizes our own agency and exaggerates our helplessness. We have bestowed upon the material realm a dangerous power it would not otherwise have. And we have made money the holy grail of this realm.

Meaning of Money

By esoteric law – eloquently reframed for us by physicists like David Bohm – events in our world bubble up from the unseen arenas beneath manifestation. All forms originate from this substructure of formlessness. Our tangible realities arise from thoughts, attitudes and yearnings engendered in a zone that is not tangible at all.[5]

This is not a new idea. It has been stated in innumerable iterations throughout the annals of classical and mystical tradition, and it finds widespread agreement among modern consciousness seekers. Yet it seems to be qualitatively more difficult for people to apply it to the world of money than to other areas of life. Indeed, we have a tendency to suspend all sorts of laws and beliefs where money is concerned. We seem to think of financial matters as occupying a unique kind of reality, as in "I don't have the luxury of getting all philosophical here. I'm talking about the real world. How am I going to pay the rent?"

Though I've never heard a client say it out loud, the prevailing assumption seems to be that the *everything-is-just-energy* rule doesn't apply where money is concerned. In astrological discussions, money matters seem to have a velvet rope cordoning them off. The practitioner may be invited into this arena – indeed, the anxiety surrounding it gives rise to frequent invitations – but he is expected to handle it differently. The client wants him to suddenly suspend all symbolic interpretations and go literal.

By contrast, as regards relationships, I find that people will nod knowingly when you suggest that they *create their own reality*. As regards to their career, too, they tend to be fully open to the notion that internal drives are at work. Similarly, in terms of their spiritual lives they have no trouble at all seeing their current state as the result of unconscious energies assembling in cosmically appropriate ways.

But to suggest that the same processes are at work in our financial lives is to provoke an automatic defensive posture. The client's lower chakras go on red alert. She may move into an animal crouch, as if her meat were about to be grabbed away.

---

[5] See *The Field of Being: Collected Thoughts on the Evolution of Human Consciousness* by Don Nix (iUniverse 2009).

When all is said and done, surely this is the most interesting thing of all about money.

In our more sanguine moments, were we to apply the precepts of humanistic astrology unconditionally, we would have to conclude that even money is just an end product of aboriginal energies that have nothing to do, ultimately, with the physical world. They aren't born there. They just end up there.

Transits

This is to say that if we want to use astrology to assess what's happening in the world right now, we have to apply our axioms consistently. If reality is a construct of human consciousness, then financial reality must be no different. The way money enters and leaves our lives is no more arbitrary than anything else. The lessons money teaches us are as soul-generated as any other life teachings.

The oddly exclusive status we grant to money tells us a great deal about the current state of the collective unconscious. In our era, the attention we pay to our material needs and wants has crowded out the attention we pay to all other concerns of life.

To reach any meaningful understanding of the years ahead we must confront the preternatural importance we have given to money in our philosophical vocabulary. Not to dwell on it as a moral problem – these years are not about ethical judgments – but to see it as a gross imbalance that the transits are here to address. The harsh angles being made by Pluto (breakdown) to Saturn (elimination) and Uranus (abrupt departures from the past), though they may be expressing themselves through financial crises, are not *causing* those crises. The planets are only markers, mapping out a series of profound changes the human animal is slated to go through.

By cosmic logic these changes are being expressed in terms the current human mind can understand. Ours is a world where material concerns have become the predominant way to define experience, so these are the terms through which we're experiencing the transits.
The real change afoot has to do not with what money does but with what money means.

Haves and Have-Nots

The majority of people on Earth live hand to mouth. During the upcoming years, the have-nots of the world will be pressed by material hardship on a scale unimaginable to the relatively tiny proportion of the global population with enough financial security to worry about losing it.

According to Gwyn Kirk of the AGAPE Foundation, a billion people in the world live on less than a dollar a day; another billion live on less than two dollars a day. The world's wealthiest 946 people, identified by Forbes Magazine in 2006, comprised about 0.0145% of the global population, with a net worth figured to be $3.5 trillion: about 3% of the world's wealth. The U.N. estimates that just 500 rich people in the world earn more than the 416 million poorest people.

Then there's the rest of the First World, the merely middle-class. As the have-nots scramble to survive, many of this latter group will spend the next few years pumping their vital energy into stock quotes, interest rates and retirement funds.

The Karma of Money

Contemplating the contrast between the First and Third Worlds as regards privation – or the perception of it – is a sobering and instructive exercise, and it would certainly broaden our perspective to add it to our meditation practice. But it wouldn't be enough. Not just because merely wringing one's hands in anguish about the starving masses is unhelpful to them. But also because, in a spiritual sense, it's unhelpful to *us*. Pondering where we are not doesn't tell us where we are.

We need to take responsibility for where we find ourselves during these critical years. If, as truth seekers, we believe that time and place are never arbitrary, it follows that where we live is no accident. Each of us ends up where we are for a precise set of soul-driven reasons. The country we live in is, for better or worse, the perfect setting for the intentions of our higher self. In this view, if you live in the USA you were fated to grapple with the weirdness as well as the opportunities that America represents. Your soul expressly chose, for its own karmic reasons, to develop against the backdrop of a financially neurotic society.

Numbers vs. Image

America's fixation on money has resulted in a curiously skewed self-image. For all that they attribute to money more *realness* than it deserves, most Americans are strikingly out of touch with the reality of money as it plays itself out in collective life.

One of the most telling symptoms of this disconnect is the degree to which the country's most beloved national story, the tale of Horatio Alger, flies in the face of the way America actually works. The myth declares that in this land of opportunity (which phrase is implicitly understood to mean *opportunity to make money*), any poor kid can strike it rich. Indeed, there is supposed to be no such thing as social class. But the truth is the USA is closer to the Third World than to Western Europe in terms of income disparities. Statistically, the gaping abyss between rich and poor in America is comparable to that in Brazil and Central Asia.

A society's self-image may be flagrantly inaccurate, but its numbers do not lie. Money speaks volumes about what a culture values. What does it say about a country that lavishes half of its discretionary spending on the military? Every day $500 million of American taxpayers' money goes to pay for the occupations in Iraq and Afghanistan while expenditures for the common good (healthcare, schools, etc.) are whittled down to the bone. The American president has been forced to insist that he won't sign any health care bill that adds any amount to the national debt, but he is never asked to make such a promise when it comes to troop escalations or bank bailouts.

These skewed priorities, bizarre discrepancies and widening gaps between fact and fiction in the national identity are signals of collective illness. A doctor whose patient presented contradictions this cockeyed would have reason to be concerned about an imminent nervous breakdown.

Pluto, the planet of breakdowns of every stripe, is bringing these distortions to a head. All of the planetary players now assembling are there to bring a wildly imbalanced situation back into eventual balance.

CHAPTER 3

FOUR POINTS OF THE CROSS
2010

For seven years, I kept the chart of a date in the summer of 2010 tacked up on my bulletin board. Over the years leading up to it, I'd often look at that piece of paper, its edges now curling and its ink faded, and try to imagine how on Earth energies that explosive would manifest. It felt like I was looking at something out of science fiction. And then: Boom! 2010 was here. The chart was no longer speculative. It was reality.

It was the stunning geometry of its planetary placements that had astrologers everywhere in a thrall of speculation. That August, for example, two of the most powerful planets in the sky, Uranus and Pluto, were going to line up with Jupiter, Saturn, the Sun and Mars, to form a Cardinal Cross, with the Pluto-Uranus relationship as its anchor. The charts from the Summer of 2010 kicked off a riff of globe-altering transits that summed up the potential in the years upcoming: the people of the world (Uranus) were going to get the chance to realize how much power (Pluto) they have.

Astrologers have long expected the current epoch to be rife with historic change, analogous to the social change of the1960s. Back then, the planet of transformation (Pluto) and the planet of revolution (Uranus) were in an earlier phase of their current cycle. Analogous, but not an exact repeat; given how much the world has changed since the days of flower power, the Beatles and Vietnam.

Humanity has been through the sexual revolution, the discrediting of the Mother Church and the tech revolution. The green movement and the global financial meltdown have disabused us of much of our naïveté. Environmental degradation and freak weather events have caused unprecedented numbers of refugees to pour across national borders, changing the world's collective assumptions about national identity, as have globalization and the consolidation of the world's wealth.

The nature of war itself has changed. Patriotism has been trumped in this new era by the reactivation of ancient religious feuds, and by the desire to wrest control of certain ever-more-precious finite resources (among them, the minerals used by electronic gadgets and the last of the world's oil). Ten years into the new millennium, the world's superpowers have shifted positions. Uncle Sam is now in hock to China for a trillion bucks, and the former empires of Europe are teetering on the brink of bankruptcy.

In April of 2010 an oil rig exploded in the Gulf of Mexico, invoking outrage and grief in Earth lovers worldwide. A heated public discussion sprang up about corporate greed. There were hints that the concept of income inequality would break through the threshold of collective consciousness, a theme that would erupt explicitly six months later, at the winter solstice.

Over the course of 2010, as explosive planetary pictures formed, broke apart and reformed in the sky, the psychic environment on Earth intensified. Ecological warriors, political activists and spiritual seekers were galvanized. Dots got connected in many minds between the urgent events taking place and the myriad ancient prophecies associated with this era. Many people who had felt aimless and discouraged before now felt fired up and ready to do their part, in whatever form their unique skill set directed them.

This was happening despite a new level of chaos being reflected in the mirror of the mass media, with official agencies and profit-seekers scrambling to exploit the burgeoning feelings of uncertainty and peril in the populace. Tuned into the power of the Cardinal Cross, many people were starting to feel more alive than ever before.

ALL IN THE SAME BOAT

(originally published in *Skywatch*,
February 2010)

The world is melting. And I don't mean just polar ice caps.

February 2012 marks the conjunction of Neptune with Chiron to the degree of
arc. Neptune is the planet of dissolution; that is, it does what hot tea does to
sugar, and what an emotional melt-down does to our self-control. Neptune
dissolves, erases and effaces.

On a personal level, Neptune is associated with the little ego-effacements we
endure in the course of living: those moments when our sense of competence
disappears and we just wimp out. Mentally, Neptune can throw us off-message;
make us sloppy, ungrounded and confused. Such experiences weaken our focus
on the external world. This we do not like at all.

Part of the reason we don't like it is that we've been conditioned not to like it.
Modern societies define strength in terms of robust activity and competitive
accomplishment. Humbling is for 15th-Century nuns, not for us. We equate
humbling with humiliation.

But we will miss the point of Neptune transits entirely if we measure ourselves in
terms of Type-A activity. These transits have nothing to do with worldly success
per se (though they don't preclude them; they're just not about them). Neptune is
about spiritual awareness. If it has to, it will weaken whatever stands in the way
of soul wisdom.

Walls

The Neptune conjunction is happening in Aquarius, the sign of collective
intelligence. The most obvious place to look for this blurring and effacement
right now is in the human collective. False separations are melting; illusions of
superiority that make one group think it is different from other groups are
gradually being erased. Neptune is trying to get humanity to see its inter-

connectedness.

This planet, named for the god of the sea, makes its statements in watery terms: it floods, erodes and wipes out. It isn't just the deltas and habitats of Earth that are threatened right now. Also being wiped out are the effective geographical boundaries that separate countries. Neptune is bringing to the surface the fundamental arbitrariness of apartheid of every type.
It's showing us the madness of the USA's attempts to keep Mexicans from crossing its border with an actual wall. It's making us look again at Israel, whose blockades and checkpoints have kept the people of Gaza trapped in their bombed-out peninsula, and whose leaders are now building a wall to keep out African migrants.

Such efforts are not only cruel but stupid. They are doomed to fail. While Chiron in Aquarius makes the wound of class and race divisions more and more obvious, Neptune is making our efforts to divide ourselves from each other as futile as building sand castles at high tide.

Cap and Trade

The world has been taking a crash course in Neptune symbolism since it opposed Saturn (consensual reality) in 2004-07. This was the transit that saw climate change cross the threshold from questionable theory to common knowledge. In 2009, Jupiter (dissemination of knowledge) added its promotional skills to the campaign, and the balance was tipped: for more and more people, global warming suddenly got very real. At the tail end of the year, in Copenhagen, the great powers of global officialdom admitted *en masse* that climate change posed a unique threat to life on Earth.

People are listening up in a new way.

The acceptance of climate change has opened the door to the acceptance of other aspects of our poor stewardship of the Earth, as well, such as species extinction and the increasing shortage of clean water. To admit to the truth of these issues is a huge leap of consciousness.

Sometimes the truth hurts, as we know; and letting all these things sink in has, over the past couple of years, has left many of us shocked and numb (negative Neptune).

We have been thrown off our bearings, and this makes us vulnerable. In this state we need to be particularly selective about what information we plug into. Should we listen to the big-power G12 delegates who convened in December – the guys who were driven to Copenhagen in specially commissioned stretch limos? Should we listen to the talking heads on TV – who portrayed the protestors there as irresponsible criminals?

To avoid being overwhelmed by the magnitude of what is happening, and to be of any use to our world, we need to cultivate an eyes-wide-open realism. This starts by disabusing ourselves of the illusion that America's elected officials and pundits – funded, as they are, by deep-pocket interests – have a workable plan. Granted, the powerful interests of the world have their stories ready about our various global crises, and it is these stories that fill the airwaves. But in order to make use of this information, we need to decode it.

The "cap and trade" schemes being cooked up by Western powers and Wall Street bankers would allow mega-corporations to profit from the pollution they cause. While the conscience-driven activists who poured into Copenhagen from all over the world were gassed with chemical weapons and thrown in jail, the delegates inside the polished halls busied themselves with setting up an international speculative market that would buy and sell carbon emissions. It really is something out of a Stanley Kubrick parody, when you think about it.

If what we want is an understanding that is as vast as possible, we must establish a clear-eyed geopolitical perspective, then put what we know into cosmic perspective. These two levels of understanding do not conflict with each other. They are both true, and they are both more necessary than ever.

Cleaning Up Our Act

With denial out of the way, we face the knotty problem of facing the emotions that tend to arise when information this daunting begins to sink in. Fear, despair and helplessness are no fun, and we don't like feeling them. But if we have made the spiritual decision to say *No* to denial, it is our responsibility to negotiate these feelings if and when they come up.

By allowing ourselves to feel them, I don't mean to say that we should stay stuck in them. That doesn't help. It doesn't help the Earth, and it doesn't help us.

But the sense of catastrophe we are feeling does have a meaning. We are feeling this urgency for a reason; in the same way that the warning light on the dashboard of your car is there for a reason. Its *raison-d'être* is to point to something important. The various systems collapses of the years 2008-23 are pointers to show us how ignorant we have been, so that we can clean up our act.

If we could anthropomorphize for a minute and consider the situation from Neptune and Chiron's point of view, we might see global calamities as the only way the recalcitrant human race can get hip to the fact that *we're all in this together*. The cosmos realizes that humanity somehow missed the memo on this one; as a corrective, it is stepping in. If it takes global warming and the breakdown of world financial markets to make us realize how interconnected we are, so be it.

When we assimilate this understanding as it applies to groups of people – for example, the wackiness of human groups trying to erect racial caste systems to try to prevent miscegenation – we can't help but extend it further, to every buzzing particle of life on the planet. We start to realize that separating devices of all kinds are man-made ideas. Not Nature's idea.

As the Bioneers say, "It's all alive. It's all intelligent. It's all connected."

Our fellow Earth-dwellers from the vegetable, animal and mineral kingdoms can teach us a thing or two. It doesn't matter to the flora and fauna whether humanity calls their habitat Rhodesia or Zimbabwe. The Earth's minerals don't care which superpower owns the rights to them. Earth's river and ocean systems don't give a fig about how we categorize their tributaries. The mountains that loom over the plains don't care what colors are printed on the flags men stick into them.

All On Board

We will be hearing a lot of "I told you so" from the world's visionaries in the years ahead. Those prescient souls who saw these crises coming decades ago are increasingly having their voices heard.

It has never been more obvious that necessity is the mother of invention. As the waters rise and the droughts spread, so are the profiles of once-dismissed theorists such as the hippie-engineers who develop clean cooking stoves for third world populations; the African conservationist who has just been awarded a Goldman Prize; the urban planners whose advocacy of rooftop farming was once met by blank looks.

The women's spirituality movement, which was seen as silly at best or blasphemous at worst to mainstream thinkers, up until a few years ago, is now informing scientists, who call it the Gaia theory. We don't hear the embarrassingly ignorant phrase "tree-hugger" too much anymore. What we hear of is thousands of young people graduating from green programs in college campuses worldwide.[1]

Earth-lovers who saw the writing on the wall have waited a long time to assert themselves in fully creative ways. Now, under the Aquarius conjunctions (collective activity) they are pooling their resources. The sustainable agriculture folks are joining forces with the clean-energy researchers; the anti-strip-mining activists in West Virginia are supporting the Nigerian farmers under siege by Shell Oil. Interconnectedness is the name of the game.

Butterflies, businessmen, spotted owls, soccer moms and Brazilian child street hawkers: we are all in this together, watching the old world get washed away.

---

[1] Many of the graduates of such programs seem to recognize that their relatively affluent upbringings allowed them to choose to acquire this knowledge, as a means to back up their idealism. If it seems surprising that this group lacks the sense of entitlement typical of their age, it makes sense astrologically. Born when they were and raised where they were, the most insightful of them are aware of the sense of responsibility for the state of the planet reflected in the Cardinal Cross. At some level of consciousness, all of us know that we were born under a certain set of circumstances for a very specific set of reasons. The world situation is, in every case, the perfect backdrop for our soul development – not random, not a thing apart.

MASTERPIECE OF DISINGENUOUSNESS

(originally published as a blog,
March 2010)

If you tried to invent something to symbolize the Aquarius conjunction that's been dogging the US Moon for a couple of years now, you'd never come up with anything more perfect than what actually happened. Up in the sky Neptune (universality) has been orbiting alongside Chiron (healing) and Jupiter (reform) in Aquarius (medicine). And what do we get? Health care reform.

Now that Jupiter has sped ahead and left the conjunction, the reform piece seems to have dropped out, and it's just Neptune and Chiron again. As the transit wafts along into its third year, it's time to take stock of some of the other dimensions of its symbolism.

Neptune is about illusion: it teaches that things are never as they appear. As a Buddhist truth, this is pretty unarguable. But in the absence of spiritual maturity, the fullness of the idea doesn't translate, and we get stuck in the transit's dark side. We become vulnerable to deception: a crippling (Chiron) of our ability to discern the real from the unreal (Neptune).

There is nothing wrong with stagecraft *per se*, of course. When it's used consciously, it becomes an art form. But when stagecraft is not seen as such by its audience, negative Neptune takes over. This is what's happened to American politics.

Systemic Illness

The agencies set up to inform misinform instead, with a mess of flashy distraction and deliberate lies. The bills that pass are the results of bought-and-paid-for politicians brokering backroom deals. The national conversation has all the dignity of a food fight in a grade school reformatory.

But these are symptoms only. As a fever can be symptomatic of a whole-body disease, the corruption and ludicrous incivility of America's current political discourse are symptomatic of an all-encompassing social illness.[1] To arrive at an understanding of it, we need to float up above the fray and cop a planet's eye view.

From the moment we turn off the TV and leave the propaganda behind, we see in the health care debacle a set of meanings very different from what the pundits have been saying. First of all, we see a bill apparently rooted in GOP principles – in that it's market-based and eliminates any chance of buying insurance from the government – that the *Democrats* passed and the *Republicans* unanimously stonewalled. This should be our first signal that there's something fishy in how it's being served up.

Brothers Under the Skin

Before the propaganda went into full swing, it was clear that the majority of US voters wanted a public option. Democratic politicians – who are billed, per the script, as champions of the working stiff – appealed to this majority in their campaigns. Once elected, however, they did a little bait-and-switch number: they changed the plan to one that would subsidize the insurance companies, claiming that they lacked the votes for a public option. The fact that they still had a clear majority was empirically verifiable, but they shamelessly refused to hold a vote to prove it.

The truth is, of course, that these guys had just raked in record-breaking amounts of campaign money from the insurance industry, just as their counterparts across the aisle had. Towards the end, drug companies were actually hunkered down with the Democrats in unpublicized meetings, lending a hand to help the bill pass. But the public didn't see this part on TV.

What the public did see was what they've been trained to expect: the ol' two-teams-mixing-it-up trope, displayed with increasing degrees of acrimony. Like TV wrestlers breaking fake rebar over each other's heads for the amusement of a boozed-up crowd, the Democrats and Republicans are putting on a show. Health-care, like many another high-profile issue, has been presented as a rousing, nasty, "Left-vs.-Right" blood match.

But if we want to learn anything from the Neptune (drama, masques) transit, and that of the Cardinal Cross, we need to look beyond this cartoon narrative.

No way did Republican politicians truly believe the bill was "socialistic." They

---

[1] See *Soul-Sick Nation*, op. cit. p 30.

knew quite well the opposite was true. But they were pledged to the script. As for the Democrats, at the same moment that Obama was declaring the bill a victory for "ordinary working folks," in another part of Washington the insurance execs, who had just been promised 32 million new customers, were throwing themselves victory parties.

And the show goes on.

Behind the Hoopla

As suggested by the Pluto-Saturn-Uranus T-square of 2010, the reasons for this charade go as deep as we dare to look. The multi-billion-dollar spectator sport that is American politics is designed to distract the public from the singular truth of US society: the one Jim Hightower was referring to when he said, "The true political spectrum in this country is not right to left, but top to bottom."

Most Americans are so brainwashed by the right-to-left narrative that they can't imagine asking any other question except *should the bill have passed or not?* But the partisan madness surrounding this issue, orchestrated to compel our undiluted attention, is not where the significance lies.

The significance lies in the fact that our politicians are funded by corporations through the lobby system, and that the media is too.

To overlook this fundamental fact in all the culture-war hoopla is to lose sight of the power of these times, as signified by the most critical of current transits, the epochal Cardinal T-square. Once sucked into the official narrative, we neglect to ask the trenchant questions. This happened to the tea party bunch, who had their script handed to them by Fox News, and obediently transformed themselves into a vicious mob. And it happened to the *Anyone-who-doesn't-back-Obama-is-a-traitor* liberals, who likewise accepted the terms of debate that had been dictated to them.

Either too dumbed-down by the way issues are framed to ask *Qui bono?* or so dispirited that they zone out in angst, most Americans neglect to use the power of their minds to repudiate the nonsense, the power of their votes to throw the bums out, or the power of their numbers to demand reforms of public benefit.

But the era is demanding that we address the fact that the country is a plutocracy. It's a fact that we'll either be subsumed by or do something about.

MAKING TRANSITS YOUR OWN

(originally published in *Skywatch*,
June 2010)

The Full Moon this month is a lunar eclipse, an exaggerated Full Moon. And it's not just any eclipse. Its chart features a tight Grand Cross made up of no less than seven planets. We'll have Saturn, Uranus-Jupiter and Pluto-Moon in a T-square, with the Sun-Mercury in Cancer supplying the final vertex to make it a full Grand Cross. The reason predictive astrologers are watching this chart like a hawk is that the extreme tension in such patterns is often associated with dramatic world events.

But humanistic astrologers see things somewhat differently. We don't see transits as operating by cause and effect. It isn't as if the eclipse will *cause* this or that to happen. It just describes the great themes afoot, telling us what time it is. Moreover, it's not particularly empowering to sit around waiting to react.

In order to learn from this or any other transit, why wait to see what the group mind will cook up by way of illustration? We don't need the news in order to engage with the eclipse.

Tale Told by an Idiot

Then there is the fact that the mainstream news is highly unreliable as an indicator of significance. The commercial subtexts and outright falsehoods streaming into people's living rooms day in and day out make most of what's shown on television more mind control than teaching tool. As far as the promotion of consumer goods is concerned, the mass media displays a diabolical psychological genius and a state-of-the-art aesthetic sophistication. But artistically and intellectually, we would have to consider it an embarrassment and a failure.

It is true that if we carefully decode the welter of distorted reporting, we may find clues in the media with which to parse transits. But as interpreters of meaning, TV and radio are worse than worthless. Those who want to connect with cosmic messages must maintain a skeptical distance from our society's highly paid savants, the talking heads. What TV tells us is going on in the world is a far cry from "the way it is," as Walter Cronkite used to say.

Consider the way stories are prioritized on American television. It's not as if the crisis of the Euro had nothing to do with Americans because they don't hear as much about it as they hear about the juvenile infighting of their own two political parties. It's not as if the slaughter in Central Asia isn't happening.[1] But on May 28th, 2010, when the US death toll in Afghanistan reached the grim figure of 1,000, the big-city newspaper where I live featured a local sporting event on the front page.

It is time to engage, deeply and authentically, with the era we have incarnated into. This means telling the truth to ourselves. Some of us may do so by aligning with path-showing teachers, by joining groups that speak truth to power while providing safety-in-numbers, or by choosing allies wisely. We can all do so by seeking out reliable information.

When we access clean data and stay connected to the moment, we attract the truth. We draw to us exactly the right people and opportunities to help us make sense of our unique role, and perform it boldly.

The Big Four

During the Cardinal Cross years, try to feel the planets' energies in your belly. Especially when a transit emphasizes the Moon, as this month's does, the economic and political climate will be palpable on a direct, emotional level by all who are not shut down.

In order to make the most of these teachings, look at the houses in your chart where the four cardinal points fall: Aries, Cancer, Libra and Capricorn. If you follow the degrees of the planets in an ephemeris or on the internet, keep abreast of their progress through the signs, and consider what planets or angles they are aspecting in your chart. These placements represent the crossroads you're

---

[1] A report from 2009 estimates that over the past three years the War in Afghanistan – or, more accurately, the war in Afghanistan-Pakistan – has been responsible for the deaths of 700 civilians and 14 "suspected terrorists." That's about fifty of the former for every one of the latter. One would think that more Americans, still reeling from the trauma of 9/11, would see their government's current murder spree of Muslim innocents as highly dangerous to themselves, in that it could not help but fuel anti-American rage among Islamicists worldwide. With barely any pundits of national stature connecting the dots in this way, we have to ask ourselves how useful the mass media is.

standing at.

For the world at large, these four vertices represent the lessons humanity is being taught right now:

–Uranus (conjunct Jupiter from June 2010 – January 2011) expresses Cardinal fire. This is the energy we feel, for example, in a rousing street demonstration that speaks truth to power.

– Pluto in Capricorn expresses Cardinal earth, cool and mercilessly realistic. It is telling us: *Eliminate the corruption in your monetary systems or they will fall apart like a house of cards.* It is saying *Either save this planet or you will not survive.*

– Anything passing through Libra (as Saturn currently is, through late 2012) regulation, contraction. This is Cardinal air, so the lesson is that we take the responsibility to review our moral and social laws, such as governmental limits on industry.

– The summertime Cancer transits (which include, every year, at least the Sun) express Cardinal water, the most emotional of the four. For those open to it, it will feel like a reminder that neglecting our planetary home amounts to a kind of planetary matricide.

If you keep a journal or make notes in your calendar, pay attention to what happens for you, internally and externally, under key transits like these. If you do rituals, ask for a message about your place in the world moment. If you have your chart read, ask your astrologer to describe your life purpose.

Difficult to Ignore

These transits are hell-bent on change, and the world's dying institutions will not withstand their assault. Issues that have been heating up already will demand to be acknowledged: global debt (of which Greece, Portugal. Italy, Ireland and Spain; much of Asia; all of Africa; and not least the USA are bellwethers), resource depletion and systems collapse.

For those who are receptive to what's trying to happen, the stale bromides of conventional wisdom will chafe. The little lies of everyday life will feel unbearable. Platitudes from our pundits and politicians will vex us, like toxic food in the belly that wants to be purged. The injustices and corruptions of the world will be increasingly difficult to ignore.

Uranus in Aries

The conjunction in mid-2010 of Uranus and Jupiter, fresh from their ingress into Aries, makes the fire corner of the Cross the most palpable of the four right now. It should put the spark of rebellion into all of us, and our goal should be to express this as mature, self-aware rebellion. Certainly we will find no lack of things to rebel against. This energy is often unconscious; and we have good reason to make it conscious this month because Jupiter's presence will amplify it.

Regardless of what transits are happening, each of us has a lifelong relationship with Uranus, which feels like a champing-at-the-bit urgency. Your natural way of channeling it is indicated by the planet's placement in your natal chart. Every seven years, Uranus' electric urgency takes on a new set of issues, and natives born under its aegis break away from whatever that sign represents. *En masse*, a generation is consigned to buck the trend in that particular way.

For those of us born under Uranus in Cancer (1949-56), it was our parents' version of domesticity that felt unbearable: we couldn't get away from it fast enough. For the Uranus-in-Leo generation who came along next (1955-56 to 1961-62), it was about repudiating old forms of creativity: new forms had to be invented that looked like nothing that had come before. As for you Uranus-in-Virgo people, you know who are you are. You find conventional attitudes towards work and health intolerable – and Goddess bless you for it.

In those natal charts where Uranus is pronounced, there is an explosive urge to repudiate complacency. Now that Uranus has moved into Aries, the first sign of the zodiac, we're going to have a crop of babies whose defiance will be pumped into full-speed-ahead action. And for those of us already grown, these skies are bestowing – and demanding – that we rebel from inauthentic agencies and ideas with fiery enthusiasm.

Everyone a Risk-Taker

During the Cardinal Crossroads (2008-23) we'll need to know ourselves exceptionally well, as high-risk athletes, cliff climbers and stock car drivers do. We'll need to know our limits because we'll be driven to push them further.

Most of us won't play out these energies physically. Like tournament chess players and suicide hot-line staffers, the high stakes may be psychological. If we are artists, the stakes may be aesthetic or conceptual. Like Bjork's, whose Uranus is on the Midheaven to the degree.[2]

It's never been more important to live through your chart. There are revelations to be had.

---

[2] She was born November 21, 1965, 7:50 AM, Reykjavik, Iceland.

THE SOLSTICE CROSS

(originally published in *Daykeeper
Journal*, June 2010)

To say that the Full Moon this month packs a punch is something of an understatement.

Full Moons always bring to a head whatever's been building, both in our own little internal worlds and in the big, wide, external world. But this particular Full Moon, on June 26, 2010, is an eclipse, which adds potency to whatever is culminating.

More significant still, the Moon and Sun will be joined by five other planets, including the T-square among Uranus, Saturn and Pluto that has been leading us into the 2012-15 years. It is not merely a Full Moon but a Grand Cross. Though not all are in Cardinal signs yet – Uranus and Saturn have retrograded back into mutable signs – this eclipse will be our introduction to what some astrologers are calling the Cardinal Climax. In the popular mind this period has revolved around the mythic year 2012.

What does it mean? On perhaps the most obvious level, it means that our doddering old social structures (Saturn) are up against two of the most powerful planets in the sky: Uranus and Pluto, whose functions are to shake up and break down that which is no longer of use. The obsolete remnants of the old paradigm are rotting away.

Saturn vs. Jupiter

It's not that Saturn will be vanquished. Perish the thought; we need its form and cohesion. This is the planet that glues individuals and societies together. But clearly Saturn's old expressions must be removed in order to get the new era underway. Our job is to let this happen. How do we do this? Simply by being conscious that it must happen.

The mysterious purposes of Uranus (the Great Awakener) and Pluto (the

Transformer) are vaster and more sublime than the human ego. These evolutionary forces will, with increasing intensity over the next several years, expose the corrupt structures of the pre-millennial world. To build a healthy post-millennial world, we'll need to harness Saturn's energies effectively to erect replacement structures.

Such as laws (Saturn in Libra) to regulate the flailing financial industry.

In the chart of the USA, Jupiter (expansion) is conjunct the Sun but square (in conflict with) Saturn (contraction, discipline); which reflects a childlike assumption that what goes up need not come down.[1] Thus, our national belief that big is better, and more is merrier. At this point in American history, that misguided Jupiter-Sun conjunction has devolved into a greed-is-good mentality.

The Goldman Sachs executives now squirming under the spotlight personify the USA's unbridled Jupiter, which is crying out to be reined in. A healthy dose of Saturn is desperately needed right now. The campaign to regulate the lending industry is an example of using restrictive energy for constructive ends.

But there is tremendous tension between the planets in a Grand Cross, as illustrated by this sorry reality: despite the obvious need for financial reform, Wall Street calls the tune in Congress through entrenched economic and political power networks (Pluto). The struggles in Washington and around the world between the energies of the old and the new (Saturn opposed to Uranus), between power and authority (Pluto square Saturn), and between ordinary people and entrenched cartels (Uranus and Pluto) will create much drama during the years ahead.

US Saturn Return

It seems odd, at first blush, that there is relatively little outrage among struggling working stiffs in the USA about the lopsided distribution of the country's wealth. But it isn't so odd when we consider the Sun conjunction in the US (Sibly) chart. That Jupiter-gone-wrong not only creates grotesque affluence; it creates the craving for grotesque affluence in those who are unlikely to ever achieve it.

I am thinking of the GOP-voting working poor, who see themselves as foes of curbing corporations, and who see the idea of taxing billionaires as being somehow a threat to their own freedom. In what seems to be an economic version of Stockholm syndrome, this segment of the population, though impoverished themselves, harbors a clear disdain for poverty.

I don't know if all of the Tea Party folks are wannabe plutocrats (it's hard to tell, amidst the welter of confused philosophical principles that underlie the Tea Party worldview); but it is clear that most of them heartily dis-identify with the poor and disenfranchised. As regards the inherent unfairness of America's outrageous income disparities, the attitude seems to be: *I don't care if it's fair or not. I just want my shot at the big bucks.*

For Americans a big subplot of the Cardinal Cross period is the US Saturn Return, which will peak in 2011. As everyone over thirty has had the chance to discover (whether they've made the discovery is another question), the Saturn Return is a transit of maturity. This one will put great pressure on the country's natal square between Saturn (lack) and Jupiter-Sun (plenty), one manifestation of which is an economy reeling between bubbles and busts.

Transiting Saturn will force a hard look at the battle in the national psyche between expansion and contraction. We can see this in the budget cuts that are tearing states like California apart. Reeling from financial crises brought on by the refusal to implement common sense options (such as taxing Big Oil for drilling offshore, or reinstating the vehicle license fee that Governor Schwarzenegger repealed as an election ploy), California, like many other states, is instead decimating lifesaving services for its neediest citizens.

A truly mature use of Saturn would never promote such draconian measures – not because of ethical considerations (that's Jupiter arena) but because of dollars-and-cents pragmatism. If the policymakers who are cutting home care to almost half a million elderly, sick and disabled Californians were accessing Saturnine wisdom—that is, if they were really serious about being efficient, conserving resources and saving money—they would factor in the reality that by removing critical support from these citizens they are guaranteeing an overload in emergency rooms and hospitals that will end up costing far more than home care.

Collective Illness

The system is broken, and not just because of lack of money. Monstrous sums of wasted wealth are being flaunted right now in California, even as funds for the poor are slashed. The two leading Republican candidates in the gubernatorial campaign are busy spending a total of $90 million and counting. The contrasts on display here are like those of a dark parody.

What is being revealed is a systemic breakdown of a collective that has grown pathologically out of touch with reality. The strange acceptance of our plutocratic system even by those most at a disadvantaged by it, and the rash and ill-thought-out (negative Uranus) cuts (negative Saturn) by politicians interested in quick fixes, are two examples of a national Jupiter stuck in arrested development.

What, *me* grow up?

June's Grand Cross will be a jolt of clarity for all who have eyes to see it. We are heading into a period during which Americans will have to endure the same painful self-scrutiny (Saturn) of our national values (Libra) that individuals in their late twenties—and again, in their late fifties—have to face, once Natural Law tells them it's time to act like an adult.

PANDORA'S WELL

(originally published as a blog,
June 2010)

I know I'm not alone in feeling perversely gratified that the oil has made its way
to the white sands of Florida. Certainly I wish no ill to the local tourist industry,
any more than I wish more suffering to befall the fishermen in Louisiana (some
of whom, screwed and angry, are calling the compensatory pittance BP has
offered them "shut-up money.")

But there is a bitter justice in the fact that the slick might become visible in
Pensacola. It feels just and right that more and more humans will have to see the
desecration up close.

Normally we can get away with pretending our waterways are not being
poisoned, day after day, by industrial pollutants, because the toxicity is relatively
invisible. And we can defer thinking about the occasional catastrophe when we
hear the anchormen say, as they did after the 2007 San Francisco spill, "The oil is
floating well away from shore. Nothing to worry about. It's headed out to sea."

I say, bring on the tar balls. Let brown streaks leave their mark on white sand.
Let yucky sludge ruin expensive sandals.

We have upped the ante so high on our tolerance for the intolerable that it took a
trauma like this to rouse us out of our complacency. Now we cannot look away.
We are watching more than an oil slick spreading. We are watching a sea change
in our thinking about human civilization.

Insults

The insults to which our society submits the environment are being seen by many
people as if for the first time. The public has been watching TV reports for two
months now about the horrors created by "Pandora's well," as geologist Jill

Schneiderman[1] calls it. People are hearing that it has turned marshland into "dead zones." They are seeing photos of oil-soaked pelicans suffocating on the sand.

Over the two years that Uranus (rude awakenings) has been opposite Saturn (big business) there has been a shift in how people define corporate accountability and social acceptability. With the DeepWater Horizon incident this trajectory has crested. There is a mythic quality to the disaster; everything about it is larger than life. This is not surprising, given that when the disaster began, Jupiter (exaggerated size) had moved into a key position in the sky. The big gas giant, whose dark side is excess, was conjunct Uranus (explosions) and opposite Saturn (failure) when the rig blew up.

Negative Jupiter manifests as hubris. The ambitions of the oil-drillers – who are still operating a dozen other deepwater rigs of equally fatal size, right now, lessons unlearned – were all out-of-proportion to common sense. It is now well known that BP did not subject its stupendously ill-advised project to even the barest minimum of testing or planning. Misused Jupiter expresses itself in puerile recklessness.

Short-cuts and Lies

The oil company's petition to drill was riddled with short-cuts and flat-out lies. As Naomi Klein[2] has observed, in BP's assurances to the feds of how little risk the drilling would entail, they talk about Nature as if She were a predictable, agreeable junior partner - sort of an unpaid subcontractor. After the explosion occurred, they scrambled to put together clean-up strategies that were so astoundingly ineffective they'd be comic if they weren't so hideously tragic. The spirit behind these failed fixes – even their names – seems to derive from a bad action movie. "Top kills," "junk shots" and laser-directed robots with diamond saws? It sounds like little boys dreaming up cool comic-book rescues. Goddess forbid the oil executives would admit, even now, that they don't know what they're doing.

Through its malfeasance in obtaining the green light to drill, its incompetence in safeguarding the operation, its botched efforts to clean up the mess and its

---

[1] See her article, "Pandora's Oil Well" on the website earthdharma.org from May 11, 2010: http://jillschneiderman.wordpress.com/2010/05/11/pandoras-well/

[2] The best article I have read on the subject is Klein's "Gulf oil spill: A hole in the world," *The Guardian* UK June 18, 2010: http://www.guardian.co.uk/theguardian/2010/jun/19/naomi-klein-gulf-oil-spill

dishonesty in spinning the disaster to the public, BP is embodying the skewed perspective that allows these disasters in the first place. That is, the blind imperiousness of unfettered corporate power. Their approach expresses contempt for the safety and welfare of living systems, and an oblivious condescension towards Nature Herself. The world is bearing witness to the all-around cluelessness of the unbalanced Masculine.

Public Response

The Cardinal Cross years are upon us. Pluto, planet of subterranean (as well as submarine) riches is now T-squaring Saturn (responsibility) and Uranus (revelations)/Jupiter (global implications). Together they have ushered into the group mind a blowout drama that is bringing up many urgent questions at once. From the point of view of consciousness evolution, these questions are the reason this had to happen.

The disaster has triggered an unusually emotional public response; people are viscerally engaged. They are thinking about the role of cars in their lives. The phrase "oil addiction" has been coming up a lot. Many have started thinking differently about water.

There is a growing sense among the populace that if a bay is fouled miles away, our personal relationship to water is accordingly compromised. From an ecological perspective, this is not sentimental hyperbole but scientific fact; and clean water is fast becoming the most precious resource on the planet. More people die from polluted water every year than from all forms of violence, including war.[3]

The physical and esoteric meanings of water parallel each other. We learned in biology class that humanity's ancestors were single-celled sea creatures, and that all waters find their way eventually to the sea. On a symbolic level, water is the elemental home base from which we all arose, and to which we will all return.

To assuage the anguish that the clean-up crews and the oil companies and the government have failed to assuage, we can press into service, right now, the symmetry between the physical and the mystical meanings of water. As

---

[3] According to Anders Berntell, executive director of the Stockholm International Water Institute, on the website AlterNet in an article from March 19, 2010:
http://www.alternet.org/water/146101/polluted_water_more_deadly_than_war

astrologer Adam Gainsburg and other supporters of the Unity Wave[4] have suggested, one way to spiritually engage with what is occurring in the Gulf is to connect with the waters of our bodies. Such an exercise can help us come home to the universal matrix that water represents, to resonate with it, to pledge allegiance to it. This ritual promotes a healing that is appropriate to the injury at hand.

Wounded

Since April 20th, 2010 I have heard many people speak of this travesty to the Earth as a wound. Watching that remarkable undersea video of the oil spewing forth, it was hard not to be put in mind of a gushing, bleeding wound. This image is pure Chiron, which has been conjunct Neptune (the collective unconscious) since 2008. At the moment of the explosion, Chiron had just entered Pisces, the most universal of the water signs, for the first time in 41 years.

Because it departs so uncomfortably from our psychological assumptions, Chiron is one of the most problematic symbols in astrology. It dares to propose that although human pain is a fact of life, when we follow its lead fearlessly pain becomes soul medicine. Understanding the distinction between pain and suffering, which is also essential to Buddhist thought, is the key to Chironic healing. If we miss it, we're in the same boat as the student of Pluto who reads *death/rebirth* as merely *death*.

The Gulf disaster is one of those learning moments for humanity, created by the group mind. It has escorted us into the summer of the Cardinal Climax, a season long heralded as a time of revelation.

---

[4] Visit the website UnityWave.com.

A BRAND-NEW MOVIE

(originally published in *Daykeeper Journal*, July 2010)

Imagine you're a movie projectionist, watching, for the zillionth time, a corny movie with a stale old plot. Suddenly, it comes to a halt with a loud snap. The film in your old-fashioned reel projector has broken and is dangling onto the dusty floor. Your first impulse is to stare at it in panic, incredulous-to lament the damage, to fret over the interruption of your assignment, and to worry about what your boss's reaction will be. But you don't indulge these thoughts. Instead, a gleeful smile spreads across your face as you realize that you're the one who gets to choose the replacement film. You turn to the collection of movies in the archives, pick out your favorite movie and thread in the reel.

Such is the opportunity we find ourselves in this summer and in the years ahead. There is radical change in the air; there is breakdown all around us. If we're smart, we'll take advantage of it.

The universe is bound and determined to instigate wild disruptions of our individual and collective habits. We can see this from what the planets are doing in the sky right now. What is not fated is how these disruptions will manifest. If we ourselves channel the energy, on purpose, with clarity and soul-intention, we can use our creative wills to steer the changes in life-affirming directions.

During this time on Earth we are being given the chance to play with powerful forces. But it's just an opportunity, not a *dictum:* there's no cosmic gun to our heads. We don't *have* to get conscious and engage with the energy. Free will reigns supreme, here as in all things; we can try to sit back and pretend we're passive observers.

But it won't work very well. Our resistance to what's trying to happen will create suffering.

The Conscious Path

The conscious path, by contrast, may involve pain - in the positive-Saturn sense, of *painstaking* effort – but it will not involve suffering. We can either keep watching the tired old movie that's already in the projector, or we can replace it with a new one of our own choosing.

Taking up the mantle of conscious choice will prove to be well worth it. Global events are hurtling forward at mind-boggling speed. If it seems to you that things are literally moving at an accelerated pace, you're not alone; time really is moving faster.[1] This speeding-up of reality is also clear in our personal lives (especially obvious with people whose charts contain planets in Cardinal signs). Personal dramas are more dramatic. The need to make critical decisions seems more urgent.

The key configuration in the sky this summer 2010 is the Grand Cross, the most stressful configuration in astrology. With Saturn, Uranus and Pluto in a T-square, and the quickly moving Sun, Moon and personal planets in Cancer supplying the fourth piece of the puzzle, the energy we are feeling is tense and insistent.

We may miss the mellowness of previous summers. We may feel nostalgic for years past, when the world wasn't being blindsided by critical issues peaking all at once, as it is now. But these global stresses are exactly what humanity needs to motivate phenomenal bursts of growth.

The Mother

The solar eclipse on July 11, 2010 puts the spotlight on Cancer, the sign of mothering, empathy, caring, and connectedness. On a personal level, it highlights the importance of simple kindness in our life. High-level Cancer inspires us to treat every sentient creature as if it was a treasured child of the universe. Cancer, at its best, opens our hearts to every being who comes our way as if they were a treasured family member.

On a global level, the Cancer archetype is putting the emphasis on our connectedness with Mother Earth, whose ongoing defilement by the oil industry raises many troubling questions. Blaming the rapacious profiteers of Big Oil (a manifestation of Pluto in Capricorn, one corner of the Cross) is easy enough to do – as is pointing the finger at the corrupt government officials whose failure to

---

[1] Uranus, which defies our normal experience of time, is conjunct Jupiter right now, and both planets are opposed to Saturn, the planet of chronological time. Our perception of linear time is changing.

protect our environment can be traced to deep-pocket corporations (Saturn square Pluto).

But the deeper we look at these transits, the more likely we are to find our own oily footprints in the sand. There are many stories hidden within the chart of the Deep Water rig explosion on April 20, 2010,[2] that suggest how ordinary people have accepted and maintained the ecological mess we find ourselves in.

For the USA, these changes are especially pointed. The T-square between Saturn, Pluto and Uranus has been hammering the Venus/Jupiter conjunction in the US (Sibly) chart. This configuration pins down the issue of American values like a butterfly in a scrapbook.

USA in Crisis

Venus is the planet that asks: What do we value? Jupiter asks, What do we believe in? The devastation in the Gulf has America squirming over the contradictions inherent in the way we do business, both as producers and consumers.

We are struggling to reconcile a national philosophy that purports to honor the interests of common welfare with an economy that bows unreservedly to the interests of business elites. We are struggling to reconcile our desire for cheap, accessible oil with the hideous ramifications of its extraction, transportation and combustion once converted to fuel. We are reluctantly facing up to the idiocy of risking the health and survival of life on the planet in order to support an energy infrastructure that is growing extinct. All this destruction, for a product – oil – that will soon run out for good.

In addition to a crisis of values, the USA is in a crisis of intelligence; that is, of information and its assimilation (Mercury). The New Moon of July 2010 falls at the midpoint of an exact opposition to the Sibly Sun and Mercury. The timing here suggests that the four weeks that follow will be dominated by questions about the information Americans get and do not get, and how this information is assessed.

The many lies that BP told and is still telling the public about the spill, the cover-

---

[2] For a detailed interpretation of the explosion chart, see "Disaster in Deep Water: The Astrological Message of the Gulf Coast Oil Crisis," *The Mountain Astrologer*, August 2010 issue.

up operations BP launched that are now coming to light – propaganda which was repeated by the media – are collectively symbolic of this crisis of intelligence. It is a crisis that is thematic in the US (Sibly) chart, whose spine is a natal Mercury opposition.

We are being challenged to consider the implications of living in a world where official lying has become the norm. What does our tacit acceptance of this lying do to our personal integrity, and to our own psycho-spiritual growth? What toll does it take on our collective psyche? And what harm have our mass self-deceptions done to the planet we live on?

The Saturn corner of the Cross is demanding that we look at the lack of responsibility we have expressed towards Nature. With Uranus and Jupiter opposing Saturn, many people are feeling they must put themselves forward, in whatever way is natural and appropriate to our talents, and respond to the urgency in the air.

In our visualization this month, the movie we choose should have a charismatic star – us – who meets with courage whatever comes to pass.

Honoring the Gods

(originally published as "Shifting
Currents" in *Skywatch*,
July 2010)

When planets change signs (make *ingresses*), there are shifts in the ethers. The more we sensitize ourselves to the ingress, the more we benefit from its energy. When the planets do something noteworthy, like enter a new sign, station direct or retrograde, or lend their heft to an important transit like the Cardinal Cross, it only makes sense to honor the gods they represent.

Thinking Archetypally

For those who see their spiritual practice in terms of engaging with universal laws, honoring the gods is a handy metaphor. It renders these energies less abstract, helping us to cultivate a relationship with them. If we don't take it too literally (as, alas, so many fundamentalist religionists do), a little anthropomorphizing can go a long way. It allows us to go deeper with our understanding of the planet than our intellects alone can go.

It allows us to tap into a part of ourselves that is, in fact, already in touch. Notice how children, who think archetypally by instinct, understand the meaning of characters' behavior in fairy tales. They know, without being told, that the haughty young man in the story is being very unwise when he insults the old beggar woman. From legends worldwide, people of all ages know that one honors the god when he or she comes to call, even – maybe especially – if she appears in a frightening disguise.

When we allow ourselves to think archetypally we get the most benefit from astrological transits. If we are fortunate enough to be visited by Uranus, the wild-eyed god of liberating change, should we bolt the door? Just the opposite: we should bring out wine and flowers. If Mars is doing something significant in the sky, should we hide under the bed? On the contrary. We might put a red cloth on the altar and lay upon it a prayer of thanks for the courage he bestows.

Some transit trackers like to ritualize ingresses with a candle, which brings spiritual energy to the moment. When you strike the match, think about the planet you're invoking, and what it means to you. Sweeten your prayer with thanks. Sincere gratitude brings out the best in the gods.

If your life has been a roller coaster since Uranus entered Aries (May 2010) this is your chance to check in with the Great Awakener and thank him for the freedom he is bringing you. Practically speaking, it makes sense to appeal to the essence of the planet rather than forcing it to hit you over the head with a 2-by-4…. which it will, if you try to ignore it.

The essence of Uranus is liberation. When we resist his teachings, we feel panicked and chaotic; when we understand and accept what he's about, we feel the thrill of living in the moment. Our best bet is to proclaim your openness to being changed. Open a window in a room where they're usually shut.

Chiron

On April 20, 2010, Chiron ingessed into Pisces, sign of the oceans, a matter of hours after the Deep Water oil rig explosion. For eight years Chiron in Pisces will be an undercurrent of the tumultuous period ahead that is dominated by the Uranus-Pluto square. Neptune and Chiron will both be teaching us about the nature of illusion.

Mars enters Libra

Keep in mind that, whenever Mars moves into a Cardinal sign during the years upcoming, it adds fuel to the tense configuration in the sky. Mars is a provocateur, agitating and energizing whatever it touches.

At the end of July 2010, Mars will oppose Uranus and conjunct Saturn. There will be action, there will be high drama, there will be martial force unleashed. Our job is to keep it constructive.

The global themes that have been festering will be shaken up like a smoothie in a blender. Mars's involvement here exaggerates the Aries theme of activism that underlies the Cardinal Cross years. We should be prepared for anything.

No Twiddling

These transits do not support sitting at home twiddling our thumbs. This is not to suggest that everyone should sail to Gaza on a flotilla, or join an agitprop theatre

– although such creative expressions of righteous feeling will appeal to an increasing number of people. What it does suggest is that the spark of action is enlivening all of us, each in our own unique ways, and that it is a call to be heeded. Leadership – signified by the Cardinal signs – can express itself in a myriad of different ways. In whatever way the impulse expresses itself in you, pay attention to its promptings. These transits are about agency. They are dispelling passivity, and replacing it with a healthy pride in our individual capabilities. Their lesson is that we are agents of the world we want, and of the lives we want to lead.

AT HER SERVICE

(originally published as a blog,
July 2010)

Sometimes feeling overwhelmed is a good sign. Under skies like these, to feel overwhelmed means we're not shut down. Personally and globally, July and early August 2010 should raise urgent questions in every one of us.

The oil rig holocaust of April 2010 gave the collective mind a definitive image with which to illustrate the Cardinal Cross period. The boys at BP, bless their villainous little hearts, have made millions of people think about the relationship between Planet Earth and the life forms She supports.

Big truths are afoot – truths we have collectively failed to process, or even admit to – about the kind of world we've created for ourselves. It's a world where humans have given up their power to nonhuman entities – corporations – that have been legally defined as persons. It's a world where newborns have 180 man-made chemicals in their umbilical cords. It's a world addicted to soon-to-be-extinct dinosaur ooze.

It's a world where life-and-death realities like these are still pushed to the margins of media discussion, ceding the stage to unending expostulations about money and politics.

Fate of the Earth

Is it not bizarre that the fate of the Earth isn't at the core of all public discourse? You'd think planetary survival would be the first thing that any serious aspirant for public office would address. But with the exception of candidates for the Greens Party, politicos would mostly rather talk about Barbara Boxer's hairstyle.

As for the voters, in this age of peak oil and systems collapse you'd think we'd be assessing our leaders for vision and courage; but instead we end up choosing between two deeply insincere contenders in elections that have been auctioned off to the highest bidder. In theory, We-the-People are the creators, judge, jury and *raison-d'être* of the democracy we live in. But in practice we act as if our contribution as citizens consisted of nothing more than rooting for one guy while condemning his rival.

It is an approach to collective life that is insufficient to the point of fatal.

Pluto's square to Saturn in Libra is making clear that most of the political and economic ideologies now in use are anachronistic. This shouldn't surprise us, given that they date from a pre-ecological mindset. As the Zeitgeist movement[1] points out, socialism, capitalism, neo-liberalism and colonialism all buy into a common illusion: that we can go on exploiting the planet's resources forever and ever, like a spoiled child who hasn't yet learned the concepts of karma (Saturn) or balance (Libra). Even the most sacrosanct -*ism* of all – nationalism – will have to be reexamined if Earth is to survive.

The corner of the Cardinal Cross that involves Jupiter (ideology) and Uranus (acceleration) suggests that we don't have time to spend a few decades tweaking our favorite old belief systems. For there to be a shift to new beliefs, there must be a shift in collective thinking about what it means to hold beliefs in the first place.

Uranus Square Pluto

The long square between Pluto and Uranus forms the core of the Cross that coalesced this summer, 2010. The relationships between these two planets form the longest arm of the Cross, which will peak between 2012 and 2015, with a period of assimilation through 2023. Under its influence, our 20th-century-style perspectives will lose their credibility, clearing the stage for post-millennial ways of looking at things. The trouble is, of course, that the old -*isms* are taken so seriously by their adherents – and no less so by their detractors – that, for most people, alternative viewpoints seem downright unthinkable.

A profit-driven society like ours doesn't put a lot of stock in ethics, philosophy or independent thinking. We aren't encouraged to use this part of our mind creatively. Instead we learn to align ourselves with some kind of team, as if life were a soccer match. And only a consensually agreed-upon team. (The Tea Party movement has recently been thus anointed, and now styles itself as the team where "independent thinkers" belong.) Then we parrot our team's vocabulary, and we imagine we have a viewpoint.

---

[1] Peter Joseph's argument about the inherent destructiveness of the global economic paradigm is nail-on-the-head brilliant. See http://vimeo.com/10707453.

In the USA, this boils down to a war between media-sanctioned pairs. One is supposed to be either *for* the candidate on the Left and *against* the one on the Right; *for* capitalism and *against* socialism; or *for* communism and *against* democracy; etc. It is stunning how reductive the public conversation has become.

Mediated Reality

Issues of huge moral and global import – such as the fact that the USA is pumping more money, not less, into its aging weapons infrastructure – are discussed, if they are mentioned at all, solely for the purpose of attacking or applauding one or the other side of America's political duopoly. Rather than responding with human feeling, with intelligence, or – Goddess forbid – with simple common sense, we quickly label the great problems of our day in terms of which party's administration they're happening under. As for international matters, they get labeled in terms of whether the country in question is an ally or foe of Washington. (For example, when an adulterer is stoned in Iran it makes the headlines of US papers, but when it happens in Saudi Arabia, it warrants barely a mention.)

As a stand-in for our own lack of imagination, we have created a pundit culture whose talking heads reflect this binary worldview back to us. We get no more surprises from Glenn Beck and whomever he's debating this evening than we get from a meal at McDonald's. Watching these faux debates on TV has the numbing feel of witnessing punch-drunk fighters stumble through their last round, aspiring to nothing, so much as to not fall down.

Whether it's liberals-vs.-conservative, labor-vs.-management, East-vs.-West or some other pair, none of the conventional debates leave room to confront the most relevant reality of all: that the planet is in peril.

Dead End

The horror in the Gulf, as well as the mass poisonings from gold mining in Nigeria, unchecked logging in the Amazon and a multitude of other devastations that go on every day everywhere on Earth, are the results of an approach to the environment that has become the norm. From this skewed perspective the collateral damage to flora, fauna and whole ecosystems caused by offshore drilling, strip mining and other industrial abominations are not aberrations. They're factored in, as "acceptable risks," by the corporations and by the consumer-populace that allows them to happen.

It is disingenuous of us to act all incredulous when we hear of an accident at a nuclear facility like Chernobyl or at an offshore oil rig. Such events are not merely probable; they are inevitable. This is what karma is all about. You put something out, you get something back. This is the message of the Saturn corner of the Cross.

The level of consciousness that has allowed humanity to tolerate ecocidal insults such as these has reached a dead end, and so have the ideologies that allow us to ignore them. As ecologists already know, there is an infinitude of bold new ideas out there – e.g., renewable energy potentials like solar, tidal, geothermal, that exceed current energy consumption by thousands of percent – that are kept from implementation only by the dead weight of the old paradigm.

The years between now and 2023 are intense enough to bury it.

Those of us who were born into these years were meant to use the creative minds and the wise hearts Nature gave us. In living through our charts, we put them at Her service.

Tinderbox Moment

(originally published in *Skywatch*,
August 2010)

As the month of August 2010 begins, the Saturn-Uranus opposition has just peaked for the final time, after two years of spinning us dizzy. Mars is conjunct Saturn and opposed by Jupiter, which is conjunct Uranus; and they are all squaring Pluto (dismantling) in Capricorn (nation states, the economy).

These transits have the feeling of a wad of combustible material ready to burst into flame. All the ingredients are there: Saturn is stasis; Uranus is revolution; Pluto is break down; Jupiter is international scope. And Mars is the spark.

The most literal form an explosion can take is geological. Fittingly, a few weeks ago the story broke about a huge undersea methane bubble at the Gulf rig site, the ignition of which could cause a tsunami.

Explosions can also take financial form. In his writings about the global economy, Andrew Palmer has described this period as "a tinderbox moment."

The Dollar

This past spring 2010 saw bank runs spreading like wildfire from Greece to Portugal and Spain, giving the lie to the European Union's claim of economic and social cohesion. Despite the shock-and-awe economic rescues cobbled together by Europe's governments to save its debtor states, the Union is straining at the seams. These transits augur disintegration on many levels, not excluding that of political unions.[1] During August of 2010, we have not only Pluto, but Uranus, Saturn, Jupiter and Mars – any combination of which are quite capable of cleaving unions – all configured together to create an extraordinarily fraught

---

[1] The situation makes me think of something astrologer Liz Greene wrote in the late 1970s. Transiting Pluto was approaching the Sun in the chart of the USSR at the time, and she saw it as signifying that that Union would go through "a break-up." Hard as this was to imagine at the time, so it happened, as soon as Pluto moved into position.

moment.

The USA is a notoriously isolationist nation, and most Americans seem to think Europe's troubles have nothing to do with them. But this is as shortsighted as imagining that because we can't see oil in our drinking water it means the disaster in the Gulf has nothing to do with us. If Chiron going into Pisces tells us anything, it is that what's going on in any one part of the matrix of life has impact upon the whole. The fact that on April 20th 2010 the planet of wounding (Chiron) entered the most universal of water signs (Pisces) while conjunct the planet of oceans (Neptune) is perhaps the most telling feature of the Gulf explosion chart. The Chironic warning at the root of the calamity was this: that we deny at our peril the interconnectedness of all things.

This includes social systems. Americans are not yet rioting in the streets; but like the Greeks they are living in an economic tinderbox, their enormous debt being the most obvious point of comparison. Pluto began opposing the US Venus and Jupiter (money, expansion) in 2008, just as Wall Street hit the skids. Since then, Pluto's partners in the Cardinal T-square have assembled. The whole pattern has been slowly gathering strength, hammering the US Sun cluster in Cancer.[2]

The historic transits harrying the US (Sibly) chart indicate that beyond the worries brought on by unemployment, surreal federal debt and bankrupt state governments, something even more fundamental is looming for the country. The USA is undergoing an identity crisis tantamount to an individual going through a nervous breakdown. Given the country's self-concept as proud masters of the material realm, this breakdown is being played out financially.

Pluto's opposition to the country's Venus (resources and value) is not merely changing spending habits; it is gutting assumptions about worth. Even if Pluto were the only actor in this planetary line-up, it would be more than enough to threaten, for example, the perception that US bonds are the safe haven they have historically been. With all these other planetary heavyweights involved as well, America's meaning as a financially viable entity is being rocked to the core.

The dollar's status as the world's reserve currency is no longer unquestionable, and it is clear that Washington's borrowing behavior cannot continue as it has.

---

[2] The money supply in the United States is contracting at an accelerating rate that now matches the average decline seen from 1929 to 1933, despite near-zero interest rates and the biggest fiscal blitz in history.

American pundits may talk about the economy "getting back on track" and "returning to normal," but the transits suggest this attitude is delusional.

The world is not going back. It is going forward, and it is headed there fast.

Post-Isolationism

The change in America's relationship to China in recent years has been absolutely stunning, though the shift seems not to have penetrated the USA's collective consciousness. A vague but fervent Sinophobia[3] left over from the 1950s appears to be afoot; as well as, perhaps, a sense of shame – often an ingredient in Pluto transits – connected to being in debt to one's ideological enemy.

These confused Cold-War attitudes only serve to obscure the harsh realities of the USA's precarious financial position. But it won't be possible to postpone much longer. China, to whom Uncle Sam owes a trillion and a half dollars, is working on ways to reduce its dependency on the US Treasury. It sells more now to European than to American customers.

The failure of most Americans to consider the implications of their massive deficit is on a par with their failure to consider what's going on in the rest of the world. The truth is that at this point in human evolution, isolationism is an anachronism. The human race is on an evolutionary trajectory that leads beyond the illusion of physical or psychic separation from the entire web of creation.

Speak No Evil

In addition to this pummeling from the Cardinal Cross, the transit spotlight remains on the USA through the Neptune-Chiron conjunction. For several years this pair has been harrying the US Moon.

This transit has been a teaching about mass denial.

Americans have been exposed to an avalanche of evidence about how deluded we are as a culture, having witnessed during this period everything from the unmasking of the banking industry to the myriad corruptions of Big Oil and the

---

[3] Consider the case of the California parents' group that took to the airwaves in July to protest the Chinese language program being offered at their children's school. Their fear was that learning Chinese would expose their little ones to "communist propaganda."

collusion of our government in these corruptions. And we have been presented with plenty of opportunities to wake up from the delusion.

Where the economy is concerned, Americans' delusions are legion. Deeply ingrained in the collective imagination is an image of the country as a great cornucopia of uninterrupted plenty (US Jupiter conjunct Sun in Cancer), a font of endless growth. We can see where this imagery comes from. Cancer, an emotionally conservative sign with more attachment to the past than the present, governs food, protection and security. Though the USA's aid to developing countries is miniscule compared to other industrialized nations,[4] the nation still sees itself as a benevolent breadbasket for the world.

Shock and Fury

As economist Ambrose Evans-Pritchard has written, there is usually a lag time between economic shocks and social fury. When people are hit with a drastic cutback in their resources, at first there is a stunned interval; then an eruption into a backlash against the established orders.

The wild card here is consciousness. Those observers who see things in terms of human evolution are finding nothing surprising about what's happening, nor do they see cutting back as necessarily unhealthy. The bigger a perspective one takes, the more likely one is to see global economic changes as a cosmic corrective for the excesses of an old world we are leaving behind.

---

[4] More than half of the US aid budget is spent not in the poorest parts of the world but in middle-income countries, in the Middle East; and for military and strategic purposes, not to feed people. Only $3 billion a year goes to South Asia and sub-Saharan Africa.

No More Normal

(originally published in *Daykeeper
Journal*, August 2010)

Here's a stunning synchronicity that followers of current transits will appreciate. One week after the Grand Cross in late June 2010 , an article in marketoracle.com reported that financial markets were about to make "the Death Cross:" Wall Street's term for a bull market that's turning the corner into bear territory.

August 2010 features one of the most explosive configurations of the Cardinal Cross period: Mars conjunct Saturn opposed to Jupiter and Uranus.

This transit means business.

Centered in the Chart

Financial shocks are probable under skies like these. Economies all over the world are in turmoil, and government infrastructures are creaking and crumbling like old houses in a storm. It is very important to keep our heads about us and watch the flow of events for big-picture trends. The bigger our perspective, the more we will be able to respond creatively to what is happening.

For years now, astrologers have been talking about the Cardinal Cross period as an era of breakdown and renewal. This summer's eclipses ratcheted the energy up to a new level. And as chaotic as things have already been, a new element of upset is being introduced now by Mars, the saber-rattler of the solar system. A well-functioning Mars provides courage, which is just what we need right now. A low-level Mars manifests as panic and hostility.

It's not that we will necessarily personify one or the other of these extremes; people are not caricatures. As Mars and his cohorts' energies course through us and challenge us to respond, we will probably find ourselves vacillating back and forth between the constructive use of martial energy and its sloppier forms. But when we deliberately use our wills to stay centered – taking ourselves back, again and again, to our highest potential as expressed by our charts – we will be just fine.

In fact, we will be more than fine. We may feel more alive than ever before in our lives.

Who Do You Trust?

This month is an exercise in rigorous responsibility: that is, in being responsible with our energy. We need to be hyper-conscious of what we're putting out, and of what we're taking in from the environment. We should be wary of going overboard with fear – even if people around us are afraid – at the same time that we should be wary of burying our heads in the sand.

At this point, we know that if we're interested in the deeper meaning of events, the official explanations of what's going on in the world do not serve us. Politicians will say whatever they think will get them through the mid-term elections; pundits will say whatever boosts their ratings; central banks will announce recoveries in order to stabilize the public mood; corporate spokes-flacks will say whatever they think will get them off the hook for their industry's abominations against the environment. Since Pluto went into Capricorn in 2008, these social institutions have been exposed as untrustworthy at best and criminal at worst.

If what we seek is wisdom, the only way we will learn anything from disingenuous sources is to listen to what they are saying as if it were in code. For example, if we want to know which way the financial winds are blowing by listening to the news, we must listen between the lines. We hear that the economic czars are dumping trillions of dollars' worth of cash into the global financial system. But what does this really mean?

It doesn't mean they have magically created more wealth. It means that they have created more debt; financial as well as karmic.

It does not mean that the economy has returned to normal.

There isn't going to be a return to normal.

More Alive

Transits this powerful have one main purpose: to shake us out of our lethargy. It is for this reason that astrology links high-stress aspects like these with earthquakes and other telluric events. Certainly we have had no lack of volcanoes, forest fires, unseasonable storms and tectonic bucklings since the Cross began. But literal shake-ups are only the most obvious manifestation of the symbolism involved. On the level of global consciousness, fissures are appearing in the bedrock of group assumptions.

This is happening because it is time for it to happen. For those who are awake to them, these transits are psychological earthquakes – designed to destabilize our relationships, our spiritual lives, our work routines and our sense of what it means to be alive. In August 2010, with the Cardinal Cross undergoing one of its peaks, some individuals will find enlightenment– if not bliss in the Buddhist sense, then a bursting out of denial that allows them to call on their ingenuity in new ways; ways that serve their own higher purpose, and that of the Earth.

LAW OF CURE

(originally published as a blog,
August 2010)

The WikiLeaks story hit the headlines under one of the most powerful Full Moons of the year: July 25th 2010. Mars, the planet of war, was conjunct Saturn, a combination associated with the army. Saturn was within hours of making its last exact opposition to Uranus – a contest that had been going on for two years.

I guess we found out who won that round.

Uranus is made of stronger stuff than Saturn, which governs the establishment and its various self-protective agencies. Saturn maintains stasis by tightening up and shutting down; whereas, Uranus, like a military ambush, depends on the element of surprise. Explosive and defiant, Uranus uses out-of-left-field tactics to compel change.

This summer we are experiencing an extra-potent phase of the Cardinal Cross. A tug-of-war between Saturn and Uranus forms the spine of the planetary configuration, with Mars bisected by Pluto (secrets). As soon as Mars (ignition) moved into position, it was inevitable that something would burst into the open – something that the powers-that-be had been trying to conceal.

Secrets Revealed

What have we learned from the 90,000 files released by WikiLeaks? Many observers of what's been going on in Afghanistan have known since the beginning that the occupation was doomed. What the leaks showed us was the extent to which the generals knew it, too.

They not only knew they were losing, but that they had no chance of winning. Yet with hideous cynicism they were willing to keep on destroying lives, decimating resources, and reducing to smaller and smaller bits of rubble what was left of the second poorest country in the world.

The presence of Pluto (cover-ups) in the transit picture suggests that however reasonable the official war arguments (Saturn in Libra) were imagined to be, the reality was and is riddled with ugly secrets.

A few chilling examples: from WikiLeaks we hear about the existence of Task Force 373, which is – not to put too fine a point on it – a death squad, created to murder not only suspected insurgents (whatever that means) but, apparently, the occasional unarmed motorcyclist. We hear about an incident where French troops used machine guns to strafe a bus full of children. We hear about Polish troops massacring a village wedding party out of revenge for an earlier insurgent assault.

What came to light on the Full Moon of July 2010 was a pattern of official lies that, to Pentagon-watchers of a certain age, sounded strikingly familiar. It echoed the spin concocted for that other war – the one from the last time Uranus and Pluto were in hard aspect, in the mid-60s: the one in Vietnam. The strategy then was to lie about the strength of the native resistance, to deliberately misclassify civilian deaths as combat deaths, and to send in ever more men and guns.

Newly Engaged Public

As the Moon began to wane, the spin machine began to hum. Pentagon and Capitol Hill flacks tried to neutralize the threat to their control posed by a newly engaged public. The spin-meisters seem to have been so taken off guard that their clumsy attempts at damage control contradicted each other. Out of one corner of their mouths, they opined that the WikiLeaks data were no great shakes: It's old news, they sneered. *Nothing to see here, folks, just move along.* Out of the other corner of their mouths, they described the intel as so dangerously sensitive that Julian Assange had put "the lives of US and partner service members at risk" by releasing it.

One was sorry to hear Obama echoing this despicable nonsense, but not surprised. As astrologers know, a predictable karmic arc is finishing up here. The first iteration of the Uranus-Saturn opposition was Nov 4th 2008, the same day the new president came into office vowing to throw his weight behind the occupation. Two years later, his project has started to come undone: Uranus (rupture) has ripped the mask off the war's public face (Saturn).

Our hidden faces must be disclosed if we are to transform ourselves. As a group, the realities behind our official stories must be confronted, sordid though they may be. Those who take to heart the principle known in Chinese medicine as Law of Cure – whereby toxins must be pushed to the surface before an organism can heal – may find themselves not only unafraid of, but yearning for, the next phase of this process of breakdown. We might find ourselves welcoming a new set of revelations that shows this abominable war for what it is.

Tea Time

(originally published as a blog,
August 2010)

Have you noticed that every time you think the culture wars couldn't possibly get any wackier, they get wackier? Saturn, the planet that is supposed to keep us sane and grounded, is under stress. For the past two years it has been slapped around by Uranus and Pluto, and it's now opposed by Jupiter (exact in May and August, 2010, and again in March, 2011). Jupiter represents our beliefs, and Saturn is our reality structures. The battle between them is particularly obvious in the USA, whose group soul is entering its Saturn Return.[1]

It's as if ideology (Jupiter) were vying for prominence with documented fact (Saturn). To paraphrase cartoonist Tom Tomorrow: The American media is rife with denials of reality (global warming is a hoax), distortions of reality (the country is going socialist) and wholesale rewritings of reality (Obama isn't a citizen, and the Founding Fathers never intended to separate church and state).

The Cardinal Cross of which this opposition is a part became inflamed when Uranus went into Aries (anger, activism) in June 2010, and was joined there by Jupiter (exaggeration). Anger was hot and high among the masses, towards whatever agents of authority (Saturn) they imagined were responsible for their troubles. On the face of things, this rage falls into two camps: the Left who blame corporations and the Right who blame Obama. At least, so goes the conventional narrative.

Public's Rage

But America's factional showdown isn't quite that pat. The truth is that both "conservative" and "liberal" Americans were blasted awake in large numbers by the Wall Street meltdown and subsequent bail-outs that took place under Pluto's

---

[1] The Saturn Return is a transit of maturity, experienced by every entity that lives at least three decades. It takes place when the placement of Saturn in the sky matches up with the placement it was in when the entity was born.

ingress into Capricorn in 2008. In one fell swoop, the US populace realized, pretty much *en masse*, that their government was in bed with moneyed elites. It was at this moment that we saw the rise of the teabag folk: a group of self-described patriots who considered themselves not "conservative" but thoroughly anti-establishment.

Those volatile months of 2008-09 constituted a critical moment in American history. The natives were restless: appalled, furious, and – most dangerous of all, from the point of view of the powers-that-be – fueled with a spirit of independence. The ruling class must have been quaking in their Guccis. They knew the public's rage could have crested into a full-fledged attack on the entire system, and that the only way to forestall that danger was to corral people's ire into the narrow confines of party politics. That is, into an attack on the Democrats.

Thinking quickly, the big-money think tanks swooped in and started funding Tea Bag rallies. Then Fox News started choreographing them. In the elections that followed, reactionary candidates wooed their votes. Before you could say "Patrick Henry," the erstwhile revolution had been declawed and neutered. Its colorful working- and middle-class adherents were recast as safe, anti-incumbent conservatives.

Two Teams

For the moment, the danger to the status quo has past. The old right-vs.-left trope has re-established itself, with everybody obediently dividing themselves down into two teams, thereby to vent their spleen against each other instead of at the tiny clique of fat cats at the top. But the public mood is still deeply unsettled – especially with Neptune and Chiron about to conjoin on the country's Moon again in November – and the transits to the country's Sun are just getting started.

In 2022 the USA will experience an exact Pluto Return, in the house of money. Between now and then it will become more and more obvious that the country is not a democracy but a plutocracy. (An astonishing report on CitiBank's website actually discussed the international economy in these very terms, baldly stating, "The World is dividing into two blocs – the *Plutonomy* and the rest.") The Cardinal Cross is a call for us to get real about the whole rigged game.

In this context, it's clear that the Tea Party phenomenon has a meaning that reaches beyond the ignorance and fear of many of its proponents. Granted, these folks have a long way to go before they can be taken seriously as proponents of positive change. For that, they'd need to expand their notions of personal freedom to a rather more all-inclusive portion of humanity (to the uninsured, let's say; not to mention immigrants, nonwhites, non-Christians, and anybody else who doesn't look like them and live the way they do). And to show a modicum of discretion as regards the idiot ideologues they follow (e.g., Glen Beck and his "I-have-a-better-dream-than-Martin-Luther-King-Jr." rally). And to lose the silly hats.

But those of us who seek to understand what these transits are up to need to remember that any form of protest (Uranus) against a bloated (Jupiter), corrupt (Pluto) government (Saturn) is an authentic expression of the zeitgeist.

I say let's bring our own crumpets and crash this Tea Party.

CAT OUT OF THE BAG

(originally published in *Daykeeper*
Journal, September 2010)

As transit trackers knew, July and August 2010 were fated to be explosive. Mars, Saturn, Jupiter, Uranus, Saturn and Pluto were staring each other down in the sky as Proposition 8 (the California ballot initiative to ban gay marriage) was overturned, wildfires raged in Russia and record-breaking floods inundated Pakistan.

To search for the meaning beneath watershed events like this, we look at the planetary patterns that accompany them. Here, in coded form, we find the underlying themes.

Mars and Saturn

For years now, astrologers have been keeping a particularly sharp eye on the 2010 Mars-Saturn conjunction, a pairing traditionally associated with war. The WikiLeaks story hit the headlines right on time, under the Full Moon in July, with the Cardinal Cross in full bloom.

Pundits immediately labeled the released intel "a new Pentagon Papers" and pounced on the story, echo-chamber-style, hoping to cash in on it before the public's attention moved on to the latest Congressional Caribbean-vacation-home scandal.

Like the quickly-moving second hand of a clock that meets up with the minute and hour hands, Mars' position triggered the momentous outer-planet configurations that will take us through the Uranus-Pluto years ahead (2010-15). Just as the WikiLleaks story broke, Saturn had reached its last exact opposition with Uranus (cat-out-of-the-bag surprises) while T-squaring Pluto (secrets, fatalities). WikiLeaks founder Julian Assange was talking about a second big spill of intel at the last exact square (this cycle) between Saturn and Pluto on Aug 21.

It was time to talk about things nobody had wanted to talk about.

Denial and Death

Also revealed by the transit picture was the theme of mass denial, the kind that has stonewalled any in-depth discussion of Afghanistan for almost a decade. The Neptune and Chiron conjunction that has been beleaguering the US Moon for the past two years (peaking for the last time in November of 2010) signifies a group mind at war with its own illusions. It is no easier for groups than for individuals to admit to self-deception. But judging from this epochal conjunction on the national Moon (public mood), a painful (Chiron) arousal from geopolitical somnolence (Neptune) is part of America's learning curve.

We can also infer here an instructive point about the nature of Pluto, a major player in the transit picture. Though we think of it as the planet of death, Pluto doesn't create breakdown; it just takes advantage of the rot that's already there. And though we think of Pluto as the planet of secrets, the realities it governs are in fact hidden in plain sight. Like the elephant in the middle of the room, Plutonian subject matter is only invisible to the extent that we choose not to see it.

Accordingly, the 90,000 WikiLeaks reports came as a surprise only to those who had been willfully blind. Observers of the chaotic violence going on in Central Asia have known for quite a while that the Taliban was stronger than ever, that the puppet government in Kabul was corrupt, that the Pentagon wasn't reporting massive numbers of civilian deaths, and that Pakistan was a very bad choice for a puppet state.

Money and War

It is noteworthy that it was Mars, planetary ruler of all things military, that served as the trigger for the Grand Cross in August 2010. This is a cosmic hint that we'll be asked to look deeper and deeper into a dark story of which the WikiLeaks intel is only the tip of the iceberg.

Unlike with Vietnam, most Americans seem to lack a strong moral opinion about the bloodshed in Afghanistan. It is probably the financial implications of the WikiLeaks revelations that have motivated this denial as much as anything. It is no wonder that struggling taxpayers had not wanted to look, until WikiLeaks forced them to, at the fact that the Pentagon was losing the sinkhole of a war they'd just been asked for another 60 billion dollars to fund.

Mundane astrologers foresee extreme economic instability in the years ahead. Pluto resides in the second house of money in the US (Sibly) chart, and is heading towards its first-ever return. It was expected that America's financial values and self-image would be turned upside down and inside out, as Pluto hammered the country's Sun by transit.

This aspect is notorious for pushing to the forefront whatever realities a given culture least wants to look at: realities that exist just beneath the crust of collective consciousness, kept there by fear, cultural pressure or both. At issue here are the powerful moneyed networks that link the US government, big business, and the armaments industry – a subject that our officials and pundits don't want to touch with a ten-foot pole. But in a period of systems collapse, it is not to official commentators that we should be turning to ask the right questions. The WikiLeaks exposé may have nudged the public itself one step closer to asking the necessary questions about the relationship between money and war.

Will America's soul-searching begin to include questions about the role of militarism in the national economy? So far there has been scant discussion about the hideous irony whereby most Americans, broke and getting broker, seem not to mind that 1.09 trillion of their tax dollars go to the wars in Iraq and Afghanistan.

Cultural taboos are curious things. They are kept in place by silence, sucking the power out of a populace the way psychological repressions suck the power out of individuals. But the transits overhead are powerful enough to chip away at embedded social constructs, and we know from experience that asking just a few questions about highly-charged secrets tends to unleash many more questions, all in a torrent.

Such as the staggering sums of cash with which fancy weapons are built which are never intended to be deployed; weapons that continue to be funded because the arms industry bankrolls US Congressfolk. And then there is the unknowable amount of money that goes to pay the salaries of the hundreds of thousands of brand-new intelligence workers, minted since the "war on terror" began.[1]

Forecast: Expect cats to jump out of bags.

---

[1] Not just mercenaries but analysts and desk spies, this vast army of secret-clearance employees, on the Pentagon payroll either directly or indirectly, is reported by the *Washington Post* to consist of about 900,000 people.

Big and Small

(originally published as a blog,
September 2010)

Jupiter is playing an interesting role in the sky. It is exactly conjunct Uranus and opposed to Saturn (May 2010 - March 2011). Governor of quantity, abundance and in-your-face obviousness, Jupiter works by exaggeration: it makes whatever we've overlooked expand, so we can no longer miss it.

Saturn, meanwhile, works in just the opposite way: it compresses and shrinks things, forcing us to pay attention through the perception of lack.

Gas Giants

As cosmic teaching tools, these two gas giants have the same valence. Despite the tradition that sees Jupiter as the good guy and Saturn as the bad guy, all archetypes are equal once we get away from our human value judgments. Moreover, Jupiter has a dark side. It can create sloppiness and a sense of entitlement. The Jupiter conjunction to the Sun in the US (Sibly) chart is one reason American politics are such a big, splashy mess.

Depending on how well we use it, Jupiter (growth) and Uranus (explosions) can mean explosive growth.,. On a collective level, we're being invited to consider the seismic shift that's occurred in the way we conceptualize size. Our shared attitudes towards scale and proportion are being shaken up. In *Eaarth* (sic)*: Making a Life on a Tough New Planet*, for example, Bill McKibben makes the case that "In the new world we've created, the one with hotter temperatures and more drought and less oil, Bigger is vulnerable, mammals get smaller in the heat, and so should governments."

Moving Faster

The issues the world is dealing with now are huge (Jupiter), and they are coming at us fast (Uranus). On the personal level, I hear clients and friends using the word "overwhelm" a lot lately, and I think it would help if we realized this is not just our own weird, subjective perception. Saturn (chronological time) has been trumped by Uranus (acceleration): time really is moving faster, and Jupiter is adding magnitude to the drama. We should forgive ourselves for sometimes feeling inundated.

It is a challenge to stay engaged.

I think the bigger the numbers are that are bandied about on the news, the more our mental grip on them starts to slip. Wrapping our minds around the trillion dollars that wealthy Americans have saved thanks to Bush's tax cuts, for example, at the same time that many of the non-wealthy are facing financial ruin, may represent just too ambitious a stretch. The Jupiter-Uranus conjunction can make us feel like the cartoon character whose head is exploding.

Facts and figures are not easy to assimilate when they are this big, brazen, and blasted at us through the megaphone of the media. When we hear, for example, that global military expenditure stands at over $1.5 trillion annually – a number so bloated that it strikes us as morally obscene (Jupiter) – our minds may go fuzzy or shut down entirely, in self-defense against the prospect of snapping from outrage or despair.

It's a very complex amalgam of energies that we're being asked to balance here. The planet of *big* is opposing the planet of *small*. Jupiter's opposition to Saturn is forcing us to accommodate the specter of extreme abundance vs. extreme dearth. In the same newscast where we hear about Meg Whitman spending $119 million in her quest for the governorship of California (out-of-control Jupiter), we are told that millions of Nigerian children are dying from starvation (Saturnine depletion at its most merciless). When trying to entertain realities this atrociously skewed, the best we may be able to muster is a distressed incredulity.

Opposition

To use astrology to maintain perspective in troubled times means setting aside the terms and assumptions of the social world, for a moment, and going back to the archetypal level. The contrasts we are seeing represent opposition in every sense of the word, both literally – the 180 angle between two celestial objects across the zodiacal circle from each other – and in terms of meaning. Oppositions work by pushing each pole to extremes, which creates enough stress to trigger leaps of consciousness.

Saturn's job is to squeeze a situation to a nugget of concentration to get us to admit to a reality we took for granted before; Jupiter's is to blow it up like a forensic photograph in search of understanding. Moreover, Jupiter, the planet of ethics, is being asked by Saturn, the planet of definition, to define itself. We are being forced to get clear about what, for us, constitutes morality.

WHEN LOSS IS GAIN

(originally published in *Skywatch*,
October 2010)

The transit that defines our era – the long, slow square between Uranus (revolution) and Pluto (renewal) – is getting ready for its next chapter. The geometrical friction between them will characterize the next six years of life on Earth. As they make their way towards that historic 90 degree angle, Uranus and Pluto are putting more and more pressure on the US (Sibly) chart, whose Cancer-Libra square completes the pattern to make a Grand Cross.

Like quarter Moons, waxing squares between any two planets get their meaning from the conjunction that preceded them; in this case the paradigm was struck in the mid-1960s.[1] By astrological law, the themes laid down in 1965-66 are being played out again in a cosmic echo. Among the explosive themes being reprised here is that of the Vietnam War, which notoriously polarized the USA and raised geopolitical consciousness all over the world.

Though the American government would just as soon forget it, Uncle Sam's attenuated botch-job in Southeast Asia is on plenty of minds right now as the morass in Afghanistan parallels it on several fronts.

American taxpayers are in a mood of reassessment about the occupation of Afghanistan, which is now bleeding into Pakistan – not only militarily but also in terms of a vague understanding in the public mind.

This reassessment is being played out against the backdrop of out-of-control factionalism between various subcultures within American society: a civil war of ideas being waged even less civilly than that of the mid-60s.

---

[1] The two were opposed to Saturn at the time. Now they are square each other – and, in 2010, also in a T-square with Saturn. The key astrological ingredients are the same, just rearranged.

Then and Now

US forces are losing ground month after month in Central Asia, while Washington pumps out encouraging press releases to the public to avoid the perception of defeat. But at the topmost levels the powers-that-be are split about what to do. The WikiLeaks files released at the Full Moon in July corroborated the suspicions of observers everywhere, by laying out the damning facts and figures beneath Pentagon spin.

Their publication marked another parallel with Vietnam: When Daniel Ellsburg leaked the Pentagon Papers, that war was at about the same phase in its downward spiral as this war is now. Among the occupying powers, a discussion is opening up about the military feasibility and the financial capability[2] of continuing the indefinite occupation of another country with a fierce native resistance.

The situation calls to mind a dark joke that was making the rounds in the late 60s: "Let's just arbitrarily declare victory and withdraw." It is a testament to how jaded – or pragmatic – Americans have become that, in 2010, this proposal seems less like an ironic joke than simply a good idea. The only thing that might need tweaking is the "we won" part. Observers on every side of the issue know full well that the USA is losing.

The American populace is less ignorant than it was in the years of drive-ins and sit-ins. Though mass denial is still rampant, it is much harder for the pro-war crowd to justify their saber rattling than it was in the 1960s, and it is getting harder by the month.

Archaic Enmity

In order to condone the mass murder (including that of civilians, a fact of which Americans can no longer pretend ignorance) and the targeted assassination of "insurgents" and "suspected terrorists" – a vague, all-encompassing class of enemy that is stateless, geographically mutable and geopolitically amorphous –

---

[2] As for the moral feasibility, one doesn't expect to hear that discussion from the leadership of the countries occupying Afghanistan. But citizen peace groups are stirring anew. Among the issues they are trying to bring to the attention of the wider public: the May 21st 2010 decision by a federal appeals court in Washington that detainees held by the USA in Afghanistan are not entitled to the hard-won right earned by prisoners at Guantanamo, to challenge their indefinite detention. Prisoners at Bagram Air Base were declared to exist in a "theater of war" and therefore not under the jurisdiction of the US civilian courts.

those Americans who buy into their government's propaganda need a different armory of self-deceptions than the ones that sufficed back when the Uranus-Pluto cycle began.

When Uranus and Pluto conjoined in the mid-60s, Americans were in the thrall of a primitive anti-Communist fear campaign, one that persuaded all but the most independent-spirited citizens to accept the now-discredited Domino Theory.[3] Now, with Uranus and Pluto again in aspect but this time in a waxing square, the enemy is imagined to be nothing less than an entire world religion: Islam.

Reigniting archaic enmities that have lain dormant for centuries, Washington is pitching itself against the same Islamic bogeyman that gave Europeans nightmares 500 ago. Then as now, endless wars against The Turk drained Christendom's national military coffers and bankrupted its states.

Not-So-Secret Motives

The West's current anti-Islam campaign, however, is driven by motives that have little to do with ideology. As imperial misadventures usually are, Washington's suicidal tenacity in Afghanistan is driven – no less than every other colonial power that's tried (and failed) throughout the ages to control Afghanistan – by the bottom line. Ever motivated by the lure of strategic transit rights, the US government is now said to be also after the vast mineral deposits that lie beneath that unforgiving terrain.

If we did not already know this from reading between the lines of the news stories, we'd be able to guess it from the astrological evidence. Pluto, the god of subterranean wealth, was moving into position when the news of these discoveries broke. For the ancients, the god Hades/ Pluto presided over those ores, minerals and jewels hidden beneath the Earth.[4]

---

[3] What a difference a quarter-cycle makes. Consider the hearty welcome Vietnam now gets, as a lucrative trading partner from Uncle Sam, its former mortal enemy. So much for the Domino Theory, that dread scenario that struck such fear in the hearts of true-blue Americans during the 50s and 60s. All-but-unquestioned at the time and the premier justification for the deaths of three million Vietnamese, the Domino Theory proposed that all of Southeast Asia and beyond would "go red" if the USA lost the war.

[4] And under the sea. Note Pluto's placement in the chart of the Gulf oil rig disaster (see "Disaster in Deep Water," op. cit., p 97).

The third covert rationale for this war is equally Plutonian (that is, not exactly classified information, but so distressing to think about that it is seldom discussed): to provide the US arms industry with continuous support. Nonstop fighting, nonstop funding. Keeping the country in a state of endless war insures that the munitions makers will keep receiving endless Congressional appropriations of astronomical amounts of tax payer money.

Sheep from Goats

As the transits that define our era approach exactitude, the chaos in Central Asia may acquire the symbolism of a great cultural dividing line, as did Vietnam. Afghanistan will require the citizens of the occupying powers to think about where they stand.

The wars NATO is fighting will render increasingly obvious the gaping abyss between the interests of the militarists (Pluto) and the interests of ordinary people (Uranus). As we witness ever more torturous justifications from the war's apologists, we may see a corresponding resurgence of the peace movement that ignited consciousnesses in the 1960s.

In the meantime, the fact that the USA is losing this fight is a goddess-send for the cosmic learning curve that it represents. To be disabused of great destructive lies is a wholesale gain.

Sniffing Out the Truth

(originally published in *Daykeeper*
Journal, October 2010)

Sniffing Out the Truth

The dogs and cats of Sri Lanka were nowhere near the coast when the tsunami hit in 2004. They had split, seeking higher ground.

Humans, too, can smell what's going to happen. Though we act as if we've forgotten it, we too are animals. We too are born with an awareness of the natural world, and on some level of consciousness we all know we're part of the rest of creation. But it is a peculiarity of the proud modern psyche that we identify disproportionately with our minds, and dis-identify with the rest of our beings. The resulting imbalance painfully throws us off.

We do tend to recognize the authority of our body and spirit when we're in desperate straits, however. In the many parts of the world right now, where essential social systems are collapsing, basic survival has necessitated a marshaling of all aspects of the human organism, including our primal animal intelligence. People struggling with floods in Pakistan, blockades in Palestine and starvation in Nigeria are calling upon all the resources at their disposal to stay alive.

How ironic it is that in the relatively privileged First World, untouched as yet by mass life-and-death catastrophe, our estrangement from our essential natures is the more noticeable.

Crossroads

Humanity is on the cusp of a period of wrenching change. If, at this moment in our lives, we are blessed with circumstances that permit the luxury of introspective work, now would be an ideal time to consider that we are made up of more than just our linear minds. Many of us have been conditioned to neglect our corporeal intelligence and allow our inborn spiritual knowing languish.

Society has rewarded us primarily for figuring out how to figure things out.

But it is through the non-mental parts of our identities that we're cognizant of the enormous changes the world is going through right now. Our best bet is to listen to these guides: our inner animal, viscerally hip to what's what, and our soul knowing, with its hotline to the All-That-Is.

These parts of ourselves not only know what's coming. They already know what it means.

Mental Noise

Our minds, by contrast, could cause us trouble, and need to be used with care. The potential to get confused on an intellectual level will climb sharply in the years ahead. If we try to maintain our sanity by mental and ideological assessments alone, we're goners.

In the USA the societal conversation will get even nuttier than it is now, conducting fear-driven ideas like a wire conducts electricity. The sophisticated techniques of the mass media, polished to a high sheen, are poised to submit all the world-altering changes upcoming to the manipulations that are its stock in trade. These include giving distracting nonsense prime time, keeping key questions from getting any airtime at all, and reducing every issue to a cartoonish contest between polarized positions. We will need to make a concerted effort to avoid getting caught up in this noise. The more we get into our bodies and follow our intuition, the better off we'll be.

This is not to say we should deny the intellectual function that is the jewel in the crown of humanness. To believe in unconditional cosmic appropriateness is to believe that each of us, for our own mysterious reasons, chose to incarnate not as a raccoon or a dragonfly, this time round, but as a miraculously complex creature with a brain – to use, ideally, in the service of our spiritual aspirations.

But because of the cultural conditioning we've soaked up along the way, we have become attached to certain ideas that pull us away from truth – both our own inner truth and our awareness of universal truth. We have identified ourselves with false presumptions about what constitutes realism and sanity.

Received Wisdom

In order to stay sharp and responsive in the troubled times ahead, we need to notice these assumptions as they reveal themselves in our daily lives. What lies do we ingest with our morning coffee?

We may be listening to a talk show on the radio while driving to work, and hear a military expert come on the air. As he fields questions from his respectful host, we may hear this blandly authoritative gentleman opine that a certain number of civilian casualties are inevitable in war. His opinion is intoned with a neutral sobriety, shored up by the high rank of his office.

I submit that the better parts of our being – the animal part and the heart-engaged part – are repelled to hear a statement like that. These parts of us, if allowed voice, might react by saying, "It is obscene to think of the murder of human beings that way. What if the people in that drone-strafed wedding party were my own family? What if they were this military expert's own family?"

I believe it would be a healthy exercise for us to honor, in that moment, the part of ourselves that instinctively rejects what the esteemed general is saying. I believe that it would be life-affirming to condemn his opinion as a sacrilege. Whether we make this declaration privately or publicly, it would strike a blow for our sanity. What's more, to the extent that everything is energy and the power of healing energy knows no bounds, I believe that to make this declaration would strike a blow for the sanity of the world.

Few deny that the US economy is bottomed-out, its infrastructure in shreds. Fewer than ever deny that the already-nine-years-old war in Afghanistan has met none of its goals, whatever anyone imagined these to be; only death and ruination. And yet, every day, some politician or other can be heard talking as if it were a valid option to continue the occupation indefinitely.

If we were fully in touch with our body-spirit-intelligence we would no sooner go along with such consensual insanity than a cat would eat rancid meat.

Earned Wisdom

When we are in an integrated state, our mind joins together with our body and spirit intelligence, and resonates with authentic perceptions. To these perceptions our mind contributes insight, our body contributes moment-to-moment experience in the physical world, and our spirit contributes the knowing derived from living through our charts. Unlike those drilled in by advertising or government propaganda, these are perceptions we have earned. These are the ones we should honor.

Pretend Politix

(originally published as a blog,
October 2010)

How appropriate it is that, just as Neptune (pretense) conjoins Chiron (wounds) for their last hit on America's Moon in Aquarius, it's election time in the USA.

Negative Neptune manifests as addiction, self-delusion and the passive acceptance of unhealthy situations, which the shrinks have delicately termed *enabling*. I propose that we all take a pledge not to enable this November.

Specifically, I mean that we disabuse ourselves of the fantasy that the Democrats will or can save us from the Republicans. Generally, I mean that we stop pretending that the grotesque games played by the two major parties reflect anything real.

Even using the word "politics" to refer to the Dem-vs.-GOP charade feels increasingly wrong. What most Americans mean by the word (from *polis*: "city"; cities being where the wheeling-and-dealing goes on [if you don't count Bohemian Grove]) has nothing to do with how their country actually works. If it did, politics would be a genuinely interesting topic. Instead, the word's meaning has been reduced to the mock battles waged by the two halves of our national duopoly: the No-Apologies Plutocrats (Republicans) and the Kinder, Gentler Plutocrats (Democrats).

Staged Contests

Each of these teams is subsidized by the exact same legalized bribery, a.k.a. the lobby system, involving the exact same corporate interests: Big Armaments, Big Insurance, Big Oil, Big Pharma and All the Other Big Guys, in virtually equal numbers of billions of dollars. Yet the supposed distinctions between the two parties are portrayed as Earth-shatteringly definitive and critical. Whatever thin party differences the impresarios of Pretend Politix can find – differences based on pure theory, not facts and figures – are orchestrated into religiously staged contests, otherwise known as elections.

It's not that this rivalry isn't serious business. It's just that it's pretend.

By means of nonstop, high-glitz news coverage, the election season monopolizes the public discussion just as football does in football season. The analogy between Pretend Politics and big-money athletics is drawn quite deliberately by the media, which has trained voters to see the whole show as a gladiator sport. Its media advocates range from the reasonable and personable – e.g., Rachel Maddow – to the flagrantly despicable – e.g., Glen Beck. But whatever their intended message, the greater significance of these commentators is that they collectively legitimize Pretend Politix. And they have done it so thoroughly that most Americans don't think of their country in any other terms.

Diversion

Truthdig columnist Chris Hedges calls it "junk politics." Gore Vidal calls it "show-biz politics." What is it for? It's a diversion. It is what keeps Americans from thinking or feeling too deeply about the astounding inequities perpetrated by their government-sanctioned corporate overlords. Inequities which, were they to be considered outside of the bubble of Pretend Politix, would appear barbaric and preposterous.

Such as the fact that, after precipitating the meltdown that has created a chronic unemployment rate of 20%, the financial sector still calls the shots in Washington. Or the fact that while millions of Americans have been pitched out of their houses onto the curb over the past three years, their government is seriously considering preserving tax cuts for families earning over $250,000. Or the fact that while white-collar criminals make bonuses the size of a Third World country's GDP, one out of seven American citizens lives in poverty. Pretend Politix has so diverted the national mindset that, even among that struggling one-in-seventh voter, the rich-white-guys' game still drives the narrative.

Good reasons to reject Pretend Politix range from its ethical repulsiveness to our own financial self-interest. But such is the power of group-think (note the placement of US Neptune in the 9th house) that, in a country as obsessed with money as the USA, where public coffers are so bottomed-out that schoolteachers have to cough up their own money to buy books for their students, the public sits back and accepts as perfectly normal the obscene avalanches of cash wasted by Pretend Politicians mounting their campaigns.

There are linguistic reasons, too, to spurn Pretend Politix. Anyone who holds out the hope that language might mean something – that words are vehicles to express the moral dimension of humanness – can't help but recoil from the tritely earnest hypocrisies that stumble out of the mouths of politicians from Left and Right, their obvious artificiality an insult to human intelligence and a crime against language. Corrupted further by each repetition, the cliché-sodden teleprompter speeches that have become the norm in Pretend Politix should automatically disqualify the speaker and everything s/he stands for from being taken seriously. The fact that they do not is a testament to how low the public's standards have sunk.

Jerry-Rigged

And then there are the political reasons to repudiate Pretend Politix. Mainly, that it nowhere addresses the single most relevant fact of American life: the fact that the system is jerry-rigged to serve corporations. If politics did address this, everybody's approach would shift. If the federal government were seen to be no more or less than what it is – the centralized bureaucracy of a corporate state – liberals both phony and genuine would save themselves oodles of time and energy. If that central fact were named in political discussions, we'd understand in a New York minute why the nation's priorities are upside down.

There'd be no more barking up the wrong tree where political or economic reform was concerned. There'd be an end to the celebration of personalities: our smart, good-looking president would be taken down from his pedestal, and his role in the system would be examined. His crestfallen fans would not be standing around in listless naïveté, scratching their heads in incredulity about his bailouts and stimulus money having gone to Wall Street instead of building schools, libraries, public transit, and green jobs.

What's the alternative to investing in the trumped–up pep rallies, the inane faux debates, and the sentimental patriotic baloney of Pretend Politix? We can't even begin to answer this question until we leave the circus behind, turn off the fog machine, unplug the TV.

Choosing Realness

When we wrench ourselves out of Neptune's shadow, we open up to Neptunian inspiration. Once we make the break, we'll know at once that we've made a wholesome move. Like fresh air into the lungs, ideas that have realness in them will start coming our way. There are some vitally alive, ingeniously original energies floating around in American society right now (try Ralph Nader again; he's still telling the truth), and in other countries (check out the anti-corporate Scandinavian firm Kraft & Kultur).

We don't have to look far afield for inspiration. Thanks to the vacuum created by our repudiation of Pretend Politix, we will attract into our lives those ideas and people that are exactly appropriate for us. We may find ourselves invited into a humanitarian group (Aquarius) operating on a global level, or to a regional organization lobbying for solar and water power for our local community. We may find ourselves inspired by a neighbor who's redirected her domestic wastewater, or by a friend who's started an anti-consumerism magazine.

These ideas are signs of the times. They are products of the moment, given the cosmic crossroads at which we stand. Individuals who are living through their charts right now are on fire with ideas like these. Even if we do not yet see ourselves as way-showers, there are leaders among us serving as role models.

It may feel so good to ride this current that we never go back to the network news.

The Magical Glory

(originally published in *Skywatch*,
November 2010)

"Illusions give such color to the world," wrote F. Scott Fitzgerald to a friend, "that you don't care whether things are true or false as long as they partake of the magical glory."

This is a beautiful description of Neptune, the planet that dominates the skies in late 2010. Neptune bewitches us with either transcendent imagination or self-delusion, depending on how well we know ourselves.

This is the test we are facing, with Neptune (illusion) and Chiron (wounds) conjoining while stationing back-to-back. Stations strengthen transits, and this inscrutable double station is particularly powerful because it is so rare. This is the last time in our lifetimes that Neptune and Chiron will occupy the same degree.

Know Thyself

Every spiritual tradition worth its salt has the same core concept: Know Thyself. Repetition has made this dictum into a cliché, but it remains the quintessential truth of consciousness work. Nor is it as simple as it sounds, for it has a catch. If we want to follow it sincerely we have to distinguish our self-delusions from our essence.

Workable variations on the Know-Thyself theme are everywhere available. Buddhism offers techniques for noticing our delusions and then transcending them. Psychotherapy uses the talking cure to expose their sources in childhood. EST, the Landmark forum, The Secret et al. propose that we isolate out our stories, drop them and get on with life.

The one thing that's indispensable with this process is a scalpel-sharp self-honesty. Whether we follow a methodology or go it alone, every seeker who aspires to transcend her psycho-spiritual limitations will be challenged, sooner or later, to answer the question: Who am I without my autobiographical pictures?

This is the question the Neptune-Chiron conjunction[1] is asking us, and we can winnow them down to three steps. In the absence of an organization, a coach or a self-help book, try following the transit's instructions:

1. Identify where you've been in denial.

2. Let go of denial.

3. Change.

Astrology makes Step #1 easy. Take a look at your own chart, and consider where Neptune is right now. What house is it transiting through? What aspects does it form to your natal planets? These tell you which of your delusions are aching to be revealed and released. It will have been in the same general part of your chart for a while, given how slowly this planet moves along its orbit (Neptune takes 168 years to go through the zodiac).

In an attempt to connect us deeper into ourselves, Neptune and Chiron sometimes seem to leach the meaning out of the department of life represented by the house through which they are transiting. The life experiences in question will have perhaps been feeling attenuated, thin and lifeless. This is because the illusions attached to them have zapped their vitality. Although this part of our life may not have changed in an objective sense, to us it may have started to seem false, silly, even absurd.

This transit makes Step #2 – releasing denial — attractive, mostly because it makes holding onto denial so hard.

The Transit through the Houses

Neptune's transit through the sixth house, for example, can make our work feel pointless. Or it may be our physical health that registers the malaise; using vague, vacillating symptoms to prompt a more subtle attention from us. Chiron, meanwhile, is about hurting; though its intention is to use hurt as a marker, like a pointer in a power point presentation. If we follow where the transit is pointing, we'll see that a truth about ourselves wants to emerge. It has been trying to emerge for several years, but has been mired in denial.

Together, Neptune and Chiron are demanding that we go beyond self-pity and

---

[1] Broadly speaking, the conjunction's range is 2009-12.

victimhood. They are daring us to summon up the spiritual courage to do Step #2. If we do, Step #3 is a snap: it happens automatically. And it transforms our lives.

If Neptune and Chiron are transiting your seventh house, you know painful relationship patterns are the issue. This is an invitation to identify them and drop them. If the transit falls in your fourth, ancestral ghosts – possibly from the mother line – can now fade into mist. Their work with you is done. If in the 12th ghosts from even further back, from previous incarnations, can lose their hold on you. Usher them out with respect.

If the conjunction falls near the top of your natal chart, take the plunge into those unsettling career issues that may have been prickling under the surface for decades. If you're not doing work that feeds your soul, you have been suffering. Do a ritual this month that affirms your intention to make your vocation into an avocation. If the transit is in your second house, you're being called to adopt a more subtle understanding of money and self-support – more subtle than the collective attitudes you've been absorbing.

If Neptune and Chiron are in your third house right now, painful mental patterns are ready to be confronted and eliminated. Distraction and chronic escapism are common addictions of the mind; they siphon off energy that we could be using for imaginative thinking. If Neptune and Chiron are in your eighth house, ask yourself whether there are episodes from past intimate relationships that have been serving or inhibiting your sexual vitality. If the conjunction falls in your fifth house, consider your self-conception as a creative person. Where have you been kidding yourself? Your view of your own artistry may have been either self-inflating or self-deflating. Whichever the case, forgive yourself for harboring them and surrender them to the cause of authenticity.

Neptune and Chiron in the ninth house means you're being asked to own up to delusions you might have had about teachers and teachings, and to release them despite your fear of demon doubt.

In the eleventh house, the conjunction is inviting you to admit to false friendships, and/or to having been seduced by groupthink against the better interests of your life purpose. If this transit falls on or near your Ascendant, allow the self-portrait you've been cultivating all your life to melt off you, like grimy old curb ice dissolving under the noonday Sun.

These thumbnail delineations are not meant to be exhaustive; just to plant a seed. This conjunction represents liberation, and your higher self wants it to happen. It is fated to happen, and astrology tells us it's meant to happen now. But if it is to happen gracefully we need to collude in the process. We need to help it along, by being conscious. Otherwise we open ourselves up to the shadow side of the transit, which swamps us in dark Neptune – confusion and anxiety – and dark Chiron – wounds without meaning.

Both Chiron (aboriginal pain) and Neptune (empathy) are subtle archetypes, easily misunderstood. Part of the reason we so often go wrong with their teachings is that, in the modern world, we don't hold compassion as a high priority, and we don't value the process by which pain leads to compassion. We can't imagine that pain could serve any purpose. Our conventional healing modalities, even many New Age ("Be happy!") ones, bristle at the very idea. Even when we do concede that past hurts deepen us, unless we make the distinction between pain and suffering, Chiron's wounds smack of pathology; the notion of honoring them may strike us as masochistic.

So a great deal depends on the approach we take to this transit. Our degree of openness to leaving conventional attitudes behind can make the difference between despair and magical glory.

Tempest in a Teacup

(originally published in *Daykeeper
Journal*, November 2010)

Even when only partially accessed, Neptune inspires artists, sweetens love
affairs, and supports seekers of personal growth.

November 2010 marks the swan song of the transit of Neptune and Chiron to the
US Moon; and the best chance we will have, in our lifetimes, to understand its
meaning.

In secular societies like ours, where there are few healthy outlets for the planet's
sublime yearnings, the self-deceptive side of Neptune is particularly dangerous.
Chiron's involvement suggests that behind the deception there is pain. For those
who look for meaning in the cultural currents during these years of cosmic
crossroads, the Neptune-Chiron transit provides a rare window into the group
psychology of the USA.

Illusion is a cosmic constant, not something that we can evaluate as good or bad.
Self-delusion, on the other hand, causes major problems. Neptune is an emotional
planet, resistant to reason. Its placement in the US (Sibly) chart exacerbates this
tendency, making us prone to fantastical extremes. The Tea Party movement – if
"movement" is the right word – is a testament to what misapplied Neptune
(mobs, enthrallment) can do when fueled by Chironic wounds.

Propaganda

The tea-baggers began to take on steam just as Neptune came into orb of the US
Moon in March 2009. In addition, as astrologer Scott Wolfram has pointed out,
the transiting Moon will be on top of the country's natal Neptune during the
elections in November 2010: a remarkable double whammy that will make the
lessons of this pairing hard to miss.

The Left has been trying to get the word out for a while now about the real power
behind the teabag juggernaut. But it was only a couple of months ago that Jane
Meyer's article in *The New Yorker* (8/30/2010) expanded in detail the role played

by the Koch Brothers, a quiet pair of ex-John Birchers who have poured
hundreds of millions of dollars into tea bag actions. It was these guys who
brought in the requisite marketing and strategic savvy to slickly professionalize
the tea-baggers, all the while packaging them as a homespun grassroots
phenomenon. Then Fox News was brought on board to sell it.

You have to wonder what future historians will make of Fox. With a few
centuries' worth of hindsight, what will be made of the way this enormously
popular network exhorts its millions of viewers to vent their ire at appointed
targets rather than to use their intellects; the way it promotes the baser emotions
at the expense of the more generous emotions of which we humans are capable;
the way it manipulates fear as a crowd-control device? Although one rarely hears
the word *propaganda* applied to what Fox does, this is a textbook case.

Seduced and Scapegoated

Neptune rules seduction and bewitchment, and the US Moon represents the
nation's vulnerable inner child. This helps us understand why the public mood
has been so impressionable, over the past several years, to grand-scale
charlatanism. The presence of Chiron tips us to the sense of helplessness that
ordinary Americans are feeling as their old sureties crumble under the
Jupiter/Uranus-Pluto square. As we know from considering the successful
propaganda campaigns throughout history, where there is collective pain
(Chiron) there is a desire to target scapegoats (Neptune). In the Teabag scenario,
government is the scapegoat. Thus, the anti-incumbent rage sweeping the country
this election season.

But there was a tense moment there, just after the bail-outs, when the potential
existed for Main Street's anger to settle upon corporations instead. This potential
was glimpsed and averted by the Koch Brothers and their cohorts. The tea-
baggers were persuaded to focus their ire on the federal government because the
power of Big Money was behind the persuasion. They had Fox to get the word
out for them. By contrast, as Ralph Nader has said, governments don't advertise.

The Dream

"The American Dream," as a phrase, is an apt summation of this transit to the
USA. It hints at the potential to shake off the fantasies (Neptune) from which
ordinary people (Moon) have been suffering (Chiron). These fantasies include
the idea that safeguarding the interests of corporate behemoths somehow helps
rank-and-file workers; and the related idea – and this is where irrationality loops

out into full-blown magical thinking – that the existence in US society of an obscenely rich one percent holds out the hope to the other 99% that they, too, will someday catch a ride on the gravy train.

The disaffected Americans now protesting the wrongs to which they believe Obama and Nancy Pelosi have subjected them identify deeply with the whole panoply of American Dream imagery. Neptunian confusion and its close cousin, ignorance, enshroud the tea-baggers like fog. From all appearances, not only are these folks unaware that their movement is funded by billionaire oil interests, but in their passion they seem not to have realized that many of the policies opposed by those same interests – such as the bill to extend unemployment benefits – could someday prove a lifesaver to the tea-baggers themselves. Neither pragmatism nor self-interest is likely with Neptune-Moon combinations.

Group Madness

Thanks to the highly organized cheerleaders who give them their sound bites, the tea crowd worldview has morphed from an embrace of the probable, to an entertainment of the possible, to a fear of the patently absurd, such as the notion that healthcare reform would open the door to a Marxist takeover. Through nonstop repetition, guys like Hannity and Beck have done much to enable even the most counter-intuitive notions to gel into fevered conviction.

Any issue that could endanger the profits of the movement's benefactors is pitched by their allied pundits and politicos (who are jumping on the bandwagon so fast it's surprising its wheels don't fall off) as a threat to democracy – even an obviously democratic issue like the retention of net neutrality. To sweeten the pitch, the whipped-up crowds are told that they, the true patriots, are bold grassroots activists. They get to have their cake and eat it too: they get to keep their self-image as just-plain-folks while being flattered that they're courageous, radical thinkers.

There's no madness like group madness. The planet Neptune, traditionally associated with poisonous vapors, can indicate plagues. The USA is currently experiencing a psycho-political epidemic embittered by the wound of disempowerment (Chiron). How do we inoculate ourselves against it?

By divesting ourselves of delusion, and by responding to the reality underneath collective lies.

To get on Neptune's good side – its liberating side – we need to observe the situations from afar, a vantage point astrology is very good at helping us assume.

This means living through our charts, from which position it is impossible to give our power away.

The Peace within the Flood

(originally published as a blog,
November 2010)

Why did the Goddess invent grief? What is its purpose?

Most of us think about this powerful energy, if at all, only in terms of the specific things that trigger it for us. And how to avoid them. But in late 2010 the skies are asking us to consider grief in a different way.

The swan song of the Neptune-Chiron conjunction is conditioning the psychic environment right now. It is giving us a chance to consider grief without fear, dismissal or judgment. We are being invited to open up to a universal human emotion that most of us feel ambivalent about, at best; ashamed of, at worst. Most of us are afraid of grief; and that fear turns it unhealthy.

But true grief is not unhealthy. Sweet, aching, spontaneous grief is a cleansing force like no other. Like ocean tides that clear the beach and pull everything back to the sea (Neptune), grief washes away our emotional detritus and connects us back to Source. Chiron's role here is to teach us that when grief is allowed to keep moving, it heals.

Emotional Pain

This is an unusual transit and it poses an unusual challenge. It is daring us to drop our attitudes about emotional pain and simply feel it. By acknowledging sadness, and observing it from a distance, we allow it to work its magic. This is a tricky exercise: there's a fine line between respecting a feeling and indulging in it. We must let grief open our hearts, but steer clear of becoming mired in it (which creates depression: grief with no life in it). The key is understanding grief as a trans-personal energy, bigger than our egoic selves. When we realize this, we can strike the right balance, and earn Neptune and Chiron's reward: an enriched empathy.

Intellectual intelligence won't help us here. This transit is about our emotional intelligence. When we are identified with this part of ourselves, we may see grief very differently from how we were raised to see it. We may start to question the way we were taught to hold back our tears. We may start to see as very strange that people in the throes of sorrow are hushed and secreted away. We may start to see it as a statement of how emotionally unsophisticated we are, as a culture, that people in grief are relentlessly told to be happy, to smile; and that those who acknowledge grievous situations are accused of "being negative."

It takes courage to admit that certain aspects of life on Earth are sad. It is honest to mourn the fact that the world isn't more loving. It is indeed grievous that people are not kinder to one another. Why deny it? It is an unarguable shame that we humans do not live up to the potential that we know we could express. Why dismiss these recognitions of the truth? Recognizing them as true is a testament to our being aware; and awareness can never steer us wrong.

Pisces Ahead

This transit is getting us ready, as all transits do, for what is to come. After their rendezvous in November 2010, Neptune and Chiron will ingress into Pisces, of which more anon.

Those readers with emphasized Neptune or Chiron in their charts, or with Pisces dominant, will be familiar with this phenomenon. But all of us are picking up on energies from everything around us, like an insect with wiggling antennae, actively taking everything in.

Our psychological filters are weak right now. The sense of separateness that keeps us from identifying with the rest of humanity and its sufferings is not as robust as usual. We may feel chaos flooding in, inducing a fear of psychic drowning. Just reading the headlines may feel overwhelming. Such feelings are utterly justifiable, and not inappropriate. But the fact that feeling inundated is forgivable doesn't mean that it's inevitable.

The teaching here is to venture beyond the normal reaction. To trust what is moving through us, to know it is taking us somewhere, and to find the peace within the flood. When we reach that state, we realize that grief and joy are flip sides of the same coin.

APOCALYPSE NOT

(originally published in *Skywatch*,
December 2010)

In December 2010 we get a big blast of the Uranus-Pluto square, the transit I've been calling the longest arm of the Cross.

Whenever a more fleeting planet (Mercury, Mars, Venus, the Moon) passes through the early degrees of a Cardinal sign, it triggers the Cardinal Cross. The quicker planet acts like a finger plucking a harp string, causing reverberations that make a distinct sound. If we listen, we'll hear transformation. Personally and collectively, we are transforming.

But there's tremendous tension in the air, as people react with fear to the drastic cultural shifts that are the raison-d'être of these transits. To not freak out, we need to see these changes in context – in the biggest context we can imagine. The involvement of Uranus in the Cross does suggest drastic shifts, but Uranus's cycle is long and slow – it takes 84 years to go around the zodiac – which tells us that we won't get anything we haven't been prepared for. And Pluto, the planet of death, exists only to usher in rebirth.

The concept of destruction for its own sake does not exist in astrology, nor in Nature.

Civilization and its Discontents

It's time to reconsider what we mean by *civilization*. This is a word associated with Capricorn, the sign occupied by Pluto between 2008 and '23. It's going to kill off the outworn assumptions we harbor about what constitutes an advanced society.

In the Western world, schoolchildren learn that industrialization, modern science, capitalism and imperialism are all benchmarks of civilization. I don't think it's ever stated as such; it's just something we absorb with the ABCs. We're given to understand that the contemporary world represents the pinnacle of human thought and behavior, whereas the ancient world roiled with chaos and barbarism. Everywhere, that is, except in classical Greece and Rome. (And, interestingly, in Mesopotamia, which my generation was told was "the cradle of civilization;" but this accolade seems to have changed with the political winds. Once the Western powers began to covet Middle Eastern oil, they decided that Iran, Iraq et al. were deeply *un*civilized after all, and that they needed the Great Democracies to enlighten them via military control.)

The transits overhead are daring us to question this assumption. What if it was all propaganda?

The mass mind is going through wrenching shifts of viewpoint (Pluto) about how human groups organize themselves (Capricorn). To more and more people it is becoming apparent that the industrial revolution has resulted in ecological devastation; that capitalism has resulted in plutocratic inequalities the world over; that imperialism and colonization have resulted in gross injustice. And that the Goddess-worshipping societies of the pre-historical world bore little resemblance to our stereotypes of brutish "cave men" with clubs.

When you think of a civilized society, what sort of images come to mind? I think of the availability of rest rooms downtown. And clean public spaces. I think of the quiet library near my house, and the bench in front of the hardware store that has no advertising on it. It's there just so people can sit down.

If we were to ask this question of regular people all around the world, what types of answers do you suppose would turn up again and again? I bet a lot of people would say that it was the richness of a culture's art that made it civilized. Or the value a state places upon education. Or how well its leaders used reasoned moral arguments, to inspire the citizenry to deploy its highest capabilities.

Some might propose that what counted most was how highly a society prioritized peace over war.

I doubt we'd say that what made a society civilized was having a booming GDP.[1] Yet that seems to be the key criterion you read about in official circles.

---

[1] Even if we did say that wealth was the main marker of a civilized society, the question that needs to be asked is: Whose wealth are we talking about? When the experts issue their proclamations about a country's overall financial health, what part of the demographic are they referring to? In the USA, whenever there's a spike in the wealth of Wall Street traders, big investors, high-earning professionals and CEOs, we're told that "the economy is on the mend"... even though the average worker may be doing worse than ever (like right now, for example).

The proud new ascendant powers, China and India have been asserting their vigorous economies as proof of their worthiness to enter the club of civilized nations. And in the USA,[2] schools have been pumping resources into business curricula as fast as they can, while de-funding the humanities. Lip service is still given to the kinds of values that the humanities nurture – democracy, empathy, tolerance and free speech – but less and less investment is made in the training that fosters such values.[3]

As to the prioritization of peace over war, given the amount of money the USA has invested in the armaments industry – including the billions it makes in weapons sales to other countries – by this measure America is the most uncivilized nation the world has ever seen.

Organic Decay

But this trajectory cannot be sustained. By Natural Law, that which is non-life-affirming cannot go on past a certain point, and we are reaching that point. Many aspects of human civilization are dying. It isn't the capacity of humanity to be civilized that's dying; it's just the non-life-affirming aspects that are dying. They have to be sloughed off so that we can become re-humanized. We are coming to the tipping point of a long, slow learning curve.

The processes denoted by the Uranus-Pluto cycle – devolution, social change and evolution – are organic. To conceptualize these transits in terms of sudden mass destruction is too simplistic. Action movies work that way, but Nature doesn't. The changes represented by the Cardinal Cross may be mammoth, but they are natural and perfectly sequenced, one phase segueing into the next. We're being given all the time we need to understand and assimilate what we need to learn.

---

[2] The US (Sibly) chart's Sun occupies the fourth corner of the Cross, that of Cancer.

[3] Martha Nussbaum, in *Not for Profit* (Princeton Books, 2010), says we are raising "useful profit-makers with obtuse imaginations."

Political Animals

(originally published in *Daykeeper
Journal,* December 2010)

How do we keep our integrity in insane times? Here's a rule of thumb that covers
all contingencies: Aspire to the highest truth, in every situation.

Astrologically, this translates as living through the center of the chart. This
means identifying with our essential selves, whether our upbringing taught us to
do so or not; whether our friends are doing so or not; whether our country's
leaders and spokespeople are doing so or not.

It can get confusing when we take into account how many "selves" we have.
Natal charts are complex amalgams of different planets in different signs: the
Moon is our emotional needs, Jupiter our idealism, Mercury the opinions we
hold, Venus our personal values, *etcetera.* Being true to the self should beg the
question, "Which part of myself?"

When we are in the moment, responding fully through every part of our chart, the
sense of unity trumps our inner fractiousness. But when we're not, the many
levels of truth that the self perceives – intellectual, emotional, political, esoteric –
sometimes seem to clash with each other, even cancel each other out.[1] For
example, it often feels as if there's a contradiction between seeing things
politically and seeing things spiritually.

Different Lenses

Have you ever been blissed-out at a meditation retreat in the mountains or by the
ocean? In that context, doesn't the *sturm und drang* of elections and culture wars
feel utterly faraway and absurdly unreal? In those circumstances we feel that the
sublime wisdom of our guru is the only thing that's real. But once we get back to

---

[1] Eckhart Tolle teaches that when we find ourselves confused between our feelings and ideas at any
given moment, it's the feelings that we should trust.

our daily routine and plunge into the social fray, we might feel the opposite.

Once we're home again and following the news, we might find ourselves, say, in an argument with someone who had more important things to do than vote in the midterm elections (in which it is speculated that the GOP would've lost the House if all of the eligible young voters had voted). Which shocks and appalls us. So now, suddenly, it's the "naval-gazing" that's unreal. Now we feel what's *really* real is paying attention to one's immediate cultural and political environment.

But these two layers of existence are not at odds. As suggested by the '60s catch phrase "Think globally, act locally," there are different tiers to our human existence, which different parts of ourselves are sensitive to. Political understanding is a lens that we can polish to a high clarity, or not use at all, depending on our ambitions and proclivities. Spiritual understanding is another lens, which, similarly, we can polish or not polish.

The natal chart offers many lenses for viewing ourselves and the world; and clues as to whether the person will emphasize the political over the spiritual or vice versa. Also, depending on what's going on with our transits, the emphasis may shift. A person who normally thinks of herself as apolitical may be drawn to engage actively in her societal matrix if her chart is being triggered by an epochal configuration like the Cardinal Cross. Assuming her activism is fueled by animal instincts, clear-thinking intellect and cosmic connectedness, it will enrich her spiritual understanding rather than detracting from it.

Ultimately it is not about which point of view we assume, but how fully engaged we are.

Another Solstice, Another Cross

Each equinox and solstice throughout the Cardinal Cross years will have the effect of turning up the heat under the Cancer cluster in the US (Sibly) chart. When the planets closer to the Sun hit the current degrees of transiting Pluto and Uranus, the opportunity arises to glimpse deeper levels of truth, collectively and personally. Americans who aspire to the political truth will get to strip one more layer of nonsense off their national self-image. It's an invitation to confront the nastiness of decay.

In US culture, as in every culture, nationalistic identification inclines us to believe government spokesmen. That is, *our* government's spokesmen. Nationalism – and its high-drama cousin, patriotism – are almost universally seen to be virtues. They dictate our point of view so thoroughly that even progressive thinkers are hypnotized by them. Notice how otherwise unemotional men – especially men – are considered high-minded and noble if they sniff and snuffle a little bit when saluting the flag.

But during this time of cosmic crossroads, a good many of our assumptions about what constitutes civilized virtues are biting the dust. Many thinkers are proposing that we must move beyond our identification with nation-states if we are to survive as a planet. For Americans, this would mean viewing our country's machinations from a wider point of view, even as we continue to confer meaning on our American-ness.

Pluto and Government

Take, for example, the so-called "war on terror," a powerful propaganda conceit that doubles as a military campaign. When we allow ourselves to parse the word/concept of "terror" apart from its post-millennial buzzword status – that is, independent of the meaning the US government wants us to give it – we see Pluto in Capricorn at work.

Terrorism, the use of violence and threats to intimidate or coerce, has been around for a long time. What is noteworthy about the current use of this word-concept is that it has been taken over by the state, which has claimed exclusive rights to its definition. This definition presumes, of course, that only the government's enemies can be terrorists. But the overuse of this term since 9/11/01 has inadvertently thrown attention on the fact that governments claim the right to monopolize the perpetration of violence.

Classic examples of this monopolization include the British vs. Irish nationalists, the Pentagon vs. the Vietnamese/Iraqis/ Afghans, and police forces everywhere vs. dissidents. As geopolitical writer Andrew Palmer has pointed out, where violent groups arise which have not been state-sanctioned, they're tagged with this word, isolated, and turned into a propaganda plus for the government. The ruling party of Israel uses the word *terrorism* as often as the White House does. It came in very handy when the IDF was massacring innocents in Gaza during the winter of 2008-09, billing the slaughter as an assertion of law and order.

Thus is the state's own terrorism not only permitted by a hoodwinked citizenry, but welcomed by most of them. The group's inner child (signified by a national chart's natal Moon) needs to believe that its parent figures are keeping it safe. Under the guise of "security," this need keeps the US populace from protesting their disempowerment. It is because of this aspect of group psychology that the Bush administration's curtailment of American civil liberties has not been reversed. It is the reason the TSA screenings at airports are overwhelmingly accepted by the masses, despite their degrading nature, statistical contraindications, and potential to cause cancer.

The use of the noun "terrorist" as a linguistic bogeyman appeals to this same layer of the group psyche. Like a toddler who wants his parent there to fend off nighttime monsters, this aspect of the populace is reassured when the Pentagon says that "several suspected terrorists" were killed in Afghanistan. Logically, the phrase "several suspected civilians were killed" would be at least as accurate. But it wouldn't play as well in Peoria.

Political and Spiritual

Whether we call it spiritual awareness or political awareness or something else, it's all about awareness. One is awake or one is not.

Do you believe that there are no accidents? Then everything in our reality must be there for a reason. To declare a belief in this *dictum* is to believe, with no sense of blame attached, that everything in our environment, from our wardrobe to the weather, is a part of a meaningful gestalt: our very own cosmic learning curve, none of it arbitrary.

This total meaningfulness includes other people and their doings. If we are inhaling second-hand smoke from our neighbors, clearly the reality we created includes our neighbors' nicotine addiction. If we are paying taxes that go towards the slaughter of human beings in other countries, then our reality includes what our government is doing. Whatever exists in our life is there to enlarge our awareness.

I suppose it could be argued that, free will being what it is, we could then decide to either respond to it or not. This argument might sound more persuasive in ordinary times. But these are not ordinary times.

FILTHY LUCRE

(originally published as a blog,
December 2010)

Here at the tail end of 2010, there's an unsavory aroma in the air. With Pluto
(decay) opposing the US Jupiter (increase) and Venus (wealth), money's on the
mass mind.

Our terminology around money says a lot about our ambivalent feelings about it.
Money is associated in vernacular English with pollution and corruption: we
speak of people being "dirt poor," for example, and "filthy rich." I thought of this
last week when I read that researchers have found dangerously high levels of the
carcinogenic chemical bisphenol-A on dollar bills.

In the USA, the potent charge attached to money is indicated by Pluto, the planet
of taboos, in the second house of the national chart. All taboo subjects require
euphemisms. For example, people who find "sexy" a naughty word tend to coyly
substitute "sensual."

New Coinage

Accordingly, a tortured new coinage entered the English language with the
Mercury-Pluto conjunction (propaganda) in early December. The Federal
Reserve, whose use of numbers economist Laurence Kotlikoff has called "Enron
accounting," has announced a scheme to buy up government debt that they call
"Quantitative Easing." It's a trillion-dollar program that Ben Bernanke wants us
to know is *not* what it looks like – i.e., printing money out of thin air (comedian
Jon Stewart said: "Oh right, Ben. We're not printing money; we're *imagineering*
money.") As astrologer Jim Perilman has pointed out, Benny B.'s natal Jupiter is
opposite his Sun: he's a naturally inflationary guy.

It is not only the USA that's in money trouble, of course. National borders mean
nothing to Pluto, whose entry into Capricorn in 2008 inaugurated the global
financial meltdown. The Uranus-Pluto square, exact seven times between 2012

and 2016[1] is wreaking havoc everywhere on Earth, exposing Big Money's smoke-and-mirror games wherever they are to be found.

Money Trouble

The Eurozone's currency crisis is spinning out of control. Last month's bailout of Ireland – Celtic Tiger, we hardly knew ye! – has deepened suspicion worldwide that the Euro is crumbling. In London last week, Prince Charles's limo got mobbed by rioters as he made his way to the theatre. They aren't too happy about the austerity cuts over there.

The dollar is in deeper trouble. America's Saturn Return (stringent challenges) in the tenth house (international credibility) is peaking through 2011, lending credence to predictions that the dollar will lose its status as the global reserve currency. The International Monetary Fund is fully aware that the USA is broke, but seems to be hoping nobody reads its reports. And since any mention of taxes is career death for politicians, and the mass media only reports the nonsense they do mention, most Americans seem to have no idea that keeping taxes at their current level rate is fiscal suicide.

Anger and Intrigue

The global scenario is one of self-destructive debt (Pluto), untethered speculation (Uranus) and unavoidable austerity (Saturn) – all of it increasingly associated with banks. As far as profits are concerned, the bankers are coming out on top, as they always have. But to the public they are coming off as villains.

Hollywood, always a good indicator of the mass mood, is once again putting out movies with evil Gordon Gecko characters. But something has shifted since the mantra "greed is good" was first ascribed to Wall Street, in the 1980s. Back then, it was presented as a shocking bit of fictional dark humor. Now, since Pluto entered Capricorn, it has been borne out by real-life events. Now no one's laughing.

As Mars gets ready to join Mercury in its opposition to the US Jupiter, in mid-December, an outpouring of public outrage has erupted over the linking of unemployment benefits to tax cuts for millionaires. With Mars and Pluto involved, you know there will be intense power plays; and you suspect that whatever appears on the surface will be covering up layers of intrigue.
My hunch is that the threat to cut millions of jobless Americans' benefits was

---

[1] These take place June 24, 2012, September 19 2012, May 21 2013, November 1 2013, April 21 2014, December 15 2014 and March 17 2015

craven stagecraft. I don't believe the GOP would have dared to actualize a policy so flagrantly anti-populist. It would have not only cost them their jobs, but risked triggering Washington's worst nightmare: a mass uprising.

Consider FDR, whom history lauds as a great hero of progressivism. He was all too aware that if he didn't offer concessions to the working class, there'd be riots in the streets. Avoiding revolution is one point upon which both ruling parties of the American plutocracy fully agree.

Trickle-Up

The pundits, meanwhile, are using the issue to begin a timely discussion about ethics and decency (Jupiter). Moreover, it's refreshing to hear them making the very pragmatic observation that since the Bush cuts went into effect in 2001 all the wealth has trickled up, not down. In other words, the tax-cut apologists' central premise has been shown not to work. And as everyone who's gone through a Saturn Return knows, functionality is the first and last criterion for anything under this transit.

On the other hand, it did work in terms of its plutocratic intent. The richest 1% of the US population has already scored about a trillion dollars since the breaks began. And it is working in terms of its cosmic intent, too. Ordinary people (Uranus) all over the world are smarting up about where the power lies.

Chapter 4

Into the Streets
2011

Neptune was about to enter Pisces, the sign in which both the creative and destructive sides of water are maximally strong, when the tsunami struck Japan on March 12, 2011. The disaster was an astonishingly apt summation of the combined symbolism of all the major planetary players: Neptune (flooding), Uranus (earthquakes) and Pluto (nuclear reactors).

Uranus, which also governs revolutions, was back in Aries (activism) that spring, provoking pro-democracy riots in Europe and in Asia, North Africa, the Middle East, and even the American Midwest, where the big business-backed government (Pluto) was pitted against the unions. The eager entry of NATO into Libya's civil war and the assassination of Osama bin Laden forced many people to reconsider the collective values implicit in their membership in a nation state.

Throughout 2011 the USA was going through its Saturn Return, the transit that tests an entity's standing in the world. A heretofore almost unimaginable idea started to gain credence: that America's global status as a superpower was slipping away. As the global roots of the financial crisis were revealed, the concept of nationalism itself started to feel more and more anachronistic. Old-fashioned patriotism was being replaced by the raw, unvarnished profit motive of multinational corporations, and in many minds a new understanding began to gel about workings of the world's centralized financial power structure (Capricorn). The use of national debt and "sanctions" to control the fate of non-allied countries started to gain currency as coercive models, every bit as destructive as military warfare (Pluto).

Just before the autumnal equinox of 2011, with the square of Uranus and Pluto closer to exactitude than it had yet been, the USA celebrated the tenth anniversary of its first great myth of the new century: Nine-Eleven, an event no less mysterious (Pluto) and explosively divisive (Uranus) in 2011 than it was a decade earlier.

Amidst the building tension was an uptick of reactionary populism worldwide:

the EDL in England, the Front National in France, Fox News in the USA. At the other end of the spectrum was Occupy Wall Street, a direct and explicit challenge (Uranus in Aries) to the global financial status quo (Pluto in Capricorn) that spread like wildfire after its birth on September 17th in Manhattan to cities and town squares across the world. Something in the zeitgeist that had been stewing for quite a while had been named, at last. And just like 9/11, it was identified with a set of numbers: 1 and 99 percent. It was as if the energies being symbolized were too big for words alone.

Feelings and ideas about income inequality, about the corruption of the political process, and about the skewed priorities of modern consumerist societies burst into public discussion after having festered for years, unvoiced in public discussion. Explicitly revolutionary, the OWS movement disdained the terms offered up by conventional politics. Full-throated, it spoke from outside of the box.

Like a blast of cold, fresh air, a new freedom was rushing into humanity's shared consciousness. Economic and political thinkers were not the only ones stimulated. On the inner planes as well, people were being invited to break out of old patterns of thinking and feeling. By turns stressful and exciting, the transits of 2011 functioned as an inner quake-tsunami; an inner Molotov cocktail.

Explosive and disruptive in the outer forms they took, the transits were nevertheless understood by many meaning-seekers to be essentially about balance and re-ordering. They were offering humanity the chance to rewire its spiritual intelligence.

Sharpening Our Attention

(originally published in *Skywatch*,
January 2011)

With the quicker moving Jupiter exaggerating the fire of Uranus in Aries, we are being challenged to consider the implications of living an inspired life. All Aries transits are about breaking out the superhero cloak and leaping into the fray. The impulse is to move beyond our limits, overtly, passionately, and courageously.

And recent months have deepened our sense of why such courage is necessary.

Common Thread

All over the world, alert human beings are working on the same basic learning curves. They may be using different words and coming from different points of departure, but they are all expressing the same thing: that if Earth is to survive, humanity needs to acquire knowledge quickly and boldly.

Environmentalists are organizing their analysis around overpopulation, resource depletion, climate change, species extinction and the advent of peak oil; which, according to some analysts, will be reached around 2012 – the year Uranus and Pluto first square each other to the exact degree. Geopolitical observers are bringing our attention to the systems collapse underway in, for example, almost every country in Africa; and to the corrupt regimes worldwide whose pseudo-governments are showing themselves to be threadbare, such as in Pakistan, Haiti and Afghanistan. Economists are pointing out the cracks and fissures that have appeared since 2008 (when Pluto entered Capricorn) in the international financial system.

Not all of the voices being raised are coherent. We are also hearing from jihadists whose idea of seizing the day is to blow up marketplaces; from Zionists whose vision of choice is Palestinian genocide; and from Christian zealots warning us that Armageddon is nigh because of our tolerance of homosexuality. We have survivalists building up militias in the woods, and *deus ex machina* hopefuls waiting for deliverance by UFOs.

The visions being received run the gamut, from visionary to mindlessly destructive. But they share a common thread: the idea that the human race is teetering on the edge of something.

The astrological approach holds that whatever is not life-affirming must be abandoned now, so that the greater whole can thrive.

Butterfly Effect

Most of us would immediately agree that widening our knowledge about the world we live in is a good thing. Who wouldn't want to have their consciousness raised? But let's think a minute about what this entails. As Adam and Eve found out, knowledge can lead to complications.

In times of critical change (Uranus), acquiring knowledge must be accompanied by spiritual wisdom and moral responsibility (Jupiter). The kind of learning world citizens need now isn't merely about information intake. It involves sharpening our attention about the relationship between ourselves and the wider world. This means getting real about both our collective and personal realities, and looking for the interface between them.

For holistic thinkers the idea that everything in the world impacts every other thing is not merely an abstract concept. Environmentalists talk about the butterfly effect: the idea that a seemingly inconsequential event like the flap of a butterfly's wings can impact distant telluric systems halfway around the world. Those of a mystical persuasion go the whole distance with this idea, applying it to human thought, feelings and spiritual impulses as well. The mysterious interconnectedness of all things applies to everything in the universe, and it starts at home. Where do we, as unique individuals, fit into the way things are? What impact does our lifestyle have on planet Earth?

We hear, for example, that in the not too distant future, clean water will be as precious as oil is now. If we allow ourselves to learn a bit more about this daunting fact, it could change our lives. We might discover, for example, how much water goes into the production of an 8-ounce piece of beef.[1] That might get

---

[1] It takes 630 gallons, because of the staggering amounts of water required by the grain crops consumed by the cattle. The "water footprint" in affluent countries is around 1,800 gallons per day per person.

us feeling differently about our hamburger habit.

To believe that the universe is inextricably interconnected is to understand that the tiniest little things we do make a difference. What used to seem like an unremarkable choice no longer seems unremarkable. Will we bring our own tote bag to the grocery store, remembering that plastic bags are accumulating in the oceans, choking the fish?

No Pointing Fingers

A typical first reaction to hearing disturbing information that involves complicity on our part is to indignantly defend ourselves against presumed blame. ("It's not my fault they used slave labor to make my iPod!") This makes sense if our goal is political point-scoring or face-saving. But if our goal is sharpening our awareness, then pointing fingers has nothing to do with anything. Neither blaming others nor blaming ourselves[2] (feeling guilty) has any relevance.

Guilt feelings are the last refuge of the well intentioned. At first blush, they seem an innocuous enough response; maybe even sort of limpidly noble. But the more we sharpen our awareness, the more we realize that feeling guilty is no response at all. It's a substitute for responding. It's a diversion.

If sharpening the attention is our goal, we must begin with the simple acknowledgment of our role in the interconnected world. We acknowledge that it is our destiny to be alive here and now. We accept that we have a role to play in these mad times. We open up to them, perils and all, and instead of fear we feel the thrill of learning.

At that point, the transits begin to fuel us.

---

[2] Some psychologists propose that the reason we blame others is because it's less painful than blaming ourselves, and that the former is a cover for the latter. But energetically, blame directed at others and self-blame are made of the same stuff, and both are beside the point in this context. Taking responsibility in the archetypal sense means making full use of one's Saturn, symbol of the law of karma.

PIGGY BANKS

(originally published in *Daykeeper
Journal*, January 2011)

Uncle Sam is in the middle of his Saturn Return as 2011 begins, and Pluto is opposite the US Jupiter, getting ready to square Uranus in the longest arm of the Cardinal Cross.

Heads We Win; Tails You Lose

This conflux of transits is meant to drive home the lessons of the epochal Uranus-Pluto square, which has been building since 2008. The fact that they are hitting the US (Sibly) chart so pointedly just as the year begins tells us that the decay (Pluto) inherent in our social institutions (Saturn) will be shaken up (Uranus) and rendered egregiously visible in 2011. The events we'll be seeing have this essential purpose: that of bringing to the fore aspects of our system that have become so skewed and toxic that they threaten the country's overall health.

It is a point that will not be left to our imaginations.

We have here an emphasis on the US Saturn in the tenth house (government) and on the country's natal Pluto (absolute control) in the second house (money).[1] This leaves little doubt about which aspect of the American system is ready for rehab. It's about the distorted distribution of valuables in this, the richest country in the world.

The national Saturn Return continues through 2011, peaking a second and third time in March and August. To get a sense of what to expect, we can look at its first hit, on December 3, 2010. That was also the week Mercury conjoined Pluto in the sky, provoking the long, ongoing opposition between transiting Pluto and the US's Jupiter (expansion)/Venus (money) conjunction.

---

[1] The USA will be having its first-ever Pluto Return in 2022, when the teeny-weeny planet of great big power reaches the degree of the zodiac that it was in on July 4th 1776.

It was then that the American Congress went through that perverse debate about who deserved the country's resources more: the gentry or the rabble.

Distorted Logic

With welfare rolls burgeoning and soup kitchens feeding record numbers, the nation watched Washington wrangle over whether three million jobless folks would be cut off from their unemployment benefits vs. whether those making over $250,000 a year would be able to keep their tax cuts. A grotesque political power game was played out, pitting the funds that laid-off, outsourced Americans need to survive against the windfall[2] given to that tiny section of the population who already reap almost a quarter of the total national income.

The scenario flies in the face of ordinary logic. But we might posit an astrological logic afoot here: it's a testament to how distorted things have to get in order to require transits this extreme.[3] The intensity of the Uranus-Pluto square, symbolic of radical dismantling, is precisely matched by the insanity of this debate.

Saturn, the planet of pragmatism, governs rubber-meets-the-road empirical evidence. Let's put morality aside for the moment. Even from the purely practical point of view, everything about the sordid money dust-up in Washington last month spelled disaster for the debt-addled nation; and forgoing dollars-and-cents realism is not a good idea for an entity in the throes of its Saturn Return. The voodoo-economics of trickle-down, the favored argument still clung to by Republicans advocating millionaire tax cuts, have produced not a shred of evidence that they work.

Money Talk

Money is a staple of American discourse. So are the links between money and power—no surprise, given the USA has Pluto in the second house. But just because the populace talks and thinks a lot about financial issues doesn't mean

---

[2] The Bush tax cuts have so far bestowed roughly a trillion dollars on the richest five percent of Americans.

[3] This may sound backward to those who understand the relationship between transits and their worldly circumstances in causal terms. But if we believe that planetary cycles and events coincide through synchronicity rather than through cause-and-effect, it is equally valid to propose that the Uranus-Pluto square is the effect of the system's need to break down, as it is to propose that the system is breaking down because of the Uranus-Pluto square.

we see them in perspective. Americans are obsessed with money, but the consciousness about it seems to be in arrested development.

The transits to the country's chart are intense enough to break through this stagnation. Whenever humanity can't see the forest for the trees about something, the cosmos has the Rx. Right now it's hauling in Uranus (shocks) and Pluto (excavation) to give us a reality check. With a Saturn Return for good measure, to force us to take responsibility.

It is hardly a secret that the rich are getting richer in the USA, the poor are getting poorer, and the former are in firm control of the country's agencies of authority (Saturn) and power (Pluto). What does seem remarkable is that the plutocratic nature of this state of affairs is not universally described as such.

The cold, hard facts are everywhere available. Every night on the news, nonwealthy Americans hear evidence of the insane differences that exist between their own situation and that of their elected representative, tech stockholder, Big Oil exec or college administrator. The American who does still have a roof over her head, a job and insurance is reminded at every turn of how close she is to losing them. The contrast between the lifestyles of the haves and have-nots is the explicit or implicit subject of a plethora of media discussion and spectacle, from celebrity-crib reality shows to welfare mothers on Oprah.

Yet somehow the egregious irony of the situation is never seriously analyzed in the media. And the technical term for it – plutocracy: a nation ruled by its wealthy minority – is never used. You can listen to pundits talk about the economy all day long and never hear it. There seems to be an unspoken agreement to avoid, at all costs, stating the obvious. This is consistent with the nature of Pluto, the planet of secrets hidden in plain sight.

Wall Street Blues

Pluto doesn't create problems, it exposes them. The current series of transits began when Pluto first went into Capricorn (monetary systems) in 2008 while opposing the USA's Venus (money). It was then that the workings of Wall Street suddenly became front-page news. Over the months that followed, Americans watched as the global economy was brought to the brink of collapse.

At that point, controversial corporate policies such as outsourcing jumped to the blazing forefront of public conversation. It became common knowledge that by moving almost half of American manufacturing offshore, Wall Street and the multinational corporations had struck it rich, while the domestic work force was slipping into double-digit unemployment.

As 2011 began, the conversation became polarized. Powerful moneyed forces have moved in to stage-manage the Tea Party "movement" for their own purposes, and the debate has become confused. But the institutions that caused the financial meltdown are still very much in business. Still fattening themselves greedily at the trough, bankers are giving new meaning to the phrase *piggy bank*. The disparity between their wealth and that of the 30 million global denizens who lost their shirts is greater than ever before.

Like Hitler?

Living systems in the throes of Plutonian decay can grow extreme, The rhetoric that surrounds them careens towards hyperbole. We can see this both in the attacks upon and the defenses of the financial industry. As Wall Street's spokesmen react to the current mass mood, one detects a note of panic; the mildest possible proposals to regulate their excesses are eliciting wildly fevered reactions.[4] Hedge fund manager Stephen Schwarzman, for example, has protested that taxes on private equity would be tantamount to "Hitler invad[ing] Poland in 1939."

It is a curious thing that the industry that's making the very wealthiest Americans even wealthier – the finance industry – is one that doesn't design, build or sell a single tangible thing. This does not, in and of itself, signify fraud. But the fact that it strikes us as baldly counterintuitive is one more clue that our definitions of worth and value are due for an overhaul. This is exactly what Pluto (makeovers) is supposed to do as it passes through the house of money.

---

[4] Certain plutocrats infer different meanings from their minority status than the rest of the country does. In a newsletter to his Wall Street colleagues, hedge-fund manager Daniel Loeb recently railed about how efforts to regulate the financial industry flew in the face of "every American's constitutional right to be protected against the persecution of the minority." Thus did the good banker, apparently without a trace of irony, declare himself a member of an oppressed minority; that is, the minority of the richest one percent.

IN THE BELLY

(originally published as a blog,
January 2011)

I love Imbolc, halfway between the winter solstice and the spring equinox. It's a neither-fish-nor-fowl time of year, a bare flicker of a sabbat, as tentative as the new green shoots contemplating their debut above the crust of the soil. Imbolc was once a holy day, as were all seasonal turning points in the Great Wheel of the Year.[1] It was celebrated by the ancient Celts as the end of the Dark Time.

The word Imbolc means "in the belly": that's where our impulses are, during these delicate weeks of proto-spring. In the dark belly of the Mother a new consciousness is taking shape, on the verge of being born.

In 2011, a major ingress occurs the week after Imbolc, one to which the subtle energies of this time of year seem peculiarly well suited. On Feb 8th, 2011, Chiron returns to Pisces, a tenure that will last until February of 2019. If we want to handle this nine-year transit with grace, we will need to develop a deeper understanding of the so-called wounded healer, a planetoid so new (it was first sighted in 1977) that its meaning is still settling in. And we need to get to know the sign it's in, Pisces, better than we ever have.

Pain vs. Suffering

Chiron is about pain, the kind of pain that calls us to attention. Like Buddhism and many other traditions, astrology can be used to draw a distinction between pain and suffering, between grief and depression, between empathy and enmeshment. These distinctions will be important to keep in mind in the years ahead, when Chiron will be showing us our ailments, and the world's, as part of the dissolution of the old paradigm. Like an expert diagnostician, Chiron reflects back to us our own condition. Its transits show us where we have been hurting,

---

[1] Co-opted by the Christians, Imbolc became Candlemass and was later fully secularized as Groundhog Day.

without even realizing it.

Chiron's shift from Aquarius to Pisces alters the mass mood in subtle but all-encompassing ways. The planetary rulers of both of these signs, Uranus and Neptune respectively, have to do with impulses that exist beyond the individual: they both pull us out of our egos.

But Chiron's tenure in Aquarius (2005-11), an air sign, was conceptual, whereas the waters of Pisces are spiritual and psychic. In Pisces, Chiron will invite us to register global realities from a deeper place than the mind alone can go.

We've spent the last few years gathering the information about, for example, global warming. The next few years will be spent absorbing the implications.

Transpersonal Feelings

Pisces, often thought of as an emotional sign, is not really about personal feelings. It's about transpersonal feelings. While it is true that our emotions can more easily express what Pisces knows than our thoughts can – feelings are better suited to speak the watery language of the fishes – Pisces is not really about the personality at all. It's about the relationship between the personality and the higher self.

With Chiron in Pisces, put out the intention to embody the bliss that comes of losing the self while staying centered. If you have a lot of Pisces in your chart, you're already familiar with this challenge. With Chiron in this placement, we'll all be asked to revel in our openness to That Which is Bigger Than Ourselves… at the same time that we remain true to our uniqueness.

Things Start Breakin' Down

(originally published as a blog,
January 2011)

The longest arm of the Cross, the transit of revolutionary (Uranus) and deep-structure (Pluto) change, is upon us. The rebellion in Tunisia has spread to Egypt. Yemen is seething, Jordan is restive, and the Saudi royals are getting very nervous.

As the resentment among the populations of these long-simmering Arab states boils over, the Uranus-Pluto square feels far less theoretical than it did even a few weeks ago. We are watching, in real time, the clash between ordinary people (Uranus) and the cartels that control them (Pluto). In corridors of power all over the world, there's a mad scramble to decide how to respond. First-World politicians and pundits who have built their careers on platitudes about democracy are getting the chance to put their allegiances where their mouths are.

At six degrees of Capricorn, Pluto is opposed to Jupiter (international affairs; ideology) in the US (Sibly) chart as 2011 begins, heading straight for the US Sun. It will be interesting to watch the reaction of Uncle Sam to this turbulence in nations that serve as its regional proxies. What will ordinary Americans make of it?

Geopolitically naïve in the best of times, xenophobic in the worst, most Americans have historically been clueless about this part of the world. They seem to blandly accept Washington's deep abiding friendship with Saudi Arabia, never mind that the place is a feudal monarchy where you can get your hand chopped off for stealing a sack of grain. Mubarak's Egypt, too, was labeled a "friendly" regime despite the fact that his people suffered for thirty years under the iron thumb of a military dictatorship notorious for its torture chambers and secret police.

Good Guys and Bad Guys

For Americans who watch the mainstream news, the word *dictatorship* is identified not with Egypt, Tunisia, Bahrain, Saudi Arabia or Jordan – but with Cuba. This isn't because Cubans themselves consider their country a dictatorship, nor is it because Americans would find the term apt, either, were they to actually go see the place with their own eyes. It's because the Cuban government doesn't kowtow to Washington.

The engine behind the US government's good-guy/bad guy evaluations is petro-political and military, not ideological. For all the State Department's high-minded huffing and puffing (the US (Sibly) chart's Sagittarius rising is big on moral posturing), Washington's interest in Egypt has nothing to do with democracy and everything to do with the Suez Canal.

Moreover, Egypt has proven handy as an out-of-the-way place to stash torture victims. Although it's been public knowledge for years, this dirty piece of business has been all-but-absent from the public discussion of the Egyptian situation, unmentioned both by US media pundits and by the man-on-the-street. It's hard to believe that Americans could delude themselves into imagining that Washington picked Egypt for this hideous purpose without any knowledge that Mubarak was already an experienced expert, notorious for torturing his own state enemies.

Too Many Worms

The Obama administration is being criticized for being inconsistent and stumbling in its reaction to the revolution, as if that were the worst of it. Apparently, the really relevant issues – including the shameful practice of rendition, and the strategic importance to Washington of Egypt's geography – have been designated off-limits to analysis. Too many worms in those cans.

While juntas that pose minimal strategic risk to the US ruling class (such as Burma) elicit all manner of holier-than-thou condemnation from Washington, the repressive Arab dictatorships – absurdly termed "moderate" in official euphemism – have been given a pass. The power of that magic phrase *US ally* is such that senators who regularly heap calumnies on Venezuela's leadership have not batted an eye about Uncle Sam's brutal puppet regimes in the Middle East and North Africa. Under the past six US presidents, there's been not a peep of dissent in Congress over the bankrolling of Mubarak and his thugs, who ranked second only to Israel as a recipient of our military aid.

From self-described conservatives among the US populace, the response to such uses of taxpayer money has been inconsistent to the point of schizophrenic. Whether through rank hypocrisy or good ol' American ignorance, their attitudes defy moral logic; even pragmatic logic. They're outraged to the point of apoplexy about the expenditure of even a couple of million dollars on something like social services for immigrants, yet seem serenely unperturbed by the 1.3 billion dollars a year, for the past thirty years, that was spent propping up a despot in Egypt.

Uranus-Pluto Square

Now that the tinderbox is starting to explode, things will start moving very fast. It will become harder and harder for the propagandists' story lines to keep up with global events. There will doubtless be efforts on the part of the USA and its allies to halt the momentum of other popular uprisings (which extend, at this writing, to Libya, Iran, Algeria and Pakistan) inspired by the success in Tehrir Square, and to play dirty tricks behind-the-scenes to control them – in the name of "stability." But such attempts will increasingly strained

We can expect media distortions in those countries, like the USA, where the powers-that-be have much to lose from genuine democracy. But in the age of the internet, global opinion is hard to control, as has been boldly demonstrated by WikiLeaks. Too much is happening. During the Cardinal Cross years The Old Guard is going to have a real struggle staying one step ahead of change.

Astrological symbolism will help us keep our heads above the fray. From the planets involved, we can see the energy in the streets of Tunis and Cairo as an example of explosive (Uranus) evolution (Pluto) at work. Seen as a manifestation of this transit, even the most disruptive events are revealed to be nothing more nor less than a new chapter of life on Earth unfolding.

Uranus and Pluto were conjunct in the sky during the mid-1960s, as the Rolling Stones sang, "Things start breakin' down." That conjunction has now evolved into a square, as the collective consciousness of the '60s has evolved into that of the 2010s. If humanity stays on course, these breakdowns will turn into breakthroughs.

LEAKING AT THE SEAMS

(originally published in *Skywatch*,
February 2011)

February 2011 features a cosmic lesson about leakage (Neptune), making it a good time to consider the ongoing saga of WikiLeaks. The explosive (Uranus) and taboo (Pluto) nature of this international (Jupiter) drama has raised its significance to the level of contemporary myth, and made Julian Assange a major star. That's what happens when somebody is plugged into the world moment.

As we will see, Assange is a Uranus-Neptune-Pluto figure. Natally and by transit, he represents the disruptive and uncontainable energies of the three outer planets, all of which threaten the status quo (Saturn).

The relationship between these three archetypes is hinted at by their placement in the solar system. Uranus, Neptune and Pluto all orbit beyond Saturn, the planet of law and order. Saturn governs that which is in-bounds; the planets beyond Saturn govern people, activities and ideas that are out-of-bounds.

Officialdom never knows what to do with outer-planet-driven individuals. These folks are larger-than-life, and inspire intense reactions. They tend to be vilified as evil and dangerous by some, and put up on a pedestal by others. Not unusually, the miscreant is demonized at first, and later transformed into a savior figure by history.

This is what happened to Daniel Ellsberg, the man who leaked the Pentagon Papers back in the Nixon era. An arch-enemy of his government in the 1970s, he has been lionized ever since by peace activists, historians and artists. In a marvelous irony, the State Department – which is, even now, busy building a case against the Army private suspected of passing those cables to WikiLeaks – is actually promoting a documentary celebrating Ellsberg as a hero.[1]

---

[1] *The Most Dangerous Man in America: Daniel Ellsberg and the Pentagon Papers* was selected in January 2011 to be one of the 18 films that will tour the world this year as part of the State Department's American Documentary Showcase program.

Neptune and Chiron

The Neptune-Chiron conjunction has been with us since 2005, and though it has technically finished peaking it is having another surge this month. Chiron moves into Pisces (spilling, spreading, undermining) on February 8th, 2011.

Neptune seeks to escape confines, like grains spilling out of a punctured bag, or water leaking out of a cracked vase. Neptune's trajectory is from boundaried to unboundaried, from being enclosed to floating free. And Aquarius (ruled by Uranus) is associated with technology. Neptune in Aquarius puts together the planet of unification and universalization with the sign of science, to create the infinite realm of shared ideas that is the internet.[2]

With these archetypes being provoked by current transits, it is clear that if WikiLeaks hadn't already been on the scene, the cosmos would've had to invent it. Or to put it a different way: though Assange created WikiLeaks, it was the Uranus-Pluto square and the Neptune-Chiron conjunction that created Assange.

World Outlaw

With the WikiLeaks scandal, we find cyber space having its first international showdown. Like in an old Hollywood Western, the corrupt sheriff figure (corporations, certain national governments and militaries) is facing down the renegade outlaw (Assange and his posse, including the mysterious hackers' group that calls itself Anonymous) as the world watches in real time.

The outlaw is symbolized in astrology by Uranus, which is square the Sun in the 9th house (publication) in Assange's natal chart. This is the aspect of a Prometheus: the mythic maverick who stole fire from the gods to give it to mortals. If you have this square in your natal chart, you probably colored outside of the lines in kindergarten.[3]

Assange's astrological profile fits into the Cardinal crossroads transits like a hand in a glove. The epochal Pluto-Uranus square aligns tightly with his natal solar square. With a chart like a Molotov cocktail and a karma with information

---

[2] The Uranus-Neptune conjunction of the early 1990s established the internet as the primary symbol of this archetype for the modern age.

[3] Assange has Saturn in Gemini opposed to a Jupiter-Neptune conjunction.

dissemination, he is a personification of the celestial time bomb we have been calling the longest arm of the Cross.

The way astrologers got hold of Assange's chart is of a piece with the rest of this remarkable drama. A tipster who asked to remain anonymous contacted *The Mountain Astrologer Magazine* with his birth time.[4] The chart that came to light combines martyr imagery (Moon in the 12th house) with a heavy dose of cloak-and-dagger stealth (Ascendant and Moon in Scorpio, Pluto opposing his Sun, and Venus in the 8th house of secrets).

In the weeks before the eclipse at the winter solstice, astrologers were speculating that a juicy global scandal would bubble up from the Mars-Pluto conjunction leading up to the Full Moon. It was during early December, when transiting Mars (attacks, criminality) was opposing Assange's natal Venus (women) – which rules his 7th house of (open enemies) – that he was arrested for actions that, in the Swedish legal system, constitute rape.

Perhaps the most telling thing about the WikiLeaks affair is that Assange was at first tut-tut-tutted-but-tolerated by the officialdom – back when he was only embarrassing governments. But the minute he took on the banks, his powerful enemies moved in for the kill.

Sky Mirrors

If we see the patterns in the sky as mirrors of the lessons humanity is slated to learn, we will be able to watch the world's big, splashy dramas from a healthy distance. This way, we will not only be safe from distress and reactivity, but we will deepen our wisdom.

To consider Assange's role from this distance is to understand some of the key themes of our era. One of these is the breakdown of old models of governmental and military authority. As the Pat Tillman case and Bradley Manning's leaks (Neptune and Chiron) have made clear, old-fashioned Establishment stonewalling isn't working as well as it once did. Pluto in Capricorn

---

[4] *The Mountain Astrologer* Magazine's Mary Plumb writes: "[We] felt that the circumstances through which we got the information, and some other details, suggest that this is an authentic time. Our source clarified what s/he saw: 'The birth record (is) from the registry which has appended to it a copy of the birth certificate but the hour was not on the certificate but on the record in the registry files.' Because of ink that was a bit smeared, there is a question of whether the time of birth was 2:05 pm, 2:06 pm. or 2:08 pm on July 3, 1971, in Townsville, Queensland, Australia (19S09 146E48)."

(containment) and Uranus in Aries (popular defiance) are threatening the conventional entitlement protocols that world leaders have used for as long as we can remember.

Individuals who assume larger-than-life public significance, as Assange has, are no longer merely persons, archetypally speaking. Their characters and actions take on a dual meaning. On one level they are human beings with character traits, just like anyone else, whose personality and learning curve can be delineated from their horoscope. And on another level, they are walking embodiments of the cosmic energies that make the era what it is.

As the repository of collective feelings and ideas, Assange symbolizes many things right now. He has become a hero to one group of observers, comprised of hackers, free speech advocates, anti-corporate and anti-militarism activists et al. And he is a dangerous villain to another group, comprised of companies like PayPal and MasterCard (and sites like Twitter, that depend on advertisers like PayPal and MasterCard), as well as patriotic homeland-security enthusiasts (like Sarah Palin) who live in the nations whose dirty secrets Assange has scooped. He is a loose cannon and a security risk – if by "security" we mean the ability of governments and militaries to control how much information is known by ordinary people.

The fact the WikiLeaks episode means many things to many different observers is a testament to its importance as a multifaceted symbol, one that is still evolving. As products of a cyber-age, Assange and his website are changing the rules of international relations. He has inaugurated a global cyber-warrior dynamic, whose latest victory is the Facebook-and-Tweeter-driven revolution in Egypt. He is the hero of our first postmillennial spy caper: waged not with bombs and cyanide but with stealth hacking.[5]

WikiLeaks is proving itself powerful enough to embarrass superpowers (the USA, China) and prompt the cable crazies (Fox News) to propose that Assange and his staff be assassinated. When the status quo gets this worried, chalk up 25 bonus points to Uranus (revolution), Neptune (universalism) and Pluto (evolution).

---

[5] According to astrologer Eric Francis, his hacker name was 'Mendax', from *splendide mendax*, or 'nobly untruthful.'

Lurching Towards the Crossroads

(originally published in *Daykeeper
Journal*, February 2011)

Word has it that Facebook is filing an IPO. It appears Mr. Zuckerberg's key partner will be none other than Goldman Sachs,[1] the most notorious of the financial industry players, whose shenanigans triggered the global financial meltdown. This is a telling augury about the state of the union as 2011 gets underway.

In February, Pluto, the planet of corruption and breakdown, passes through the 5th and 6th degrees of Capricorn. Pluto's long-running opposition to the US (Sibly) chart's Sun cluster will hover around the national Jupiter (ethics, principles) all year. As we approach the exactitude of the Uranus-Pluto square, the American Devolution continues apace.

Bewitched

As sky watchers, we know the Cardinal Cross offers the potential for a wholesale national makeover. No other transit in our lifetimes is as capable of gutting the dying group organism that is the USA, and ushering it into a state of rebirth. But the longer the country delays excavating the rot at the core of its system, the more difficult the upcoming years will be. Given the current cocktail of crises, including unsustainable debt, endless wars and addiction to cheap oil, it will take a very sharp turn of the corner to point the nation back towards economic health.

America's self-image as a Mecca for the little guy continues to be referenced in the dreams of working-class patriots and in the platitudes of ruling-class politicians, but in practice the country is a plutocracy. This reality must be confronted if the nation's proud ideals are ever going to find their way into the

---

[1] As soon as Obama was elected, the former heads of Goldman turned up in his administration like bad pennies, and made haste to undermine the regulations then being discussed to prevent another crash. Their obstructionism has been so successful that, as Treasury Department Inspector General Neil Barofsky recently told Congress: "We are still driving on the same winding mountain road, but this time in a faster car."

country's day-to-day workings. The US Pluto Return that peaks in 2022 is pregnant with this potential.

For a large part of the US population, confronting this reality seems to be very painful. Seduced by the commercial media while struggling to make ends meet, most Americans are too bewitched by the fantasy of the American Dream to perceive the grotesque financial disparities that exist here. An inordinate number of citizens are angry, but not at the wealthy elites who rip them off. They are pissed off at the educated elites who keep telling them about it.

This tendency to look but not see is a symptom of the absence of spiritual health. To the extent that we can speak of a group entity as having a soul, America's economic crisis is fundamentally a spiritual crisis.

The Internet Revolution

The other collective theme that will be activated in February belongs to the air element and is mental in character. The passage of Mars and Mercury through Aquarius puts the focus back on the six-year sojourn of Chiron and Neptune (mass trends) in Aquarius (advanced technology), a transit that has overseen a revolution in the way humans relate to each other.

In an astrological context, we can use the word *revolution* here, not hyperbolically but technically. Astrology links Aquarius and its planetary ruler, Uranus, with revolutions of mass consciousness: accelerated changes in the zeitgeist that are drastic and unprecedented. Since Neptune and Uranus came into mutual reception,[2] portable electronics have transformed human interaction. What has changed is not just our mode of communication, but the way we think about communication. The whole meaning of sharing ideas has undergone an unprecedented shift.

This revolution has had its epicenter in the USA, whose Moon (the populace) the Neptune-Chiron conjunction is crisscrossing (2009-12).

It's a good time to stand back and look at what it all means.

---

[2] Planets are said to be in mutual reception when the sign each is in is ruled by the other planet; i.e., Uranus has been in Pisces, which is governed by Neptune; Neptune has been in Aquarius, which is governed by Uranus.

Connected

Since the entry of Neptune (limitless dispersal) into Aquarius (technology) in 1998, the number of hand-held gadgets has exploded, as have the number of functions they're used for. A sense of urgent necessity seems to surround the purchase of apps for functions of life that were app-unassisted just a few weeks before. And the length of time between when a new device hits the shelves and when a new one comes along to replace it is shorter than ever.

The human capacity to access, store and exchange information has been catapulting itself forward at a speed that outpaces our understanding of its implications. This is a revolution moving too fast to be charted. It is obvious that it is transforming our social habits, but how is this transformation affecting us epistemologically and neurologically?

As subjective participants in the cyber-revolution, we are hard-pressed to cop a perspective on the changes sweeping us along. A few scientific studies have come out recently on brain changes among wired youth, but investigations into the psycho-sociological implications of these changes are few and far between. One gets the feeling that scholarly observers have yet to catch their breath, even enough to formulate the right questions.

Along with astrologers, artists are stepping in to hold up a mirror to the times. It seems to me that the movie "The Social Network," which reflected the buzz of contemporary life both in content and in form, was as hugely popular as it was because of our urgent need to understand what is happening to us.

There is also a new documentary coming out, "Connected," that looks at technology's effect on interpersonal relationships. "I used to love the way people connected on the street," the director, Tiffany Shlain, said of a recent trip to New York. "Now I see everyone looking down, texting." She says she wouldn't have been surprised to see even the Statue of Liberty holding a torch with one hand and a smart phone with the other.

Time Change

We hear that "six months in digital time equals a decade of pre-digital time" (with "six months" changing to three months, then one, etc.) What is the impact of this mind-blowing phenomenon on our subjective experience of the flow of life?

The astrology of the situation is suggestive. The archetypes involved (Uranus and

Neptune) refer to realms beyond that of linear time (Saturn) – just as the actual planets Uranus and Neptune orbit beyond the astronomical realm of Saturn.

And Chiron, which forms the bridge between Saturn and Uranus, is in Pisces now. This strengthens the tendency of people to space out and become disconnected; it also strengthens our tendency to become inspired. As we meet and greet others ceaselessly through our tiny little screens, will we become more truly connected (Pisces) with our brethren (Aquarius), or just be going through the motions of connection, while feeling more isolated than ever before?

There is no turning back from our headlong dive into the cyber sphere. Only our spiritual consciousness will determine whether we find ourselves or lose ourselves in the plunge.

COME HELL OR HIGH WATER

(originally published in *Skywatch,*
March 2011*)*

*[Editor's note: This essay was written and titled 3 weeks before the Japanese
tsunami.]*

For terrestrial life, water is important to the point of being definitive. And it is
becoming more so.

For at least part of the month of March 2011, no less than six planets — the Sun,
Mercury, Venus, Mars, Chiron and Uranus — will be in Pisces, the wateriest of
the three water signs.

This is our preview for the upcoming epoch-defining ingress: Neptune's launch
into Pisces, the sign of its rulership, for the first time in 168 years.[1]

The Mother of All Illusions

Pisces can manifest as confusion or bliss, depending on how we approach it.
We'll have the choice to either float on top of the chaos or drown in it; it all
depends on the depth of our understanding. Pisces is said to govern illusion, but it
also promises to steer us through illusion - all the way to the other side. This sign
represents the part of the human spirit that pierces through the illusion of
separateness.

According to many sacred traditions, separateness is the mother of all illusions:
the illusion whence all other illusions arise. What makes Pisces exceptional is
that it refuses to be taken in by separateness. It sees right through the various
barriers that purport to divide us. It doesn't honor the much-touted differences
between white and black, haves and have-nots, Norteños and Sureños, I and thou.
From Pisces' point of view, all such demarcations are nonsense.

---

[1] Neptune's entry into on April 4th 2011, It will return to Aquarius in Aug 2011, and then ingress
back into Pisces for the duration in February 2012.

Every sign is the guardian of a particular truth; a special wisdom that is its specialty. The one attributed to Pisces, the last sign of the zodiac, can be seen as the last word on truth:

Distinctions are apparent, interconnectedness is fundamental.

Single Origin

In Pisces, Chiron (wounds) is offering us a teaching about how much we have hurt ourselves, *en masse*, by pretending we can deny our interconnectedness.

As if throwing a plastic bottle into a river were an act of disposal.

As if Chevron's dumping 18 billion gallons of oil into the rain forest has nothing to do with me, because it's happening so far away.

The key symbol of this interconnectedness in the physical world is the ocean. When we look at a world map, landmasses look like islands floating in a unified sea. Two-thirds of the globe is covered with water. The great continents seem almost like an afterthought.

Along the same lines, consider how our worldview expands when we gaze at a photo of the Earth from space. If we look long enough at that NASA photograph of our singular blue planet, the much-touted differences between all the various countries seem like no big whoop. We may start to see the whole business of nationalism as tragically shortsighted, even ridiculous. (Especially since you can make out, just by looking, how the continents used to fit together. Africa looks like it fits right into the cleft of the Americas, like pieces in a jigsaw puzzle.)

The all-surrounding seas give the lie to the isolation pretended by national borders. And Pisces, which governs the seas, gives the lie to the appearance of isolation between people and things. Everything does indeed fit together, and has a single unified origin.

Chiron and Neptune

Chiron has been using this oceanic metaphor as a teaching tool for several years already, since it began orbiting alongside Neptune. It has been showing us that we're all in the same boat.

This understanding is the central, over-arching theme of human consciousness development. Gradually, inexorably, we are moving away from our investment in separateness, towards the acceptance of our interconnectedness.

During these years of Cosmic Crossroads we stand at a major juncture point. For its nine-year sojourn in mutable water (2010-19), Chiron will continue to mirror back to us the craziness of our efforts to close ourselves off from each other. When Neptune moves into Pisces next month and stays there for fifteen years, we will be shown not only how painful this is, but how futile. Examples of such futility abound. They include Western Europe's attempts to impose quotas on Eastern European immigrants, the USA's efforts to stem the tide of refugees from Central and South America, Israel's walling-in of Gaza, and the containment of civil war refugees in camps throughout Africa. All attempts on the part of one group to try to build fences and walls against another group will increasingly appear inhumane and pointless.

Learning Curve

The skies suggest that we have the chance right now to experience a spike in our learning curve. Another way to say this is that it will become harder and harder to stay in denial.

In starkly literal terms, it's going to be very difficult to avoid the physical reality of water. The floods that inundated Pakistan in 2010, and Sri Lanka, Brazil and Australia as 2011 began, are only going to get more intense. And the seas are rising.[2] Scientists report that a further two-degree rise in global temperature will cause enough melting to inundate the existing coastlines on every continent.

Although many people seem blind to water's warning, on the level of the collective unconscious all of us are aware of it. Our melting ice caps and flooded islands are triggering an archetypal teaching: the warning inherent in the story of the Great Flood, a universal image that resides deep within the human imagination.

Like canaries in the mine, the world's low-lying countries, such as the aptly named Netherlands, are taking steps by necessity. The Dutch have looked far enough in to the future to develop a 200-year plan to adapt to the rising waters. Like in the folk tale of the prescient little boy who saved his village by putting

---

[2] Climate scientists believe that if greenhouse gases persist unchecked, global temperatures will be 9 degrees Fahrenheit over the pre-industrial era before 2100. An increase of 2 degrees would mean the loss of most of the world's coral reefs and the disappearance of most of its mountain snow packs. See *Hot: Living Through the Next Fifty Years on Earth*, by Mark Hartsgaard.

his finger in the dike, Dutch engineers are widening rivers, creating barrier dams, repairing old dikes and building new ones.

Precious and Rare

At the same time that salt water is creeping inland, fresh water is becoming scarce. What happened in Bolivia in 2000 should serve as a warning to us about the kind of power plays that could arise in a water-deficient future. In a move that would have seemed – just a few years before it happened – too far-fetched even for a science-fiction novel, the monster corporation Bechtel made a deal with the corrupt Bolivian government to privatize the public's drinking water. Until street protests in Cochabamba forced an end to the policy, Bolivians were charged even for collecting rainwater from their own roofs (a movie about the incident has just come out, called *Even the Rain*).

It is becoming clear that water will be the new oil.

Before we recoil with foreboding from this idea, we need to remember that one of the features of a rare commodity is that it is valued as precious. Mystical thinking has always held water as precious, and primal, as the matrix element whence all else manifests.

Associated by astrologers with psychic pick-up. water is the element that most easily conducts emotions and intuitions. Scientists are coming to similar conclusions, as shown by the astonishing studies by Japanese researcher Masaru Emoto (*sic*) of water crystals.

If the element water is dominant in your chart, you may find yourself appreciating water in extraordinary new ways. Particularly if you have planets in Pisces, the years to come will help you understand that part of your life purpose is to embody what water knows.

WOUNDED WATERS

(originally published in *Daykeeper
Journal*, March 2011)

Chiron's re-entry into Pisces on February 8, 2011 represents a cosmic mission: to get us in touch with our feelings. But not our unique, personal feelings. Pisces is about the kind of feelings that we share with everyone else. When we feel these, we know how the whole group intelligence is feeling. We become engaged with our fellow humans.

And if we confer sentience upon non-human beings – upon even earthworms and trees and rocks and stars – then we must extend this idea even further, and propose that Pisces represents an emotional connectedness with every single thing in existence. Every molecule, every ion, every micro-dot of "empty" space. Pisces knows what the Bioneers are talking about, when they say, "It's all alive; it's all intelligent; it's all connected."

Pisces is a transpersonal sign, not a personal sign. It's not at its best when we try to enclose its truths within our own little personality. It is confounded by the boundaries entailed in living as a singular ego. When stuffed into the too-small package of our individuality, Pisces just leaks out. It never got the memo about there being an operative distinction between *me* and *not-me*.

It's only when Pisces is understood to be about the spiritual dimension that its weaknesses become its strengths, and its strengths become its wisdom.

Burning Sea

Chiron's ingress into Pisces in February 2011, its second this cycle, is a sneak preview of the once-in-168-year ingress of Neptune into Pisces. Together they will offer us a teaching about the inextricable unity of all things.

Chiron's first entry this cycle took place on April 20, 2010, a day that will live in infamy for all who feel themselves to be children of the Earth. That was the day the DeepWater Horizon blew up in the Gulf of Mexico. To look at the astrological chart of the explosion is to see the whole eight-year transit of Chiron in Pisces in microcosm. The event was replete with Piscean symbolism: the ocean, the martyrdom of flora and fauna, the sacrifice of living things for corporate profit.

It is perhaps easier in retrospect than it was at the time to see the Chironic teaching behind this environmental tragedy. It put millions of ordinary people in touch, through deep feeling, with something beyond themselves. All over the world people were watching the devastation on their TV screens, day after day, together, in real time. Heartfelt responses poured forth, and were pooled together in a unity – from letters-to-the-editor writers, poets, journalists and bloggers – all declaring themselves advocates of our Mother planet.

Amidst the horror and grief, something profound took place: a massive collective pledging of allegiance to Nature. Most of the paeans that were written and shared made reference to the Earth as a living being: an integrated body, whose rocks are her bones, whose waters are her blood. Though the disaster has left the headlines, its multitudinous reverberations continue to spread, extending outwards like concentric circles from a stone thrown into a pond.[1]

Empathic Advocacy

In the years ahead, the impact of our dead rivers and poisoned deltas, our polluted streams and extinct marine species, will become undeniable. An immediate and everyday example of our negligent stewardship of this most primal of resources is the scarcity of clean water, which is growing in urgency as a global problem.

We are being inaugurated into a period in which we will move into a response to this problem that goes deeper than mere fact-finding. The Chiron ingresses into Pisces, together with Neptune's entry in April 2011 into this, the sign of its rulership[2] are introducing to human awareness a new way of looking at water.

More precisely, it's a new way of *feeling* about water. These transits have the

---

[1] The studies that have been done since the disaster are evidence of its continuing impact as a consciousness-raiser. For example, research on the toxin Corexit (!) used during and after the "spill" is raising alarming questions. Senator A. G. Crowe from Louisiana has launched a petition drive to address the issue.

[2] Neptune will stay in Pisces until 2026, apart from a brief retrograde period in Aquarius between August 4, 2011 and February 2012.

power to inspire sensitive souls to undertake a peculiarly Piscean form of activism that we might call empathic advocacy. More and more people will respond to the toxicity of the world's waterways as a loving parent would respond to the wounds of her child, or as a child would respond to the wounds of its mother.

The Great Flood

In earlier essays we have discussed the Great Flood story, a tale that resides deep in the collective unconscious. The image is of a deluge (Neptune) whose purpose is to all-but-destroy an irremediably wounded (Chiron) human race, giving the few survivors a chance to start all over again. Since the opposition of Saturn (structures) and Neptune (melting) in 2006-07, the mass mind has been inundated with the latest iteration of the legend. We are awash in the imagery of breaking levees and flooded cities. Animals and birds are migrating away from the planet's climate-compromised zones, seeking higher ground,.

The Great Flood myth is experiencing a renaissance, in our era, in order to supply us with a coded multidimensional teaching. It is giving us an image of vengeful water, of gigantic floods that wash everything clean. We are being prompted to purify that which we have made toxic, and to take responsibility for the guardianship of our planetary home.

On a physical level, geological and meteorological water emergencies over the years ahead will force us to understand and revere the laws of water. At the same time, we will be absorbing this lesson on a trans-physical level. Our enhanced attention to water will show us the extent to which we are all psycho-spiritually bound together. Neptune and Chiron in Pisces will make it inescapably clear that all beings are drops of water in the same cosmic sea.

SHOWDOWN IN WISCONSIN

(originally published as a blog,
March 2011)

The revolution has reached Wisconsin.

All in the scope of a bare few weeks, the world's mind has been blown by the jasmine rallies in the Middle East and Africa, student protests in the U.K. and anti-government eruptions in China and Pakistan, among other uprisings all over the globe. The epochal transits that have kept astrologers buzzing for the past several years are bursting into fullness. This home grown American uprising is the latest milestone in a long destabilization process, cosmically designed to rend asunder humanity's sense of stasis.

Provoked by retrograde Saturn (resistance), the square between Uranus (rebellion) and Pluto (decay) is moving in for the kill. Among Pluto's manifestations are agencies of control that are so deeply rooted in the group mind that they have become a way of life, even for – perhaps especially for – those whom they dis-empower. Two examples of such agencies: dictatorships that have eliminated all political opposition for 40 years, and plutocracies so riddled with corruption that reform has heretofore seemed impossible.

The transit series I have been calling the Cardinal Cross is destabilizing Jupiter (values) and Saturn (authority issues) in the US (Sibly) chart. Astrologers were not surprised to see a Jasmine-Rally-like protest sprouting in the USA. What is a bit surprising is that the drama is taking place in a part of the country more closely associated with apple-pie county fairs than with guerilla politics.

Uranus vs. Pluto

In the role of Uranus we find Wisconsin's schoolteachers and other public employees, whose dramatic camp out in the state capitol alerted millions of observers to the governor's efforts to crush the unions. Personifying the role of Pluto, we find those chilling *eminences gris,* the Koch Brothers, and their paid mouthpiece, Gov. Scott Walker (whose bland, wholesome cover was blown in Feb 2011 by a prank call that purported to be from David Koch, in which the boy scout-faced governor admitted that he'd considered hiring *agents provocateurs* to disrupt and discredit the protest).

Representing Pluto on an institutional level, we have the propaganda machine comprised of Fox News and rightwing radio, which have come out against the workers. At first blush, their taking this stand seems utterly counterintuitive. How do these self-professedly populist commentators manage to side with The Man, in fight after fight, and still maintain their credibility with thousands of Americans as the voice of the underdog?

Greedy Teachers

The enormously well-funded, well-oiled machine that is the corporate media makes full use of the dark psychological urges governed by Pluto. These originate in the viscera – Pluto is an emotional planet, not a mental one – and relate to the human fear of failing to survive. Plutonian impulses tend to lurk in the shadows of semi-consciousness, as if aware that they wouldn't pass muster with our rational thinking and ethical values.

These impulses are what give the attack on the unions its ugly power. Fear, rage and envy are being used by the state and its cheerleaders among the talking heads, to pit one group of struggling citizens against another. Frustrated and infuriated Fox viewers are being exhorted to repudiate the hard-working teachers – essentially, to blame the lousy economy upon them – for having the gall to expect a decent living. The *cri de coeur* here seems to be, "Goddammit, *I* don't have a secure job; why should *they*?"

Making schoolteachers the enemy must have been the easy part. Appealing to the anti-intellectual insecurity of its listeners has always been a winning strategy for Fox. Last week, railing against how high teachers' salaries were, Megan Kelly affected a sneer when pronouncing the phrase "50 thousand dollars," to imply that the figure was obscenely unwarranted. Her voice dripped with scathe when she condemned the teachers' "guaranteed paid summer vacations."

It is beyond ironic that these same commentators take the exact opposite tack where taxing millionaires is concerned. "$250 thousand dollars a year is not all that much money," said one of them recently, without a hint of irony, while defending the fat-cat tax cuts.

Deserving Millionaires

Presumably, the interests of the bailed-out hedge-fund crowd, unlike those of teachers and firefighters, are deemed worth safeguarding. In the upside-down moral universe of American plutocracy, the value of Wall Street's work – all those arduous hours spent speculating, foreclosing and trashing the global economy – trumps the value of educating children, putting out fires and policing the streets.

Thus, the oft-heard apologia for executive compensation: *We have no choice but to offer the rich-and-successful all this money, in order to stay competitive.* In one of the more twisted justifications for the increasingly feudalistic income gap in the USA, the common folk are being told that their country would suffer a "talent exodus" if those bloated CEO bonuses were to be reined in.

Economic Injustice

It was when Pluto entered Capricorn in 2008 that political and economic injustice started to break through the floorboards from beneath collective consciousness into open discussion. In the USA, a poorly educated and dis-informed public has so far largely embraced the narrative of a political establishment that stonewalls genuine social change and condones sociopathic greed. But this scenario is unraveling. Uranus reenters Aries on March 11th 2011, to be inflamed even further by Mars's ingress in early April.

As impoverished autocracies across the globe boil over with citizen revolt, the American populace is having a harder and harder time staying in denial about the gaping abyss between rich and poor here at home. With Cardinal trigger transits accelerating the Cross throughout the spring of 2011, the realization is dawning that there's something wrong with the way free market capitalism prioritizes private wealth (Pluto) over individual human lives (Uranus).

The word *crisis*, etymologically linked to *crossroads*, implies decision-making. The Cross spelled out in the sky right now is a prompt to each of us, to respond – not merely to react – to the tensions in our world. This response may be one of thought (air), emotion (water), action (fire) or creative gesture (earth); but it must be a response.

The only way to do this is to get into the moment, which is where every transit tries to get us to go. Awake and in present time, we are able to truly consider what's at stake, to draw on our powers of discernment and to stand up and be counted, using the unique resources that make us who we are.

Terra Infirma

(originally published as a blog,
March 2011)

In any given era, humanity gives rise to just the right number of heroes, geniuses and saints to keep itself balanced and alive on its checkered evolutionary journey. When in crisis, it gives rise to Cassandras. Our epoch is chockablock with them. Some of them even announced the very date of the earthquake in Japan.

Our prophets include climate-change environmentalists, anti-nuclear activists, telluric scientists and astrologers, who for years now have been talking about the likelihood of earthquakes (Uranus) and nuclear disasters (Pluto), as well as water catastrophes (Pisces). All those who are not asleep have heard the warnings. We're past the point of incredulity now; being shocked is insufficient. Consciousness seekers need to be considering the meaning of violent shocks to our collective system, like the one on March 11th, 2011 in northern Japan. To respond, rather than to react, means taking in the significance of these instances of human suffering, and bringing to bear our highest understanding to fathom their implications for spiritual growth.

Cosmic Timing

Three elements – earth, fire and water – are contained within the symbolism of this record-breaking quake and tsunami. The irradiated Japanese atmosphere supplies the fourth: air. The initial geological spasm occurred mere hours before Uranus hit the explosive Aries point, the singular degree that starts the zodiacal cycle like a bullet from a gun. The news that five nuclear reactors were imperiled hit the news when the *ingress* [entry into a new sign] was exact.

The Gulf disaster of 2010 had the same relationship to the ingress of Chiron into Pisces, a transit that reflects back to us our own wounded condition. The doomed oil rig blew up the very day Chiron crossed that zodiacal threshold. These ingresses indicate juncture points at which the consequences of humanity's environmental folly are exploding in our face.

Nuclear Karma

At this writing, at least two of Japan's reactors are dangerously unstable, giving the crisis a reach that extends far beyond the local. This latest disaster was meant to wrench every one of us, everywhere in the world, out of our slumber. Its purpose was to provoke questions, life-or-death questions.

Such as: At what point did people start getting complacent about nuclear power? When did the compelling image of the Doomsday Clock – once a looming symbol in the collective imagination – disappear from public discussion? It is time to start listening again to Helen Caldicott, one of our modern saints.

There are so many ironies stacked up here as to signify the presence of a pointed collective karma. For a start, it seems so bizarre as to defy plausibility that the only country in the world to have had an A-bomb dropped upon it has, over the six decades since then, built 55 nuclear plants on its tiny, unstable land mass – composed of islands that are more prone to earthquakes than anywhere else on Earth.

What we might think of as the exact opposite of a healthy response – that is, a response to having themselves experienced this unholy weapon – seems to be driven by a perverse unconscious logic. Obviously the Japanese are not alone in expressing the dark side of Pluto; its manifestation as a kind of death wish is a universal in the unevolved human psyche. But where this uniquely Plutonian weapon is concerned, Japan seems to be serving as a canary in the mine.

There are many levels to Pluto's rulership of nuclear energy, the most literal being the timing of the planet's sighting in the sky – in 1930, at the advent of the atomic age. Another is the extreme degree of toxicity involved in its production (Pluto governs pollution), which creates detritus so dangerous that it is impossible to dispose of safely. Another is the secrecy (Pluto is about underground maneuvering) in which the plans were hatched to build the first A-bomb.

The most terrible manifestation of this symbolism, and thus the most difficult to consider, is the ultimate apocalyptic potential for life on Earth of this deadliest of human concoctions. In atomic weaponry, Pluto, the god of Death, has offered us a uniquely modern image for the opposite of creation.

Uranus and Pluto

All of these dimensions of the square between Uranus (technology) and Pluto (mass destruction) have been prodded awake in the global consciousness by the disaster in Japan. Anti-nuclear activists have been energized worldwide. Less than a week after the tragedy, Germany has closed all of its aging nuclear plants for the time being in response to demands from the public; France and Britain's governments are feeling similar pressure. There are signs even in China of a resurgent anti-nuclear movement.

It is becoming more and more important to eschew fear, and use the urgent energies upon the Earth in the most conscious possible way. This is how immeasurably destructive power is transmuted into life-affirming creativity.

DEATH METAL FLYING

(originally published as a blog,
March 2011)

The confetti had barely been swept up in town squares all over the world after the triumph in Egypt. The American public was distracted elsewhere, trying to find a job or keep a job. And suddenly we were in another war.

The approach throughout March 2011 of Mars, the god of war, to the Aries point – the red-hot degree set off by Uranus on 3/11/11, the day of the monster quake in Japan – called up disasters of a less natural variety: military ones. The week after the quake, the USA strong-armed the U.N. into passing a resolution to allow its cruise missiles to attack Libya.

Kinder, Gentler Warmonger

The response from the American public was mixed, as they watched their president send forth the Tomahawks, aircraft carriers, destroyers, nuclear submarines and F-16 bombers. Some noticed that he hadn't waited for Congress to declare war, nor attempted the kind of long, drawn-out justifications that made Bush's military incursions so blatantly disingenuous. He just went ahead and sent the death metal flying.

The *no-fly zone* (one of the Pentagon's more opaque euphemisms) was declared under the banner of "humanitarian intervention," a sentiment around which all who watched Moammar Khadafy's hideous attacks on his own countrymen could rally. Moral imperatives are very tricky, however, when deployed geopolitically. In a military context, contingencies are as slippery and interconnected as strands of spaghetti on a plate. Try to isolate just one and you get a whole pile of them coming at you, making a big mess.

Selective Morality

The questions begged by Washington's morality argument are legion. Why does the mandate apply here but not to the Ivory Coast? Or to the Congo, with its thousands of rape victims and child soldiers and disappeared dissidents? Or to Uganda or Zimbabwe or the Sudan, where innocents are being murdered by dictators who are surely no less certifiably insane than Libya's?

How do Washington's moral imperatives apply to the bombing of Libya by Reagan in 1987 that killed Khadafy's two-year-old daughter? Do they explain why the corrupt monarchs Uncle Sam is choosing to support right now – in Yemen, Bahrain and Saudi Arabia, where protesters are bleeding blood just as red as that of the rebels in Libya – aren't eliciting the same degree of righteous outrage as is the madman in the caftan?

And how does the international peacekeeper argument apply to the fact that the USA is by far the biggest manufacturer and seller of armaments in the world?

White Knight

Since the equinox, the Sun has been triggering the Cardinal Cross in the early degrees of Aries, lighting a fire under the US Jupiter: the planet of ethics and ideology. Every American is being forced to ask herself: In this complex, troubled world, how do right and wrong shake out?

Transiting Saturn is opposed to transiting Jupiter now, as well. It is not only dogmas that are breaking down; it is our most cherished ethical ideals. These transits warn us against facile moral positions. Americans in particular are being asked to look more closely at their country's use of idealistic truisms (Jupiter) to justify policies of dominance and control (Pluto).

Would that it were as simple as good-guy-vs.-bad-guy. But this supposed white-knight crusade on the part of the US military smells rankly of unintended consequences and hidden motivations. And as the ones whose taxes are paying for it, Americans ought to be asking themselves whether this bloody expenditure is really likely to help the people of Libya. Does recent military history suggest that the intervention of a Western power into an Arab civil war will bring peace? Is this attack likely to endear the USA to that part of the world?

Petro-Power

In 2003, Washington's hideously cynical decision to bomb Baghdad was framed, first, as a vengeance ideology (something to do with 9/11; it was never clear exactly what), and later as an enlightened-government ideology (introducing American-style elections at the point of a bayonet). But the ideologies employed were never the point, and they showed themselves to be fungible. The warmongers used whatever sales pitch they could get to fly.

What does seem to be clear about the tragic situation in Libya is that the petro-powerbrokers would very much like to secure a foothold into a strategically critical region. The forces behind the UN resolution seem to be beefing up their own hand-picked contingent amidst the fracas, with an eye to giving the French, the Brits, and the USA (say, aren't these the same folks who divvied up the Arab world between themselves in the last century?) control of the oil spigot to Europe. A reliable puppet state there would also allow them to keep an eye on those other pesky revolutions in the area.

Mars and the Cross

Mars enters Aries on April 1st 2011, making it a part of the Uranus-Pluto square. Later that month it squares Pluto just after stationing. The preceding weekend anti-war protests are planned for cities across the USA. These build on recent demonstrations where students carried placards asking, *Why is there no money for our schools but always money for another war?*

Pluto in Capricorn oversees the breakdown of authoritative systems that are too old and corrupt to survive. During the decay process, the falsehoods at the core of these systems become increasingly obvious. They can no longer be hidden within the folds and recesses of cultural habit. Those institutions fall apart that once sheltered the old guard, whose well-worn power plays become clumsier and more artless. Techniques of control become threadbare.

The forces of deep change are ascendant. Not cosmetic change. Rebirth-style change.

The Quake Within

(originally published in *Skywatch*,
April 2011)

It happened on the very day Uranus (shocks, shattering) moved into Aries. On March 11th, 2011, the tectonic plates under the Pacific Ocean buckled and northeastern Japan was devastated by the biggest quake-tsunami in its history. At this writing the peril of nuclear reactor meltdown looms as the most far-reaching of the quake's attendant dangers.

For many years we have been talking about the possibility of sudden telluric disasters under this square between Uranus (disruption) and Pluto (destruction). We have also talked about the sensitivity of the Aries Point[1] a zodiacal hot spot over which Uranus will hover throughout 2011.

It is not only astrologers, of course, who have been sounding the alarm. And not just about earthquakes.

Scientists have predicted that by 2030 we will see a perfect storm of global food shortages, water scarcity and near-prohibitive oil prices. Environmentalists have been supplying us with nonstop updates about climate change. Demographers have been talking about mass migration across national borders, an enormously destabilizing global phenomenon that is provoking all manner of reactivity from politicians and xenophobes, but precious little practical consideration.

All of these upheavals fit the symbolism of the Uranus-Pluto square, the transit that colors the period between 2008 and 2023. Uranus is wrenching us away from whatever we've seen as normalcy, while Pluto is breaking outworn structures down into their constituent parts.[2] The tension between the two will peak when

---

[1] The Aries point is the first degree of the first sign of the zodiac. The mind-blowing precision of the ingress on the very afternoon the quake happened goes a long way towards reinforcing astrologers' respect for the potency of this singular degree.

[2] Pluto's association with nuclear destruction is reflected not only in terms of the atom from which such bombs are derived, but also in the uniquely thorough way they break down physical form - all the way down to the atoms that make it up.

they form a 90-degree angle seven times between 2012-15.

A philosophical decision is before us here, one that all transit trackers will have to make about the years ahead. How does one acknowledge energies this daunting and not react with panic or escapism? What is the highest way to handle the mass events we are hearing about? And what inferences can we draw about our own reasons for having incarnated into these times?

For a certain kind of seeker, making guesses about external events is not enough. The goal is, rather, to absorb the transit's information intently, and bring it home to the core self. This means applying its power to the unique resources and karma encoded in our own individual birth chart, the record of who we really are. It means using these historic transits to take in the meaning of the changes happening in our lives right now; changes which parallel the ones happening in the news.

Can we detach ourselves from the buzz of outer events enough to do this?

Literal or Figurative

Most aficionados of astrology use it primarily to track outer occurrences. Certainly the general public thinks of astrology this way. What else is it good for, they reason, except to foretell the future? But if we consider the underlying implications of this expectation, we'll notice that it is based on a fundamental assumption to which conscientious thinkers should decide whether or not they subscribe: that events in the physical world are the *sine qua non* of reality.

Humanistic astrology, by contrast, proposes that literal events are not what life is all about. For us, literalism is just the cosmos' way of making things easy to understand. It isn't that the outside world is not a perfectly viable stage upon which energies can express themselves. But there are others.[3]

The use of astrology to predict literal occurrences exclusively relies on another assumption, too: that events are fixed and immutable, neatly lined up in a queue somewhere in an established Future, patiently waiting for Time to catch up with

---

[3] If we posit that the physical world correlates to the earth element, it follows that the worlds correlating to the water element (emotions and intuitions), air element (ideas) and fire element (inspired action) must be equally real. No one of them should get more realness points than any other. To be theoretically consistent, we'd have to concede that if an astrological archetype expresses itself through any one of these realms, it could express itself through all of them.

them. But what happens to this assumption if one believes that humanity creates its reality anew at every moment, via free will. If the future is generated at every moment, then there are no specifics to predict. So what's there to predict?

We predict energy flows. Raw, pre-manifest energies, which make time-sensitive patterns. Energies that can be molded into form by intention and intelligence.

If it is believed that everything in life is a symbol, then events must be symbolic, too. We suggest that they arise in order to symbolize certain cosmic lessons. From this point of view, our job as astrologers is not to predict what a transit has "in store" (the phrase suggests stocked-up supplies in a pantry, packaged and ready to be dispensed and consumed), but to translate the patterns in the sky so as to reveal what we can learn.

Inner Landscape

Presumably the literal earthquake of March 11,[th] 2011 has done its work of driving out of many astrologers' minds any skepticism that might have been there, as to how powerful this transit is. Now, the mission, for those who choose to accept it, is to undertake the inner work. This means applying our unique gifts to grapple with the larger meaning of the shattering, wipeout and breakdown symbolized by the earthquake, the tsunami and the destabilized nuclear reactors.

And how it is manifesting subjectively, within our psyches.

We can do this by taking note of what areas in our own natal chart are being highlighted by the planets involved in the Cross. Then we look into our hearts, asking ourselves whether we feel a transformation occurring in that area of life. We can also press our intellects into service, connecting the dots between what our studies have taught us about the particular astrological metaphors being signified, on the one hand, and the facts "on the ground" – what's going on in our lives – on the other.

How can the Uranian image of an earthquake be used as a cosmic teaching tool? There is a reason why we use the phrase "Earth-shattering" to refer to emotional and psychological growth spurts in our personal lives. If Uranus is now in your seventh house (one-to-one relationships), is there any wonder that you feel an earthquake rattling the foundations of your marriage?

We know that Pluto governs death and rebirth. So, taking our cue from Pluto's placement in our chart, we ask ourselves what's going on in that arena of our life that feels like death? If Pluto is currently transiting your fourth house (the home), it is telling you that something in your domestic life must be let go of, so that you can move on.

It's All Connected

Collective catastrophes certainly compel our attention, and they exist in a realm – the material realm – that we can all observe together; we can all agree, together, that these things are real. But energies powerful enough to shatter tangible structures on the physical plane are capable of nonphysical changes that are no less real, and no less transformative.

When we wrap our minds around the particular energy afoot, and try to tune into it using our own singular intelligence, then we are truly paying attention. We are focusing not so much on what will happen as *why* it happens. We are setting ourselves up to respond to the energy in the air, in a way that is maximally authentic. We are freeing ourselves from the perils of herd mentality.

And we are getting in touch with what our soul always wanted for us.

The Natives are Restless

(originally published in *Daykeeper
Journal*, April 2011)

Rising to a high flame in April 2011, the Uranus-Pluto square is already turning into a game-changer for the USA, whose (Sibly) birth chart the transit confronts with both barrels.

As astro-trackers know, the earthquake and tsunami that hit Japan on March 11 occurred only a few hours before Uranus hit the Aries point. Uranus will be flirting with this degree of the zodiac the rest of this calendar year, as it moves retrograde and direct.

Astrologers expect shattering group events to take place whenever Uranus, the planet of quakes both literal and figurative, slams up against Pluto, the planet of breakdown. The astrological antecedent of what is happening right now was a cultural earthquake, not a geological one. It took place during the mid-1960s when Uranus and Pluto were conjunct.

This time, because of the transit's cardinal emphasis and the degrees involved, the US (Sibly) chart is being hit head-on. Uncle Sam's natal Cancer-Libra aspect is being completed by the Aries-Capricorn aspect, and together they are boxing in America's consciousness. The transit is compressing and squeezing the USA into a new level of understanding itself. It's a troubling, exciting, appalling, exhilarating time to be a citizen of the red, white and blue.

Global Unrest

Uranian defiance is alive and well in the American heartland, where a callow and corrupt new governor is doing his best to dismantle the unions, arguably the one remaining institution remaining to the American working class to protect it against the ravages of systemic greed.

In Ireland, angry voters wreaked vengeance for their shattered financial expectations upon the country's ruling party, which had been in power for 61 years. In Pakistan, protestors are up in arms about the murder of two locals by an

American CIA contractor, who has infuriated the populace by claiming diplomatic immunity. In China and elsewhere, pro-democracy demonstrations are being nipped in the bud – so far – by the hard-line autocrats in charge.

In oil-rich Bahrain, whose Washington-supported monarchy hosts the US Fifth Fleet, much of the violence against protesters is being perpetrated by foreign mercenaries from US ally Saudi Arabia. The ultimatums aimed at Libya and Bahrain from the White House that were issued at the equinox, on the Full Moon March 19th 2011 (which was also, with dark appropriateness, the 8th anniversary of the war in Iraq) should be viewed very skeptically. There is a world of Plutonian subterfuge beneath the new saber rattling. With Mars on the rise there is more need than ever for Americans to do their homework before green-lighting the Pentagon yet again.

Pluto Stationary

On April 11th 2011, Pluto makes a retrograde station just two days before its exact square with Mars. Two things make this situation noteworthy: 1) Planets are very strong around the time of their stations; and 2) During the years of the Uranus-Pluto square, whenever any of the more fleeting planets – especially Mars – transit through the Cardinal signs, the power of the Cross will be triggered.

In this case, the power of Pluto and Uranus combines with the force of Mars (rage, militancy). In the US (Sibly) chart, where the longest arm of the Cross makes a Grand Cross with the natal Sun-Saturn square, the addition of Mars to the mix is especially compelling. There is already plenty of anger simmering in the US populace, and plenty to be angry about.

Americans are still limping along in a protracted recession caused by the chicanery of some of the highest-paid individuals in the world, while those same individuals rake in record-breaking bonuses and get elected to high office (witness white-collar criminal Rahm Emanuel finessing the mayoralty of Chicago). The number of families on food stamps has reached 43+ million, an all-time-high of 14% of the population. Yet the country's wealthy are doing better than ever before. While small business owners watch their companies go belly up, Tiffany's, Nordstrom, and Saks Fifth Avenue are booming.

And what assistance are Americans getting, in these hard times, from official channels? Instead of being represented by actual public servants, they are represented by a political class that consists – with exceptions so few you can count them on the fingers of one hand – of corporate servants.

If American voters wanted to serve their own best interests, all they'd have to do is pay attention to what their representatives do rather than what they say. The same politicians who cry "It's about jobs"[1] whenever a microphone is in front of them tend to be the very politicians who defund the social services and programs that create jobs; including, recently, meat inspection, railway construction and the Small Business Administration. The self-styled conservatives who repeat the "jobs" mantra *ad nauseam* tend to be the very folks supporting the busting of unions, retaliatory lay-offs and out-sourcing on the part of their big-business sponsors.

All things considered, it's hard to think of a time in its history when the US citizenry had so much justification to feel outraged.

Righteous Anger

It is an homage to Mars when anger is acted out appropriately; that is, consciously and creatively. We have been seeing a lot of high-level Mars lately. Even among many self-professedly "apolitical" Americans, dire conditions have inspired armchair complainers to reinvent themselves as bold activists.

When informed of how their tax dollars are actually spent – that is, when apprised by sources other than right-wing pundits, who would have them believe that all their money goes to abortions and immigrant services—Americans have gotten angry. Hearing that their government spends 54 percent of tax dollars on the military (a military that accounts for 47 percent of the world's total military spending) heart-engaged citizens have been responding with the positive side of Mars: that of creatively self-assertion in the face of an intolerable situation.

As a world, we are in the midst of an era that is full of extremes, and the transits this month are extreme to match. With Mars and Pluto setting the tone, it is time to allow the urgency of current events to stoke our own courage. Nothing emboldens like tragedy, calamity and grotesque injustice.

---

[1] Unemployment is supposedly down to 9.4% in the spring of 2011, but this is probably due to significant numbers of job-seekers dropping out of the system altogether.

PERSONALITY POLITIX

(originally published as a blog,
April 2011)

It's that time again. Soon the American airwaves will be in a frenzy with the 2012 campaigns.

Ambitious candidates are hitting the ground running, with strategists and stylists in tow. Media networks and advertisers are licking their chops at the guaranteed spike in viewership, as they get ready to spend a year and a half convincing the public that nothing exists in this big, wide, troubled world outside of the American presidential election.

Obama will soon arrive in San Francisco for a $35,800-per-plate fundraiser. His wealthy local supporters will doubtless do the best they can for their man, despite his spotty delivery on early promises. Such as transparency, for which he was just given a prize.

Disappointments

Like his Nobel, this latest prize, for openness in government, was clearly awarded for the ideals he represents, or used to represent, rather than for what he has done. (In an irony worthy of parodist Steven Colbert, the transparency award was bestowed in a ceremony that was closed to the media and omitted from his public schedule. Not to mention that his administration censored 194 pages of their internal emails.... about their efforts to make government more transparent.)

Another disappointment for many was Guantanamo Bay; which is not only still open, but soon to be the site of military tribunals, against which Obama righteously campaigned during his first presidential run.

But those who have been tracking such contradictions will have lost count by now. The unions, whose picket lines Obama promised, in 2008, to "put on a comfortable pair of shoes" and join, have watched him stand mutely on the sidelines while they fought for their lives in Wisconsin. The peace activists who hoped he would rein in the Pentagon have seen the military budget rise 20 billion dollars higher than it was under Bush. The progressives who expected accountability have seen more whistleblowers prosecuted under this administration than in the past forty years. Those who fully expected him to clean up the slime through which his predecessor dragged the honor of the presidency have heard, from WikiLeaks, that in his first months in office Obama quietly pressured Spain to drop its investigation into Bush's torture of detainees.

What does it all mean? Does it mean that Obama is not a smart and well-intentioned man? I think most of us would say No, it doesn't mean that. Then what *does* it mean, that such a worthy man has such policies?

Know Too Much

It means we're using the wrong criteria to frame our question. If we really want to make sense of this person's role right now, and what he's likely to do upcoming, assessing him as a good guy – via personality politics – won't help us any more than deciding he looks great in a suit. The fanciful notion that a given politician would, or could, fix everything because he's a fine, upstanding individual is, at this point in American history, as silly as trying on a poodle skirt we wore in the 1950s. We are different people now, and it no longer fits.

The USA is at an awkward age. Like a kid who's too old to believe in Santa Claus but too young not to put out cookies and milk for him on Christmas eve, the USA is midway between an old way and a new way of seeing its leaders. Personality politics is the old way, and it's comfortable, as familiar perspectives always are. But the realities of America's show-biz elections have defeated its plausibility.

The new way of seeing institutions of power, which is arising during the Pluto in Capricorn years, is troubling, as new perspectives always are. Not only because of its merciless demand that we confront the implications of what our system has become; but also because we can't be sure what our new perspective will be. We can't be sure of anything under the Uranus-Pluto square. Except that our old ways of seeing won't work.

We know too much now.

Jerry-Rigged

We know about the lobby system, an institution whereby legalized bribery determines what laws get passed. No doubt most Americans wish they could chalk up the Abramoff scandal to bad-apple exceptionalism, but they know that his outrageous scams were only quantitatively – not qualitatively – different from the hustles that occur on Capitol Hill every day of the week.

Despite varying degrees of denial – which covers a broad spectrum in this society of unevenly informed citizens – Americans by and large understand quite well that their politicians are sponsored by business interests. Especially after last year's Citizen's United ruling, where the Supreme Court wiped out any last vestige of limitations on corporate campaign contributions, it has become well nigh impossible for the public to sustain any illusions about the role of Mammon in national elections.

It is painfully obvious to most Americans that a candidate proposing deep-structure change, like Ralph Nader or Barbara Lee or Dennis Kucinich, would never be allowed to occupy anything other than a marginal position in the system as it is. We may bitterly complain about it, ruefully accept it, or succumb to soul-numbing apathy about it. But we can't really tell ourselves it isn't true. Not anymore.

Not when the most appallingly cynical realities get thrust in our faces every day, such as political parties talking about "branding" and "re-branding" themselves. It is by now such a commonplace to talk about elections as if they were just one more facet of American capitalism that the public has become inured to it. Most probably find it hard to imagine there was ever a time when elected officials were not spoken of as products for sale.

Rules of the Game

Americans have come to expect disingenuous positions from their representatives, not sincere beliefs. We don't bat an eye when Newt Gingrich calls for bombing Libya and then, as soon as the opposition agrees with him, promptly comes out against it. We don't go slack-jawed with incredulity when we hear Senator McCain vote against the very bill he himself sponsored a few months before. We understand and accept all this as the rules of the big exorbitant game.

But we can't have it both ways. That is, we can't (not without inviting a cognitive disorder, anyway) be aware of the current rules of the game and at the same time rely on personality politics. We can no longer kid ourselves that anything less than a systemic approach will help us negotiate the critical cultural shifts of the Cardinal Cross years.

Emotional Buzz

Of course, personality politix is sexier. We like the emotional buzz of identifying with our candidate's presumed moral standards. We feel validated by condemning his rival's repugnance. We like assessing our guy's easy smile, his debating style, his interest in basketball. And we very much like comparing our opinion with what others think. Thus our obsession with polls; as in high school, when we couldn't be sure our outfit looked good until we knew whether all the other girls liked it.

It's not as much fun to listen to experts – from whom we might actually learn something – discuss a politician's actions or voting record. We'd rather not think about what special interests are in his corner and why. But which perspective tells us more about what we need to know?

A system that is riddled with rot must be transformed. To do that, we need to do two things. We need to adopt a perspective that can look at our political system as an entirety. Then, we need to face the truth of what we're seeing.

This is when magic happens. In energetic law, facing the truth and transformation amount to the same thing.

Spiritual Sound Bites

(originally published in *Skywatch*,
May 2011)

From now until 2025, the world will be treading the waters of Neptune in Pisces. On April 4th 2011 Neptune glided into the sign of the oceans, where Chiron had been waiting for it. That week, Japan dumped 15,000 gallons of radioactive water into the Pacific Ocean.

Recall that a year previous, in April 2010, BP's Deepwater Horizon rig blew up in the Gulf on the very day of Chiron's last entry into Pisces. Thus has the theme of wounded waters announced itself as a key teaching of the Cardinal Cross period.

Environmental horrors like these are uniquely attention-grabbing, which seems to be part of their cosmic intention. But it is the symbolic meaning of a polluted sea that grabs us on a soul level, and it is on this level that we need to begin our search for a response. To heal these abominations we need to understand mass psychic unconsciousness.

Psychic Pollution

Chiron (woundedness) and Neptune (impressionability) in Pisces sensitize us to circumambient mental and emotional noise. All around us, the content of the collective mind seethes and roils like the ocean. And like the actual sea, this energetic sea is susceptible to being poisoned.

If we want to be part of the clean-up crew, we must recommit to our life purpose (i.e., *Know thy chart*), meanwhile taking care to add no more negativity to humanity's pooled experience. This means staying open, while at the same time avoiding the spikes of anxiety and reactivity that attend groups in crisis.

How do we stay open, yet avoid the negativity all around us? It's a daunting paradox. But then, this is a daunting era. To keep our wits about us while we do our soul work, we have to vigilantly identify group fears that enter our energy field. Then we allow them to wash over us and pass through us, so they cannot carry us away.

To begin, we have to know pollution when we see it. Such as the noise streaming forth from our infighting politicians, noise that is growing increasingly hysterical. So are the End-Time predictions of various religions, and the fear-driven pictures from pop culture. Regardless of their lack of merit, these pictures are all charged up with the insistence of the collective voice. Times of crisis have a habit of bringing up every fear known to humanity.

Reincarnation

Since all fears ultimately derive from the fear of death, let's cut to the punch and talk about it.

I see it as highly likely that human beings were created by the same force that created everything else in the Universe. If this is true, then our consciousnesses must have the same access to cosmic intelligence, and our physical beings must follow the same rules. Maybe it's the Taurus in my chart, but to me it seems only logical that if Nature thought her laws were good enough for pigeons and potatoes, she'd apply them to human beings, too. I think it must be true that, like every other living thing on Earth, human beings get recycled.

We know that organic systems are wired to get rid of their built-up toxins, decompose and self-re-create. Everything in Nature decays and then gets reborn, into a new form. I realize that to many people reincarnation seems like a wild and crazy leap of faith. But to me it seems no more than consistent to posit that, like fallen leaves in damp soil, our bodies break down and our constituent parts mutate into new forms, releasing our spirits to take off for parts unknown.

Spooked by Death

If we could view death from Mother Earth's point of view, would we see it as a tragedy? I think that despite our charged feelings on the subject, most of us would agree that death is inevitable and natural (unless you subscribe to the very weird theories of early Christian propagandists). Moreover, from the point of view of spiritual astrology, death is miraculous, as are all processes governed by the outer planets (Chiron, Uranus, Neptune and Pluto). We don't think of the tail end of the Pluto function – dying – as any less miraculous than its front end – being born.

But in the post-Enlightenment, secular West, we're terribly spooked by the idea of dying. Not just ourselves dying, but of anything dying. Like all fears, this one derives from ignorance. We can't think clearly about death because we humans are, compared to other sentient beings, staggeringly out-of-touch with cosmic truth.

We're brought up to believe that we have precious little in common with flora or fauna. We seem to imagine we're not part of the warp and woof of the planet we live on, an insanity that has gotten to the point of poisoning the sea and – as the latest news from Japan suggests – even the rain.

Our Ancestors

But I don't believe this insanity is permanent and ineluctable. And I don't think we were always this clueless. I very much doubt that aboriginal humans saw themselves as apart from the great life-death wheel. I think they looked around and saw how things worked, and drew conclusions from the parallels. They saw dogs shedding their winter fur in the summertime, forests self-recycling after a fire, and the ocean cleansing itself with every wave. Everywhere they looked, they saw the creation and destruction of form – while the whole of Life kept on going.

They noticed that each thing's underlying essence (e.g., bear energy, rabbit medicine, essence of green bamboo) remained inviolate, even though its outer shell morphed into some new shape. I think it's very probable that they believed in reincarnation as a fundamental and universal given, humans not excepted. And they saw that the endings and beginnings of cycles blended one into the other, supporting each other, as rotting leaves on the forest floor fertilize the soil where the new saplings are taking root.

At this point in human history it would help us immeasurably to get back in touch with this perspective. It would shed a lot of light on the world's current paroxysms. It would remind us that whole civilizations have death phases and renewal phases, and that these interpenetrate each other; with the dregs of old societies fertilizing those to come.

End-Time Pictures

When (not *if*) we find ourselves caught up in the death throes augured by the Cardinal crossroads, our best bet is to keep in mind humanity's allegiance to Nature's eternal laws.

To forget them is to risk flailing around in panic, in which state we tend to grab at whatever idea is around. This will, unfortunately, become easier and easier to do. There will be an increasing number of emotionally charged theories blasting from the television and flitting around the internet; there will be toxicity in the mass mood, born of confusion and unprocessed emotion. There will be a lot of chasing around after something to blame.

A great hunger is building for explanations. In response, there will be no dearth of quickly graspable parables on offer: Hollywood-packaged modern myths, like the film "2012." People want their predictions nice and simple, framed in good-or-bad terms as in an action movie. But we won't assuage any of our anxiety by reducing the vicissitudes of human evolution to a cartoon.

Fundamentalist religions – which claim to possess more legitimacy than science fiction movies, but which appeal to the same instincts – are having a field day with the apocalyptic buzz in the air. There have always been priests, in every religion, who frighten their parishioners with tales of heaven, hell, deliverance and Armageddon. When social systems are breaking down and the populace is freaked out about the future, there is a bull market for apocalyptic scenarios.

These can be entertaining, like a good yarn. And if viewed with detachment, they can be psycho-sociologically instructive: they tell us where the mass mind is at. But identifying with them emotionally and intellectually is dangerous.

Truth Stories

To see these scenarios as Truth stories undercuts our spiritual intelligence. Getting attached to End-Time pictures interferes with our ability to entertain subtleties, such as the Natural Law about endings blending into new beginnings.

Worse, buying into the polluted sea of fear stories prevents us from manifesting elegant and creative realities. I think we can concoct a future more sophisticated than reptilian extraterrestrials (The Earth invaded!) and vanquished super-villains (We got bin Laden!).

What will it take to create a more copacetic collective future? It will take consciousness. The process starts and ends with individual consciousness. That's where each of us comes in: living through our charts, as if the fate of the Earth depended on it. Which it does.

Money Season

(originally published in *Daykeeper
Journal,* May 2011)

Mercury is no longer retrograde, depriving astrophiles of their favorite excuse for things going wrong. On the other hand, Neptune is now in Pisces, giving anyone who's looking for a planet to blame plenty of justification for confusion.

The second third of spring, every year, is dominated by Taurus, the earthiest of the earth signs, with the Sun and usually some of the inner planets, too, singing the money song. This is the season for getting back in touch with what we need for physical survival.

But with the Cardinal Cross in the background, our focus on materiality is waxing compulsive, especially for Americans.

Pluto (plutocracy) is in the second house (resources) of the US (Sibly) chart, the astrological signature of financial obsession. Pluto always pushes the issues of its resident house to extremes. And right now we have not just natal Pluto but transiting Pluto involved: an inherently extreme condition is being pushed to an even more extreme condition. Since 2008 when Pluto in Capricorn (monetary systems) started opposing the US Venus (finances), the country's extraordinary relationship to the material plane has become more and more dysfunctional.

In 1980 the richest tenth of American families controlled half of the nation's income. In 2011, the top 1% controls double that amount. And the top *one-tenth* of the top 1% have made the biggest advances of all.

The scenario is so skewed that a new way of speaking about it has had to be deployed, as if to disguise its inherent craziness; e.g., calling executive pay-and-perks packages "compensation" (as opposed to what ordinary folks get: plain old wages). When called upon to justify the policy of rewarding the already-rich with ballooning salaries and bonuses during a global recession, companies these days have been invoking the "talent drain" argument: If we don't pay our CEOs a king's ransom, we'll miss out on hiring the best and the brightest.

Could there be a more stunningly tone-deaf statement for a corporation to come out with, in a period when everybody but the fortunate few is in financial crisis?

Third-World Superpower

Almost as great as the disparity between rich and poor in the USA is the disparity between the financial facts and the collective self-image. Most Americans equate patriotism with the belief that their country represents the epitome of equality and fairness (Saturn is in Libra in the US (Sibly) chart); the assumption is that access to wealth is evenly distributed, despite staggering amounts of evidence to the contrary.[1] A fog of incredulity protects the myth that the little guy has as good a shot at wealth as his well-connected brethren.

But the country is growing less naïve by the day. As the Cardinal Cross slams into the US Sun cluster, the country's Horatio Algier fantasies are being bombarded by a battering ram. The poor and middle class are watching their social services go from paltry to non-existent, at the same time that the very richest among them receive bigger and bigger pieces of the American pie. No longer the exclusive knowledge of academics and statisticians, these disparities have moved from being a subtext of the public conversation into being its main text. Even *Vanity Fair*, hardly a radical rag, has an article on the income gap in its latest issue.

This is causing a wrenching disconnect in the group psyche, as a cherished part of the national imagination is being contradicted by evidence that can no longer be denied. When such contradictions (Pluto opposite Sun) occur to individuals, the identity crisis can be devastating.

Unions

In the political arena, financial self-interest has grown fanatical. Last year the Supreme Court's *Citizens United* decision opened to full throttle the spigot of corporate cash into political campaigns. Since then, the moneyed class has been emboldened to go whole hog. As we would expect from a transit spearheaded by Pluto, subtlety and shame have been thrown to the winds.

---

[1] Extreme financial inequality is not just unfair; there is also a body of scholarship suggesting that it causes economic depressions. It does so by creating a bias towards asset bubbles and overinvestment while holding down consumption, until the system becomes top-heavy and tips over, as happened in the 1930s. Right now the profit share of corporations is at record highs across the USA and Europe.

In February 2011, with Pluto's opposition to the US Jupiter within a degree of exactitude and Uranus closing in on the Aries point, Wisconsin's governor made history. Backed by two of the deepest-pocket players in American politics, the Koch Brothers, Gov. Walker did what no politician had done since the union busting of the early 1930s. He introduced a bill stripping state workers of their right to collective bargaining.

American unions have been in steep decline for the past several decades.[2] But they remain the only significant counterbalance working people have against the forces of plutocracy. The all-out attack upon them marked a surge in the income gap wars.

Pluto Opposite US Jupiter

Through November of 2011, transiting Pluto will be finishing up its exact opposition to the US Jupiter.

The America's Jupiter is the repository of collective ethical values. It's the container where the country keeps its sense of what is right and just. Beginning in earnest around the 2010 summer solstice, Uranus, Pluto and Saturn have been ripping its lid off. These transits are asking, What do Americans really believe, underneath what they say they believe? What makes a society ethical?

The opportunity exists for the USA to confront its previously unexamined truisms, to repudiate its morally bereft behaviors, and to move towards a vision of true national integrity. This might include the idea that a truly civilized society is one in which the most vulnerable segments of the population are cared for, and in which the financially powerful do not exploit the powerless just because they can.

---

[2] In 1960, one in four American workers was in a union; now it's one in eight. The primary reasons for the change seem to be the erosion of American manufacturing, largely through outsourcing-as well as the increasingly close ties between big business and the lawmakers on their payroll, who enact labor laws without teeth.

Moral Ambiguity

(originally published as a blog,
May 2011)

I do not have the stars-and-stripes flapping in the breeze this balmy spring evening. I don't have my "We're Number One" T-shirt on. I'm not giddy with jubilation about the fact that my country just shot Osama bin Laden in the face.

President Obama claims that "justice was done," somehow glossing over the associations the word *justice* has with charges, public trials, evidence and so on. Does it matter, if we flout international laws by sending hit men to smoke people on foreign soil? Does it matter, if we violate our own Constitution by waging war on Libya without Congressional approval? Apparently, if the cause is popular enough, it doesn't matter. I guess those Americans who think that what happened in Abbottabad is an example of "what makes America great" took away different ideals from 5th-grade Social Studies than I did.

The assault occurred at the Beltane New Moon 2011, with Mercury, Venus, Mars, Jupiter and Uranus all in Aries. This planetary grouping bristles with the potential for subterfuge, violence and militarism. But, like every other daunting transit of the Cardinal Cross period, we were given it to learn from. Of course, this is only possible if we open our ears and eyes; not a strong suit of the American public.

Most Americans did not ask questions about the strange events of September 11, 2001 at the time, and they are not asking questions about them now. The public seems to prefer watching earnest airheads on TV ask questions (and not questions that genuinely seek information – just questions that play *gotcha*, to score political points). We like to let our pundits do our non-thinking for us.

American Showdown

At first blush the Osama killing seems like a classic American showdown, the kind we could find between the pages of any X-men comic book. But it is highlighting a jarring ethical divide for the US public. Transiting Pluto, the most critical piece of the longest arm of the Cross, is approaching exactitude in its opposition to the US Jupiter (ideals): the group mind is at a crossroads of moral ambiguity. Many people are feeling profoundly disquieted by the shift; others are cleaving blithely to the old simplicities. But my sense is that all of us are experiencing this one in the gut, where we keep our deepest notions of right and wrong.

Neptune, now in its glory in Pisces, is also about ambiguity – which comes in two flavors. There is the reasoned kind of ambiguity, which opens us up to the subtlety of nuanced understanding. Then there's the blind kind, where our sense of self gets lost in a fog. We slip into the latter when, for example, we become hypnotized by the media's engineered version of events.

To resist this, we might notice that those elements of the Abbottabad attackthat are attracting the fewest questions are far more interesting than those being repeated *ad nauseum* on the news. One example: I found myself wondering about the unnamed women and children who had to watch Osama get shot in the head. One of them was apparently his twelve-year-old daughter. The White House has been changing its story about this child from day to day. This ought to make us even more curious.

The existence of these tragic bystanders parallels the killing of Moammar Khadafy's youngest son and three grandchildren a few days ago. The White House didn't devote much time talking about them, either. And I haven't heard a peep in the mass media about the murder – all-but-forgotten but newly relevant – of Khadafy's baby daughter in 1986, by a US missile strike (does it not chill the blood to imagine this man's feelings about America right now?).

Collateral Damage

It's pretty clear why these specimens of collateral damage are being given scant air time. It would complicate things for the American public to think of their designated Evil Ones, bin Laden and Kadafy, as human beings with actual flesh-and-blood daughters. The fact of their humanity (in the literal, not the ethical sense) does not justify or diminish bin Laden's or Khadafy's crimes. All it does is complicate things. It throws off the narrative, by leading us to other thoughts.

It might lead us, for example, to think about the millions of lives destroyed by Uncle Sam's wars. This, in turn, might get us thinking about how the Iraqi and Afghan and Pakistani widows and orphans must feel right now, watching clips on Al-Jazeera of Americans gleefully singing "The Star Spangled Banner."

And then we might start thinking about the disparity between the number of Arab dead and the number of US dead in the World Trade Center. This is not to say that crimes against humanity can be quantified. But any line of inquiry that provides perspective is called for under transits like these, and we are talking about the difference between some 753,400 deaths in Iraq (WikiLeaks figures are available up until 2009) and Afghanistan, compared to fewer than 3,000 deaths on 9/11 in New York.

Thoughts that complicate things invite nuance into our thinking, and nuance creates confusion in a time of fevered groupthink. This is why, in all the brain-numbing hours of TV coverage about the extra-judicial assassination of bin Laden, we hear so little historical context. The mass media will not touch with a ten-foot pole any subject that flies in the face of the neat, dumb simplicity of the official narrative.

Such as the fact that before bin Laden and Saddam Hussein were styled as arch-villains, both spent several years on the CIA payroll. I'm not suggesting this makes them any less odious. For some of us, it makes them more odious still. But what does it make the US government?

Moral ambiguity is not easy to embrace. Nor are any of the other wrenching cultural changes upon us between now and 2023. But on a soul level, we know we are ready for them.

When Everything We Know is Wrong

(originally published in *Skywatch,*
June 2011)

Here it is, the Murravian Mantra: Only by living through our charts can we understand the world, and our place in it.

Two clarifications:

1. I don't mean that astrology is the only way to reach this understanding. *Living through the chart* is just my way of saying "committing to our life purpose." Astrology is one of the best means I've ever found, to arrive at that place; but living through the chart is a state of being, that we can get to with the help of any number of spiritual paths and modalities. We just have to be ready to be authentically and fully ourselves.

2. When I say "understanding," I'm not referring to some stash of esoteric knowledge that we acquire, as when we get a degree and hang our diploma on the wall. I mean the kind of understanding that comes from our core essence. The kind we get from tapping into what we already know.

The way sky watchers get in touch with our core essence is by continuously going back to our natal charts. We ground ourselves by remembering what those symbols say about who we are, at the deepest level of being. Then we forge a relationship between what's happening in our inner world and what's happening up there in the sky.

Neptune in Pisces

What's happening up there in the sky are year-by-year, day-by-day, minute-by-minute planetary changes. By decoding these changes, astrologers discern the meaning of the world moment. It's like watching a giant crawl-feed screen in Times Square, except that, instead of being a message from Disney or the Gap, this one's from the cosmos.

Covering roughly the same period as the Cardinal Cross is the other momentous transit of the era: Neptune in Pisces. For the duration of 2011, Neptune remains neck-and-neck with Chiron, from which it is slowly separating from an exact conjunction. Loaded with teachings about the difference between pain and suffering (Chiron), Neptune is now more universal and mystical (Pisces) in its feeling-tone than ever before.

Wistful, melancholic, ecstatic and all-encompassing, Neptune's call is bewitching. We will want to come up with strategies to keep ourselves from diving overboard into its waters. This is what Ulysses feared he might do, which is why he asked his fellow sailors to bind him to the mast: he knew about the power of the sirens' song.

What house of your chart is Neptune transiting? This is where you start, in order to identify where in your life the transit is playing itself out. Then When Neptune is strong in the sky, watch for delusion, deception or malfeasance he illusions of this particular cycle will come to a head.

Collective Illusion

We will be working with Piscean illusion for 14 years. To keep our sanity – indeed, to bring it to a higher level – we'll need to make critical distinctions between pernicious and non-pernicious forms of illusion. Everywhere we turn, we'll find that what we thought was true is in fact just somebody's story.

Neutral illusion – that is, illusion that manipulates and deceives, but without malevolence – is consciously received, does no harm and sometimes delights. The best example of this form of Neptunian illusion is art, "the lie that tells the truth." In an art gallery, we look at a canvas, a flat surface on which a series of paint marks conveys an illusion of forms in space, and we conspire with the artist to pretend that three-dimensionality is going on. If what we are looking at is great art, and we are able to let it in, the boundaries of our perception are expanded; and Neptune has done its job.

Also in the neutral-Neptune category are myths and legends, including religious tales for adults and fairy tales for children. These, too, are lies that tell the truth. Their simple imagery conveys important cultural messages that speak the language of the unconscious mind. They are automatically understood by all who hear them to be symbolic, not literal. An example is the tale about young George Washington chopping down a cherry tree and supposedly saying to his father, "I cannot tell a lie." Everyone knows it is apocryphal, a fable about the honesty of a national hero.

More insidious are those lies that we don't know are lies. Pernicious illusion is when *a story about what happened* masquerades as *what happened.* We see this with government-generated and media-promulgated narratives, which have been given a shiny gloss of credibility by the stamp of officialdom. For Americans, the most epoch-defining of these in recent times include the assassination of JFK, the bizarre events of 9/11/01, and the shooting of Osama bin Laden on May 1st, 2011.

In theory, no interpretation of a cultural event has to be harmful, necessarily, any more than a theatrical event is harmful. (Even advertising can be construed as an art form. After all, in France they even give awards to the cleverest commercials.) If the conventional narrative of the bin Laden killing were to be viewed as a modern legend, in the Rambo revenge genre, it could even be instructive. Sociologists studying the mores and values of American culture who turned their attention to the assault of the Seals-6 (apparently now trademarked by Disney!) in Abbottabad would find a treasure trove of material.

The problem arises when we buy into what we hear on TV as if it were the truth. Whatever that means.

Osama bin Laden

With Neptune in Pisces, the truth is a very slippery commodity. As Voltaire said, "Uncertainty is an uncomfortable position. But certainty is an absurd one."

In the case of this most recent cultural myth, that of the bin Laden killing, a global meaning has not yet gelled. It is far from clear whether any commonality exists between the spin America's self-congratulatory politicians are putting on it and the meaning it has for the Arab street. Or, for that matter, how it will come to be seen in Libya, or Ivory Coast, or India. Even the official American version of has already been through multiple permutations (recall that it was said at first and later retracted that Osama was armed, and that he used his wife as a human shield).

Under Neptunian skies, the lack of consensus about the meaning of this episode is more telling than anything else about it. One of the biggest question marks is how Uncle Sam's interests will now be received by Washington's erstwhile ally, the Pakistani government; and by its civilian population, who are still getting slaughtered in Pentagon drone attacks. What is the meaning, for these people, of the fact of bin Laden's death, and of the way he died?

Which is more likely to become the more globally dominant legend: bin-Laden-as-martyr, or the purge-of-the-antichrist spin popular in the USA?

As reactions to the assault came in from governments around the world, we saw the subjectivity of truth exemplified. Washington's staunchest rival, Beijing, has been eager to capitalize on the strain between the Obama administration and Islamabad. Their spokesflacks heaped fulsome praise upon the Pakistani government for being a brave and true fighter against terrorism.

Meanwhile, the sheiks of Saudi Arabia, supposedly Washington's staunchest allies, issued a statement so cautious it could only be called a non-statement, calling the death a "step that supports the international efforts." The sheiks know they're sitting on top of a powder keg: their subjects, anti-American and desperately poor are watching the Arab spring revolts erupting everywhere else but in their own feudal petrocracy. The behooded kings must be quaking in their designer sunglasses. They know it's only a matter of time before a spark from nearby uprisings ignites a blast under the House of Saud.

In Cuba, Fidel Castro decried the way "Osama was executed in front of his children and wives." In Palestine, the event was protested by both Hamas and non-Hamas Arabs as the murder of an "Arab holy warrior." In the USA, John Yoo, the Justice Department official who made torture legal under Bush, gushed that the killing was a success generated by the "tough decisions" of his former boss.

We are watching myriad stories bouncing off of each other, like refracted shards in a kaleidoscope.

No More Cause-and-Effect

For those who deeply integrate the Piscean lessons of the coming era, old notions about cause-and-effect will come to seem very limited. When we consider the probable effects of the bin Laden killing, we need to remember that the great Neptunian Law of Unintended Consequences trumps all human plans, guesses and purposes.

Where did this long and violent story begin? It depends on who is telling the tale. One way to find meaning in this miasmic saga might be to ask ourselves how future historians might tell it. We cannot know now, in 2011, whether history will unquestioningly attribute responsibility for 9/11 to Osama bin Laden. History makes mincemeat of our cherished certitudes.

We all know this, yet we seem to forget it every time we read about a new discovery in the newspaper.

Scientific announcements about the age of humankind, for example, or about the danger of cell phone radiation, tend to be disproved every few years – completely discrediting what was accepted as gospel before. And the history books are constantly being rewritten: in this morning's paper I read that journalists are now debating whether the poet Pablo Neruda actually died of cancer after all, or whether he was killed by the same Kissinger-financed assassins who murdered his friend Salvador Allende.

Perhaps Osama bin Laden will ultimately be remembered by some scholars less as the mastermind of the WTC catastrophe – about which there remains all that curious evidence showing the CIA knew about it well in advance – than for his early *communiqué* to Washington; the one most Americans didn't get a chance to see, because it was censored in the US media as soon as it was leaked. In it he demanded 1) an end to foreign troops in lands sacred to Islam, 2) an immediate halt to the bombing of Iraqi civilians, and 3) that the USA stop bankrolling Israel against the Palestinians.

I am not suggesting that, after questioning the official story, we should swing over to a different point of view and cleave to it just as tightly. Under transits like these, certainty is a lost cause. I am suggesting that there's a lesson here about the folly of there being only one story to anything.

"It's the best possible time to be alive, when almost everything you thought you knew is wrong."
–character in Tom Stoppard's Arcadia

WEAKENING THE BONES

(originally published in *Daykeeper
Journal*, June 2011)

As we enter the second half of 2011, the USA is moving towards the last peak of
its Saturn Return, a crisis of maturity that happens every three decades.

Anybody out there having your Saturn Return? You are, if you're around 28
years old, or fifty-seven years old... or 235 years old, as is the USA.

Those who have been through this transit to their personal charts know what a
stiff challenge it is. When Saturn returns to the position it was in when we were
born, we get tested to see how grown-up we are. We are forced by circumstances
to answer to our conscience, that inner taskmaster who holds the keys to our self-
esteem. If we abdicate responsibility or space out on our goals, we feel like silly
young punks, who want nothing so much as to be a person of substance.

The US's Saturn Return is a major part of the Cardinal Cross period, the long
series of transits that will decide America's status as a world leader. Peaking
three times in 2010-11, this part of the collective learning curve has to do with
the values professed by Libra, in which sign the national Saturn resides.
Prominently placed at the top of the chart in the tenth house of international
reputation, America's noble Saturn holds certain ideals to be terribly important.

But that doesn't mean they are easily integrated. Saturn squares the Sun in this
chart. The Saturn Return is bringing to a head the most difficult conflict in the
national character. All those Libran goals we learned about in American history,
and that we continue to hear bandied about in idealistic speeches, are being put to
the test right now. These include impartiality, justice and legality.

Tenth-House Libra

The image the USA proudly projects to the world (tenth house) is adamant about
rule of law (Libra). But the Sun cluster, squaring Saturn from the third quadrant,
reveals a self-protective entity whose instincts prioritize comfort and security
(Cancer). How do these two get along? Awkwardly, as indicated by the 90-

degree angle that separates them. With the Pluto-Uranus transit triggering this dynamic and the Saturn Return making it globally obvious, the USA is being forced to confront its cherished commitments.

We hear a great deal of high-minded bloviating from our elected officials when other countries flout international treaties. We hear outraged pundits roundly castigating any number of global autocrats who drop the Libran standard and operate outside the law. But Saturn cares nothing about public pronouncements. The cosmos is only interested in how the native himself behaves. In this case, the question is: Are we practicing what we preach?

Libra is an air sign, which inclines it towards clean, unemotional judgments. Behind the concept of Libran justice is the notion that subjective influences should not influence the balancing of the scales of justice. How well has the White House been honoring the Libran mandate?

Rule of Law

Consider the case of Bradley Manning, the young soldier imprisoned for disclosing government secrets to WikiLeaks. Is his treatment an example of high-functioning Libra? Held in an isolation cell for 23 hours a day, stripped naked and deprived of sleep, Pfc. Manning is being subjected to the kind of hideous mistreatment that Washington condemns tyrants for doling out to those who disagree with them.

It was in March, 2011, when the US Saturn Return was peaking for the second time, that State Department media spokesman P. J. Crowley declared, at a seminar at MIT, that Manning's treatment was "ridiculous and counterproductive and stupid." Two days later he was fired.

There are so many ways in which Bradley Manning's punishment must be considered appalling. Anyone with water signs in their chart would be sickened by its cruelty; anyone with earth would be repelled by its counter-productivity. From a fire standpoint it is appalling by virtue of its moral repugnance. At issue here, however, are the ways that it is appalling from an air point of view. When we consider the USA's Libra Saturn, we have to conclude that what is happening to Bradley Manning flies in the face of everything the country is supposed to believe in.

When Obama was in San Francisco on April 21, 2011, a group of Manning's advocates crashed the president's fundraiser. Obama responded: "If I was to release… information I'm not authorized to release, I'm breaking the law.. He [Manning] broke the law." First of all, as journalist Bob Egelko has pointed out, in fact the president does have the authority to declassify whatever documents he chooses; he wouldn't be "breaking the law" by releasing them. Secondly, the Pentagon Papers, which Obama and his apologists claim were a whole different kettle of fish from the WikiLeaks cables. They were classified top secret – a far more restrictive classification than applied to the Manning material.

But the most egregiously Libra-flouting piece of Obama's response was this: Bradley Manning is still awaiting trial. Isn't he legally presumed to be innocent?

Mine is not a particularly Libra-driven chart; I find the Manning case loathsome mostly for other reasons. But the USA is up against its Libra karma right now, and it is by Libra standards that it must primarily be judged.

Unintended Consequences

It was also in March, just before the equinox, that Washington ordered up missile strikes in Libya without bothering with Congressional approval. The US public seemed utterly untroubled by this violation of Constitutional law (Libra), thanks to a confounding dose of strong collective emotion (Cancer). Americans were sufficiently horrified by Khadafy's violence to the protesters – with whom the US public was primed to identify at this particular moment in history, given the recent triumph in Egypt – to brush aside the laws of their republic.

Here again, the US (Sibly) chart's Sun won out over its Saturn. In this case, a flood of fierce, protective feeling (Cancer) won the day. The loser in this contest was the cool rationality of Saturn in Libra, whose strong suit is to weigh the pros and cons of any endeavor. As the nuclear submarines and F-16 bombers swung into action, caution (Saturn) was thrown to the winds. The popular mood in the USA is still blithely impervious to the prospect of unintended consequences that might be incurred by a new war in the Middle East.

Extra-Judicial Assassination

Then, Osama bin Laden was killed in Abbottabad. Here we see group feeling triumphing even more fulsomely over any pretence of legality. In fact, Obama could even invoke the word *justice* in his televised announcement without the slightest risk of anyone quibbling about its actual technical meaning (public trials, juries and evidence).

The US public came down on the side of Cancer (domestic security) once again.

Even more so than with the Manning case or the decision to bomb Libya, in this instance the government's extra-judicial action met with an unambiguously jubilant response. There were a few critics, but they were mostly just the Obama-baiters, doing their predictable partisan thing. I heard no one in the mass media advocating for Saturn in Libra.

The Bones of the Chart

Saturn represents our boundaries; it's there to correct our excesses and keep us honest. It provides an underlying structure, giving us solidity in a chaotic world. The USA desperately needs a well-functioning Saturn right now: with its Sun caught in a Uranus-Pluto T-square, the next few years are going to be uniquely chaotic. At the moment, however, the country is adhering only very selectively to the laws enshrined in its Constitution – that much-touted document considered so sacrosanct by theoretical patriots.

Ignoring the rules of Saturn's game comes with a price, and never more so than at the Saturn Return. By blowing off those laws that serve as the cornerstone of its collective integrity, the USA is weakening its bones.

Safeguarding Our Sanity

(originally published as a blog,
June 2011)

I thought of Neptune, the Great Dissembler, last weekend when I heard about the yogi Swami Ramdev, whose protest against corruption in the Indian government (Pluto in Capricorn) took a Neptunian turn. Accosted by the police during his hunger strike, the yogi fled into the crowd disguised as an old woman, covering his black beard with a white shawl.

The big transits in June 2011 surround the summer solstice, which trines Neptune in Pisces – the first time in our lifetimes that we have experienced this winsome water trine. And, as it has since 2008, the first few days of summer set off the explosive Cardinal Cross. As we have seen, global dramas financial, political and revolutionary cluster around the degrees where Uranus and Pluto are currently transiting.

The configurations in the sky are becoming very intense indeed. In order to receive them in a healthy way, I recommend we make use of the notion of sanity. Transits this potent are a signal that we need sanity more than we need anything else.

Changing Course

More than ingenious technology, more than lots of money, more than cool friends or charismatic leaders, we're going to need sanity over the years ahead. Especially considering that we are living in a world where attention seems to magnetize around ideas and people who express the opposite of sanity. Case in point: Donald Trump and Sarah Palin sitting down together for a photo op at a franchise pizza outlet. Ladies and gentlemen, I give you Meaning-Challenged Media Magnets.

Around the same time as the Palin-Trump powwow, scientists from the International Energy Agency convened to release their estimate of greenhouse gases, though few among the public were paying attention to that meeting. The IEA declared that worldwide emissions had increased by a record amount last year.

So despite all the cant we've been hearing, from every quarter, about the world going green, the truth is that if this year's emissions rise by as much as they did in 2010, according to the IEA it will be all but impossible to hold global warming to a manageable degree. The incalculable suffering that humanity faces unless we change course is, according to Lord Stern of the London School of Economics, "a risk any sane person would seek to drastically reduce."

Sane Enough

Are we sane enough to seek to reduce it? This is the question that lies behind the issue of human choice in our era. Will we seek to reduce this risk, each of us, in whatever way we can? "In whatever way we can" means in whatever ways might be appropriate to our own unique situation. It won't do any good if we try to address the situation by mimicking somebody else's approach. Learn from, yes. Mimic, no.

More so than the idea of right and wrong, the idea of sanity has legs. I think it will prove far more useful during the years of the Cardinal Cross than the promotion of any particular ideology or behavior. After all, everywhere we turn we see the pointlessness of trying to foist any one idea or course of action upon people. As astrologers, we know such attempts are doomed. Think about it: how could a singular approach be right for every person, given that everyone's chart is by definition unique?

The notion of sanity, on the other hand, is one-size-fits-all.

LEAPING THROUGH THE PORTAL

(originally published as a blog,
June 2011)

Greece is in flames. The cradle of Western civilization is exploding with the Cardinal Cross. And glimpsed sneaking away from the mayhem: none other than Goldman Sachs, whose world-famous (this was before they became world-notorious) consultants helped Greece mask its debt crisis with the same credit-swapping tricks that trashed Wall Street. I swear, not even the snarkiest black humorist could have come up with a scenario this outrageous.

We are seeing a stunning encapsulation of everything astrologers have been expecting, as the summer eclipses trigger the showdown between Uranus (revolution), Pluto (breakdown) and Saturn (debts come due).

Since the advent of the industrial age, humanity's had the bit in its teeth, all hopped up by our fancy new technologies (Uranus) and enthralled by their immense power (Pluto). But when we fail to factor in the potential results (Saturn) of what we're doing, we get the kind of thing that happened in Japan on March 11th 2011.

Elsewhere in the karma department, the US's Saturn Return is peaking during 2011. Everywhere Uncle Sam turns, chickens are coming home to roost. *Karma* is an overused term, but astrologers have a very precise meaning for it: the results of processes we set in motion. That's what we mean when we talk about Saturnine Law.

Sins Redeemed

Buried beneath the big news stories on the eclipse in June 2011 was a disquietingly touching item about the war in Vietnam, that military morass that kick-started The Sixties for many insular Americans. It was announced that Washington will join together with the Vietnamese government to clean up the defoliant Agent Orange, with which the Pentagon laid waste to that nation's terrain fifty years ago.

Here we see the Cardinal Cross offering up another parallel between our own era and that of the last rendezvous between Uranus and Pluto (1965-66), this one with a Saturnine twist: an invitation to take responsibility for crimes committed when the Cross was born.

And on the day before the summer solstice, yet another old sin came forward to be redeemed. A group of Native Americans was awarded the largest settlement ever approved against the US government. It seems Washington stole or squandered billions of dollars' worth of royalties intended for American Indians in exchange for grazing and other leases. The suit had been pending for more than a century.

Feel the Questions

During the years upon us, the eclipses that fall within the degree range of Uranus and Pluto square are acting as a series of portals of consciousness: opportunities for drastic breakthrough. There are individuals all over the world who are making extravagant leaps of awareness right now.

It takes courage of a special kind to take this leap. Depending on the potentials within your own chart, these leaps could take various forms: active, private, whimsical or deeply solemn. They might take the form of unplugging from the internet for a week, as a means of reclaiming your brain.

They might take the form of questioning conventional wisdom about current events; asking yourself, for instance, whether this latest quest for regime change in Libya has anything to do with the fact that that country has the largest oil reserves in Africa. They might take the form of letting yourself feel – in your belly (governed by Cancer, the sign of the solstice) – the significance to the World Soul of a massive drought in China, a country that is home to 20% of the world's population.

Don't get stuck in "But what can I do about it?" Activism may be in the cards for you at some point; but the first step, for the purpose of this exercise, is to feel the questions. To defy the urge to deny. If we can obviate our usual blocking mechanisms and simply let the thought in, we are answering the call of the times. Musings like these stimulate the part of us that aches to be connected to the planetary moment.

The next time a significant transit – an eclipse, a Full Moon, your birthday – takes place, use it as an invitation to think up your own thought-seeds. Focus your attention on these as you would on a koan or a mandala. Use them to get a running-start leap through the portal.

SPILL IT? CLEAN IT UP

(originally published in *Skywatch*,
July 2011)

It always struck me as so quintessentially American, that Pottery Barn metaphor that Colin Powell and Thomas Friedman used to refer to Iraq: "You break it, you own it." (You wonder whether a public speaker elsewhere in the world would have chosen a less explicitly commercial metaphor; such as, oh I don't know, a mother saying to her child, "If you spill that milk, you're cleaning it up.")

Buzz-phrases that catch on as solidly as this one did clearly resonate with something deep within the collective imagination. "You break it, you own it" has wormed its way into the American vernacular. It even has its own Wikipedia page.

The phrase makes a great exercise for students of the US (Sibly) chart. Via the imagery of home furnishings, the Pottery Barn metaphor supplies the symbolism of Cancer, in which sign the US Venus, Jupiter and Sun reside.

But it is Pluto's placement that gives "You break it, you own it" its power. America's Pluto (annihilation) falls in its second house (possessions). Deep within the national unconscious, the ideas of destruction and ownership are inextricably fused.

Longest Arm

This July 2011 Uranus' square to Pluto is barely a degree away from exactitude, the strongest it has yet been.

With the solstice eclipses, the square was kicked into a new level of fervor. As the world rolled its eyes in disgust and dismay, Pluto's two most salacious expressions, sex and corruption, found tawdry expression in the failure of Anthony Wiener (the N.Y. Congressmen caught sexting) and Dominique Strauss-Kahn (the IMF director arrested for assaulting a hotel maid) to keep their appetites in their pants.

But it is the square's impact on the world's governments that is making history. Rebellions (Uranus) against entrenched corruption (Pluto) are now threatening an astounding number of the world's heads of state, giving the lie to those that are democracies in name only, such as India and Indonesia.

It is hard to think of a single spot on the globe where individuals (Uranus in Aries) are not up in arms against centralized institutions (Pluto in Capricorn).

Waves of Meaning

The Japanese earthquake-tsunami will go down in astrological history as one of the most stunning instances of the power of ingresses (a planet changing signs), in general, and of ingresses to the Aries point, in particular. The catastrophe took place on the very day Uranus moved into Aries for the second time this cycle, March 11th, 2011.

Like the angry ocean that destroyed northeastern Japan, the wider meaning of this catastrophe has come at us in a series of waves. The first shock wave was local, as we would expect. Its focus was the immediate human tragedy of the earthquake. Its effect was to magnetize the world's sympathy for the victims, with attention funneled to the islands themselves.

The next wave of meaning extended beyond the local. The earthquake and threat of nuclear reactor meltdown that ensued expanded the sense of threat into a significance that was, for many observers, universal and dystopian. Environmental implications started to dawn on people all over the world.

Baby boomers old enough to remember the clumsy civil-defense newsreels they'd watched as schoolchildren wondered whether their worst Cold War-era nightmares were coming true. As the aftermath from the quake in Japan was televised far and wide, people everywhere watched hundreds of thousands of gallons of irradiated water being pumped into the sea, heading towards their own shores and poisoning everything in its wake.

At this writing, July 2011, the solar dial has shifted a full quarter turn since the catastrophe, and its meaning is in a third wave. This one is far more demanding than the first two, which were merely about shock and horror. Now we are left to confront the sobering realities. Humanity is having to consider, for example, the fact that we built dozens of nuclear reactors in the world's most quake-prone series of islands. Is it not difficult, at this point, to imagine that we thought that was a good idea?

When we factor in the global frequency in recent years of climate change-induced tsunamis, and of freak storms that can no longer accurately be called "freak", surely what happened on March 11th comes to look not shocking at all but downright inevitable. The question is not "How could we possibly have seen that coming," but rather, "What kind of denial have we been in that we could have not foreseen it?"

Unasked Questions

If you think of human existence as one long evolution of consciousness, you place no small significance on the things certain segments of humanity learn from hideous blunders like the Japanese quake. You pay attention to the fact that in the months since March 11th, 2011, Germany's government has taken the vanguard position and moved to ban nuclear plants altogether, and that elsewhere in the world the anti-nuke movement has been revived after a relatively complacent hiatus. If you believe that the Uranus-Pluto years are about consciousness raising, which is signaled by questions being asked, then you infer from this event that the Cardinal Cross is doing its job with daunting precision and timeliness.

More and more people are asking whether it is possible to have nuclear power without the dangers of unimaginably toxic contaminants.

Another question lurks behind this one. What will we do when the oil runs out? Global peak oil production, speculated by some energy analysts to be reached any time between 2012 and 2020, has long been associated by some astrologers with the transits of the Cardinal Cross.

Culture Clash

In the 1960s, Uranus & Pluto (*counter-*) were opposed to Saturn (*culture*) and created the counter-culture. Right now the same three planets are creating a new set of stringent societal polarizations. One of them, Pluto, relates to nuclear energy.

Worldwide, most environmentalists are incredulous that there could still be any doubt about the folly of nuclear energy. But, predictably enough, as soon as the initial shock from the quake and tsunami died down, the nuclear power industry, in the USA and elsewhere – even, goddess have mercy, in Japan – started qualifying their contrite moratoriums and making plans to return to business as usual. Among political progressives there is, at the moment, no clear consensus on nuclear power.

But among readers of astrological archetypes, a clear theme starts to arise. Humanity is being asked to integrate Uranus (technology) and Pluto (power) with Saturn (responsibility).

Wild and Crazy

The specter of explosive (Uranus) mass death and toxicity (Pluto) that arose in March 2011 in the seas of Japan was a textbook example of Pluto and Uranus run amok, unleashed from all restraint (Saturn). Both Uranus and Pluto are associated with the breakdown of the atom. Inventing a power source for which there is no disposal plan is an example of heeding Uranus and Pluto without Saturn. Saturn's placement at the solstice eclipse, stationary and positioned right between the other two, was telling us loud and clear that Saturn, and only Saturn, can contain the wild energy of these years.

Wild and crazy Uranus and Pluto certainly are; but we would be wrong to think of them as malevolent forces. This is a mistake many beginning astrologers make. In truth the planets do not have motive or agency; they are value-neutral symbols, representing cosmic laws. Uranus governs technology and Pluto is about power. They are just doing their jobs, in this case manifesting as the nuclear power industry, cooking up ways to meet the world's energy needs.

Reining In

Saturn, meanwhile, exists to rein in Uranus and Pluto – because wherever there is enormous power, there is the potential for it to backfire enormously badly. Saturn represents the impulse towards caution which, when integrated with the other two planets, allows all three to function well.

Why do we need Saturn? It governs the legal regulations that are set up to rein in big business – cautions which would, in theory, prevent us from the kind of desecration that Big Oil inflicted upon the environment in the Gulf of Mexico in April 2010. It governs the kind of safeguards that could have prevented the financial catastrophe that Wall Street inflicted upon the world economy. During these fiascos the absence of Saturnine accountability was the object lesson.

Examples abound of modern societies that have thoroughly mastered Uranus, exemplified by all those shiny new gadgets rolling off Chinese assembly lines, and Pluto, exemplified by the unstinting production of weapons of war – but that have not mastered Saturn.

Saturn continually finds new ways to teach us that everything we do has a consequence. At this historical moment, the society that does not find a balance among all three is doomed.

Fouling the Nest

Uranus is a very fancy planet, a taker of high-concept risks. If you have Uranus prominent in your natal chart, you know what I mean. It specializes in that spark of mind-power that makes humans different from the "lower animals." Saturn, by contrast, is the most soberly practical of the planets. Its caution is based on simple rules of survival. Such as the instinctive rules that prevents birds from fouling their own nests. If modern humanity were as hip to the Saturn principle as birds are, we wouldn't have created an industry whose wastes we haven't learned how to take responsibility for.

On the weekend before the lunar eclipse of June 2011, the streets in parts of Tokyo were jammed with protesters demonstrating against nuclear power. These folks were messengers of high-level Saturn: thousands of ordinary citizens making the case that we cannot continue to foul our own nest. Three months after the Uranus ingress sent that scorching message to humanity about how dangerously easy it is to spill poison, these folks were doing their part to clean up the mess.

NANNY STATE

(originally published in *Daykeeper*
Journal, July 2011)

If you were looking for a nanny for your baby, and you had a chance to peek at
the applicant's charts while interviewing her for the job, wouldn't you be pleased
to see she had Cancer planets? Astrologers know this sign makes for great
babysitters, geriatric nurses, dog walkers, houseplant-tenders... any activity
where care is provided for living things who need help.

This is why it is so perversely fascinating that the USA, the group entity that
celebrates its 235th Cancer birthday on July 4, 2011, is being condemned right
now by some of its citizens for being a "nanny state."

On the face of it, the complaint seems to reflect a disdain for freeloading. That is,
Obama's government is being accused of allowing and/or encouraging the adult
public to act like feckless children. But there are layers of complexity here. I
think the strong emotional charge behind this strange put-down has little to do
with political, practical or financial policies, and everything to do with the kind
of hidden feelings that can be revealed by looking at the astro-psychology of the
US (Sibly) chart.

Sun-Saturn Square

In the US (Sibly) chart, America's Cancer Sun and Libra Saturn square each
other.[1] This pits the country's essential purpose – feeding, sheltering and
protecting – against its notions of authority and government.

Whenever a square aspect remains un-integrated, the ambivalence may result in a
form of psychic projection. Those readers who have the Sun-Saturn square in
their own charts may have noticed this split: Saturn can manifest as a
disapproving and resistant force, an agency or person who comes down hard as a
champion of self-sufficiency.

---

[1] I look at this chart in detail in my book, *Soul-Sick Nation*, op. cit. p 30.

I propose that deep within the American group mind, there is a helpless child who can't support itself, a frail old person who can't get up, an invalid who needs help – from which the national Saturn struggles to distance itself as far away as it can.

This natal aspect helps us make sense of the "nanny state" epithet, which is being deployed as a tactic by (mostly affluent) politicians to rile up (mostly non-affluent) voters. Instead of being assured that each and every citizen deserves guaranteed compensations for their economic losses, angry voters are being cajoled to disdain the search for succor from government. Falling right into step with the propaganda, blue-collar Tea Bag folks seem to be identifying with unconscious Saturn (withholding) and Pluto (cruelty).

In an un-integrated Saturn square, one part of the self fears what another part represents; in this case, weakness and dependency.

Trauma Victims

The vulnerability theme is one of several themes the country is slated to go through during the Cardinal Cross years, between now and 2023. The financial theme is still big in the transit picture, with the US Venus (values, money) and the US Jupiter (beliefs, credit), targeted when Wall Street took a dive, once again in the cross hairs. Both material (Capricorn) and emotional (Cancer) security are huge issues right now, what with many Americans having been unemployed so long that they've given up looking for work; while, at the very same time, the thin social services that once protected them in hard times are being whittled away.

That square in the US (Sibly) chart is our tip-off about why Americans are so sensitive to the presence and absence of government-maintained support systems (Saturn in the 10th, Cancer Sun), and these Cardinal transits are making painfully clear how vulnerable these support networks are. The country is experiencing a Cancerian trauma.

More and more Americans are aware these days of what the very young, the very old, and the infirm are aware of all the time: that human beings need support. How chillingly predictable it is that cuts to childcare and education are the first to be made as the social order breaks down. And as the plutocratic forces continue their onslaught on the neediest segments of the population, we are seeing medical care for oldsters threatened in turn.

House Republicans want to get rid of Medicare, replacing it with vouchers that would decrease the help seniors get while swelling insurance industry profits. The irony, of course, is that if the USA were to extend Medicare instead of eliminating it, the quality of healthcare would go up, and the savings to the country would be immense.[2]

Safety First

Since 9/11/2001, the USA has seen an inordinate amount of focus on public safety as a propaganda device, with a corresponding decrease in public safety as a reality. The "Department of Homeland Security" (I cannot write this phrase without quotation marks; it still seems like something out of a wacky Orwellian parody) was born of fear. It wasn't born out of the motivation to provide genuine protection for anybody. This is the shadow side of America's Cancer Sun.

Anyone with Cancer strongly placed in their chart knows the vibrational difference between the creative side of Cancer and its reactive side. The former provides authentic protection in ways appropriate to context. The latter manipulates for its own purposes the human fear of being exposed to harm.

What would a highly functioning Cancer nation do, to offer genuine protection to its citizenry?

It might build a well-supervised system of regulatory agencies, to prevent harm to the public before it happens.

The cry for regulation arose in a big way in the USA when the Enron scandal broke, around the same time as the twin towers went down in late 2001. Pluto was conjunct the Ascendant of the US (Sibly) chart during this period; this was the beginning of the group soul's unmasking. It was the lack of regulation that allowed, first, Enron, and then, seven years later, the global financial disaster.

---

[2] Obama's proposal of summer 2011, to limit the amount seniors would receive for Medicare insurance, is less draconian but also fails to address the fact that rising medical costs have nothing to do with the federal program. They have to do with the unrestricted greed of Big Pharma and Big Insurance. In a profit-driven system, medical professionals make tons of money off unnecessary tests, drugs and procedures; but no incentives exist to keep people healthy. For example, it's estimated that 95% of back pain is best relieved by physical therapy, but there's no money in physical therapy, so American patients are given big fancy MRIs and surgery instead.

Positive Cancer

Regulations and safeguards are part of the web of protections that Cancerian nurturers weave around those they take care of. In Nature, these are instinctive, as when mother birds cover their babies' bodies with their wings.

In democratic nations, in theory, alert citizenries are supposed to elect representatives who make sure the government maintains and enforces such protections. Such as the kind of environmental regulations that would keep oil rigs from exploding in the ocean, preventing a disaster such as the BP Deepwater Horizon in April 2010.

How else might a well-functioning Cancerian native use its resources to protect those in its care? It might set up an agency to prevent pipeline blowouts in residential neighborhoods, of the kind that took place in San Bruno California.[3] And nuclear reactor meltdowns.

Profit Motive

What is keeping the USA from having such a system of regulation? Certainly not lack of technological know-how. The answer is summed up by this ugly fact that made its way out of the ghastly news from Japan in March: General Electric, the manufacturer of the Mark-1 boiling water reactors used in the devastated Fukushima Di-ichi plant, had marketed the reactor as being highly profitable because cheap to build.

Herein lies the key to the dysfunction of America's Cancer pattern. As we approach the national Pluto Return in the US second house of money, we see signs everywhere that the profit motive in this country has gotten a tad out of hand.

This is not to demonize businesses. It is just that, as human beings and citizens, we should not forget that businesses are set up to try to make as big a profit as they can. It is ridiculous to imagine that capitalistic enterprises should police themselves out of the kindness of their hearts.

If we want to be a democracy, we need to act like one. This means demanding

---

[3] The blast took place on 9/9/2010, with the Saturn-Uranus-Pluto square tipped off by Neptune (gas) on the Ascendant in late Aquarius.

that these agencies be set up for the good of the public. And it means speaking up for the members of that public who don't speak up for themselves. As a mother stands up for her very young children.

Gimme Shelter

It is a principle of group charts that individual souls intentionally incarnate into certain collectives in order to learn particular lessons in common. We Americans would not have incarnated here unless we wanted to get in touch with the Cancerian values of shelter, nurture, and protection.

It's only going to happen for the country when we get in touch with these values within ourselves.

Befriend the Month Ahead

(originally published in *Skywatch,*
August 2011)

I don't have to tell you, dear reader, that astrology is great for knowing which way the wind is blowing. Not just in our own individual life, but knowing the meaning of the storms we're all being buffeted by together right now, during this thrilling, surreal, crazy-making epoch. Our ancestors engaged with the world moment by watching the Moon.

The Moon is closer to us than any other celestial body, not only astronomically but in other ways as well. As planetary cycles go, the lunar cycle is a relatively accessible chunk of time to wrap our minds around. The emotional arc it symbolizes is short enough to relate to, psychologically. Sizing up the major transits of a given month is an easy way to stay astrologically organized. It helps us feel in synch with the cosmos.

So even if you do no other kind of transit tracking, try to keep tabs on the month to come. Once we've familiarized ourselves with the twists and turns of the upcoming four weeks, the future feels less daunting. The more we do it, the easier it becomes to get a sense of the nature of the period. The month starts to take on a distinct character. We can become its ally. We can *friend* it. When we do this, we'll be aligned with whatever chooses to happen on the event level.

It Starts with Noticing

The Cardinal Cross period as a whole (2008-23) is trying to sensitize us to the meaning of our role in the larger collective. A tension exists between our own individual sensibility and the immense force of the external world, generated by global events. Keep an eye out for this theme whenever a Cross-trigger (a quicker-moving planet, such as Mars, that comes along and provokes the Uranus-Pluto square) moves into position.

How do we keep abreast of what's happening in the greater world, without buying into denial? We already know the corporate media isn't going to tell us the truth. We can't expect the increasingly tabloid-like press to describe the new realities (we're now finding out, for instance, that some of the juiciest headlines in Murdoch's *News of the World* were simply made up, out of whole cloth.

And if we think we're going to get the New Earth mirrored back from our TV screens, we will wait in vain. There is something obscenely false about the way humanitarian crises are discussed on the news. The anchor people are given things to say that are so spiritually disconnected that, watching them perform, we are embarrassed for them. How are they supposed to find the right tone of voice with which to read two sentences' worth of statistics on the Somalian famine before cutting to a commercial?

We know it isn't in the interests of the corporate media to provoke compassion or understanding in its viewer-consumers. Quite the opposite: complexities are to be avoided at all costs. Thus the grotesque dissonance between form and content, as newsreaders are given a hairdo and a script and three minutes to address-without-really-addressing issues of staggering human pathos.

The conventional narrative broadcast by the corporate media does not model compassion or sanity.

Trauma and Backlash

If we want to disassociate from the conventional narrative, we first have to identify it.

Consider the epidemic human diasporas afflicting the globe right now. According to the U.N., forty-five million people were forced from their homes last year because of systems collapse, climate crises and war. Half of them are estimated to be women and children. Many are escaping from villages doomed by poverty.

Others are fleeing civil war, persecution, war, murder, rape, and mutilation. They are making their way to the relatively functional parts of the world that are closest to them, even if that means risking their lives hanging on to an overcrowded boat in the Sicilian sea, or allowing themselves to be stacked like sardines in a hidden compartment in a truck crossing the Mexican border.

On the rise as the Uranus-Pluto square nears exactitude: politicians like Gov. Brewer of Arizona, xenophobic groups like the EDL in England, and the nativists now making gains in Switzerland, France and Italy. Even an open, progressive society like Norway has now given us Anders Breivik, the young psychopath who explained his mass shootings on July 22, 2011 as an effort to market his anti-Islamic, anti-Marxist manifesto.

In a social climate of animosity and fear, we should take into account that language can be a form of unconscious collusion. The term "illegals," for example, deserves repudiation. What must be the effect on a person's human dignity, to be identified with the noun "illegal" when you've done nothing more untoward than exist in a place where people don't want you?

I have proposed that we dissociate from the narrative at an even earlier linguistic step, by recognizing the anachronism of the term *immigrants*. and calling these unfortunates what they consider themselves: refugees. Continuing to use the word "immigrant", with all its connotations of estrangement and suspicion, is one of the ways that people who aren't yet directly afflicted by the catastrophes of the postmillennial world are able to distance themselves from those who are.

It's a means of denying, for a bit longer, the reality that in the era we live in, instability is not the exception but the rule.

Our Brother's Keeper

We won't be able to keep up the pretense for much longer. Those of us living in the still-relatively-privileged parts of the world will find it harder and harder to distance ourselves from our struggling brethren.

Geopolitically, we are all connected in the experience of global suffering. Everywhere we look, we see the First World's own consumerism causing the Third World's anguish. Two examples among many: the drugs whose violent sales networks are destroying civilization in Latin America exist to satisfy demand up north, in the putatively civilized USA. And the endless wars in Central Africa that are fought over columbite, the mineral used to make cell phones for customers worldwide, destroy the lives of those in whose homeland it is mined.

To ignore these connections is to shut down a part of our consciousness. As the Cardinal Cross and Neptune in Pisces (2011-25) do their work, the perverse attempt on the part of one group of human beings to estrange themselves from their fellows will come to seem more and more arbitrary and grotesque.

CLASS WARFARE

(originally published in *Daykeeper
Journal,* August 2011)

Uranus in Aries (populist rebellion) and Pluto in Capricorn (breakdown of the social order) are off and running. The tension deriving from the square between them, ignited by the involvement of Aries planets every spring since 2008, has exploded worldwide in sporadic dissent in places like Saudi Arabia and Iran to out-and-out revolution in Tunisia and Egypt.

For several years astrologers have been anticipating the Uranus-Pluto transit's impact on the US (Sibly) chart, into which its geometry fits like a hand into a glove. Uncle Sam is a marked man. So it makes you wonder why the USA has not experienced martial conflict against its own governing regime, such as is going on in town squares and villages elsewhere in the world.

Mars is T-squaring the longest arm of the Cross this month, and astrologers are keeping a close eye on the global hot spots. One of these is the USA, which is in the middle of its natal Mars Return (action, anger). These transits suggest demonstrative rage.

In the newspaper this morning, I read that the California state university system – which was once the jewel in the our crown, fulfilling the promise of excellent, free education for all – just held a meeting at which they raised the fees for a second time this year, over the objections of desperate students who are already drowning in debt. At this same meeting, the regents gave large pay raises to executives who are paid from state funds.

I know I am not the only one asking: Where is the outrage?

The planetary picture is one of an explosion (Uranus) of mass anger (Mars) at the wildly disproportionate way America distributes its ample resources (Pluto). Yet we have seen the signs of no mass movement here. With Americans broke, angry and ripped off, and the transit acting like a bellows to the flame, we might well ask: Why isn't everybody in the streets? *[Editor's Note: Six weeks later, Occupy Wall Street convened in New York.]*

Mind Control

One feature the existence of the American media, an immensely sophisticated and far-reaching enterprise which serves as an arm of the country's controlling interests. The US (Sibly) chart's Mercury (opinion) is opposite Pluto (power) in the two money houses (second and eighth). When we see these two planets opposed in an individual's chart, we allow for the possibility of mind control.

Consider the way the mainstream news has co-opted the phrase "class warfare." By appropriating these highly charged words, and by dulling their significance with repetition and insincerity, the pundits and politicians have done a pretty good job of distracting the US public from noticing what could be an otherwise very dangerous thing to notice: that a war between the classes is exactly what's already going on.

It is not a class war with guns and tanks,[1] but in every other way it's a class war. In a country where almost a quarter of the total income generated goes to the top 1% of its citizens, would it be that surprising to see a military war break out between the haves and the have-nots?

Income Inequality

Notice that the phrase "class warfare" tends to come up whenever the Democrats trot out their halfhearted proposals to tax the rich.[2] At this point, a righteous Republican will hurl forth his salvo, accusing the Democrat of waging CW.

Clearly we're supposed to infer that the phrase means something bad. But why is the charge implicitly a slur? After all, it is supposed to express the fact that one class (let's call it "most of us") is taking umbrage at the fact that the other class (let's call it "the very wealthiest") is hogging all the wealth and power. How is that so out of line?

---

[1] Not yet, anyway. But it is no wonder that the powers-that-be are so nervous these days. With their fevered leak prosecutions (Obama has targeted whistleblowers more aggressively than any previous president), their extravagant "Homeland Security" and TSA departments and their ever-expanding surveillance network, the American government is taking no chances of having its large, unwieldy populace become disaffected to the point of armed rebellion.

[2] That is, to tax them a token amount. Not tax them so much that the Democrat's own net worth is threatened, or that of his corporate sponsors, but just enough so the Democrat can go on record as having made the proposal.

Even just a few years ago, you didn't often hear the phrase "income inequality." But now that the USA is in its Saturn Return, in Libra—the sign of the equality/ inequality spectrum—we hear it everywhere. Saturn's placement in the US (Sibly) chart (natally square the Sun: ouch) indicates that the issue it represents is the country's Achilles heel. We are very touchy about living up to our Libran ideals of fairness and equality. As a nation, we make big, bold claims to being the world's greatest democracy. But the facts don't hold up to the ideal. They don't even come close.

What's it Worth?

This summer 2011, Pluto is again opposed to the US (Sibly) Jupiter, going retrograde. During August it will move onto the midpoint between America's Jupiter (social class) and Venus (money); while Uranus (popular unrest) exactly squares that midpoint, moving retrograde.

Since this transit cycle began, Americans have been experiencing a breakdown of their sense of what things are worth. The value of their work, their houses, their possessions and aspirations has been grotesquely distorted-and so has the American self-image with which that value has been identified.

Have you ever asked yourself: What would happen if CEOs made – oh, I don't know – let's say *only fifty* times more than their workers make – instead of *500 times* as much, as they do now? That would still be an awful lot more. They'd still be, you know, very rich. And without all that locked-up private wealth, employment and commerce would rise. The whole economy would be healthier.

Musing about questions like this leads us to wonder whether maybe class warfare, rather than being what the Democrats are doing when they try to tax the rich, is what bailed-out banks are doing, when they buy government bonds instead of making loans. Or what Microsoft is doing, when they take government funds given to them to create jobs, and instead invest it for themselves. (Later, we may see Bill and Melinda Gates at a charity ball, fulsomely praised by beaming NGO staffers for their selfless philanthropy. Classy!)

High Praise

I suspect the reason the Republicans get any traction at all from crying "class warfare" is *not* because of the "warfare" part of the phrase. American popular culture thrives on violence. No, I think it's the word "class" that sends the shivers up people's spines, in both Congress and the listening audience. There's a word scary enough to shut up the liberals.

This is because "class" is something the USA is not supposed to have. If you think we have it, you must be a socialist... which is code, in this same belief system, for *traitor*. Carrying the linguistic analysis one step further, we might find that, for some Americans, the word *traitor* has a charge not dissimilar to the word *Devil*, judging by the intensely virulent, emotional energy with which it is deployed in partisan debate.

Of course, all of these fraught insults crumble into nothingness if you don't believe in the assumptions they're based on. If you don't believe in the Devil, then being likened to Mephistopheles will not have the same sting as it would for a fundamentalist Christian. If you don't believe in nationalism, then being accused of treachery to your nation will not strike you as a fate-worse-than-death.

And if you don't believe that it's shameful to call out class injustice in a society where only 32% of groups paying for election ads are disclosing the names of their donors,[3] and where the state and local taxes of the middle class are rising while their services are being cut, their teachers and firefighters are being laid off, their roads and bridges are crumbling and their libraries and parks are shutting down... at the same time that the marginal income tax rate on the very rich is the lowest it's been in more than eighty years,[4] then being called a "class warrior" is not going to sound like a put-down.

On the contrary, it might feel like high praise.

---

[3] Thanks to the Supreme Court's *Citizen's United* decision, which essentially made it legal for big business to bribe legislators with as much cash as they wanted.

[4] Today the marginal income tax rate is 36%; under President Eisenhower it was 91%. Would today's GOP blowhards call good ol' Ike a "class warrior"?

Mad as a Hatter

(originally published as a blog,
August 2011)

This August 2011, Pluto is slowing down for its station opposed to the midpoint of the US Venus and Jupiter, and the rot at the core of the American system is blossoming in the summer heat. The nation's values (Venus) are being stripped raw. A twisted morality (Jupiter) is being exposed.

As individuals, we can't afford to lose our minds amidst the madness, nor lose sight of our own moral compass. To stay engaged yet sane and humane, we must observe collective psychopathy while keeping a distance from it. One way to do this is to see current events as myths, being played out right in front of our eyes.

Art mirrors life, and life mirrors art. Watching our world happen as if it were a story being told, we learn from the symbols couched in events-just as we do when we take in the truths of a parable or legend. In the news headlines, we find themes from great works of fiction; such as Lewis Carroll's enduring parody Through the Looking Glass, written 130 years ago without ever going out of print.

Crackpots

Many political cartoonists have made hay out of the fact that the current Tea Party movement bears the same name as the fictional shindig in Wonderland. As America's cultural landscape gets more and more grotesque, more and more parallels are appearing between Carroll's fictional characters and our own real-time crackpots.

We've got candidates like Mitt Romney, whose changes of position mirror the way the Mad Hatter and the March Hare arbitrarily jump up and switch places around the tea table. We've got Fox News bullies verbally abusing their opponents in the same way the Hatter insults Alice with "over-personal remarks."

We've got empty-headed blowhards like Rick Perry, whose challenges to Obama mirror the Hatter's unanswerable riddles – to which he does not have an answer himself. We've got demagogues like Sarah Palin who, when challenged, can only stonewall with mean-spirited sarcasm - just as the Hatter mocks Alice when she asks him a commonsense question.

In the story, you will recall, this behavior eventually drove Alice away. Will the American public, too, finally get sick of the insanity, and get up and leave the table?

Duopoly

A first step in doing so would be refusing to buy into the jerry-rigged duopoly that drives American politics. All Americans know, on some level of consciousness, that no social change can come of the farcically hyped-up contests between the two major parties, both choreographed by the same cabals. It is understood that the system is set up to silence any contenders outside of a few handpicked Tweedledums and Tweedledees.

During a recent debate about the country's tailspin into financial chaos, it was interesting to see outsider Ron Paul play the role of Alice. He was the only speaker who mentioned military spending, and he was met with eye-rolling dismissal by the other Republicans. They actually smirked when he proposed reconsidering the wisdom of the wars in Iraq, Afghanistan and Pakistan – which a new Brown University report says could end up costing $4.4 trillion.

Let's write that in numerals: $4,400,000,000,000.

When Mars slammed into the Cardinal Cross and ignited the US (Sibly) chart in early August 2011, Democrats and Republicans approved their much-touted "compromise" which, while cutting services for the unemployed, the poor, the elderly and schoolchildren, leaves tax breaks for the very wealthy intact and the war budget untouched.

Dark Laugh

The USA's penchant for stupefyingly selfish leaders and fatally ignorant citizens will only get more absurd as the Uranus-Pluto square plays itself out. During its peak years (2012-15), the corruptions of America's political and financial institutions will be laid bare for all to see. It's essential that we avoid outrage fatigue. Anger and incredulity can take us only so far. It's time to ground ourselves in the larger meaning of cultural breakdown.

Sky watchers achieve this perspective by isolating the cosmic lessons encoded in astrological archetypes. Another way is to track what's happening through the lens of apposite fiction and myth.

We may find it not only appropriate, but healing, to respond with a dark Carrollian laugh to these latest incarnations of Wonderland lunatics.

Got to Serve Somebody

(originally published in *Skywatch*,
September 2011)

Both Virgo and Pisces are misunderstood signs. Every time the sky hosts an opposition between them (for example, twice a year when the Sun passes through these signs and the Moon is full) we have a chance to get underneath their reputation from being difficult, and benefit from their deeper meanings. It isn't that Pisces and Virgo are inherently any more problematic than any other zodiacal pair; it's that our society doesn't value the impulses they represent – impulses which we are brought up to believe will steer us in the wrong direction.

Both these signs minimize the ego. Neither buys into society's messages about success, messages that tell us to focus exclusively on Numero Uno, and that we're undermining ourselves unless we do. Neither Virgo nor Pisces prioritizes individual aggrandizement over collective good. Their special genius is to pinpoint flaw (Virgo) and acknowledge suffering (Pisces), both of which prompt acts of service.

It is a shame that such urges are given short shrift in the modern world, where empathic communion with our fellows and the ability to do humble, diligent work, are, at best, dismissed – and at worst, disdained.

Natural Instinct

During the tenure of Neptune in Pisces (2011-25) we'll get a series of Virgo-Pisces oppositions annually in late summer. Neptune – and, until 2019, Chiron too – will be opposed by the Sun and the bodies orbiting closest to it, which will be passing through Virgo. This polarity is an invitation to reflect upon our attitudes towards service (Virgo) and compassion (Pisces). What are we to do with our instincts to help and to empathize, in a culture that failed to encourage these qualities in us when we were growing up, and fails to respect them now?

This is what we do: we gently distance ourselves from the limitations of our upbringing, and look around, with clear eyes, at what's really happening.

Unmitigated by cultural nonsense and groupthink, the here-and-now itself will rouse our true natures to respond appropriately. First tentatively, then enthusiastically, our inborn resources will rise to the fore. They've been waiting with bated breath for an invitation to do their part.

The healthiest kind of self-critique (Virgo) under this opposition begins by retiring our old stories. This is the first step in making ourselves available to the era we inhabit. The fact that ours is an era replete with immense and ubiquitous crises is not random. The cosmic plan has provided opportunities galore for us to explore our capacity for helpfulness and empathy.

But there is a step even before this. In order to distance ourselves from obsolete cultural pictures, we have to know what they are. To be of use during the Cardinal Cross years, we have to root them out. Even the most independent-minded of us has absorbed any number of collective fantasies over the course of being socialized into our tribe. To pierce through these stories and become fully functional, we need to ask ourselves: Do the ideas in our heads about what's "normal" compare with what's really going on?

It's ironic that this is harder to do for those of us in the still-somewhat-operational First World, where food and clean water are available and our nights are uninterrupted by missile-firing drones. The down side of a non-life-threatening lifestyle is that anachronistic mass assumptions seem to stick around longer.

What's Normal?

One of these is the assumption that, sooner or later, the economic conditions of the 1950s will come back, and that life will settle into a Leave-it-to-Beaver or Brady-Bunch-style "normalcy." (It says a lot that we have to go back a couple of generations in order to find an exemplary sitcom that portrays a dumb, happy nuclear family: the kind that represents *ür*-normalcy to many nostalgic Americans. As exemplars of domestic normalcy, Ozzie and Harriet have been replaced by dark, dysfunctional clans [e.g., "The Riches," "Arrested Development"]. Even more revealing, of course, is the fact that we have to turn to television to find them, rather than to factual reality).

In other essays we have considered the fact that those of us who live in the relatively functional regions of the world are going to be less and less able to isolate ourselves from the disasters that are rocking other regions.[1] Americans,

---

[1] In 2011, some 1,500 people, including women and children, drowned in the Mediterranean Sea

especially, a notoriously insular tribe, seem to be shrouding themselves in the belief that the post-WWII years of booming industry and unquestioned consumerism represent base-line reality. According to this worldview, today's economic, military and meteorological crises are merely temporary aberrations.

But it is increasingly difficult to find a spot on the planet to which Brady Bunch "normalcy" bears any resemblance. Included in this shrinking pool we might still count patches of the USA and Western Europe – and even in these patches, the pool is shrinking month by month – and isolated pockets of stability such as Singapore. Just about everywhere else, things are in a state of emergency: either in an out-and-out systems collapse, as is true in the narco-economies of Latin America; in continuous war, as in Iraq and Afghanistan; or in dire privation, as in drought-stricken Ethiopia. Most of these stricken countries are struggling with multiple catastrophes at once: right now almost every African state is in a state of crisis that is chronic, acute, or both.[2]

Humanity and Inhumanity

As the old ways devolve, we are seeing the inevitable rise of reactionaries such as the American Minuteman movement and the English Defence League. These groups are testaments to the fact that the word *reactionary* does not mean merely "extremely conservative." It describes a state of reaction – as opposed to one of response – driven by fear and resulting in overcompensation.

A reactionary tries to push away and repudiate the source of his phobia. The postmillennial specimen of this breed is motivated by a dread that the world's calamities will spread to his own home town, like a plague virus. Thus the cruelty shown to the sea-tossed asylum-seekers who approach the shores of Australia and Italy seeking safe quarter, only to be turned away.

Inhumanities like these vie with expressions of humanity everywhere we look. The choice to identify with either one or the other confronts us every day. We are constantly being asked to choose: this is the meaning of the crossroads in esoteric thought, and of the geometrical cross in astrology. If we believe that the purpose of life is to learn, then our goal is to choose the humane way. If the world's chaos is a phase in a great collective growth arc, our goal must be to keep our sights trained upon where the evolutionary trajectory is leading.

---

trying to reach Europe.

[2] Crises in Afghanistan, Libya, Sudan, Somalia and elsewhere drove 800,000 people to flee their countries in 2011.

In the case of the Virgo-Pisces axis, the consciousness shift has to do with deepening our response to the suffering among us. The efforts of the reactionaries – those desperately trying to dis-identify from the masses – is becoming increasingly far-fetched, awkward and implausible.

The realization will come to every one of us sooner or later, no matter how many lifetimes it takes. Victims of catastrophe are not Others, but alternate versions of ourselves.

Dreams Only Money Can Buy

(originally published in *Daykeeper
Journal,* September 2011

Intense transits make it easy for us cultural observers. They make appalling trends impossible to miss.

Pluto, which intensifies everything it touches, has been opposing US (Sibly) chart's Venus–Jupiter conjunction since 2008; Sept 2011 is this transit's last hurrah. Pluto moves at a snail's pace, but triggers changes more radical than any other planet. Its approaching square with Uranus is zeroing in on America's values. The national psyche is being forced to ask itself, "What do we believe in?"

The American public is undergoing not just a credit crisis (Venus) but a credibility crisis (Jupiter). With Pluto and Uranus hammering away at the Sibly's Cancer cluster (security), all the malarkey being spun from the highest echelons of power is coming up against the credulity of an increasingly hard-pressed populace.

Doublespeak

Fox News came out with a new double-speak campaign this summer, 2011. Suddenly "rich people" were "job creators." It was the kind of ham-fisted propaganda that seems doomed to backfire. After all, most of Fox's viewers are pretty clearly from the *non*-"job creator" classes; that is, middle class and blue-collar Americans – groups that are having a rough time of it right now.

I wonder what goes through the minds of, for example, former GM workers in the audience, as they listen to Megan Kelly intoning the new euphemism. These folks' life savings are disappearing as their houses decline in value, and their last-resort social-services safety nets are being cut to ribbons as federal money disappears. Indeed, their hardships probably started when the "job creators" shipped their jobs overseas.

Pluto (breakdown) and Uranus (explosion) have their first of seven exact hits in June of 2012. When combined with the Sibly's natal Sun-Saturn square, the four planets form a full Grand Cross. The three main expressions of the Cross in US society are:

– the growing income gap;[1]
– the reduction of jobs, services and savings of middleclass and working people; and
– the record amount of secret money flooding into elections[2] and lawmaking,[3] undermining what everyone insists is a democracy.

It's hard to imagine the con game continuing at this volatile a level for very much longer. There is a predictable arc to the putrefaction process (governed by Pluto), whether we're talking about the decay of a corpse or the devolution of a society. The symptoms become more obvious as the breakdown progresses. The smell gets noticeably worse.

Mass Neurosis

To deny is a human defense mechanism. We lapse into denial when something is so wrong and absurd we cannot assimilate it. It pains us to let it in (hence the phrase "painfully obvious.") But there are ways to stand back from the situation at hand, far enough back to see a whole society as just one more life form, one that goes through the same kind of creation and decomposition process that any other entity goes through. From this perspective, we start to see that it is not the toxicity of the situation that causes pain. It is our denial of the toxicity that causes pain.

If a psychiatrist saw her patient exhibiting self-harming behavior, she would identify it as an illness. She would interpret wildly displaced anger the same way.

---

[1] Income inequality, as measured by the Gini Coefficient (sociologist Corrado Gini's measure of statistical dispersion), is reaching the same extremes as in the Roaring Twenties, just before the Depression. Our grandparents, too, saw subprime debt built up as an attempt to buy off the poor. Easy credit has been used throughout history as a palliative by governments that are unable to address the deeper anxieties of the non-wealthy.

[2] The epitomical example of this trend is the 2010 *Citizens United* ruling by the Supreme Court, that disallowed any restrictions at all to be put on the amount of money corporations could funnel into US elections.

[3] *The San Francisco Chronicle* reported that 2/3 of the US senators drafting new financial regulations hold stock in banks of other companies affected by the legislation.

So what does it mean when a whole group of people, thrown into poverty because of the decisions of corporations, allows their government to give away billions of dollars to those same corporations; who then turn around and use the money to reward their own top-tier managers with billion-dollar bonuses?

We are in denial if we imagine that the American system can be turned around via cosmetic changes. Until the national conversation moves below the surface, we will just become a more frenzied and neurotic population, displacing our rage upon ourselves through self-harming mechanisms like addiction and obesity.[4] Or upon our peers, with gun violence,[5] or with the kind of emotional violence that is exemplified in tabloid scape goating (consider the over-the-top hatred that was aimed over the summer of 2011 at the domestic villain *du jour*, Casey Anthony, who was widely believed to have murdered her daughter).

If Uranus, Saturn and Pluto have anything to tell us right now, it is this: societies that cannot reform themselves must break apart. Without being admitted and reversed, the corruptions of American society will end up in systems collapse, along the lines of what is happening in Africa and Asia. Andrew Palmer, an observer of African economies, sees Somalia, now spinning out of control with anarchy and famine, as the USA's canary in the mine.

As distressing as these scenarios are, astrologically speaking they are simply demonstrations of Natural Law. Denying them inhibits our ability to be useful to the collective and to ourselves.

American Dream

When Pluto is active, it doesn't make sense to get all shocked and appalled at the sight of breakdown. We expect breakdown. When Pluto is in the second house, as it is in the US (Sibly) chart, we expect breakdown to express itself financially.

---

[4] What does poverty mean in a society where so many poor citizens are obese? There is a reluctance to talk about this lamentable correlation; one risks coming off as callous, or worse. But I don't think we should allow a fear of being accused of blaming-the-victim to keep us from noticing a grotesquely obvious modern phenomenon.

[5] The rise in American militia groups—posses of just-plain-folks packing M16 assault rifles and M60 machine guns—is a dangerous example of displaced rage. Styling themselves as guerrilla warriors defending their constitutional rights, these trigger-happy citizens are mostly financially disadvantaged Americans who have been betrayed by the new global economy.

And with the US Jupiter in Pluto's crosshairs, it is not just the economy that is at stake. Jupiter in a national chart represents our collective morality. Before the national soul can experience rebirth, it must subject its obsolete values to a mercilessly honest reappraisal, and start over from scratch in the ethics department.

This does not mean returning to the American Dream of borrowing against imaginary equity to finance reckless consumerism. As the Cardinal Cross morphs into the US Pluto Return, the karma of materialism will be everywhere apparent. It is no longer going to be possible to exist on dreams that only money can buy.

Patriots for Truth

(originally published as a blog,
September 2011)

On this tenth anniversary of you-know-what, I don't want to write about 9/11. I've written before about the explosive transits of that day, as have many other astrologers,[1] and about the implausibility of Washington's account of what happened. It was the first Big Lie of the 21st century, and has amassed so much refutation that a cultural movement has arisen to hold it.[2] What I want to look at now is the nationalistic energy that dominates the public conversation every September since 2001, the emotive form of which is a strangely compulsive patriotism.

There was a lot of verbal tribute being paid today, 9/11/11, about those who died in New York ten years ago. Even the comics in the Sunday paper gave it a mention. Some strips featured the characters taking off their hats. Some showed family members embracing each other.

I appreciate the solemnity in the air. It's a rare thing to witness America slowing down and taking off its collective hat, in a mass ritual rooted in unselfishness. It's something to savor. You can sense people making the effort to recapture that brief, transcendent moment a decade ago, when a magic blend of grief and shock forced the US populace into its collective heart. Our tormented, secular society was provided with an opportunity to reach something like spiritual communion.

As an astrologer, I credit the importance of a person living in a certain place. Like all other points of karma, the fact that we identify with one nation and not another is anything but random. But where the 9/11 mourners lose me is the definitive distinction they seem to draw between the tragic significance of their own countrymen dying and that of people in other countries dying. I hear about the three thousand Americans killed in New York that day and I think: Far more

---

[1] See especially Richard Tarnas, PhD, "An Astrological Perspective on the World Trade Center Attack" in the archives at stariq.com.

[2] One of the best known of these is 911Truth.org.

258

than three thousand civilians have been killed in Iraq. And in Afghanistan, by Pentagon drones; right now, this week. And I think: There is a famine spreading through Somalia that is killing a hundred children per day.

Experience tells me that pointing this out is all but universally unwelcome, especially around September 11th. This is understandable. It is always grotesque to compare one atrocity with another. It is unseemly to respond with anything other than respect to people who are in the throes of genuine grief, as so many Americans are in this month of remembrance.

Founding Fathers

The founding fathers are mentioned a lot these days. Their ghosts seem to loom over this anniversary. I interpret their ideas quite differently from the way my neighbor in the Tea Party does, but we both see these 18th-century gentlemen as being central to any discussion of American patriotism.

When I read the political writings of Thomas Jefferson and John Adams, I am amazed, every time, by the prophetic quality of their vision. They could not have imagined body scanners at modern airports, or the prospect of having their data mined by Facebook; but they could and did imagine the general tendency of governments to use fear to curtail a citizen's freedoms, and they didn't like that at all. Benjamin Franklin and Tom Paine clearly foresaw the danger it would pose to a democratic republic if citizens were forbidden to criticize their leaders. They passionately denounced the practice of one citizen calling another "traitor" for questioning official pronouncements.

Among us today are the postmillennial equivalents of those bold gents: Prof. Judy Wood,[3] for example, and the members of Architects & Engineers for 9/11 Truth (see RememberBuilding7.org).

With profound respect for the importance of this milestone in American history, I too salute those souls who incarnated into this landmass with me during this critical era, for these first decades of this century are the moment of truth for America. I also salute those souls who died ten years ago under mysterious circumstances. And I take my hat off to those patriots who show up for the task of uncovering what really happened.

---

[3] See "Where Did the Towers Go?" on drjudywood.com.

Seeing in the Dark

(originally published in *Skywatch*,
October 2011)

A time of Dark Mysteries, Scorpio has a strong seasonal character. It is governed by the planet Pluto, governor of taboos and secrets. Halloween, or Samhain (pronounced *SOW-en*) in Wicca, is our annual celebration of the human desire to know forbidden things.

Pluto, god of darkness, is in his glory, inviting each of us to take on unsavory material. We're being asked to confront charged issues in order to transform them through the light of consciousness. In our personal lives, psychologically difficult matters are nag at us. We are being dared to dig beneath the surface of the very things we least want to look at.

The Unspoken

On a collective level, the Pluto corner of the Cardinal Cross is calling our attention to secrets hidden in plain sight. What are the key taboos of our day? What are the biggest issues given the least discussion?

I think we'd have to say that, for Americans, a big contender for the prize is the money the nation is shoveling into the death pit of war. To call it ironic that this much money is being spent in this particular way,[1] when the country's gargantuan debt is causing all hell to break loose, is an understatement. It feels insufficient to describe as counterintuitive the fact that while entire states are going belly-up, the Pentagon budget is rising.

The outrageousness of the situation is so extreme that normal logic doesn't suffice to explain it. But Plutonian logic does.

---

[1] According to the Watson Institute of International Studies at Brown University in June 2011, $4 trillion and counting has been spent in Iraq and Afghanistan.

The clue that Pluto is afoot is the lack of discussion. The disparity that exists here between the degree of America's financial investment in war and the paucity of public debate about it is so striking as to suggest inverse proportion. This is a defining feature of Pluto. It is the governor of any issue that dares not speak its name.

The Dark Continent

"Do you think they'd be bombing the place if its main export was broccoli?"
–Kevin Danaher of Global Exchange, in March 2003, just before the Pentagon's assault on Baghdad.

The latest place to make the Pentagon list is Africa, once dubbed The Dark Continent by the great empires of the West. The true darkness here is that of ignorance and unconsciousness, on the part of those non-Africans who have been raping and pillaging Africa for hundreds of years.

England, France, Italy and the USA conducted more than eight thousand bombing attacks on Libya between March and September 2011. Were the good citizens of these countries to reflect upon the fact that Libya possesses the largest oil reserves in all of Africa, it would probably not take long for a substantial number of them to connect the dots and discern a pattern.

Oil is obviously the engine behind NATO's involvement. But to call it "obvious" needs qualification. The geo-military role of oil is obvious only in the Plutonian sense: hidden in plain sight. It is taboo for governments and their media arms to mention it. It is utterly left out of the official accounts. My belief is that in the absence of propaganda to the contrary, everyone would see as clear as day that the Great Powers – as these NATO governments used to call themselves – have laid waste to any sovereign government unlucky enough to have the sticky black stuff beneath its soil.[2]

Kill the Bad Guy

But among a media-hypnotized populace, the fantasy prevails that the evilness of a given foreign leader constitutes an open invitation to swoop in and bomb his country to smithereens.

---

[2] An article in the 8/22/11 *New York Times* business section made no bones about it: "Colonel Qaddafi proved to be a problematic partner for the international oil companies, frequently raising fees and taxes and making other demands. A new government with close ties to NATO may be an easier partner for Western nations to deal with."

Not all evil foreign leaders, mind you. Not those of, say, Saudi Arabia, one of the most brutal oligarchies on Earth. This is a place where a king's promise to grant women the right to vote (though not right away: three years from now) is being lauded as an enormous step forward; where courts can sentence a woman caught driving a car to be publicly whipped; and where any hint of dissent is met with imprisonment, torture and execution. The reason the Great Democracies of the World don't touch a hair on the head of this despicable regime is clear to all. We have been granted petro-privileges.

But the Let's-kill-the-bad-guy scenario is sexier, and it has so seized the public imagination that there seems to be no brain space left over to consider anything else. Such as the implications of the fact that Libya's "rebel fighters" have been directed by NATO's own ground forces and commando units.

Americans like their morality neat. They like their foreign policy presented to them in no-frills, good-vs.-evil terms, just as they remember from Sunday school and children's cartoons. It is a story line designed to streamline complex ideas for ingestion by juveniles. In its simplicity, it presumes the absence of any more complicated intellectual function.

Tyrants and Their People

One of the most insidious features of the kill-the-bad-guy approach to warfare is that it blurs any distinction between a dictator and his populace. By limiting their focus to Gaddafi as an individual, Americans have been able to ignore the effect upon Libya's citizenry of all those US Tomahawks and nuclear submarines.

What else do we miss, by framing the military assault upon Libya as a noble, tyrant-eliminating crusade? We blind ourselves to the lessons of history. With all the emphasis on Gaddafi's wickedness, geopolitical context goes out the window. The citizens of the NATO countries – after all, it is we who are financing the slaughter – are prevented from seeing the campaign as one more example of straight-up colonialism.

This assault on Libya is just the latest salvo in what was called in Victorian times "the scramble for Africa," a series of invasions perpetrated by the same Western powers. Indeed, Gaddafi rose to power 42 years ago on the wave of the Libyan people's backlash against domination by Italy.

X-Ray Vision

It could be argued that the very reason for the darkness of this era on Earth is to force truth-seekers to learn to see in the dark. Many souls are meeting these transits' challenge right now, piercing through the ambient noise of cultural corruption and social nonsense with a bold (Uranus) X-ray vision (Pluto).

We do so by asking questions.

Such as, in this case: From what set of assumptions does the notion derive that because Muammar Gaddafi is bad, destroying the country he rules must be good? As to whether such assumptions have been proven valid by global events, we need only remember that this Libya story uses the same argument that was deployed by the same Pentagon cabal eight years ago. Remember when all objections to the USA bombing of Baghdad were countered by the non-sequitur about Saddam Hussein being a torturing brute?

We might further ask ourselves: Does a familiarity with military history suggest that war is a good idea, or that warmongers are friends of the human race?

By asking common-sense questions, it is possible to stay engaged yet unscathed by the violence and mendacity of these intense times, even to be inspired by them. It is possible to use the perversions of mass thinking as a grindstone, against which to hone our own independent thinking sharper than it has ever been.

It is possible to see clearly, whether or not the Sun is out.

Sharing the Dark Crown

(originally published in *Daykeeper*
Journal, October 2011)

With Uranus squaring Pluto in the sky, it strikes me as a good time to propose an update to an old astrological maxim. In the name of Uranus (challenges to tradition), I suggest we re-think the traditional planetary rulership of oil.

Astrological textbooks associate oil with the planet Neptune, governor of lubricants. But recent developments in global history are mirroring back to us a distinct meaning shift as regards this ancient black goop.

Black Gold

Since the advent of the Industrial Age,[1] the archetype of oil has become darker, more dangerous, more compulsive – in a word, more Plutonian. I propose we extend oil's governance from Neptune alone to a joint rulership with Pluto. Let them share the crown.

The designation of Neptune as a sole ruler ignores one of the most definitive and evocative of oil's characteristics: that the stuff is dug up from underground. It is Pluto that governs underground riches,[2] such as precious jewels, minerals and ores. In the collective imagination, oil has for the past several decades replaced spice, gold, silver[3] and gems as the premier symbol of global value.

Oil has nudged aside traditional valuables not merely in terms of financial worth. It is the new top signifier in iconic terms, too, as evidenced by one of its nicknames: black gold.

Identified by many astrologers with the Neptune-Uranus conjunction of 1820.

Pluto (his Roman name; the Greeks called him Hades) was the god who presided over minerals and jewels from subterranean mines. On a psycho-spiritual level, this hidden world of invisible wealth is symbolizes the valuable energies we keep sequestered away deep within our beings.

Gold has been traditionally linked with the Sun, silver with the Moon.

Oil Fever

Moreover, there are deeper and more troubling reasons to attribute Plutonian rulership to this singular liquid that greases the wheels of the industrialized world.

It is not for its use value alone that countries want oil, any more than it is for practical reasons that people have always coveted gold. Consider the role of "gold fever" in political history, myth and literature. The extremism with which these resources are desired slips easily into pathology, with fatal consequences. I would argue that a Plutonian resource is one that has acquired connotations of death and destruction.

The colonial adventures of the old European empires were motivated first by spice; later by gold and silver, sugar, tobacco, slaves and diamonds; then by natural gas and oil. In the 19th century, the USA took over as global superpower, riding high on the wave of the Industrial Age, whose complexly interconnected systems of manufacture, infrastructure, transportation and distribution depend – with absolute singularity – upon this one product (muck from the decayed corpses of long-since-extinct creatures. Doesn't the whole thing sound kind of science-fictional?) In fact, as we are only now starting to realize - some with dread, others with jubilation – the industrial model of societal organization would die overnight without oil.

The US (Sibly) chart features Pluto in the 2nd house, which indicates an obsession with control over whatever resource is deemed the most valuable in any given epoch. A cursory glance at recent American foreign policy bears this out. Washington has used its military might to sate its desire for oil wherever in the world it is to be found.

Kill the Tyrant

As I write these words, October 2011, the USA is in a new war. According to what we hear on TV, Uncle Sam is saving another country from another villainous dictator. We are being told that this is why all those F-16 bombers have been tearing up the people, buildings and landscape of Libya. I would argue that this story, now being met with childlike credulity by even the most well-informed and best-intentioned Americans, would be met by a healthy skepticism were it not for its incessant repetition in the media. It would simply have no legs.

In the US (Sibly) chart, Mercury (information) opposes Pluto (absolute control), giving rise to a mass media so powerful that it can transform otherwise life-affirming human beings into lemmings to the battlefield. It was ten years ago, three months after 9/11/01, that the White House conceived of attacking Iraq. Messrs. Cheney, Wolfowitz, Feith et al used the media to convince the US public to go along with their plan by explaining that, as the world's self-delegated good guys, we needed to eliminate the vile Saddam. The same propaganda gambit, of course, is being used right now.

It's been a sobering ten years, however. The American public found out that the rationales behind the Iraq war were lies, that the short military "cakewalk" they were promised turned out to be anything but, and that the war had become very, very expensive.

Expensive Wars

Appealing to collective psychology to guess the public's thinking about Libya, we might expect that the expense factor would rankle quite a bit. After all, for everyone except a tiny fraction of the US population, the recession is getting worse. The unemployment rate is the highest since 1948, and most Americans are barely scraping by. Human nature being what it is, many are grabbing at straws for someone or something to blame. The Tea Party crowd is reacting with hair-trigger outrage to any federal expenditure that could be vaguely construed as a waste of money.

So it might seem logical to expect that the reactionary pundits on mainstream TV and radio, notorious for pouring gasoline on the flames of popular anger, would be champing at the bit to talk about the hundred million dollars (so far) that the Pentagon has spent bombing Libya.

But this is not the case. The news channels play the songs their funders give them, and questioning the wisdom of the Defense Department budget is not in the lyrics.

Here Comes the Cavalry

Neither is providing the complete story behind the 7,459 bombing attacks[4] that have descended upon Libya since the autumnal equinox. The American media's portrayal of the anti-Gaddafi troops as disaffected citizens stops short of explaining under whose control they are fighting.

---

[4] As of this writing, at the Full Moon in September 2011.

In fact, as in every other place in the world where global powerbrokers want a regime changed, the insurrection is under the direction of Western commanders and led by Western commando units. These are the "advisers" that are occasionally referred to in media coverage; but they have been dispensing more than advice. First they froze and seized Libya's assets in Western banks; then they started handing out shiny new weapons and billions in financial aid.

Leaving this information out of the Libya story is a strategic decision on the part of the powers-that-be. Instead of giving the public the full picture, the commentary from all along the political spectrum plays up the simplistic narrative that led many Americans to approve the bombing of Baghdad ten years ago. Nothing sells like the old America-as-noble-avenger myth.

With Sagittarius rising and Jupiter conjunct the Sun in their national chart, Americans would like to believe that their country is motivated by high principle. Most seem happy with the image of Uncle Sam as the fearless cowboy galloping in to save Libya from an evil madman.

Blood for Oil

If Americans connect the dots between the horrors taking place in Iraq, Afghanistan, Pakistan and now Libya, it will be in spite of, not because of, the US media. Those who get their news from outside of the standard sources – from WikiLeaks or BBC Al-Jazeera, for example – will hear information that could make them aware of other reasons why their taxes are funding yet another war.

Such as the fact that Libya possesses the largest oil reserves in Africa. From Wikileaks they would hear that Washington was none too happy about Gaddafi's threat to re-nationalize Western oil companies.[5]

Until It's Gone

Under the longest arm of the Cross, Uranus is prodding all things Plutonian into the light. There is a window of opportunity for Americans to begin looking at Washington's military decisions differently. There is a chance here for people to go beyond the nationalistic spin and consider the human perspective.

This might entail a shift of focus from the madman in the caftan. It might lead Americans to ponder, instead, what it must be like to be a denizen of a part of the world where a dangerously coveted resource exists-one that powerful leaders, in the thrall of negative Pluto, would kill to possess. It would lead us to see Libya in

---

[5] Per the State Department cables released by WikiLeaks between 2007 and 2010.

other terms than just as an inscrutable, war-torn, faraway place. What thoughts would arise, if we looked at the Arab world as a group of human beings, very like ourselves, except for the geography?

I believe we would be inspired to ask ourselves whether the Arab people will be allowed to live peacefully while there is still oil under their land, or whether they will they have to wait until every drop is gone.

WHOSE STREETS?

(originally published as a blog,
October 2011)

The corporate media tried to ignore the Occupy Wall Street movement. Lord knows it tried. Over the past three weeks, as protests filled the streets of New York and started springing up in cities all over the country, the TV news at first played blind, deaf and dumb.

They tried to distract the public with the usual meaningless faux-controversies. But the transits leading up to the equinox were so powerful that even these non-issues came with subtexts that were inadvertently timely and on-the-mark. Consider the pertinence of Rosanne Barr's behead-the-rich joke.[1]

Even the hoopla about Obama backing a failed solar energy firm fell right into step with OWS's message. The rightwing media had a field day crowing about how foolish and profligate the government had been to lend Solyndra $535 million dollars; but, as many pointed out, when you compare the amount of taxpayer money that went into bailing out companies like AIG, the amount lost to Solyndra was infinitesimal.

When OWS became too big to ignore, the media pundits reacted, *en masse*, with a resounding "But it's not clear what they want" (a non-response, patterned after Sigmund Freud's notorious "But what do women want?" Both questions reveal nothing about the spoken-about, and everything about the unconsciousness of the speaker.). "They're protesting so many things," whined the journalists.

Why, yes, we are.

---

[1] In early October 2011, comedian and Occupy sympathizer Roseanne Barr unleashed a firestorm by wisecracking, in her darkly hyperbolic way, that corrupt bankers should get capital punishment for their white-color crimes.

Same Essential Issue

As astrologers had foreseen, all the various manifestations of the key transit of our era, the square between Uranus and Pluto, have leaped, flaming, into the American public discussion. There is an understanding among the new activists (Uranus in Aries) that the world's richest 1% (Pluto in Capricorn) use more than one mechanism to keep themselves in power.

One of them is the war machine. The march last night down the main drag in San Francisco marked the tenth anniversary of the start of the war in Afghanistan, but the chants and placards drew a link between the war and myriad other injustices afflicting human beings everywhere. "Money for jobs and education- not for war and occupation." "Tax their a$$ets." "It is a class war."

Each of the battle cries illustrates the same essential issue: the conflict between the interests of ordinary people (Uranus) and the interests of a tiny elite that controls global operations (Pluto) through money, munitions and media.

The march in San Francisco made this point through the route it took. We marched from the Federal Building, headquarters of a government that spends $3 billion every day for war and surveillance, up to a luxury hotel where service workers were picketing for a living wage. We continued down to the bay, where Occupy SF has been encamped in front of the Federal Reserve building. When the march reached the encampment, from the joyous whoop that arose you'd have thought the thirteen lost tribes had reunited on Market Street.

Poor, beleaguered Obama. No doubt realizing that a failure to exploit this latest American drama would win him the biggest booby prize in his four-year collection, he tried to strike the right tone in his statement about the OWS. The "American people feel frustrated," he said, "[because] Wall Street doesn't always follow the rules."

Blow to the Jugular

The truth is that whatever he said would have come off as lame. It isn't possible to transform a plutocracy while being its figurehead. No matter how much more intelligent and humane this president may be than his predecessor, Obama embodies a system in which "following the rules" apparently means rewarding the very swindlers whose deregulation of the financial industry caused it to implode, and assassinating the evil-guy-of-the-week with goon squads and targeted drone strikes.

The Occupy Wall Street phenomenon sprang into life on September 17, 2011, when Mars, patron of warriors both righteous and unrighteous, was opposing Pluto (powers-that-be) in the US (Sibly) chart. This stunning chart says it all. Any entity born under this symbolism would be a blow to the jugular of the US power structure.

But Wall Street itself is a symbol, and by putting it at the center of their crusade, the movement is transcending the conventional narrative. It is transcending the ugly infighting of national politics. It is going all the way, addressing the skewed state of power in the postmillennial world. The longest arm of the Cross, which will peak seven times between now and 2016, presides everywhere on Earth under a shared sky.

Under the waxing Moon, the energy of last night's march was nothing short of joyous. A sense of vitality filled the air – vitality and relief. At last, the crowd seemed to say, our benumbed country is shaking itself awake. It was a great reminder that being awake is more fun than anything.

FINGERING WALL STREET

(originally published as a blog,
October 2011)

It's hard to believe the Occupy Wall Street phenomenon is just over a month old. Long expected by astrologers, long awaited by progressives and long dreaded by the One percent, the movement hit the ground running.

It expresses the world moment so precisely that it seems to have arisen full-blown, like Athena from the head of Zeus. Germinating since 2008 when Pluto entered Capricorn, it is an organic consequence of the dirty secrets that were revealed when the economy went bust.

Four years later, no one but the willfully blind requires a bullet-point explanation of "what the protestors want." In a society where corporate criminals get six-figure bonuses while unemployment remains in the double digits (if you count the jobless who have given up looking), the question would seem to be not "Why are these people in the streets?" but rather, "Why aren't 99% of us in the streets?"

Bodies on the Ground

None of the Wall Street gamblers was punished after their greed and chicanery pitched the world into a recession; indeed, right now their henchmen are lobbying their tiny little hearts out in the halls of Congress, trying to gut proposed regulations that could prevent another meltdown. None of these One-Per-Centers went to jail; none had his ill-gotten gains repossessed. By contrast, plenty of protestors have been arrested, some violently attacked by police. Many have had their tents seized and their bare-bones equipment impounded.

Some of the OWS campers traveled hundreds of miles to make their voices heard. They have no party backing to launch campaigns, so they put their bodies on the ground. They have no corporate funding to pay for media ads, so they put the word out through Twitter. They can't afford to stay at hotels, so they bring their sleeping bags to city squares and parks – the last vestiges of public space that remain, in a society that's hurtling towards full-on privatization.

And what do we hear from the White House, as the most significant mass movement since the '60s spreads like wildfire to thousands of cities around the world? We hear about a "terrorist threat" featuring Iran, a country the Pentagon has been hankering to attack for years. And we hear about the assassination of yet another Bad Guy, this time in Libya.

Oh, and suddenly the president has decided to crack down on medical pot.

Disrupting the Status Quo

Those who observe the American media from a distance will have noticed a pattern in these news stories. They are a testament to just how big a threat the OWS movement poses to the One percent, who tend to pump saber-rattling incidents, and other issues that will play in Peoria, into the public conversation whenever they think the 99% need distracting.

It is clear to most Americans that the problems the protestors are identifying cannot be solved from within the hopelessly corrupt system of electoral politics. The power behind OWS comes from forces that exist outside of the official story, just as the outer planets that symbolize these forces exist outside the orbit of Saturn (status quo).

This cultural paroxysm, a domestic version of the Arab spring, is a manifestation of the definitive transit of the 2012 years: the square between Uranus and Pluto. Uranus works by disruption. It interrupts the complacency of everyday life, challenging society to change – like the protestors whose presence downtown disturbs business as usual. Pluto works by exposing decay, so that what is degenerating in a collective can cede the way to regeneration.

Degeneration is just as crucial as regeneration; breakdown is just as sacred as rebirth. During the years ahead Uranus and Pluto will finger what is standing in the way of evolution, so that obsolete structures can cleanly fall away. But neither of these planets presumes to offer solutions. What they do is point the finger at problems.

Staying Alert

What happens after that? Here's where human will and ingenuity come in.

The existence of each one of us is also part of the cosmic plan. All who are alive during these crucial years bring to the table a unique experience, an inimitable creative intelligence, and the ability to perform a crucial role in this world moment. When we tap into these resources, keeping our eyes and hearts open, we know what to do.

Consciousness-seekers have learned that the best way to solve our individual problems is to tap into our inner resources, while staying alert to what's happening around us. This is also how to solve society's problems. When we follow the lead of our essential beings – when we live through the center of our charts – we know instinctively how to respond as the diseased old order cracks around us, as it should, as it must.

Coming Home

(originally published in *Skywatch*,
November 2011)

Earth signs teach us how to consciously use of the plane of matter. They show us what it means to earn one's keep; they let us know what an entitlement complex looks like. During the second half of November 2011, Mars, Jupiter and Pluto will make a perfect equilateral triangle in the sky, highlighting the teachings of the earth element. This rare Grand Trine in earth offers us the opportunity to free ourselves from limiting cultural notions about wealth and poverty.

The transit has both personal and collective applications. It is coming along at a time when humanity's old assumptions about resources will not work any more. Dramatic shifts are afoot – global access to food and clean water foremost among them – to which the wealthy individuals of the world will not be immune.

Smug and Isolated

The cultural bubble that surrounds many upper- and middleclass Westerners allows us to be physically removed, psychologically disconnected and spiritually estranged from the atrocities of penury. This isolation is often considered no more than good and right by those encased in it. In fact, it's considered a birthright.

Some members of this small class of world denizens use ideology to justify their material smugness. There are religious Americans, for example, who'll tell you that there's something uniquely deserving about (white) denizens of the North American landmass. For others of this demographic, it's not so much a belief but a vague, unstated assumption that hideous extremes of physical privation happen only in other countries.

Whether conscious or unconscious, spiritual isolationism is an obstacle to the cosmic learning curve represented by the trine. One of the questions posed by earth transits is this: In a world where a famine in Somalia has killed 30,000 children, does it feel appropriate to whine about the fact that we can't afford to go out to eat as often as we used to?

Entitlement Complex

I am not proposing that we should, instead, upbraid ourselves for having a full belly, or indulge in a fear of lack. These reactions slow down our growth, and can even incapacitate us. For those who wish to get beyond them, transits in earth are an invitation to work on identifying within ourselves any vestiges of deprivation anxiety – to which Americans, who live in a culture obsessed with dearth and abundance, are particularly susceptible. Now is a good time to work on purging this fear, by catching it in action, noticing what a drain it is, and saying *No* to it.

Nor am I proposing that we discount the income disparities that exist within even the most affluent societies, dividing the citizenry up into haves and have-nots. Domestic imbalances of wealth deserve our attention as much as international ones – and are getting it, thanks to the Occupy Wall Street protests.

What I am proposing is that the First World, in general, start to re-think the strange economic exceptionalism with which we view ourselves. It's time to review our astonishingly outdated expectations of material abundance, most of which date back to the Eisenhower era and before. During the Pluto in Capricorn years (2008-23), entitlement complexes both individual and collective will become more and more ethically, spiritually and even pragmatically ill-advised.

In a very practical sense, this illusionary sense of being uniquely entitled blinds us to the world moment. To imagine that the ideal way to live is to have a big, fat house with a three-car garage is a grotesque anachronism in a world that is running out of oil. These old material aspirations are outdated to the point of toxicity. Those who expect a return of the larded lifestyles of former times run the risk of making the years ahead very unpleasant for themselves. Moreover, they are forfeiting the chance to cultivate healthy new priorities.

This will doubtless be most challenging in the parts of the world where most people live in cities, where the disconnection from our food sources is most acute. But those who look forward to getting rid of what they don't need, and who are eager to live more simply and creatively, will not only survive but flourish.

By contrast, if we are waiting for the economy to get back to "normal," we are setting ourselves up for a fall … if by "normal" we mean two dozen pairs of shoes and imported fruit in our cocktails.

Lessons in Empathy

Neptune is just about to leave Aquarius, the sign of humans in groups. From 1998 to 2012, the planet of melting has been blurring group boundaries. For those who have tuned in to Neptune's lesson, it's harder than it was 13 years ago to confine our identity to one dinky little niche of the human family. We feel more a part of the whole teeming seven billion.

Meanwhile, Chiron has just entered the sign governed by Neptune – Pisces – until 2019. Our susceptibility to the world's wounds is now very high. In order to take them in without drowning in them, we need to confront a fundamental stumbling block of the mass mentality: the illusion of dualism.

Dualism is the essential falsehood that says < *I* occupy one realm and *everybody else* occupies a different realm>. It's the big lie that holds modern culture in thrall and keeps us blind. Those who follow any kind of spiritual path must come back around to it again and again. For consciousness seekers, slaying this dragon wins the key to the kingdom.

Us vs. Them

Dualism shows up as the way we judge our experience, in big and little ways. A bad habit of the collective mind, it is considered normal. This makes it even more of a trap.

For most of us, this evaluating and judging is so incessant that we can't imagine not doing it. A cloudy day is bad and a sunny day is good. When we're ill, we view our own worth as less than when we're hale and hearty. And we buy into group judgments, those of our family and our culture, without even thinking. We harbor the unconscious assumption that poor people are less worthy of our respect than wealthy people. Pretty people have more social value than the rest of us.

The granddaddy of dualistic viewpoints is Us vs. Them. We build whole worldviews around this one, by means of intricate social and global hierarchies. A dark-skinned applicant is less valuable to the condo association than a Caucasian applicant. The death in war of one of our countrymen is more tragic than the death of a foreigner. The media panders to this schema so completely that most television watchers seem not to realize there's any other way of seeing things. If you support human rights for Palestinians, you must be against Judaism. If you criticize Obama you must be Republican. Every life circumstance is reduced to a zero-sum game.

Beyond Dualism

The alternative to dualistic thinking is experiencing life as a unity. When we live as if we and everything else were part of an unconditionally inclusive whole, we free ourselves from the trap.

One way to get there is ecological consciousness. An understanding of Earth's interconnected systems can't help but encompass unity thinking. So do any number of legends from wisdom traditions the world over (even those, like Christianity, whose appalling histories as institutionalized powers have rendered them suspect in other ways. Consider the beautiful imagery of every-sparrow-falling and every-grain-of-sand). All spiritual teachings, and the most advanced scientific theories, are founded upon the premise that everything in existence is inextricably linked.

There are innumerable variations on this theme, but there is only one truth. Consciousness is the way we interpret that truth.

Carrot and Stick

For those who are ready for it, the transits upon us in this era will give us a glimpse of what it might feel like to go find an interpretation of that truth that goes beyond dualism. The teaching is coming at us from several different directions.

Cosmic intelligence always offers us both a carrot and a stick. The stick in this case is our realization that if we stay stuck in Us-vs.-Them, we'll kill ourselves and the planet. The carrot is the feeling of peace that we feel when we know ourselves to be part of a universe in perfect synch with itself. When both Neptune and Chiron are in Pisces together, starting in February 2012, we'll enter a period during which many will take this leap, and there'll be no turning back.

When we make this leap, what's happening in the Amazon Valley, in Afghanistan, in the Congo and Ethiopia no longer feels foreign and abstract. Beyond the illusion of dualism, the truth of what people in different circumstances are going through becomes our truth, too. In this state there are no masks of separateness to maintain, no foreigners to protect ourselves against. It will feel like we have come home.

Tantrum Time

(originally published in *Daykeeper
Journal*, November 2011)

At its direct station in November 2011, Neptune is within a degree of the US
Moon. This will be the last hurrah of the conjunction that has shrouded the
American populace in a fog of confusion and illusion since 2007. Also in
November, the "bipartisan commission" convenes in Washington that is slated to
decide whether to proceed with $1.5 trillion worth of cuts[1] to hot-button social
programs, among them Social Security.

Social security. We hear those two words so often that we have become
habituated to their sound, but when we stop and think about them, they speak
volumes. In the collective psyche, feelings of security are governed by the Moon.

Fearful Child

The past several years of American politics have highlighted the most vulnerable
and childlike layer of the group consciousness; the part that resides only inches
away from sheer panic. Where social security is concerned, the fear felt by the
average citizen is about the prospect of not being taken care of when we grow old
and dependent.

The Moon is a primitive energy. Under its four-year-long conjunction with
Neptune, the US group vibration has been reverberating, lowest-common-
denominator-style, with anxiety and denial. Moon-Neptune is not a combination
from which we expect clarity of thought.

Have you ever experienced the transit of Neptune conjunct, square or opposing
your natal Moon? At its worst, it provokes a state of clueless impressionability,
where we are maximally receptive to charlatanism and deception from those who

---

[1] The focus of the committee is "deficit reduction," which could theoretically include increasing the
taxes of the wealthy and closing their tax loopholes. But at the moment the media seems to be
strategically preparing the public for more cuts.

would manipulate us through fear. In aspect, Neptune and the Moon can blind us to rational solutions that would otherwise arise, neatly and simply, from the circumstances right in front of our face.

Such as the fact that in a $15 trillion annual economy such as the USA, Medicare and Social Security could be solvent tomorrow if a few basic taxes were put in place.[2] And that they could even be expanded to every man, woman and child in the country, if there were a redirection to these programs of the funds that now support military presences in Iraq, Afghanistan, Libya, Pakistan, Somalia, Sudan and Yemen.

Neptunian Origins

It was right around the time Neptune made its first pass over the US Moon, in March 2009, that the Tea Party started to coalesce as a political force. Before then, it had the makings of a genuinely populist uprising. Its adherents came across as a bit loony (Neptune) with their paranoia about death panels and their silly hats, but there was a spontaneity and visceral realness to this crowd.

Even more Neptunian was the way these folks eluded definition. Before being wooed by the establishment, the Tea Party was a formless, leaderless reaction to the Wall Street meltdown and its subsequent bailouts. Vociferously against "government" - though not, apparently, *for* anarchy – they were all over the map with their grievances.

Then it came to pass that their uprising became a puppet movement for insiders like the Koch brothers and Fox News, who brought it into the Republican fold; and the rest is history.

Occupy Wall Street

Now that Neptune has retrograded back to within a degree of the US Moon (27° Aquarius), the Occupy Wall Street movement has erupted. There are many stunning aspects in the OWS birth chart, the most telling being the opposition of transiting Mars to the US Pluto. On September 17, 2011, the day of the first encampment, the planet of anger and assertion was opposing the planet of raw financial power (Pluto in the US 2nd house).

---

[2] Income disparity makes the country feel poorer than it really is. The OWS, with its tax-the-rich platform, is educating many Americans to the raw facts, such as that 400 American families now own more wealth than the rest of the population put together.

With Neptune strong again, we are not surprised by the formlessness and lack of singular focus expressed by the OWS. By contrast with the Tea Party, however, the multiplicity of this new movement's grievances elicits only scorn from the corporate media.[3]

Though one group has become the media's darling and the other a burgeoning threat, both of these Neptune-on-the-Moon movements lack a laundry-list-style agenda. Their meaning and focus are diffuse and all-encompassing (Neptune), and they appeal to the public on a primal and instinctive level (Moon).

Both the Tea Party folks and the OWS crowd are channeling the same archetypes – though the Moon-Neptune conjunction is stronger in the former, and the longest arm of the Cross is stronger in the latter. The first encampment in New York's Zuccotti Park took place when Uranus and Pluto were less than two degrees from exactitude.

Petulance

In stark contrast to the OWS folks, the Tea Partiers have crashed the gates of the political playing field, and have acquired enough mainstream legitimacy to be kingmakers in the coming elections. They are inside now, representing not a threat to the system, but the biggest threat to those who would change the system. It is from this standpoint that we need to understand what makes them tick.

From what we have seen of it so far, the TP agenda is an expression of the juvenile, precognitive side of the national Moon. As a symbol, the Moon is selfish by definition: its whole world is bound up with security issues and domestic matters. We can see this in the Tea Party platform, with its entitlement complex in regard to class privilege, its defensive political instincts, its self-protectiveness where social change is concerned and its emphasis on "family values" -which seem to refer exclusively to their own narrow vision of family.

The emotionalism of Tea-Partyism seems similarly lunar, in the sense of having something childlike about it. Perry, Palin, Bachman et al. have exhorted their fans to boldly self-express, and the fans are self-expressing. We have seen bursts of petulant emotionality that any good parent would chide her toddler for expressing in public.[4]

---

[3] This knee-jerk critique is more of a reaction than a response, which makes it psychologically intriguing.

[4] I am reminded of something the film critic Mick LaSalle wrote recently:

The TP demographic is becoming increasingly indistinguishable from the Republican Party base, and as election season cranks up we can expect wooing politicians to champion its interests like an over-indulgent parent humoring a spoiled child. The country will get to decide what this group is really about. Are they a battle-ready social force? Or just America's inner child throwing a tantrum?

Narcissism

The Tea Party's obsession with cutting taxes smacks of a peculiar kind of selfishness, the kind that children ideally outgrow. In youth, a certain amount of self-centeredness is developmentally appropriate; psychologists tell us that other-orientation is something we learn as we age. With maturity, we gain the capacity to understand that, for example, by contributing to a shared pool of resources we help those in need right now – as well as helping ourselves, in future, when *we* are the ones in need.

The Tea Party seems to be made up of adults who didn't get this memo. The focus is trained on a despised class of needy Others, a class they cannot imagine themselves being a part of. But you can't help but wonder about the Rick Perry fans who were burned out of their homes in Texas this past Summer, or flooded out by overflowing rivers in the South. You ask yourself whether they would go the distance and turn down federal funds in the face of these catastrophes. You wonder, moreover, what percentage of this crowd would turn up their noses at veterans' benefits, the fastest growing entitlement program in the country.[5]

A particularly ugly example of juvenile narcissism took place at CNN's GOP debate just before the autumnal equinox 2011. After Wolf Blitzer asked Ron Paul "What do you tell a guy who is sick, goes into a coma and doesn't have health insurance? Are you saying society should just let him die?", several members of

---

I think we overvalue passionate feeling in this country as some form of cleansing sincerity. Feeling something has the sensation of actual knowledge, bypassing mental work, the necessity of thought and the application of reason, not to mention actual information. I think it is significant that among people suffering from dementia, the last thing to go is the ability to have a strident opinion.

[5] This fact is almost never mentioned in all the hue and cry about government overspending, partly because vet benefits are, strategically, not counted with the rest of the Pentagon budget or war spending. But over the past decade, the Veterans Affairs budget increased 162%, to $127.7 billion per year. Contrast Social Security, which increased by only 61 percent. (Figures from Prof. Daniel Wirls, University of California at Santa Cruz.)

the crowd responded with a resounding "Yeah!"

Intellectually, too, there is a lack of responsibility here. And again, we'd give it a pass in the case of a kid who hadn't gotten that far yet in History & Current Events class. But it is from grown-up voters that we are hearing notions that bear no relationship to actual ideas or circumstances.[6]

Real Revolutionaries

Occupy Wall Street is not inside the system; its platform is emphatically outside. It is a mostly young movement, which, like the Moon, is changing every day. It is not clear to what extent it will be responded to, reacted against or accommodated by the machinery of electoral politics in this country. Unlike the Tea Party, which arose before the Uranus-Pluto square (revolution, devolution) began in earnest, the OWS is a force of deep-structure change.

It was born of the square between two planets that are, by definition, outside the establishment and a signal of its demise.

---

[6] The pinko-phobia of the Tea Party faithful – consider the slogans, "Can you see red yet?" and "Got socialism?" – seems to derive from equal parts ignorance and clinical paranoia. If challenged to name even one thriving, truly Communist state in the modern world, they would probably be hard pressed. Even socialist parties—that is, those that are socialist in more than name—have disappeared from the face of modern politics. In the USA itself, which we are told is in such peril from the red menace, there has not been a socialist party with anything like serious numbers for more than a century.

Tent City

(originally published as a blog,
November 2011)

It was when Mars (anger, militancy) opposed Neptune (confusion, pretense) as it was turning direct, just before the Full Moon of November 2011, that the tide began to turn. After being caught with their pants down for a few weeks, the media seems to have found its voice as regards the Occupy movement.

Editorials condemning the encampments are coming out thick and fast. Mayors who were on the fence before are caving in to city councils suddenly all up in their tough-guy boots. Reporters are furrowing their brows with sympathy as they listen to shop owners complaining that the presence of protesters downtown is scaring customers away from their designer scarves and perfumed soaps.

An article on the front page of yesterday's *San Francisco Chronicle* seemed intended to psychologically prep the public for today's eviction of the tent city. The photo they chose to accompany it featured a scruffy, barefoot camper looking down from his perch in a makeshift tree house, wearing a malevolent Charles Manson-like grin.

Strong-Arm Tactics

What rationale are our city fathers using to justify their shift to strong-arm tactics? It seems they are concerned about health hazards among the Occupiers. This was suggested not so much by empirical evidence, because there wasn't any, but by troubling associations some folks at City Hall have with camping equipment.

Funny thing: during Tahrir Square, you didn't hear many complaints about hygiene.

Another historical parallel we might draw is that of the tent city that sprang up in San Francisco after the quake of 1906. Back then, every park and public space was covered with survivors cooking stew over campfires in front of ragged lean-tos.

But unlike the Occupiers in Oakland last month and in New York this morning, the squatters in 1906 weren't cited for violating zoning laws. They weren't dragged out of their tents by police and beaten with batons. In fact, I imagine the officers back in '06 did all they could to help them. After fires, floods and power outages, people tend to see past the rules. Zoning ordinances mean little in a crisis.

What is being overlooked by those who are protesting the Occupy protests is that what's happening right now is a real-time, world-scale, bona fide crisis.

Hoovervilles

Unconsciously, of course, everybody knows this. The movement's middle-class foes, clinging to the shreds of their American Dream, wish the protesters would just go away. But their discomfort comes from being reminded of the ugly truths to which the Occupiers are calling attention. Those who have seen Walker Evans' Depression-era photographs may look at the new tent cities and shudder, seeing the Hoovervilles of the 1930s.

The parallel is valid. With Pluto in Capricorn (financial infrastructures) being inflamed by Uranus in Aries (militant rebellion), demonstrations against economic injustice have sprung up from East London to Johannesburg, from Rio de Janeiro to New Zealand. Europe is an economic war zone. The governments of Italy, Ireland and Portugal have been toppled; in Greece there is rioting in the streets. In Somalia and other African states the bloodshed is fueled by mortal poverty. In India there are fifteen suicides every hour due to financial despair.

In the USA, unregulated tycoons and untaxed corporate billionaires stockpile ever greater stores of wealth while unemployment and homelessness soar. Young people stagger out of school under the weight of obscene amounts of debt from student loans, while their college administrators award themselves sky-high raises.

Here in liberal Northern California, elected officials affect a solemn sincerity when explaining their policies towards the Occupiers. The other day, before the cops routed the tents, the mayor's spokes-flack seemed especially ambivalent in front of the cameras. The official eviction announcement was prefaced, as usual, with a statement about how much "we sympathize with them" (always *them*) – and ended, as usual, with a stern reminder that they are breaking the law.

Elsewhere in the news we heard that Chevron's third-quarter profits were more than double last year's, just shy of an all-time record for any quarter.

Ring Them Bells

(originally published in *Skywatch*,
December 2011)

The bells are tolling for the death of the Old Paradigm. You can hear them all over the globe. The shifts they signal are too profound to stay local, or national. The changes upon us right now are not confined to either the First World or the Third World, the Northern of the Southern hemisphere, the 99% or the 1%.

Ours is a world made up of intricately interlocking systems. Rising sea levels and other environmental degradations don't give a pin about boundaries and borders. Non-physical changes, too, are spreading like wildfire. Not even the Great Wall of China will be able to keep out the impulse that was ignited in Yemen last year when a fruit vendor, protesting his government's corruption, set himself aflame.

An epoch is coming to an end, and its death knell is reverberating across seas and continents.

Die Hard

Unfortunately, some things die hard. There are big, dying entities that are tightening their grip on the world rather than going out gracefully. Even movements that once bristled with life and promise, like the industrial revolution, tend to turn nasty when obsolete. Forward-looking members of humanity are up against stubborn resistance from adherents of the old ways.

The industrial revolution has turned counterrevolutionary. In its current, toxic form, it brought us the Gulf disaster of April 2010, and the nuclear catastrophe in Japan one year later (when Uranus was exactly where it is right now, again, in December 2011). Once world-alteringly creative, the machines-over-Nature model has turned anti-life.

But it is not about to quit on its own. The industrial approach, joined at the hip with a profit-driven approach to world management, can only continue repeating its old mistakes, enabled by a governmental system that has grown too corrupt to help us out. We should not be surprised that the US Department of the Interior has recently granted BP permission to resume oil and gas exploration in the Gulf, nor that the Japanese industry is champing at the bit to get their reactors up and running again. We will wait in vain for the powers-that-be to graciously usher themselves out. It is we who hear the bell tolling who must make the call.

Neptune

As the longest arm of the Cross nears exactitude, we see this happening everywhere. As Neptune (oil and gas) slowed down for a station in early November, thousands of environmentalists – many of them wealthy former donors – surrounded the White House to protest Obama's support for the disastrous Keystone XL Pipeline.

The uprisings we are seeing right now, all over the world, feel fated, irresistible. Yet we know that, human nature being what it is, many people will resist to the teeth their call for change. But for better or worse – depending on your point of view – resistance will become increasingly difficult. At this point, to deny what's going on is tantamount to plugging our ears against the sound of the Now.

Euro Peril

The bell is tolling for the economic models of the past.

As we saw at the Pluto ingress into Capricorn (monetary systems) in 2008, Wall Street, the Federal Reserve, the IMF and the World Bank left no country untouched by their accumulated corruptions. Four years later, Goldman Sachs's advice to their top international clients is worth our attention as a bellwether for upcoming trends. Not what they tell the public, which is that everything is going to be just fine; but what they are telling the highest tier of their clientele: to bet on a huge financial collapse.[1]

The European Union is teetering on the brink of disintegration as 2011 winds to a close. The still-nominally-solvent countries are scrambling to contain the spread of their neighbors' bankruptcy. The Euro crisis is making it all too clear that these member states are indeed their brother's keeper.

The configurations spelled out in the sky suggest that we hold on to our national provincialisms at our peril. Neptune (universal values) is about to re-enter Pisces

---

Goldman Sachs distributed a report to their institutional clients on August 16th, 2011, that the general public was not intended to see, which suggested ways to make money an upcoming period of severe economic turbulence.

(meltdown of boundaries), where Chiron (humanity's wounds) has been waiting for it. Europe is struggling with the reality expressed by this symbolism: that no one country operates in a vacuum. Nervous market commentators are using the word "contagion" to describe the probable effect of one country's financial crisis on the others. It's a coinage that sums up the collective mood. The catastrophe in Greece – which may turn out to be dwarfed by that of Italy – is being compared to a microbe that multiplies and spreads like an epidemic.

The USA itself, whose debt is anywhere from fourteen trillion dollars to many times that, is believed solvent right now only by means of the wildest possible suspension of disbelief. Pluto is still opposing America's Jupiter – a bottoming-out of credibility/credit.

Too Big to Fail

You could hear the bell tolling in New York City just before the autumnal equinox, with Pluto direct in the sky. Before his handlers could shut him up, Mayor Bloomberg gave voice to the worst nightmare of the rich: He said the poor might riot. Calling unemployment and poverty in the United States a potential powder keg, Bloomberg was speaking on WOR Radio the day the Occupy Wall Street encampment began. This was before anybody had any idea how big it would become, nor how important.

The specter of the great, unwashed hordes rising up *en masse* has struck fear into the hearts of the upper classes since patriarchy was born. It is now, at this crossroads in human history, closer to happening than it has ever been. All it would take is a single mindset shift: the simple realization, among the denizens of the world, that 99% makes for a lot more people-power than 1%.

There is a realization dawning, all at once, among ordinary people everywhere: that it is not the 1%, but the 99%, who are too big to fail.

Occupy

The Occupy movement is a manifestation of energies that had been festering below the threshold of collective awareness, waiting to explode. They erupted into public consciousness as the equinox transits set them off, like the second hand of a clock sets off the chimes on the hour.

To many astrologers it is nothing less than thrilling to see a cultural phenomenon cleave so tightly to the archetypes behind the defining transit of our time: the square between Uranus (revolution) in Aries (raw, unmediated activism) and

Pluto (demolishment) in Capricorn (corporations, financial structures). We cannot doubt the authenticity of a movement that serves so precisely the purposes of these two celestial giants.

Six years ago, writing in *Soul-Sick Nation* about the significance of Pluto in Capricorn, then two years away, I said the transit would bring fatal challenges to hierarchical models of organization. Capricorn governs the concept of layered tiers of power: hierarchies of every stripe. Astrologers have known for years that when Pluto, which breaks down whatever is distorted beyond repair, went into this sign, serious threats would arise worldwide to the vertical model of authority.

It's happening before our eyes. The deliberately leaderless Occupy movement, with its whimsical "human microphone," its *über*-democratic assemblies and its avoidance of demagoguery through rotating authority figures, constitutes a stunning rebuke to the stratified structures of the corporate-centered state.

By contrast to traditionally liberal agencies (e.g., the unions, NPR, MoveOn.org, the Democratic Party) the Occupiers are not part of the Establishment, and they don't want to join it. They are up in the bell tower, throwing their whole weight into pulling the ropes, making it known – to everyone who hasn't plugged their ears – what is wrong with the Old Order.

Think Cosmically

Nothing less than a world-encompassing perspective will help us now. Never has that great aphorism of the '60s been truer: we must act locally and think globally. Better yet, let's update it to *Think Cosmically*.

When we watch these crises from a cosmic perspective, we remember that these death knells are also baptism bells. Brand new human systems are waiting to be created from the ashes of the old.

Ninety-Nine Percent

(originally published in *Daykeeper
Journal*, December 2011)

Just as names can explode into mass consciousness, so can certain numbers. This has just happened to 99 and 1. The figures have become a chant, ringing in the world's ears.

The reality that these percentages refer to is no longer in the closet. But it's not to see why it stayed there for so long. 1% of the population owns 99% of the wealth?[1] That's crazy, right? It's a state of affairs that, when you think about it, seems so preposterous as to be something out of science fiction.

So a lot of people didn't think about it.

As denizens of the World's Greatest Democracy, our first impulse is to disbelieve it or remain willfully ignorant of this fundamental fact of the American economy. These numbers strikingly belie the stories we've been told about the modern civilized world. Even among Americans who had heard about it, the full weight of this statistic had probably not pierced the credibility barrier.

Until now. By making a slogan out of these numbers, the Occupy Movement (OWS) has dealt a fatal blow to their deniability.

---

[1] The figures have moved beyond a literal statistic into the realm of metaphor: they are now a vernacular catchphrase whose essential meaning is universally understood. Statistics on this vast and fluid topic are not verifiable in a scientific sense, but a study published by the United Nation's Development Research Institute found that the world's total wealth including real property and financial assets is owned by 2% of global denizens. Income is distributed unequally and wealth is even more unequal. Unsurprisingly, they found this wealth to be heavily concentrated in US and Europe where 90% of the world's total wealth is held. The Institute's director, Anthony Shorrocks, compared the situation to a group of 10 people, in which one person owns $99 and the remaining nine share $1.

Backlash

Scrambling to come up with a counterattack, the powers-that-be have accused OWS of incoherence. The opposite seems to be true. "We are the 99%" may be the most straightforward and succinct battle cry in history.

In fact, it is the status quo that is incoherent. When you compare the demonstrators' statements to the idiotic ramblings of our campaigning politicians, the protestors come off as exquisitely lucid. It's easy to see why OWS has higher approval ratings than any of the presidential candidates, whose 1%-friendly platforms and Wall-Street-fattened coffers perfectly make OWS's points for them.

On the local level, the backlash is even more incoherent. The mayors of Oakland and San Francisco have been flip-flopping like fish on a deck. Police chiefs have been overreacting with tear-gas tactics that backfire and increase the movement's popularity.

The cable TV pundits have been maligning the protesters as young, scruffy troublemakers, just as the hippies were condemned during the Vietnam years. For veterans of the counter-culture wars, at first blush it feels like one big rerun. But it's very different now.

Epochal Transits

For one thing, we have the Internet. The conjunction of Uranus (technology) and Neptune (global reach) in the early 90s introduced what would become a wild card in all future culture wars. YouTube and texting promote a kind of instant democracy, as we saw in Tahrir Square. When the whole cybersphere is watching, it's harder for the Man to bash heads with impunity.

But the difference between the demonstrations of the mid-sixties and those going on right now go further still. Uranus and Pluto were conjunct in 1965-66; now, they are square each other. The wheel has turned, and the issues have delved deeper.

The OWS campers aren't protesting a war, as the peaceniks were, nor a political party, as are Moveon.org and other liberal groups. They're not protesting "big government," as are the Tea Partiers.

OWS is not really a political movement at all. It's something much bigger, which is why the unions have been unable to co-opt it,[2] the corporate publicists have failed to discredit it, and the media doesn't know what to do with it.

Look in the Mirror

"We are the 99%" refers not to an opinion or an ideology. It is not an exhortation (as is "Hope and change"). It is a statement of fact: a singularly chilling fact, and one with which everyone who hears it must come to terms.

The occupiers' decision to use these numbers as a catchphrase was a brilliant piece of anti-branding. "We are the 99%" challenges the listener to look in the mirror. The phrase says, "Don't look at us; look at yourself." It doesn't say "Join our club," it says, "You are already in our club."

This creates a cognitive dilemma for those who are statistically part of the 99% but whose psychological identification is with the 1%.

"We are the 99%" invites the average worker to consider that the CEO who owns his company makes 400 times as much as he does, and to ask himself what this says about his alliances. It invites the 30,000 Bank of America workers who lost their jobs in October to consider the implications of the fact that two top B of A executives scored eleven million dollars in severance at around the same time.

It invites policemen and army recruits, foot soldiers of the state, to ask themselves which tribe they are part of – as happened in Egypt when Mubarak commanded his forces to fire upon demonstrators, only to have the troops defect.

2012-15

Movements that arise as suddenly as this one did are expressions of cultural moments whose time has come. Its birth in mid-September 2011 was augured by the transits of the autumnal equinox, functioning as a spark that hits a carefully laid fire. The fire is the longest arm of the Cardinal Cross.

Occupy Wall Street began with a localized bit of guerilla theatre and then roared

---

[2] The relationship between the unions and the Occupiers is in flux. Organized labor, whose leaders' salaries have steadily risen over the last several decades while workers' rights have sharply diminished, is widely perceived by progressives to have become part of the Establishment. But unions have been earnestly lobbying for some kind of alliance. So far the closest this has come to happening, at least in San Francisco, is OWS putting out a call to its supporters to remove their money from the big banks and put it into credit unions.

into a massive *cri de coeur*. It is an instrument of Pluto, the planet that purges muck and toxins, which is stripping away the cant that had adhered to America's self-image as a democracy (Uranus).

More than 200 years' worth of accumulated muck have all but smothered the democratic impulses that gave this country birth. It has built up in layers like tar on a smoker's lungs. OWS is asking the question that will be answered by the time of America's Pluto Return in 2022: Will the 99% give up on, or re-establish, a government of the people, by the people, and for the people?

CHAPTER 5

THE CROSS CLICKS INTO PLACE
2012

The storied year 2012 was loaded up with expectations before it began. Fuzzy interpretations of ancient prophecies and a myriad of pop culture references had millions of people on the edge of their seats.

From the point of view of Western astrology, the momentous consciousness shifts afoot are not confined to this single calendar year. But 2012 is indeed a significant marker, in that Uranus and Pluto make their first two (of seven total) exact 90° angles. The first hit, on 6/24/12 is at 8° Aries/ Capricorn.

It is not just the dates of the square's exact hits that portend radical shifts in the energy fields – the kind that tend to erupt in physical events. Long-running transits like this one are activated when fleeting planets zip across their degree range, especially in the four Cardinal signs: Aries, Cancer, Libra and Capricorn. For example, when a new or full Moon (especially an eclipse) or a planetary station falls in any of these signs, or when the Sun makes one of its seasonal shifts (as happens on the summer solstice 2012, four days before the first exactitude) the Uranus-Pluto square is likely to explode into manifestation, as when a spark ignites stacked-up kindling.

As the year 2012 began, astrologers also had an eye on Mars (armies, aggression). Setting the tone for the year to come, the warrior planet went retrograde in January; and throughout the spring it was moving back and forth in opposition to Neptune and Chiron in Pisces (chaos, pain). As the Vernal equinox approached and set off the Cardinal square, the shadow side of Mars reared its head. With the American public, three episodes in particular hit a nerve. A viral video (Pisces) exposed the horrors wreaked by African warlord Joseph Kony; in Afghanistan a US Army sergeant massacred 16 civilians; and in Florida an unarmed black teenager, Trayvon Martin, was killed by a neighborhood vigilante.

Water is another theme astrologers expect to be highlighted in 2012, given the historic ingress of Neptune (the sea) into Pisces, the sign of its rulership, early in the year. Both too little water (drought) and too much water (rising sea levels) are set to enter the world's consciousness in a whole new way. The disappearing coastline problem and its relationship to the dark machinations of geopolitics are both epitomized by the travails of the island nation Maldives (1.3 meters above sea level), whose pro-democracy president, Mohamed Nasheed, became famous in 2009 for trying to raise consciousness by conducting a cabinet meeting underwater. The subject of a documentary that came out at the spring equinox three years later, he was ousted at gunpoint in February in a Washington-supported coup.

While the Equinoctial transits were inflaming events (Aries) on the surface of the Earth (Capricorn), "Titanic" director James Cameron made history by taking his underwater film studio down to the deepest, darkest point of the world's oceans.

In the years building up to 2012, the Uranus-Pluto square has been associated with the use by political protesters worldwide of social media to circumvent governmental control. The battle between the powers-that-be (Pluto) and the voices of dissent (Uranus) continued to climb in early 2012. In China, governmental anxiety forced the shutdown of several social media websites after online rumors of a coup took off under the Full Moon in Libra (China's Libra Sun is the same degree as the Uranus-Pluto square's first exactitude).

Be the Future

(originally published in *Skywatch*,
January 2012)

Now begins a calendar year that was born with a checkered reputation already in place. Arcane eschatological imagery and cartoon-like religious and cinematic prophecies have been pouring forth for years about 2012. Now that it's here, let's try to separate the hype from the essential meanings that underlie it.

From the point of view of Western astrology the big news about 2012 is the square between Uranus and Pluto, which becomes exact for the first time just after the summer solstice. This square is the longest-running arm of the series of Cardinal transits that has been forming in the sky since 2008.

On the level of worldly events, one of the most notorious manifestations of the 2008 ingress was the Wall Street meltdown that went global. At the time, it seemed like the cataclysm happened overnight, but of course it was really decades in the making. The deregulation of the financial industry and the government-abetted corruption of the banks took place over the course of several US presidential administrations.

Rare transits like these invite us to take an even longer view. When our interpretive model is planetary cycles many centuries long, it's easier to see meaning. It becomes obvious that the economic crises upon us now have their origin in failed policies that have held sway since the beginning of the industrial revolution.

Uranus (massive disruption) and Pluto (decay) represent cosmic forces that are breaking down models of social organization so deeply ingrained in the mass mind that most of us can't imagine the world working any other way.

Digging in its Heels

The odd thing about many of the predictions that have been circulating about 2012 is that they fail to factor in what we already know about life on Earth. It seems to me that a good rule of thumb, when taking the pulse of the future, is to factor in human nature – which isn't going to change overnight.

How realistic is it to nurture fantasies of a sudden mass awakening, where everyone on Earth sees the light in one fell swoop, and drops all their fear like a hot potato?

For good or ill, it doesn't happen like that. Evolution is slow and incremental, even when in the throes of a steep learning curve. Moreover, immense change – that is, the degree of change that the world needs now – provokes resistance. The deeper the changes required, the deeper the status quo is going to dig in its heels. We can expect every spasm forward to be met by denial, at best, and by violent reaction, at worst, from agencies with a vested interest in keeping things the way they are.

Our focus should be to zone in on the burgeoning wave of health-affirming energy all around us, at the same time that we avoid being naïve about the negativity human beings tend to express when they're under threat. Both of these realities together comprise the cosmic climate of the years surrounding 2012.

Just as we need to know how to encourage the creators of positive wherever we find them, we need to know how to identify and respond to the change-resisters. They will be at least as ubiquitous.

Backlash and Vision

Resistance to change can take either active or passive forms. An example of the latter is induced escapism: large numbers of people diving into self-loss, with a little help from manipulative agencies.

When Neptune reenters Pisces in February it meets up with Chiron, their conjunction exacerbated by an opposition from Mars. We can expect the media-consuming public to be especially susceptible to over-the-top fantasies (Neptune) whose origin is some kind of pain (Chiron); for instance, paranoia about "terrorists" that expresses itself as vandalism against mosques and hate crimes against Arab Americans and other minorities. Another negative expression of this energy is reactive consumerism, fed by a no-holds-barred advertising industry (which, in the USA, has taken to ceiling-to-floor, wall-to-wall ads in heretofore public spaces: transport terminals, shrink-wrapped city buses.)

Almost everywhere in the world, we can expect the backlash expression of the Uranus-Pluto square to take the form of coordinated efforts of government, military and police agencies to crack down, *no-more-mister-nice-guy*-style, on protests and cultural critics, as began to happen with the Occupy movement when Uranus was at the Aries Point under the solar eclipse, in late November 2011.

In American politics and perhaps elsewhere, we will probably see an increase in *Throw-the-bums-out* syndrome: the undiscriminating reaction, on the part of most members of the public, against any and all incumbent officials. Whoever had the job last will be blamed for society's increasing hardships, regardless of their ideas, character or actual responsibility. This public attitude opens the field to extreme and unhinged ideologues, making for a highly unstable, unserious candidate pool.

Be Selective

We need to be more and more selective about where we put our energy. As the action ramps up throughout the year, it will prove a waste of time to engage with the elements of society that are fighting change tooth and nail, though their antics will make insistent claims on our attention as they wax ever more absurd, idiotic and heavy-handed.

We see this happening in the US presidential campaign, where contenders for the GOP nomination are coming up with ever-more outlandish statements in an attempt to grab the headlines. (e.g., Because he has not excluded abortion counseling entirely from federally funded programs, Obama is now being accused by Newt Gingrich of infanticide.)

We need to remember that, realistically, it is never more than a small minority of the population at any given time who grasp the world-altering changes required by the whole. These are the visionaries, the voices of the future. We will recognize them by their life-affirming messages, such as the recent campaign to end discrimination against same-sex couples, and the anti-consumerist movement, which we can expect to grow increasingly imaginative and committed.[1]

Our focus and support should go to these Uranian figures, and to the parts of

---

[1] Prescient pioneers in this area include *Adbusters Magazine*, the glossy quarterly magazine whose editors conceived of Occupy Wall Street, and the Bill Talen of the Church of Stop Shopping. Talen, a master parodist, has been known to collect soil from mountains that have been strip-mined. Carrying these soil samples, he and his cohorts stroll into bank lobbies with an air of having been invited by an art curator, and proceed to sculpt dirt peaks while singing; thus exorcizing the demons out of the ATMs.

ourselves that we see mirrored in them.

Threshold in Time

(originally published in *Daykeeper
Journal,* January 2012)

There is no lack of lore about 2012. Isn't it interesting, in and of itself, to see this degree of fuss made about a calendar year? But from the point of view of Western astrology, the meaning of this epoch is not about one singular year. Celestial events don't fit neatly into the demarcations of the Gregorian calendar, especially the really far-reaching ones. They are too vast to be understood within the confines of a solar cycle. But it is in 2012 that the biggest transit of our era, the First Quarter square between Uranus and Pluto, twice comes to exactitude (6/24 and 9/19), out of seven passes total. What will it bring?

What 2012 brings to us depends utterly on the level of awareness we bring to it. Only one thing is certain: whatever its outward manifestations, the year to come marks a point of no return. Though we're not at the beginning of the Uranus-Pluto transit nor at its end, 2012 is a definitive threshold in time.

The cosmos is throwing down the gauntlet. Humanity is going to have to make some critical decisions about life on Earth.

The Longest Arm of the Cross

During 2011 we watched the Uranus-Pluto square approaching its exactitude like a revolutionary advance guard. Everywhere in the world, infrastructures are breaking down. At the autumnal equinox, the square was closer than ever, and the more temporary seasonal transits made it explode into manifestation. The moment was ripe for the birth of Occupy Wall Street, an expression of the collective need for societal overhaul. OWS took off like a thunderbolt, as do all events born of outer-planet transits. Within days, the protesters' message was shaking windows and rattling walls like a tempest, all over the world.

The military-political wing of the Uranus-Pluto square first arose in the Arab world in armed clashes between dictatorial regimes (Pluto) and revolutionary elements (Uranus). Its financial wing has been reflected in global debt crises: in particular, the debt debacle in Europe, putting the cohesion of the EU itself at risk.

In the case of Italy, Ireland and Portugal, a breakdown of the economic infrastructure has caused whole regimes to topple; in England, France and Spain the people are seriously unhappy with their rulers. Here we have a blending of the two primary meanings of a Capricorn transit of Pluto: monetary and governmental systems. The Euro crisis is an outgrowth of the revelations that were presented to the world four years ago, when Pluto first entered Capricorn.

Head in the Sand

It was then that a lot of Europeans who had never before thought about such things found out how intertwined the world's financial markets are, and how inescapable their neighbors' problems were from their own. The isolationism of the USA is a harder nut to crack. What's going on in Europe would doubtless freak Americans out more than it is doing, if they paid more attention to international news.

After February 2012, when Neptune goes into Pisces to stay, it will be less and less feasible for Americans to pretend that catastrophes elsewhere don't affect them. Neptune in Pisces will emphasize the universals of existence on Earth. Walls built to keep immigrants out will start to look ever more ridiculous. Environmental policies that fail to consider the degradation of other parts of the world won't work. Separatist notions of all kinds will be rendered irrelevant. American insularity is becoming anachronistic very fast.

Cancer Suns under stress are notorious for retreating into isolationism, and we are heading into a period when the US's Cancer Sun will be under tremendous tension. Between 2012 and 2015, with an orb of several years on either side, Uranus and Pluto will be in a Grand Cross with the Sibly Sun-Saturn square. Americans will find it tempting to fall into isolationism, a national habit; but this will be increasingly precluded by the nature of the world's crises.

To the extent that the country resists the call of Neptune and Chiron in Pisces (still conjunct the US Moon as 2012 begins), Uncle Sam will be in for quite a struggle over the next four years, most obviously in terms of environmental, financial and foreign policy.

Crisis in the Old Country

The Euro crisis that started to peak in November 2011 is a good example of this interconnectedness. On the level of the collective unconscious, the news that Mother Europe could be sustaining such a catastrophe was an earthquake underneath the foundation of our notions in the Western world about the stability of civilization.

This is the kind of thing astrologers have been issuing warnings about for years, with Pluto in Capricorn – the sign we associate with civilizations and their infrastructures. We knew that when it came up against Uranus, the planet of radical shake-ups, all those old assumptions about civilization that have been taught in dusty old textbooks for centuries would be rent asunder.

There was a stunning expression of the tension between Uranus (ordinary people) & Pluto (the powers-that-be), around Halloween 2011 – just a brief little flash that expressed the transit's symbolism to a tee. The Greek president said he wanted to submit a referendum to the populace, about how to get out of their catastrophic debt.

The very mention of a popular referendum shocked the pants off the geopolitical/ financial cabals that control the world's money. Imagine, following the will of the *vox populi!*

The idea was quashed almost as soon as it began. But what a statement of the Uranus-Pluto square. The concept was pure Uranus, the planet of democratic impulses, and it was smothered over the course of a few days by the G20 powers playing the role of Pluto.

Change

But there is a deeper level of Plutonian function that has nothing to do with human power trips. Pluto is the Natural Law of breakdown and renewal, and it is being accelerated right now by Uranus' square to it.

When we study Pluto dispassionately, observing its operation within cultures over long swaths of time – think of the rise and fall of the Roman empire—we see that this is the same force that ushers everything in the universe through the cycle of birth, death and rebirth again.

Pluto does not kill so much as rip the mask off decay. It certainly doesn't cause something that is healthy and vital to suddenly drop dead. It just walks up to a corpse that's already teetering and – poof – blows it over, so that it falls crashing down. Uranus is lighting the fire underneath the whole process, quickening it and intensifying the urgency. Traditionally called the Great Awakener, Uranus is inciting revolutionary vigor in every heart ready to let it in.

Dead Giants

(originally published as a blog,
January 2012)

Astrologers have been talking about the Uranus-Pluto square for so long that we risk forgetting to be amazed when its energies play out the way they have. The momentous uprisings and financial turbulence with which the transit expressed itself in 2011 were such exact illustrations of the planetary energies as to match our wildest predictive metaphors. The epochal clash between the corrupt old (Pluto) and the revolutionary new (Uranus) is acting itself out in front of our eyes. We are living in a thrilling moment in history. As 2012 hits the ground running, deep-structure change is in the air.

Since 2008, Pluto, the planet that shows us the mortality of all things, has been especially strong whenever other planets join it in Capricorn. This is true every January, when the Sun, and often its neighbor planets too, enter Capricorn, the sign of economic theories and political structures. We see reminders everywhere that even those institutions we think of as eternal are merely temporary constructs.

Pluto asks one question of the systems governed by its resident sign: Are they promoting the healthy functioning of human beings and other living things? If not, they must go the way of everything else in decay. If a social institution has started to turn against the people it was set up to serve, it's dustbin-of-history time.

Financial Trauma

Capitalism is one of these systems. In its current state it is rotting from within. Despite the fact that most of us are conditioned to equate capitalism with modernity – indeed, with civilization itself – this economic model is no more immortal than anything else under the Sun. Under skies galvanized by the longest arm of the Cross, everywhere we look we see "free market" capitalism in its death throes.

Neoconservatives don't talk much about the dubious effects of the capitalist flood that swept over Eastern Europe after the fall of the Berlin Wall, nor about the environmental and cultural desecration wrought by China's voracious entry into the GDP sweepstakes. As for Uncle Sam, king of capitalism for the last two centuries, he is finding himself smack dab in the middle of the Uranus-Pluto square (America's natal aspects become a full-on Grand Cross when the transit is factored in).

With a self-image that revolves around material wealth, America is now going through not just a financial trauma but a breakdown of its core identity (transiting Pluto opposite US Sun). The notion of being the richest country in the world is so central to the nation's view of itself that many Americans have failed to grasp the fact that, right now, in 2012, the only thing the US economy leads in is military might and people in prison.

Indie Capitalism

In many ways, of course, robber-baron-style capitalism has been wildly successful. It has generated untold amounts of wealth for a tiny sector of humanity, and has established networks of profit that have undermined whole governments; as, for example, the donor-lobbyist-representative axis in Washington that has undermined US democracy. Follow the logic of capitalism along its natural trajectory and you get the immensely profitable business of trafficking and selling illegal drugs, which constitutes what is perhaps the most stunning financial success story of our era (worldwide, it is thought to be a four-hundred-billion-dollar-a-year industry), ranking it right up there with the oil companies and the arms trade.

But under skies like these, visionaries are challenging even the most entrenched and the least questioned of Capricorn operations. Uranus, the planet of people power, is capable of transforming the plutocratic state (Pluto) of modern capitalism. An example of this is the entry into the public discussion of indie capitalism, a radical challenge to business as usual, in every sense of the phrase.

Indie capitalism is based not on trading old value, but on creating new value. It is not globally but locally oriented. It is concerned not with quantity but quality; and its modus operandi is sharing rather than exploiting. Consider Kickstarter, the internet funding phenomenon whereby people invest creatively, observing the growth of products that mean something to them personally. In this model, says proponent Bruce Nussbaum, consumer, investor, audience, fan, helper, and producer conflate. It allows people to find and prepare their food the same way they find and prepare their music. Then they share it all.

The courage to challenge (Uranus) and reformulate (Pluto) even such a powerful phenomenon as big global capitalism may seem like a David and Goliath battle. But tackling huge power differentials like these is exactly what this transit is about. Giants are big, but they are mortal, and not exempt from Plutonian law. The symbolism in the skies suggests that when entities such as these start to putrefy, we should collectively grab our shovels and bury them.

WATER, WATER EVERYWHERE

(originally published in *Skywatch*,
February 2012)

It's a once-in-168-year event. In a year chock-full of world-altering transits, it's one of the most important. The god of the sea is inaugurating a thirteen-year-long shift in the way we look at water. To people with water-dominant charts, Neptune's entry into Pisces on February 3rd, 2012 will feel the way a drop of water must feel when it finally reaches the sea.

The archetype of water means many things. On the level of physical reality, Neptune governs drinking water, oceans and rivers, pipelines, gas and oil, leaks and spillages. Maximally strong in the sign of the fishes, Neptune will provoke all of these Earthly manifestations of the water principle, causing them to swell into group consciousness with a new poignancy.

And of course this ingress isn't happening in a vacuum. It's taking place against the backdrop of the overriding transit of the era, now getting closer by the day: the Uranus-Pluto square, the longest arm of the Cardinal Cross. The Uranus and Pluto cycle, which began when Uranus met up with Pluto (in a conjunction) during the 1960s, charts the seeding and flowering of cultural revolution. Its job is to overthrow stale, old, bankrupt aspects of collective life. The square's approach during 2011 has already introduced us to a brand new era of possibility, what with political uprisings all over the planet, a breakdown of economic sureties everywhere, and an environmental urgency that is changing the way humans think about life on Earth.

Projects Backfire

When we combine the symbolism of Neptune, Uranus and Pluto, one of the trends that arises is an explosive eruption (Uranus) of toxicity (Pluto) occurring with water systems (Neptune). We can expect water issues to lead the pack upcoming among the life-and-death issues facing the world environment.

This means keeping our eyes on developments like the disastrous Keystone pipeline, still being promoted by a coalition of the usual get-rich-quick suspects (maybe we should lobby for a law against ecocide denial, just as there is against holocaust denial). As these transits dominate the skies, we will be seeing the backfiring of a number of profit-driven water projects.

There are plenty vying for the crown of Most-Ecocidal-Idea-of-2012. One of them is BP's continuance of deepwater drills in the Gulf of Mexico, site of their catastrophic oil rig explosion in 2010. These monstrous polluters are not only still pumping, but have been sprouting leaks with impunity in recent months. Getting even less attention, in the Nigerian delta, Chevron has been getting away with murder, quite literally, in their efforts to silence local fishermen who have been struggling to stop the fouling of local waterways.

Similarly, in the Amazon rainforest, a plan to build the world's third-largest dam on indigenous land is now working its way through the Brazilian courts. In the American Yosemite, the flooding of the Hetch Hetchy Valley, a desecration that is said to have broken the heart of wilderness visionary John Muir, is once again under discussion. And this may be the year when California's long-simmering water wars finally boil over. Remember the movie *Chinatown*?

Escapism

With Neptune and Chiron both in Pisces, those who prize their sanity will need to be clearer than ever about the dangers of this archetype in its low-level of expression. We're going to need to watch out for fuzzy thinking and denial (Neptune) where deep healing is required (Chiron). Escapist longings are strong when Neptune is prominent in the sky – whether through sex, beer or prescription drugs, sleep, work or depression.

Even if we do not, ourselves, eat of the Lotus, we have to factor in the reality that just about everybody else does. We live in a world where self-medication is normative. Of relevance here are two facts. One: a new study reports that almost one quarter of American women age 40 to 59 take antidepressants. Two: the tap water most of us use is reclaimed sewerage effluent. This means it's a good bet that every time we fill our glass at the sink we're repurposing somebody else's Zoloft.

Amoebas in a Pond

Moreover, there is the psychic dimension of Neptune to consider. We move through our lives in constant contact with others, picking up the vibrations like an amoeba in a pond; we are surrounded by the messages of the media as if by polluted water. Citizens of modern capitalist societies are subjected to some kind of advertising at every waking moment, and, given the cunning and repetition of visual and aural tropes in commercials, probably in our sleep as well.

It is not surprising that the default consciousness of modern humans in groups – that is, of those with sufficient resources to be free from the incessant struggle to just stay alive – seems to be a semi-voluntary numbness. This means that those who wish to avoid drinking the Kool-Aid need to take extra precautions.

Like all outer planets, Neptune has a shadow a mile long. The warnings we get from traditional astrology about this planet's misuse are legendary. They include fraud and deceit, self-delusion and self-loss. But we would expect nothing less when we are dealing with an archetype this powerful; the bigger they come, the harder they fall. As with the Uranus-Pluto square, humanity is getting strong cosmic medicine as a function of how out of balance we have become.

Higher Neptune

That said, those who want to step out of the negative-Neptune pattern will experience the Pisces transit as a liberation. To taste the sweetness of high-level Neptune, we must cultivate a detachment from the unhealthy aspects of group life while at the same time staying in touch with what the mass mind is up to. For Americans, this might mean glancing at the cover of People Magazine with our peripheral vision; or noticing what propaganda Fox News is using this week, to cater to the prejudices of its viewers – noticing it without becoming ensnared by it.

Neptune is the symbol of the illusory nature of this world: what Hinduism calls *Maya*. With an appreciation for the cosmic lessons at hand, we can inform ourselves, as a sociologist might, about our epoch's illusions-of-choice. We might even get to the point where we approach these foibles with genuine curiosity; for, when we are not manipulated by them, the misadventures of an ungrounded collective are more fascinating than the most wildly improbable science fiction. It's about keeping our finger on the pulse of what currently passes for reality, while keeping our distance.

Like the Cardinal square above us, Neptune in Pisces has the capacity to transform the world, one individual consciousness at a time. It teaches that we are all little corks bobbing around in the same experiential sea. When we allow ourselves to open up to it, we glimpse the great truth behind material existence: unconditional interconnectedness. This is a realization that, when it comes,

comes in a flood.

Diving into the Deep End

(originally published in *Daykeeper
Journal*, February 2012)

All three of the outer planets – Uranus, Neptune and Pluto – are very strong
during 2012. The best way to avoid being swept away by their energy is to dive
right into the action and flow with the current.

Those whose natal charts have strong connections with these transits will feel a
strong pull to pay attention to what's going on in the world beyond their
personal, everyday frame of reference. For these folks, the year 2012 is a great
broiling sea, into which the sirens are calling them to pour their talents and skills.
The urge to know where they fit in may be shifting, right now, from a vague
yearning to an all-encompassing compulsion.

If you're feeling this way, it is not a sign that you are flipping out. It's an
appropriate response to the moment. Check your chart, and notice where these
three planets are transiting. What house are they in; what planets do they affect?
It is in these departments of your life that you're being called to deepen your
understanding. You are being deeply affected by events from which you may feel
unable to look away.

Evolutionary Map

Those singled out by the Aries-Capricorn aspect may feel that this riff of years,
right now, is the primary reason they incarnated. This era right now is what puts
our lifetimes on the evolutionary map. It seems that almost everyone, to one
degree or another, feels 2012 to be especially decisive, no matter what their chart
has going on and no matter how they explain it to themselves.

Americans are entering into the most expensive election in the history of the
world; we will be seeing corporate "citizens" pouring mind-boggling amounts of
money into their favored candidates' coffers. But we'll also be seeing human
citizens pouring immense amounts of time and energy into alternative scenarios.
Many people, fired up by the Occupy movement, will no longer be able to

stomach the cynical charade of hijacked democracy that they've tolerated in past elections.[1]

Missing the Boat

Square aspects between planets this powerful can bring out the very highest of a chart's potential. Pluto, which is by nature extreme, and Uranus, which is extraordinarily bold, are manifesting in world events that inspire us to respond with our whole selves: to recommit to being alive, wherever we are, whatever our context. Straddling the fence feels like less and less of an option. The great thing about world turmoil is that it prompts us to use all the resources at our disposal to engage with the moment. It's not going to be possible to just coast.

A long time ago, in the 1960s, when Uranus and Pluto were in the middle of their last powerful transit before this one, one of the catchwords among activists was "If you're not part of the solution, you're part of the problem." In this more spiritually attuned era, we might re-frame it as *If you're not living through your chart you're missing the boat.*

God of the Sea

Neptune's entry into Pisces in February 2012 begins a 14-year transit where the God of the Sea is maximally strong: Pisces is the sign of its rulership.[2] Moreover, this year began with transiting Mars conjunct the US Neptune square natal Mars, portending for Americans a double-barreled dose of water energy in 2012.

On a physical level, the systems collapses augured by the Uranus-Pluto square are likely to take place in Neptunian arenas: with gas, oil and water. Astrologers expect to see plenty of pipes leaking, infrastructures flooding and coastlines eroding.

Water, the staple of all life on Earth, will be increasingly understood to be the incomparable resource that it is. There should be a surge of consciousness as regards many aspects of this most primal of substances, starting with a calling out of the ways we abuse it: the ill-fated use by agribusiness of fossil groundwater in irrigation, for example. This may be the year that the depletion of underground

---

[1] The activists with Move to Amend, a group formed after the Supreme Court's *Citizens United* ruling in 2010, are dedicated to reclaiming democracy for actual people.

[2] Planets in the signs that rule them are like actors typecast in a role.

aquifers comes to the public's attention. More people will allow to sink into their awareness the resounding Neptunian irony that drinking water is declining while sea levels are rising. Coastal dwellers will start to feel the implications of living on the edge of the sea.

On a less literal level, Neptune's entry into Pisces is a symbolic threshold, on the other side of which we will feel ourselves connected to the world at large in new ways. This is the planet of inter-connectedness and immersion. Given the obtuse nature of the human ego, we may try to hold onto our sense of being different from everyone else, and alienated from what the rest of humanity is going through. But on a psychic level it won't fly.

Faith, Not Fear

The global crises associated with Neptune and with the Cardinal square are certainly daunting enough to give the stoutest heart pause. But there is a difference between acknowledging the severity of the world situation, on the one hand, and crumbling into a state of fear and passivity, on the other.

Under these skies, non-Pisceans will feel more like Pisceans do all the time. Our focus should be to try to understand this sign's genius – to model the very highest things about this winsome, intuitive sign – and eschew the quaking-in-our-boots part. Do you know any high-level Pisces folks? Think of the way they can look at even extremely troubling situations with a serene, undiscriminating acceptance. This isn't about condoning it, or ignoring human suffering. Quite the opposite. An integrated Piscean person just seems to know, deep in her bones, that there is a reason for everything under the Sun.

This is the model for us to follow as we launch into Phase Two of the Cardinal Cross Years. A good habit to cultivate would be to remind ourselves that our higher selves had a very distinct set of soul reasons to make the decision to participate, at this juncture, with our fellows on the Earth plane. It is immensely empowering to get in touch with the part of ourselves that realizes this. It awakens something inside of us: the inborn knowledge that we have been given all the resources we need in order to live out our chart at its highest level.

We may freak out now and again over the state of the world. That's human. But making a practice of remembering the big picture will keep us honest in times like these.

Fog Fight

(originally published as a blog,
February 2012)

Mars is in Virgo until early July, 2012. This transit is great for editing, tweaking and other kinds of incremental reform. But if unconsciously channeled, it makes us prickly and irritable. In Virgo, Mars's default is fuss and fret. What's especially interesting is that the sign opposite Virgo – Pisces – is getting a lot of action right now as well, from Neptune and Chiron. We have here the planet of aggression, rendered all skeptical and fidgety by Virgo, coming up against two mysterious forces whose *modus operandi* is passivity and indirectness.

Neptune and Chiron are blurring the clarity of what Mars is doing and what it thinks it wants. They are pouring energies from the right brain into the workings of Virgo, an otherwise straight-ahead, left-brain sign. Those who tend to use Virgo for fussing and worrying will find that these Pisces planets are providing plenty to fuss and worry about.

War of the Mutables

In the social arena, we see an orgy of fault-finding (Mars in Virgo) operating against the backdrop of an elusive, vacillating mass mood (Neptune, Chiron in Pisces) that disdains practical considerations. Examples abound of obsessive nitpicking fed by unconscious spiritual malaise. Consider the fuss being made right now about birth control by the Catholic Church, an institution that has displayed an astonishing lack of concern, paradoxically, about child rape.

For the USA in particular, the War of the Mutables is raging. America's natal Mars-Neptune square is being provoked by transiting Mars; its station in January 2012 was exact within a degree and set the template for the entire calendar year. The effect on the national climate will be to thicken the fog of emotional reactivity while inflaming the tendency to blame.

The country's ongoing political vaudeville act, recently described by no less a critic than Fidel Castro as "the greatest competition of idiocy and ignorance that has ever been", sets the scene for an endless stream of complaint unconnected to any rational methodology for improvement. "Freedom from big government," cry the GOP nominees, a call to arms that gets foggier and vaguer with every repetition. Though aggressive (Mars) in tone, it seems to be an attempt to lull and hypnotize (Neptune) their base into forgetting the facts of recent history, e.g., the role their team played in the Wall Street bailouts.

Point-Scoring

The recent fog fight over a Clint Eastwood commercial that aired during the 2012 Super Bowl is another example of outsized group feeling pitted against real-life details. The ad was a standard-issue bit of capitalist jingoism, on the order of "What's good for General Motors [updated here to Chrysler] is good for the USA." Juiced up with movie-star glamour (Pisces), it was the kind of sales pitch we hear regularly from the spin departments of both political parties. But the ever-vigilant Karl Rove found grounds in it for partisan point-scoring, and up rose a great hue and cry of impassioned noises from pundits and populace alike.

Pisces isn't about to let a little thing like *facts* prevent it from indulging in a good drama. Amidst the hooplah was a pesky bit of relevant data that managed to get lost in the fray: in fact, the company in question is no longer American. Italy's Fiat SpA now owns a majority of Chrysler.

Culture analysts of the future will surely roll their eyes incredulously when reading about societal antics such as these. As denizens of the present, we can take heart from remembering that each of us, as individuals, has a better shot at channeling these transits creatively than the group as a whole has. The only way humanity's consciousness gets raised is one person at a time.

Soul Level

The 14-year tenure of Neptune in Pisces, the sign of its rulership, is a teaching about healing on the soul level. The more we open to it, the more we will change our lives in subtle but unmistakable ways.

These transits guarantee that we will be taught, but they don't guarantee that we will learn. Learning depends on whether mindfulness is brought to bear. To the extent that we stay mindful, the impulses we're getting from any Virgo transits during Neptune's tenure will be beautifully blended with the grand, sweeping sensitivities of the Pisces cluster. Then a perfect balance is achieved, with each sign revealing its most exalted side to the other.

SEA HUNT

(originally published in *Skywatch*,
March 2012)

The influence of Pisces is all-encompassing right now. People with a lot of water in their charts are responding to it especially strongly, but every one of us is submerged in it. It is coloring the mass mood like violet watercolor in a seascape.

We're feeling it on the physical level. Our bodies are mostly water, the element of universality; if there's one thing we all have in common, it's H_2O. We're also feeling it on the spiritual level. Pisces is the sign that reminds us that we're all floating around in the same cosmic soup.

Neptune's sojourn in the sign of the fishes (2012-26) is an emotional, mystical teaching that's providing a background to the rowdier Uranus-Pluto square. Chiron is now pulling out of orb of its long-running conjunction with Neptune, but will remain in Pisces until 2019. Since its ingress two years ago, Chiron has been raising the world's consciousness about the wounding we inflict upon the Earth's oceans: it was on the very day of Chiron's Pisces ingress that BP's rig blew up in the Gulf of Mexico, in April 2010.

Moody Blues

We are also having our consciousness raised about the wounding sustained by our unconscious mind, that invisible inner sea. What will we do about the wounds we find there? How will we handle the shared pain that floats around in the collective ethers?

Looking to our culture for answers won't get us very far; a dysfunctional society is a poor role model. The Western world's philosophy of mechanistic materialism reduces the concept of "reality" to the physical world exclusively, giving the emotional world short shrift. We are discouraged from admitting our complex feelings. The group mind defaults instead to mass denial, the shadow side of Pisces.

Exploiting the situation is the Denial Industry, booming at the moment, as we can expect it to boom during the years ahead. We've got muzak in the superstore trying to numb our critical thinking, and a blue-chip pharmaceuticals industry keeping a huge chunk of the citizenry in a state of continuous low-level depression.

But for four years now, the duet between Neptune and Chiron has occasioned a healthy dialogue about the self-medications with which so many people stuff their pain. From its humble beginnings in the AA model, the consciousness around addiction is growing more and more sophisticated.

Overeating has been getting a lot of press lately (in the First World, that is, which is still affluent enough to be able to afford such a problem). And there has been a breakthrough in the discussion of chronic depression, an epidemic that Big Pharma may sometimes ameliorate but cannot cure.[1]

Moreover, with the Great Recession as a backdrop, social theorists have been emboldened to propose that consumerism itself can be an addiction. Recreational retail is no longer an easy fix for most people, and the psychological meanings attached to shopping are being reconsidered. Wags have joked about "retail therapy" for years, but the economic climate has recently been opening up people's thinking about the dark side of capitalism.[2]

In the collective psyche, chronic debt is now understood to be a social wound. The most striking example of this was the real estate bubble and bust, expressed so aptly by the 2009 Super Conjunction, with Chiron, Neptune and Jupiter (broad public awareness), solidifying the painful (Chiron) truth that people's equity in their homes had been an illusion (Neptune). (The term "underwater" to mean *irrecoverably indebted* struck astrologers as a cosmic pun: Neptune governs water and drowning.)

Chironic Approach

Although Neptune and Chiron are pulling away from exact conjunction, the influence of their merged meaning remains strong through 2012. What are they

---

[1] Chironic law suggests that there is a difference between short-term remedial effects and true healing. A recent study reports that 70% of the antidepressants on the market helped no more than placebos.

[2] Peter Joseph's Zeitgeist movement has a video out about the fatal flaws of our economic system that is entertaining, concise and profound. See http://vimeo.com/7857584.

suggesting we do with our pain?

Certainly it is unhealthy to focus on pain, either our own personal pain or the greater world's. The question we need to ask is whether we are not looking at pain out of avoidance. Many of us have been trained to suffer in silence, soldiering on through heartache as if nothing were wrong. *Keep it together*, we are told when distressed; *Don't cry*, we were told when we are children.

But experience has shown us that this cumulative suppression leads to a build-up of grief, which, after a while, gushes out in a geyser of emotional breakdown. It is only then that we notice how much pain we'd been in, and start to wonder whether we'd have suffered less had we admitted our pain to ourselves from the first. Tamping down pain only postpones its release and resolution.

The Chironic approach is, in a way, counterintuitive: it involves leaning into pain rather than away from it. This does not mean indulging in a masochistic preference for pain. It means admitting to pain, as a prerequisite for healing. Chiron invites us to concede our wounds and then work with them, as an ally.

The Chironic principle of healing is a radical departure from the conventional approach to woundedness, but it is essentially very simple:

It is to make pain more, not less, conscious.

Mourning as Inspiration

After the Gulf disaster two years ago, there was a spike in environmental consciousness. Many Americans who had spent years stewing in passive distress about the outrages of corporate polluters threw themselves into the public discussion and became engaged citizens for the first time in their lives.

The initial reaction of many people I know was a strong revulsion and grief, which, initially, made them feel helpless. Yet when perspective was retained – through discussion with like-minded observers, through prayer, through astrology – it became possible to glimpse an evolutionary purpose behind the holocaust. With a bit of distance from our feelings, we could start to see that humanity was being led through a set of understandings that had existed, up until then, only on the fringes of cultural understanding. The catharsis of witnessing a wrenching destruction forced many people awake.

Many observers reacted with outrage against the oil companies who committed the crime, and at the government agencies that enabled it. There were outpourings of lamentation in magazines and blogs, some very beautiful, mourning the oil-soaked birds, the poisoned flora and fauna, the befouled sea. Some felt the draw to political activity; others were moved to private creative exertions. It didn't matter what form the creativity took. Those who dove into the energy of the transit found that the act of opening up to a reservoir of shared emotion set something magical in motion.

Under these skies, individuals brave enough to face their pain will be led, by Chironic Law, to their organic next step. We needn't worry about what this next step will be; it's folly to second-guess Pisces. But we can be sure that whatever we find under the surface of the inner sea will make us more authentic and more alive.

AMERICA DREAMING

(originally published in *Daykeeper Journal*, March 2012)

As it has since 2008, the Spring equinox 2012 will set off the Uranus-Pluto square. At this time of year, the Sun and the planets around it enter the zodiacal range Uranus has been occupying, triggering impulses of activism and disruption.

A lot of astrological material has been written about the Cardinal crossroads, and it boggles the mind how many of the things astrologers were saying about it – way back when, years before it happened – have come to pass. The planets have cleaved to their mysterious intentions so precisely that our pronouncements upon the meaning of these epochal transits hardly need any amendment.

Slippery Fish

And now the Cosmic Playwright has thickened the plot with the entry of Neptune into Pisces. Not as obvious as the crash-bang energy of the Uranus-Pluto square, the Neptune transit adds a subtle undercurrent of feeling to the proceedings.

In the US (Sibly) chart, the Moon has been soaking in a marinade of Neptune and Chiron for four years now. This energy peaked at the Super Conjunction of Neptune, Chiron and Jupiter in 2009. At this writing, in early 2012, Chiron has pulled ahead of Neptune, out of orb. But with both of them now in Pisces, and with Neptune only three degrees from the Sibly Moon, the USA is still deeply immersed. We have here the most fluctuating sign in the zodiac, Pisces, motivating the most subjective planet in the chart, the Moon. Americans are being compelled not by their reason, but by their moods.

Given that the Moon is the ruler of the Sibly Sun in Cancer, this holds true more or less all the time. But under this transit, the vagaries of collective feeling have resulted in so much waffling and vacillating that a grand political pronouncement aired on Morning Edition is likely to have been entirely reversed by the evening news.

Pisces is not known for discrimination. When ungrounded in a moral center, its orientation flops around like a fish on deck. Consider the capriciousness of the Republican "base," warming to and then jettisoning a long string of would-be nominees. The contenders themselves, most of them now ex-candidates, have been just as slippery. The week after Neptune's ingress, Herman Cain, who had just endorsed Gingrich for president, allowed as how he'd also be "very comfortable" with a Romney candidacy. This prompted Buddy Roemer to snicker, "Romney is the one percent, Gingrich is his lobbyist, and Herman's just looking for a job."

Dreaming

The planet Neptune is associated with dreams, a word/concept with a wide reach. At the literal end of the meaning spectrum, dreams are those cinematic film clips we experience behind our eyelids when asleep. The word also refers to the fantasies and denial mechanisms that cloud our judgment when we don't want to look at the facts, as when someone busts us for not being realistic: "You're just dreaming."

It is this sense of Neptune that has given rise to the incoherent impulses that dominate America's political discourse; as expressed, for instance, in the tendency of so many struggling citizens to vote against their own financial interests. It is this expression of Neptune that has made Americans as susceptible as they are to the soporific of the corporate media.

And there is a third meaning called up by the word *dreams*, which seems to be the one advertisers and American Idol presenters are aiming for: worldly ambitions and goals. When famous athletes tell impoverished schoolchildren to "dream big," they seem to mean "Pursue a successful career." When the heroine of a Broadway show sings of "living her dreams," she means "I want to be famous." When an oncology charity talks of dreams, they mean trips to Disneyland.

Right now is a good time to look at these popular *clichés*. With the national Moon all Pisces'd-out, most public discussion is steeped in a highly emotional vagueness that tries to tug at our heartstring while making little attempt to deliver the goods.

Virgo Opposition

This group sensibility will be challenged several times during 2012, as Mars – in Virgo for a remarkable eight months – opposes every Pisces planet in sight.

Strengthening this theme of watery agitation, Mars was conjunct the US Neptune at the Mars station in January, setting up the whole calendar year to be a tug-of-war between foggy emotionalism and critical precision.

One of the lessons we can learn, as individuals, from the Pisces/Virgo challenge is that there is a difference between facile, *ersatz* feeling and deep, heart-connected feeling. The former is sentimentality, ubiquitous in American pop culture. Cheap and easy to fake, sentiment is the stock in trade of disingenuous politicians, who affect a moist-eyed patriotism at every whistle stop to try to boost their percentages in the polls.

Pure Feeling

Genuine emotion that simultaneously quickens hearts across a wide swath of the populace is much harder to find in our society. One instance of this was the outpouring of communal grief that washed over the US public just after 9/11.

A more recent instance of group feeling was the sense of celebration that was sparked by Occupy Wall Street last fall, filling parks and city squares with heartfelt excitement. Assembling to freely express what millions have been feeling for so long but have been missing in the public discussion, the OWS movement has been a massive *cri de coeur*.

Now is a good time to contemplate the difference between Hallmark-card-style Neptune and the real deal. In his discussion of sentimental art, the great art critic Northrop Frye described the distinction this way (slightly paraphrased):

> Religious or patriotic art is usually sentimental in expression because these demand loyalty, by repeating the same creed every Sunday, the same flag at every assembly. Sentimentality denies forward movement in art because it denies fresh discovery. It touts familiar values, stock responses. It's fearful because it resists as a child would, the inexorable advance through time – it tries to arrest this with nostalgia. It is the subjective equivalent of the mob's stock response to mood. It is withdrawn but not detached, egocentric but not individualized, gregarious but not social.

Inspiration

Neptune and Chiron in Pisces tell us that we have the opportunity right now to become inspired. The potential also exists to be submerged by pain and grief. Both manifestations of Pisces are flowing through the ethers. Our task is to savor he inspiration, and work with the pain.

With self-discipline, we can transform the latter into the former. It takes great spiritual fortitude, but it can be done; and for those who want to take advantage of all these transits have to offer, it must be attempted. Grief and pain can be used to give us a deeper understanding of life and of ourselves.

Iran Amok

(originally published as a blog,
March 2012)

I guess you could say March 2012 came in like a lion… if the lion was brain-damaged, gynophobic and high on meth.

In the USA, Republicans reinvigorated the 19th-century war on birth control, Rush Limbaugh called a Democratic law student who was testifying for reproductive freedom a slut, and a Montana judge sent an email about the president's mother having sex with a dog. Such is the state of American public discourse as the equinox shoots us into Phase Two of the Cardinal Crossroads.

Meanwhile, at the U.N., where Uncle Sam continues to call the shots, Iran is being cast as the next evil country to "get tough" about. That this pistol-packin' cowboy buffoonery could still be considered a viable approach to international affairs in the current world, crippled as it already is by financial, environmental and military chaos, can only strike a thinking person as completely insane.

Memory Loss

The good citizens of the NATO countries seem to be suffering from total memory loss as regards the last time they let their leaders drag them into a protracted tragic mess in the Middle East (and the war in Iraq is by no means over. Overseen by the biggest embassy in the world, CIA spies and Special Ops have a firmer foothold than ever in the country Uncle Sam has turned into a semi-permanent war zone.). Further heating up the rhetoric right now is the fact that the USA, Iran and Israel all happen to be preparing for elections at the same time. So, with grim predictability, we are seeing jingoistic, trigger-happy posturing winning the day, while appeals to reasoned diplomacy are derided as cowardly and unpatriotic.

With retrograde Mars (machismo run amok) and the Pluto-Uranus square triggered all through March 2012, we are hearing every cynical politician with a bully pulpit trying to score points with saber-rattling grandiosity. The US candidates are putting on a particularly detestable display, each trying to outdo the other with escalating threats against Iran; not excluding the president, with his dark hints about "military solutions" – an oxymoron if there ever was one.

Not surprisingly with Pluto (destruction) in Capricorn (monetary infrastructures), so far the strategies Uncle Sam has up its sleeve against Iran are largely economic. Warfare is becoming more and more a starkly financial enterprise: "sanctions" really means economic strangulation. Having failed to bring Iran to its knees through spy plots and assassinations, Washington's new plan seems to be to weaken its economy enough that the government collapses.

History-challenged Americans seem to have no clue about how chillingly the current scenario parallels what happened sixty years ago, when the CIA toppled the democratically elected government in Iran and installed the shah in its place. The coup inaugurated a 25-year-long reign of terror for ordinary Iranians, while shoveling their country's resources over to US oil companies and banks.

Seized Assets

In recent months Uncle Sam has seized tens of billions of dollars of Iranian assets. Surrounded by US-occupied countries and well aware of the abiding desire of American corporations for the oil beneath their feet, the Iranian people know all too well what really motivates this global nastiness. Contrary to media spin, the goal NATO leaders are pursuing in Iran has nothing to do with human rights, and everything to do with raw power.

It is Plutonian logic, not practical logic, that would lead an American to believe that his own country, with its stockpile of 10 and a half thousand nuclear warheads, and its unique position of being the only country in the world to have actually used nuclear weapons, should be the one to dictate international nuclear policy. Indeed, at the same time that inflammatory warnings about Iran's nuclear program blare forth from his TV set, the American taxpayer is paying for the US Department of Energy to *triple* its own nuke budget.

Washington's long-term plans for Iran are a textbook case of the US (Sibly) chart's misused Pluto (total control) in the 2nd house (resources). These plans involve casting Israel in the role of regional strongman, as a means of keeping the Middle East safe for American interests. That is, safe for the financial interests of the American 1%. In every other way, arming to the teeth a reactionary regime like Israel's represents the exact opposite of safety.

Its arsenals fattened with US-taxpayer-subsidized weapons, Israel has consistently refused to sign the Nuclear Non-Proliferation Treaty, as it has refused to allow international monitors to inspect its arsenals. But none of this arrogant bellicosity elicits a peep of protest from the American and European politicians fulsomely sputtering right now about Israel's *sui generis* "right to defend itself."

Uranus-Pluto

As the Uranus-Pluto square builds to exactitude (first hit: June 24th 2012) the air is buzzing with polarization. The essential conflict here, however, is not the over-hyped contest between the various American electoral contenders. Nor is it a conflict between one country and another. The real choice point right now is one that is activating the minds and hearts of world citizens everywhere: the one between the power of change and the forces of fear.

Though we don't hear much about them on the news, the numbers of individuals being inspired (Uranus) by the power of change (Pluto) right now are multiplying exponentially. For example, in the USA environmentalists are suing to block construction of two nuclear reactors in Georgia that would be the nation's first since 1978. In Japan, where the nuclear reactors damaged in last year's quake have sprung new leaks, clean-energy activists continue to organize and protest despite a blackout of reportage on their activities. In Germany and France, the anti-nuke movement is even stronger.

In Russia, dissidents against Putin's abysmally corrupt government have refused to be silenced, despite a campaign of suppression that has included assassination. In Syria, Yemen, Jordan and Bahrain, despots (Pluto) continue to brutalize participants in popular protests (Uranus); but the activists keep coming back, filling the city squares. Even in Israel, last month Attorney General Yehuda Weinstein declared unconstitutional Knesset bills that would sharply restrict funding for human rights groups.

Power of Change

We are living in a time when the power of change to transform the world will not and cannot be stopped. Ordinary people are far less geo-politically naive than a generation ago, and able to see global patterns for what they are. Few who have been watching the world scene can kid themselves that the conflicts of the past two years are isolated flashes in the pan.

For our part, astrologers have been saying for years now that the forces of negative Pluto can be expected to tighten their grip – not relax it – when up against Uranus, as the square reaches exactitude between now and 2015. In the months and years upcoming we need to get into the habit of taking the long view on the world situation. Bemoaning conflict is not enough; we need to remember what these energies signify.

The Cardinal Crossroads period is forcing long-unquestioned injustices, obsolete group assumptions and mass delusions to the fore. With each new global event that arises, the healthy response is to resist the fear reaction, and get in touch with the intelligence and courage that is innate in each of us.

Mars: Foe or Ally

(originally published in *Skywatch,*
April 2012)

During the spring of 2012 Mars has been completing one of its relatively rare forays into retrogradation. Any planet in apparent backward motion requires a particularly sophisticated understanding to use well, making this Mars transit doubly tricky on the collective level. Played out in society, the unconscious side of planetary archetypes gives rise to our worst stereotypes about them: hence the rule by Mars of armies, weaponry and war.

Dark Mars

The classic case of distorted Mars in Virgo took place on March 11th, 2012, when a US Army Sergeant massacred sixteen slumbering Afghan civilians, nine of them children. Among global observers habituated almost to numbness by the ongoing violence in Serbia, Mexico, the Sudan and elsewhere, here was a headline-grabber to sicken the heart.

Virgo is the sign of *service*, a word whose ancient auspices in humility and helpfulness are distorted beyond recognition in the oxymoronic modern euphemism "armed services." In the case at hand, the face of dark Mars in this placement is most obvious in the man who perpetrated the atrocity – whose unit was called, with perverse appropriateness, The Stryker Brigade. It was also expressed in the outrage his murders elicited from the Afghan civilian population.

But if we are to learn from the massacre we must look behind the singular act and consider the collective madness of which it is the tip of the iceberg. In what happened on March 11th, 2012 – the first anniversary of that other catastrophe, the quake/ tsunami in Japan – we can see encapsulated the distorted face of Mars in army life in general.

In every nook and cranny of the military culture, inculcated into the recruits 24/7, we can see the foreshadowing of atrocity. Not just in the physical drills that train these young people to kill, but also in the ideological and social rituals that implicitly train them to do so, as exemplified by the violent video games and porn that they watch on the base in their down time.

Pisces Opposition

Mars's back-and-forth movement has been highlighting the clash between Virgo and Pisces, where Neptune and Chiron are currently transiting (the former is in Pisces until 2025; the latter until 2019). Accordingly, the massacre has been raising questions about many of the dysfunctions (Chiron/ Neptune) of the world Sgt Bales and his ilk inhabit. With the planet of aggression (Mars) opposing the sign of drugs (Pisces), for example, a conversation has begun about the routine use of psychiatric meds in the military. Attention has also increased about the violent suicides[1] that are epidemic among soldiers both active and retired. Eighteen American veterans commit suicide every day. More than seventy thousand soldiers were diagnosed with post-traumatic stress syndrome between 2000 and 2011.

Among his appalled fellow citizens, calls are being made for the charge of murder to be leveled not only at Sgt Bales, the perpetrator, but also at the military commanders who sent him back, again and again, into the fray, to slog on through punishingly multiple tours of duty. On March 23rd, with Mercury retrograding back into Pisces in the sky, the army responded to the outcry by announcing that it does not track which or how many of its thousands of PTSD sufferers are sent back to active duty.

Martial anger has been lighting cultural fires in minds and hearts of all who see in this horrible incident not just a personal but a systemic disorder. With stationary Mercury conjunct Uranus – setting off the longest arm of the Cross – on the Ides of March 2012, anti-war activists took to the streets across the USA and elsewhere. The massacre of March 11th provided fuel for their battle cry: the only way to end war crimes is to end the war.[2]

Mars governs suicide in the sense that self-destruction is anger directed inward.

Since the invasion ten long years ago, an enormous abyss of ignorance remains about Afghanistan among the US government and population at large. Still undecided about what "victory" would mean in this context, Uncle Sam has been trying to destroy an enemy engendered and trained by the CIA itself, back when Afghanistan was being occupied by the Soviets. It seems to be difficult for many of the Americans who fund this ill-starred war to remember that they originally green lighted it during a wave of popular vengeance unleashed by 9/11; with Washington propagandists hoping the public would not realize that the WTC saboteurs included not Afghans but Saudi nationals, who were living in not Afghanistan but Germany. Unfortunately most of what the war's critics were saying years ago has held true.

THE SIXTIES 2.0

(originally published in *Daykeeper
Journal,* April 2012)

Are you familiar, dear reader, with the notorious transit that astrologers associate
with the rock-&-rolling sixties? I refer to the conjunction of Uranus and Pluto in
Virgo opposed to Saturn in Pisces. It peaked in 1965-66. For mad zeitgeist shifts,
you can't beat the combination of those three planets.

Astrological Symbolism for Dummies

To get its point across unmistakably, the Cosmic Encoder made it especially easy
for us: the planetary formula translated exactly into the phrase that arose to
describe the times. Pluto + Uranus ≠ Saturn: forces of extreme (Pluto) defiance
(Uranus) countered (opposition) the dominant culture (Saturn). V*oilà*: the
counter-culture was born.

Now, four and a half decades later, the next big milestone in the Uranus-Pluto
cycle is upon us. I know I am not the only sexagenarian musing about the
similarities and differences between now and the sixties.

Simple Code

Like any other war, the culture war that was the 1960s had two sides. You were
either with us or agin' us.

It was a simple matter to signal whether you were on the Uranus-Pluto team
("freaks", we called ourselves) or the Saturn (straight) team. If you thought of
yourself as part of the counterculture, you probably went bra-less. If you were
male, you grew your hair long. The code was straightforward.

When hitchhiking, you signaled your tribe with a uniform of patched jeans, and
could pretty much count on being picked up by another "long-hair."[1] Conversely,

---

[1] Both men and women wore their hair long, and both sexes wore jeans - the unisex look being one
of the identifying counter-culture innovations. Part of what we were breaking away from was a
dress code that had separated the genders by an abyss of difference.

if the truck approaching you on the highway was driven by someone with a crew cut, there was probably an American flag on the bumper, too; and you got out of the way fast so as not to get run down.

I don't recall balking at being labeled in such a simplistic way. Obsessed (Pluto) with the concept of liberation (Uranus), I think our focus was on the marvelous new discovery that an alternative could exist to the suffocating conventionality to which we had assumed, as children, we would be consigned.

The Uranus-Pluto conjunction had a long tail. By late 1972 the two outer planets had moved into Libra, with their midpoint conjunct the US Saturn. The cultural polarizing they represented had by that time been thoroughly politicized, with candidates Richard Nixon and George McGovern personifying the pro-war (Saturn) and the anti-war (Uranus-Pluto) contingents.

The polarities of 1972 were so clear-cut as to seem almost a caricature.

The Country and the Cross

In the years since then, there has been a consolidation of power in the USA, as the donor-lobbyist-representative axis in Washington became entrenched. It is now the singular engine behind the American political system, and has erased all but superficial distinctions between the Dems and the GOP.

This is the reality being pushed to the surface as the Cardinal Cross hammers away at the US (Sibly) chart. This series of stressful Cardinal transits can be seen in terms of six phases:

1. In 2008, the riff began with Pluto opposing the US Sun cluster in Cancer.

2. It reached another level in 2010 when Uranus moved into Aries while Saturn was in early Libra (the "Cardinal Climax").

3. It ramped up again in 2011 at the US Saturn Return.

4. It will become even more acute in mid-2012 as Uranus and Pluto's exact square clicks into the natal Sun-Saturn square of the USA.

5. It will finalize when Pluto conjoins the US natal Pluto.

With transits of Uranus (revolution) and Pluto (complete breakdown and renewal) we expect the essence of a situation to be exposed. With the conjunction of the 1960s, consciousness-raising forces like civil rights and the war in Vietnam forced the American collective to look at itself with a new level of self-honesty.

This new era's iteration of the Uranus-Pluto cycle will compel a collective self-examination of a similar depth. This time we can expect the exposure to be about the disproportionate power wielded by those who control the material resources (Pluto in the second house).

Post-Ideological Era

This long-range astrological schema will help us maintain perspective as we move through the upcoming election season. There is a lot of media quarreling about, for example, where the various candidates stand on "social conservative" issues such as abortion and homosexuality, but these are just noisemaker issues compared to what's really going on.

The mass media knows how much its consumers enjoy a good fight, so we can be sure it will continue to stage electoral matches featuring two teams presented as being fiercely opposed. Indeed, conventional wisdom has it that the two parties are more polarized than ever before. But in fact their trajectory is the same. Congressional Democrats have moved to the right, and their Republican counterparts have moved even further to the right.

In this strange phase of America's history, the struggle has become fundamentally post-ideological. The GOP has never pretended to be anything other than the party of resistance to change; but now neither do the Democrats, who no longer attempt to introduce new ideas. Long gone are the genuine social visions that used to come out of this party, like FDR's New Deal or Lyndon Johnson's War on Poverty.

Tea Party

Neither is the Tea Party an ideological construct. They are merely the latest version of the Pissed-Off White Guy, a contingent that shows up in every phase of American history. Mostly rural, mostly Southern and Western, and mostly male, this crowd is the holder of strong cultural opinions but not much power. That is, they see themselves as entitled to power, but robbed of it by government and cultural enemies.

Rather than shoring up the actual power – in numbers – that they do in fact have, these folks fume and obsess about the classes more disempowered than themselves: e.g., homosexuals, racial minorities, non-Christians. The Tea

Partiers' extravagant championship of democracy envisions a system just democratic enough to allow themselves to cross the line that divides the *have-nots* from the *haves*; but not so democratic that the groups they despise could cross over with them.

Occupy Wall Street

It is the Occupy movement that comes closest to naming the key players in the new American game. At first, the protesters fit neatly into the two-battling-teams formula that the media is so fond of: a fight between scruffy dissenters vs. the forces of law-&-order was just right for the evening news. But now that there's no more high-profile camping and marching, giving rise to high-drama clubbing and pepper-spraying, the TV networks have sent their reporters home.

For the corporate media to confer any meaning upon OWS outside the bounds of that standard dualistic trope would be getting too close to the truth. Any discussion, for example, of the Adbusters Magazine anti-consumerism campaign that gave the movement birth, or of the economic statistics that underlie OWS's essential premise, would be far too dangerous to call attention to. So the powers-that-be are now trying to banish the movement to conceptual Siberia by disallowing it any air time at all.

But the perspective of OWS is a manifestation of forces whose moment has come. A textbook expression of the Cardinal Cross, the initial encampment in Zuccotti Park sprang into being when the premier aspect of our era had reached its closest point yet and was set off by more quickly moving planets. Cutting through the nonsense of the official narrative, the occupiers have described the true state of the culture wars in the USA and the rest of the world. They have identified it as a conflict between the 1% and the other 99, echoing the current 90-degree relationship between Pluto (plutocracy) and Uranus (democracy).

Then, Now and Upcoming

When I think back to what life was like in the late 60s and 70s, I realize that, though most of us young hot heads didn't know what we were doing, we did know that something important was going on. We could sense that powerful forces were disrupting the status quo. The narrow, flag-waving, Communist-fearing reality structure that we had grown up was being torn asunder.

The clueless political and cultural ideologies of the Cold War years are all but gone. Certainly the diehards who would resurrect them are still among us, shrill, well-financed and well-showcased by the media; but their efforts are doomed to failure. Newer and more universal values are on the ascendency, emerging painstakingly like seedlings through of the crust of the soil; visions rising up to match the urgent realities of a post-millennial world.

Alongside them are new generations being born: a whole new crop of creative Americans wired to thrive under Pluto in Capricorn, Aquarius and beyond.

Idiot Box

(originally published as a blog,
April 2012)

Rupert Murdoch, the Australian media mogul, is back in the news. The 21st-century's answer to William Randolph Hearst (comedian Jon Stewart calls him *Citizen Shame*) has once again been dragged away from his yacht to answer questions. An investigative panel wants the what-did-he-knows and when-did-he-know-its about the bribing of cops and the hacking of murder victims' cell phones for sensational press.

Also in late April 2012, a new survey came out *in* the American media *about* the American media, concluding that – surprise! – most of the stories reported on the news are mindlessly superficial.

This was a month that saw the Sun triggering the Mercury-Pluto opposition in the US (Sibly) chart (the signature of propaganda), transiting Pluto (corruption) stationing en route to its exact square with Uranus (sudden revelation), and Mars stationing opposed to transiting Neptune (mass hypnosis). It's time to take another look at the nature of the information we take into our consciousness.

Mental Nutrition

It is odd, in a way, how undiscriminating we are about where our news comes from. Especially given how careful we are becoming about, say, the origins of our food (consider how unanimously the public rejected ground beef after the recent expose about hamburger meat containing "pink slime"). In order to stay sane during the years ahead, we need to be no less careful about how much mental nutrition vs. toxicity is in the media we consume.

News channels give the public what it seems to want, and the public grows to want more of what they are offered. It's a vicious circle of dumbness. We are conditioned at this point to desire the most late-breaking coverage possible; that is, the up-to-the-minuteness of a given event – not its meaning – is presented as its most important value.

336

Also popular is triviality – the maximum amount of airtime is devoted to the silliest possible non-events; for example, Mitt Romney strapping his dog to the roof of his car thirty years ago. The stories that get mentioned paint a picture of the world that is so meaningless and insubstantial as to keep viewers from remembering how to use their minds, let along from achieving clarity of mind.

Next!

But the perniciousness of the media lies not just in its content but in its form. On TV events are highlighted piecemeal, without context or continuity, suggesting a soulless randomness. All tarted up with exclamatory candy-colored graphics, news stories seem to be intended to appeal to an audience of kindergarteners with attention deficit disorder – which, as has been well-noted, viewers of the mass media increasingly resemble.

The viewer who hears a cursory mention of a terrible famine somewhere in the world, only to have the program abruptly cut to a commercial for fast food, risks the development of a peculiarly modern spiritual disconnection.

It is telling that it is in China right now that the vapidity of the infotainment industry is especially striking. In the efforts of this newly ascendant superpower to out-capitalism the capitalists, China is mirroring back to us the manic look-and-feel of US pop culture, rendered extra obvious via the crassness of imitation. Consider the title of a popular Chinese magazine; one little word that sums up this whole ethos: "Next!"

This breathless, up-to-the-minute approach to information not only fails to encourage a holistic understanding of what's going on in the world, but actively discourages it. Thus are the failures of the media not merely stupidly innocuous but psycho-spiritually dangerous.

We are up against the challenge of keeping our minds and hearts open amidst an onslaught of very disturbing world events, while maintaining a grounded, thoughtful equanimity. This means that, more than ever before, we require intelligence sources of the highest quality.

Digital Media

The New Media poses another problem. Digital gadgets further undercut our ability to truly absorb important information: taking the time to subject it to our personal values and ethics, so we know how to use it. In the wild world of cyber data, abbreviation and speed are valued over subtlety of thought and expression. We are kept from reflecting long enough upon anything to discern patterns of meaning in it, let alone to get in touch with our feelings about it.

We really can't afford to be drawn off focus like this. As meaning-seekers facing a rip-roaring ride over the next few years, we need our brain cells as healthy as we can keep them. This means staying vigilant about whose point of view is behind the media we are consuming. What agenda is our favorite news program pushing? Who's sponsoring the radio show we're listening to? What is Goldman Sachs's motivation for underwriting those tasteful PBS shows?

In order to stay plugged in, we need the media. But we also need to see it as no more or less than a tool, a resource – to be used by us, not the other way around.

AND A CHILD SHALL LEAD THEM

(originally published in *Skywatch,*
May 2012)

Mark Zuckerberg was in the news a few weeks ago, on the day Pluto (plutocracy) stationed during its narrowing square to Uranus (technology). Facebook's acquisition of a smart phone app for a billion dollars had the business page so excited it could hardly contain itself.

The New Yorker chimed in with a timely Jewish parents joke: "Are the Zuckerbergs now thrilled that Mark never went outside and got some fresh air?"

Social Networth[1]

When his star first started to rise, Zuckerberg struck many people as very, well, *young* to be a billionaire.[2] Before he and his ilk came along, that particular financial demographic was invariably associated in the collective imagination with old men: elderly WASP millionaires (here's another change: the <m> on that word has morphed into a <b>). These were represented in the visual vernacular by a well-fed gent with white whiskers, a top hat and a monocle.

In currency for as long as any of us could remember, that figure showed up illustrating every editorial ever written about rich people. He's the dude from the Monopoly game; he's Walt Disney's Scrooge McDuck. His origin was probably Thomas Nast's seminal cartoon of the 19th-century fat cat Boss Tweed, a corpulent Edwardian toff with a sack of money for a face. This jolly stereotype is nothing if not durable. You can still see it in political cartoons, symbolizing the 1%.

---

[1] Hats off to the wordsmiths at The Daily Show.

[2] A related issue is how little dudes like Zuckerberg pay back into the public pot, relative to their wealth, under the USA's heavily 1%-favoring tax codes. According to journalist Tim Redmond, Zuckerberg is exercising $5 billion worth of stock options out of $28 billion he will own; requiring him to pay 40 percent on that five billion but not a penny of tax on the other $23 billion. This makes his actual effective tax rate about 7 percent – far less than even low-income Americans typically pay.

But the cliché is being revised, as Zuckerberg and his peers push the age of the moneybags demographic downward. The imagery in the mass mind of extreme wealth gets younger with each new start-up that goes platinum.

This phenomenon reflects an interesting trend: a rise in the cultural stock of young people in general, which started in the rock-and-rolling Sixties.

Uranus & Pluto Then and Now

As transit trackers are aware, the energy of the 1960s is resonating strongly right now, due to what we might call a cosmic echo. The transit that gave those wild years their unique power – Uranus conjunct Pluto opposed to Saturn – is back, with its ingredients remixed.

In 2010, Saturn, Uranus and Pluto reconvened in what was called the Cardinal Climax (Uranus opposed to Saturn, both square to Pluto); and now, in 2012, Uranus and Pluto are reaching the first of their seven exact 90° angles. The seeds of social disruption, planted in the sixties, are breaking through the crust of the soil.

Generation Gap

To understand the significance of this new phase of the Uranus-Pluto cycle we need to consider the phase that began it.

When the planet of revolution (Uranus) conjoined with the planet of breakdown (Pluto) back in '65, energies were unleashed, like *agents provocateurs*, to challenge the social order. Sex was famously let out of the closet. Anything that could be construed as an establishment value got challenged, from fashion to politics.

Of interest here is the constituency that was causing the ruckus: It was the young people. The Uranus-Pluto conjunction initiated a wrenching chasm between teenagers and their parents. It was under this transit that the phrase "the generation gap" was coined.

The concept was as exciting (Uranus) as it was dangerous (Pluto) to the social order, and it caught on fast. In the Western world, the abyss between the generations spread like an earthquake fault, to every sort of family of every social class.

While it is true that there have always been youngsters who rebelled against their elders, what was different about this singular moment in history was that it became normative to do so. Whether this was ever statistically verified, I don't know; but the impact of the idea upon (especially) American culture was manifestly obvious: young and old were at each other's throats. Musically, linguistically, politically, sartorially, they occupied two incompatible realities.

The obedient sons and daughters of previous generations, epitomized by the clean, smiling kids on "Father Knows Best" and other goodie-two-shoes TV families, were now the exception, not the rule. A generation earlier, it would have been preposterous for a young songwriter to pen the lyric "Teach your parents well," as Crosby, Stills and Nash did in the late '60s.

Values Gap

Opposition to the war in Vietnam took the form of an almost-monolithic generation of young people rising up *en masse*. The war became a symbol of the stupidity and moral vacuity of the generation in power at the time: the protesters' parents. The new cultural cliché was that, if you were an adolescent or in your twenties, you were still uncorrupted enough to see clearly and act morally, which for a lot of us meant espousing anti-materialism and anti-militarism.

If you were older than young, on the other hand, you were presumed to personify not only the standard-issue cluelessness of old age, but a lamentable ethical blindness as well. Of this you were guilty until proven innocent. We were warned by Abbie Hoffman, of the Chicago Seven, "Don't trust anyone over thirty." "I hope I die before I get old," sang Pete Townsend of the Who.

We thought being young was a moral stand.

Wired World

The most momentous configuration to occur in between the time of the Uranus-Pluto conjunction (1965-66) and the Cardinal Cross years upon us now (2008-23) was the Uranus-Neptune conjunction of 1993. Here we had the planet of cutting-edge machines (Uranus) and the planet of mass consciousness (Neptune) coming together to birth the tech revolution.

In an astoundingly short time, relative to human timescales, this revolution has resulted in advanced machines (Uranus) insinuating themselves into every nook and cranny of people's lives everywhere in the world (Neptune).

Moreover, in a way that the Black Panthers could not have dreamed of when they hanted "The Revolution will not be televised," the revolution is being digitalized. Uranus (revolution) in Aries (activism) and Pluto (breakdown) in Capricorn (government) were moving into their first-quarter square in early 2011 as the uprisings in Yemen spread to Tahrir Square, a revolution that was famously enabled by the internet.

The information revolution has moved into the realm of political.

Post-Millennial Generation Gap

For those of us alive before the cyber revolution began, it was impossible to imagine the breadth of the social change it would trigger. Correspondingly, to anyone who came of age since 1993, the old pre-digital world must be well-nigh impossible to imagine. Here we have the second iteration, in my lifetime, of the generation gap.

Observing it from the other side of the geriatric line this time, I notice some key distinctions. The ethical factor, that seemed so important a distinction between old and young back in the day, is no longer part of the formula. If cultural attitudes towards materialism and militarism are starting to spike again, it is not because they are attached to any particular age group.

Young Turks in Silicon Valley are certainly not looked down upon by their peers for making oodles of money. On the contrary, in the Age of Zuckerberg, enormous, insouciant wealth is cool again. During the days of flower power, by contrast, going into business – especially advertising — was regarded as selling out.

Things have gotten a bit more complicated since then. A business or a tech degree is considered, by and large, the most "realistic" choice in these days of the Great Recession. Literature and art courses, by contrast, are dropping like flies in college curricula. The complexion of youthful idealism is very different in an economy where student loan debt, having surpassed credit card and auto-loan debt in the USA, is surging above a trillion dollars.

Digital Divide

There is a digital divide in the world right now, between societies affluent enough to wire themselves and those that are lucky to have one old typewriter per village. This is a new spin on global inequality, one that is often remarked upon by economists. But within First World societies like the USA, where access to digital technology is the overwhelming norm, the more noteworthy divide is the one between the generations.

It has often been observed, especially by us oldsters, that young people seem to understand computer technology not simply because they're habituated to it, having grown up around these machines, but because they actually *think differently*. The idea is both daunting and fascinating, and it seems surprising that more social scientists and neurologists aren't pursuing it.

Astrologers, for their part, would propose that young people growing up since the Uranus-Neptune conjunction understand the new media because the understanding is in their DNA. The internet is changing not only the ways we use information but the whole phenomenon of human intelligence itself. The new generation gap is not merely technical, nor cultural, but epistemological. Today's young people are curiously positioned, with a facility that is highly valued by the world at large. Graham Nash's call to "Teach your parents well" is being played out in front of family computer screens all over the world.

LIFE AFTER OIL

(originally published in *Daykeeper
Journal,* May 2012)

Uranus and Pluto are getting ready for their big moment. Their exact square is June 24th, the first of seven through 2015. Throughout May the aspect moves from a three-degree orb to just one. Everywhere in the world, orthodoxies are being shaken up (Uranus), particularly those relating to systems of amassed power (Pluto).

This square, the longest arm of the Cardinal Cross, is the most revelatory transit of our lifetimes. It is causing profound societal dysfunctions to be exposed: corruptions and toxicities that have been deeply harmful but curiously shrouded with a veil of silence. One of these, emerging with Occupy Wall Street at last year's autumnal equinox, is the issue of extreme income inequity: plutocracy.

Another of these Plutonian issues is the arms trade. During the next three years of the Uranus-Pluto exactitude, the dark, lucrative business of international weapon sales may take its turn breaking into public discussion. The perfectly legal sale of weapons – weapons of all kinds of destruction, both mass and one-murder-at-a-time – ranks among the three greatest amassers of international wealth. The second biggest plutocrats in the world are the traffickers of illegal drugs. The third are the oil companies.

Monopolizing the Field

In an essay from 2011, "The Dark Crown", I argued that Pluto should be considered, along with Neptune, for joint rulership of oil.

Crude oil, or petroleum, is a unique substance that has gone through an extraordinary series of meaning shifts over the last two centuries. If we look at planetary symbolism as a means of mirroring our experience on Earth, As-Above-So-Below-style, we can learn a lot about ourselves from these meaning shifts. The evolution of oil, as an archetype, so strikingly parallels the way human activity itself has evolved as to make the stuff a unique status symbol of the contemporary world. Perhaps no other substance so poignantly sums up what we have become.

With the industrial revolution, oil started to take on a world-transforming significance. Once oil started to be transformed into plastic, synthetic cloth, fertilizers – products that collectively characterize the 20th century – and fossil fuels became the number-one substance to run the mechanized world, oil began to symbolize unprecedented power (Pluto).

Pluto-style, oil has taken over the field, nudging out every other contender as a desirable commodity.

Destruction and Toxicity

Used without consciousness, no other planetary archetype is as deadly as Pluto. The obsessive quest for the global power that oil inspires is everywhere associated with death and destruction, both in the form of fatal pollution and in the form of war.

When you consider its importance to the economies of the world, it only makes sense that oil became a driver of foreign policy. Although the world leaders who design these policies rarely present them as such, a cursory reading of modern history makes it clear that superpowers like England, Holland, France and the USA make a habit of engineering regime changes in one after another oil-rich country, most recently Libya and Iran.

The most noteworthy recent example of the hideous ecological desecration caused by oil is the BP catastrophe of April of 2010 in the Gulf of Mexico; and at this writing British Petroleum continues to drill 5,000 feet down into those same fragile sea beds. At the same time, Chevron is laying waste to pristine waterways in the Amazon, and Shell Oil is doing incalculable damage in the Nigerian delta.

Drill, Baby, Drill

With the price of gas high and the election season upon the USA, hardly a day goes by that we don't hear some candidate castigating Obama for not giving Big Oil more tax breaks, and for not getting rid of environmental protections. They declare that if they're elected, they'll fight for domestic policies which will make the price go down. But these public figures should know that domestic production has nothing to do with the price at the pump.

None of the environment-gutting measures that these pro-business politicos are pushing for, such as getting rid of California's high clean-fuel standards, would lower the price of gas one penny. None of their ecocidal drilling projects, such as the one that would open up the Alaskan wilderness to the pumps, or shoot oil thru a pipe 3,000 miles to a Texas refinery, would produce a drop of oil for the USA.

The truth is that the oil would be owned by the multinational company that recovered it and then sold on the open global market, all pooled together with the rest of the world's oil supply. Big Oil's well-paid Congressional supporters know better than anybody how the system works. They know that if you have something to sell, you go where you can get the best price for your commodity and make the highest profit.

This situation could have been different, had any of the post-Wall-Street-meltdown regulations been implemented, instead of being killed by oil company lobbyists. But as it is, no regulations exist to force American oil producers to sell their products domestically instead of overseas. In fact, right now American refineries are shipping gasoline, diesel and other petroleum products abroad in record amounts. They have no reason not to. This is how capitalism works.

Pluto (manipulation) opposes Mercury (the media) in the US (Sibly) chart, the signature of propaganda. With their misleading nonsense about "energy independence", the political allies of Big Oil are pressing all the buttons of a public that's financially stressed and pissed-off. Deliberately encouraging American voters' ignorance, their ploy is to blame Democrats and environmentalists for the high price of gas.

But as energy researcher Joelle Brink points out, energy traders have been backing away from oil because of its unpredictable price spikes, and because of new evidence that reserves may have been grossly overstated. As an oil replacement, biofuels are gaining in popularity.

As always when exploitative agencies detect the next big cash cow, a complex of problems have arisen with biofuels, including gross land misuse. But the root problems here are overpopulation and poverty (e.g., in Indonesia); despite the efforts of Europe and the USA to block biofuels, using indirect land use as a pretext. Given that they do not impact food prices or pose access problems, it looks like biofuels from agricultural and post-consumer waste, algae, microbial fermentation and other renewable sources will become a major force in the years ahead.[1]

---

[1] Ms. Brinke's research finds that in much of Asia the percentage of biofuels in gasoline and

Pluto Return

The USA's first-ever Pluto Return is a useful milestone for historians and cultural observers who have been tracking this country's evolution as a superpower. Pluto (underground riches) resides in the second house (wealth) of the US (Sibly) chart, a placement expressing to a tee the symbolism of oil.

For a year or so now, transiting Pluto has been teetering on the cusp of the first and second houses. Its exact return is in 2022-23, after the Uranus-Pluto square gets finished forming a full Grand Cross with the nation's Sun-Saturn square. The way the nation has wielded its Pluto, for two and a half of centuries, is coming full circle, just as the years of Peak Oil come upon us.

Peak Oil

There isn't a clear consensus about when peak oil production will arrive; that is, the point at which the maximum rate of oil extraction will be reached, after which the rate of production enters terminal decline. There were global economists saying years ago that Peak Oil would take place in 2012; among them, astrologer Tem Tarriktar of *The Mountain Astrologer* magazine, who saw it as a likely manifestation of the Uranus-Pluto square.

There is a consensus, however, that Peak Oil is not some fantastic futuristic theory, but an urgent, real-time issue. And yet the development of healthy, efficient energy sources is still considered "unaffordable" or "unrealistic" or even "unnecessary" by an alarming percentage of the American population.

We might chalk this up to the lobbying and propaganda of the oil cartel, as well as the fear of change in the populace. Big Oil has deployed its billions in lobbyist fees to squash clean-energy legislation for generations; and much of the public seems deeply complacent in the face of the wells running dry. There seems to be a mass fantasy that bottomless oil wells exist somewhere, and we can continue this unsustainable way of life forever.

A Post-Denial World

Once enough people shake off their denial, ingenious visions of life without oil will open up like a new frontier. Given the ingenuity, financial resources, and

---

biodiesel has been raised to control escalating consumer fuel prices and reduce transportation emissions. She reports that since 2012 most of the world's major airlines completed 50% biofueled test flights. Around the spring equinox they formed a working group to increase the supply of bioaviation fuel and reduce its cost.

entrepreneurial know-how available, we could change over from destructive to creative energy sources in a New York minute.

We Americans hear all the time about new sustainable energy models being developed by inventors and engineers who see the writing on the wall. Politically and energetically, all we need is the will to change. For some, this might take the form of creating a citizens' lobby, whose first step would be to get Washington to stop Big Oil subsidies and pump the money into clean energy instead.

Granted, it is no small thing to wrap our minds around the prospect of redesigning the manufacture, agriculture, infrastructure, transportation and distribution systems now in place in the world. But a complete overhaul of the current industrial paradigm, from one of dark addiction to oil to one of life-affirming sources, is just the sort of unprecedented transformation that astrologers and other prophets have been writing about since time immemorial, when describing the power of these years of cosmic crossroads.

THE LONGEST ARM

(originally published as a blog,
May 2012)

Now is when 2012 really begins. Not in terms of the Gregorian calendar, but in terms of the biggest transit of our lifetimes. Three days after the summer solstice, the Uranus-Pluto square – the longest arm of the Cardinal Cross – kicks off its four-year-long riff of seven exact hits. June 24th marks the opening of a time-window during which our urge to grow will be far stronger than our need for stasis.

Earth will be vibrating on a new level of intensity between now and 2016. What's all this energy for? What does it mean? These questions are more useful than the *What's-going-to-happen* kind. Whatever happens is going to depend on what kind of energy we bring to bear. And that depends upon how much perspective we have.

Perspective

To get perspective, we can start by giving a thought to how many oracular traditions make special mention of this time. Of these probably the best known is the Mayan *baktun* cycle, said to end on December 21st 2012. Also stunningly vast is the *yuga* system of ancient India, in which our particular era is called the Kali Yuga, Sanskrit for "the Dark Time." (If the Kali Yuga began in 3100 BCE, as some scholars claim, this puts its beginning around the same time as that of the Mayan calendar.) There is even a theory that the Great Pyramid of Giza was built to call attention to the planetary line-up in December of 2012.

The great esoteric channel, Alice Bailey, identified 2025, the year Neptune leaves Pisces, as being the year when the Fourth Ray will come into manifestation, bringing intellectual and emotional integration to the human race. Dane Rudhyar, granddaddy of modern astrology, sees the Age of Aquarius as officially beginning in 2060. These are the kinds of correspondences that make us sit up and take notice.

Prophecies

Theories abound about 2012 and the decades to come. The rumor mill is churning. Whatever else is signified by the various theories, they are evidence that an understanding exists in the collective intelligence about this juncture point in human evolution – an understanding that may not be altogether conscious but is clearly attuned to something real.

As to particular prophecies, it's important to be discerning about what we let in. There is a lot of fear around; and when newsmen or religious leaders, or astrologers or Hollywood filmmakers, start talking about earthquakes and tsunamis and alien invasions, people get even more frightened. In this state, we are hard pressed to respond in the highest possible way to the actual crises that exist. If we're in survival anxiety we'll find it hard to respond through our charts; i.e., from the highest part of our beings. Fear pushes us down into lowest-common-denominator thinking. We cease to be true individuals, and lapse into mob-mind.

The healthiest way to approach this epoch is to open our eyes to its major themes, and keep track of them as they struggle to resolve themselves. These themes are unmistakable; only denial keeps us from seeing them. One of them is the democratization of information via technology; another is the conflict between democracy and plutocracy. Another is the petering out of the industrial revolution and the end of the age of oil.

Me and We

A key paradox of our era has to do with the dual nature of our identity; as individuals, on the one hand, and members of a vast collective, on the other. These two levels of our being each have a reality; it's not an either/or. We are independent souls *and* we are part of the human family.

As to the latter, we need to realize that the status quo is in trouble. To the extent that we identify with conventional narratives, *we* will be in trouble. The years between now and 2016 are an invitation to take a fine-toothed comb and go through the tangled knot of assumptions we hold about collective life, separating out the inauthentic perceptions from the authentic ones. Any belief systems that encourage falsehood are crumbling now, and the sooner we detach from them, the better.

There are so many raucous dramas that could compel our attention – worldwide, as well as within our individual psyches – that it's no small feat to single out any one thing. We're watching a three-ring circus except there aren't just three rings. And we aren't just watching. If we're truly living through our charts, we're participating.

Life Purpose

In light of the building Uranus-Pluto square, it was not surprising to see Occupy Wall Street in the headlines again. Just before May's solar eclipse, Occupiers joined thousands of anti-war demonstrators in the streets of Chicago to protest the NATO summit. People are getting bit by the Uranus-Pluto bug in nonpolitical ways too. Some are taking the Landmark Forum; some are committing to radical health improvement. Some are organizing around sustainable agriculture or micro-loans in India or endangered species. We have a multitude of leaders and resources available to us at this moment in history. We have righteous hackers fighting to keep the internet free; we have the environmental movement and fair trade warriors, we have visionaries leading the way in the arenas of sustainable energy and food.

The time is ripe for consciousness-seekers to step into our purpose. How will we know what this is? Easy: we will be instructed from within and without. Neither our instincts nor our circumstances will leave us alone until we honor these promptings. All we have to do is be still and listen.

THE HOT ZONE

(originally published in *Daykeeper
Journal*, June 2012)

The Summer Solstice in 2012 is dense with celestial events. With the first exactitude[1] of the Uranus-Pluto square at the midpoint of the year flanked by a host of extraordinary supporting transits, we have entered the hot zone.

This is a cosmic heat wave that's been rising since 1966, when Uranus and Pluto conjoined in the sky. We're now at the first quarter of the cycle that began back then. With this historic portal heating up the month, the dream-weaving planet, Neptune, stations retrograde on June 4th under a Full Moon, which happens to be an Eclipse. The next day is the rare occultation of Venus (there won't be another until 2117).[2]

On the 24th, five days after the New Moon and four days after the Sun announces the first day of summer, Uranus and Pluto click into the first of their seven exact 90-degree angles: the first such spike in a long crescendo. Jupiter's square to Neptune later in the month highlights the main subplot of the era, that of Neptunian illusion.[3] The Sun's T-square to Uranus and Pluto square[4] as June moves to a close gives us a peek at the kind of energy we can expect for the next seven years, whenever the Sun moves through a Cardinal sign.

Why do astrologers pay special attention to scenarios like these? In general, when transits come all stacked up this way they reinforce each other, creating a

---

[1] The second exactitude is in September of 2012 and the rest take place between then and 2015.

[2] Venus' passes between the Earth and the Sun come in pairs. As Julija Imas has noted, the Wall Street meltdown took place at the midpoint between the last Venus occultation, in 2004, and this one.

[3] See Charlatans, p. 355.

[4] The Sun is 8°23 Cancer (Cardinal water), Uranus is 8°23 Aries (Cardinal fire) and Pluto 8°23 Capricorn (Cardinal earth).

force field that squeezes events into being. But as sky watchers know, this is not just any old stack of pancakes. This is the longest arm of the Cardinal Cross, the series of world-altering formations that puts 2012 on the astrological map.

Observers of the global scene have been watching the approach of the Uranus-Pluto square very carefully, aware that certain hot spots on the world map will be hit hard.

Europe

Under the cross hairs are a number of European countries with January 1st birthdays,[5] which puts their Sun at 10 degrees Capricorn: two degrees shy of the June 24th exactitude. Capricorn is the sign most vulnerable of all to the Cardinal Cross. And as astrologer Adrian Duncan has pointed out, the chart of the Euro – the beleaguered currency itself – has the Sun placed here;[6] as will come as no surprise to anyone who's been watching the dramas taking place across the Atlantic. Pluto, the planet of death/rebirth, has been harrying that Sun for the past four years like hounds after a fox.

Greece, the poster child of the European crisis, faces an election just as the Solstice transits start to cook. Along with the economies of Ireland, Italy, Spain and Portugal,[7] Greece has been careening in breakdown mode (Pluto), with massive unemployment and immense debt threatening every aspect of their national infrastructure (Capricorn). France and the Netherlands are the most recent examples of nations whose economic woes have spread to the governmental level.

Summer 2012 represents the most critical point for the cohesion of Europe since the second World War. Monetarily, the crisis is forcing the Continent to decide whether what's good for Germany is good for the rest of the Eurozone. Politically, the crisis has occasioned the rise of ominous extremism; a point that was driven home to me when I saw a photograph of Greece's Golden Dawn party standing in salute. The gentlemen had one arm by their sides, the other extended

---

[5] Both the horoscope commonly used for England (i.e. for William the Conqueror's coronation on Dec 25, 1066), and the one for the U.K. (unifying Great Britain and Ireland, at least in name, on Jan.1st,1801) have Capricorn birthdays.

[6] See *The Mountain Astrologer Magazine*, June-July 2012, p.26

[7] The Greek people have reacted to their five-year-long recession with rioting in the streets, while in Portugal and Ireland people have been suffering relatively silently under equally brutal austerity measures. The question is whether the frustration and anger in these countries, too, will come to a boil.

straight out in front.

USA

With the Euro on life support, some investors have fled to the US dollar. But no chart I have seen gets as potent a blow from current and upcoming transits as that of the US (Sibly) chart, whose own Sun-Saturn square joins with Uranus and Pluto to form a full Grand Cross, the most stressful configuration in astrology.

Uncle Sam is being hit right where it hurts. The aspect of its natal chart that receives the hit – the difficult Sun square Saturn – is associated by psychological astrologers with self-doubt, denial and inferiority complexes.

One sign of a major downgrade in America's world status is the fevered rumor about the dollar being replaced by the yuan as the global standard.[8] Obama's discussions with the Chinese, intended to help Uncle Sam pay its out-of-control debt, may further strengthen the yuan's primacy.[9]

China

Most Americans seem not to have integrated the global meaning shift that China has undergone. The China-bashing one hears in the US media smacks of old-fashioned Cold War China-bashing; not *Yikes-we-could-actually-lose-the-superpower-crown!* China-bashing.

But geopolitical observers consider the rivalry between the USA and China to be one of the central dramas of our era. In breakneck industrialization mode, teeming with global consumers and possessed of virtually no debt, the immense Asian behemoth seems eager to accept the hyper-power baton from a beleaguered Uncle Sam. Consider the symbolism of the purchase, in late May 2012, of the giant American theater chain AMC. It was sold to a Chinese firm, stepping up to satisfy the appetites of more than a billion fans of faraway Hollywood.

Yet the transits suggest a more complicated picture. Under skies like these, the contest for hyper-power may have no winner. The chart for modern China (10-1-

---

At this writing Brazil, South Africa, India and France are in trade agreement talks with China, significantly boosting the yuan's edge over the dollar.

See Dambisa Moro's *How the West Was Lost*, in which a former Goldman Sachs economist predicts when China will surpass the USA in GDP, leading to the "redback" renminbi replacing the greenback dollar.

49, 3:15 pm Beijing) sustains a prolonged direct hit from the Uranus-Pluto square. The longest arm of the Cardinal Cross forms a T-square with China's Libra cluster, with the Sun at the exact apex.

The economic model that China is following – which all modern civilizations have so far followed – presumes that growth is not merely part of the cycle, but its constant. In this view, growth is good, period: without qualification and without interruption. The USA, with Jupiter (increase, expansion) conjunct the Sun natally, epitomizes this philosophy. China is in fevered pursuit of the same brass ring.

A poignant symbol of the relationship between the two super-rivals hinges on the commodity that will soon be seen as the single most valuable resource in the world: water. It is from the American Great Lakes that mega-corporation Nestle gets much of the fresh water that it sells, in great numbers of plastic bottles, to China, its biggest customer.

Juncture Point

The summer solstice transits indicate an extraordinary juncture point in time: a moment in history when a glimpse of the future is available. It is not that the transits promise to turn us into fortune-tellers; this isn't about predicting specific events. It's about discerning the meaning behind them.

CHARLATANS

(originally published in *Skywatch*,
June 2012)

During the years of the Uranus-Pluto square, Neptune in Pisces (2012-25) looms in the background. In June, 2012, the month the Cardinal square comes to exactitude, Neptune is exaggerated by a station early in the month and by a square from Jupiter around the Solstice.

To use this transit well requires a different kind of alertness than does the Uranus-Pluto square. Neptune is a teaching about the nature of illusion, and is accordingly elusive. It doesn't shout. It envelops us quietly, like weather.

Frauds

On the personal level, Neptune in Pisces opens us up to all sorts of outside influences as well as to our own inner inspiration. But if we aren't careful, all that exquisite receptivity melts into a woozy state of overwhelm. On the collective level, shadow Neptune can stupefy the group mind, enshrouding us in consensual delusion. Already unmoored by the radical Cardinal transit peaking for the first time this summer, the group mind is especially susceptible right now to charlatanism.

Though "charlatan" is a word usually reserved for con men and fraudulent practitioners of the occult,[1] the lion's share of the charlatanism going on in the world right now is the work of moneyed interests conning the people.[2]

---

[1] I have never personally encountered an example of this type of charlatan, though judging from the solemn warnings of most users of the term, they lurk behind every lamp post.

[2] The line between commerce and politics has become effectively erased since the *Citizen's United* decision inaugurated the age of PACs, legalizing the corruption of the electoral system.

Polluted Stream

In places like the USA, charlatanism flourishes through advertising and propaganda. At the moment, American television programmers are working overtime, hypnotizing (Neptune) the public via the gossip-fest that is domestic politics.

In Virgo until July, 2012, Mars is stirring up the daily dose of meaningless details with an aggressiveness that borders on virulence. Those who partake of the media, whether voluntarily or involuntarily (now that television sets have managed to wend their way into upscale restaurants, hotel lobbies and banks), are met with an avalanche of factoids from morning to night, revolving around which presidential candidate – each financed by the same corporate behemoths – is ahead in the latest poll.

Neptune is maximally strong in Pisces, which makes it all the more important to be wary of its shadow side, one aspect of which is a soul-deep restlessness and distractability. If we understand where these energies come from, we can better guard against them. They are the undeveloped manifestation of Neptune's higher purpose, which is to loosen our focus from the singular and allow it to reach the sublime.

Transcendent Purpose

Underneath the dizzy vagueness of Neptune transits is the potential for vast consciousnesses expansion. Neptune is trying to stretch our attention in all directions for a transcendent purpose. It makes us yearn to get beyond the specific and embrace that which is all-encompassing. When we are fully centered in ourselves, this mind state allows a universalism of vision that inspires spiritual wisdom.

The trouble comes in when we are not living from the center of our charts, and neither is the group entity of which we are a part. Then we risk losing our footing on the banks of observation, and slip into the polluted stream of mass nonsense. Thus submerged, we lose ourselves in least-common-denominator thinking.

At that point we lose touch with our personal tastes, ethical beliefs and our common sense. We may find that our priorities have inadvertently shifted to those of the anchorman on the TV screen… or, more accurately, his *apparent* priorities; given that whatever worldview he purports to represent is itself a Neptunian illusion.

Little Lies

It takes a certain kind of consciousness-seeker to study lies in order to understand Truth. This challenge is pointedly upon us whenever Neptune stations in the sky, or makes a transit to another planet, over the course of its thirteen years in Pisces. In contrast to Uranus, whose energy shocks us into noticing it, and to Pluto, whose fatal extremism compels our attention, Neptunian energy compels only in the sense that it bewitches. Its soft, fuzzy glamour seduces us unannounced. This is the source of its power.

It is no small feat to defy the myriad collective lies that serve as wallpaper in our social environment. We are up against not just the illusion-spinners but the herd mentality of the group mind itself, which promises us the safety of conformity. The most effective cultural illusions are those that have become commonplace. When I was a child, no one questioned the need to drink three glasses of cow's milk a day: the dairy industry's prescription had become the law of the land. Cultural lies reflect not only the reprehensibility of the spinners but the moral and intellectual laziness of the people being spun.

Many of the little lies we live with are transparent enough. Those perpetrated by advertising, for example, operate on a consensual basis; we can readily see through a commercial's use of sex to sell shampoo, or a billboard's use of artful design to sell a car. Part of us realizes quite well that it's a trade-off between the seller's artfulness and our own willingness to be seduced.

Big Lies

The bigger lies, such as those told by powerful agencies like governments and religions, are more pernicious while equally ubiquitous. Both little and big lies often use familiarity and repetition to work their way into the group mind. Commercials do this; so do the news stories repeated in the echo chamber of corporate news.

Both types of lies exact a pledge from the group mind to tolerate them. In the case of really big lies, the group gets agitated, even hostile, if it hears them refuted; as with the official story of 9/11.

The classic big lie is when a government sells a deadly idea to a populace who would never otherwise agree to it. Thus are military incursions sold, dressed up in patriotic terms as diplomatic missions and other feel-good concepts. The citizenry that funds these campaigns, through its taxes, would doubtless void the sale if it were framed in terms of human bodies being splintered by drone missiles.

On the first of May 2012, the American government pulled off one such stunt. The US president, who foregoes the trouble of trying his enemies in a court of law by targeting them – and any stray civilians who might be in the way — with killer robot planes, flew out for a quick handshake with his frenemy, the leader of Afghanistan. Given that this particular war has become unpopular with voters, and that elections are looming, Obama channeled Neptune in its charlatan guise. A photo op was staged whose purpose was to rebrand "the war in Afghanistan" as "*ending* the war in Afghanistan."

This PR episode will not change what's going on. The same forces will continue to control this geostrategically positioned country in Central Asia. The US military bases will remain, US taxpayers will continue to finance them and US-built drones will continue to kill.[3] What has changed is the official story, and thus the perception of many Americans under the influence of shadow Neptune.

Over the same period, Americans were consuming a flood of news coverage about a politician, John Edwards, who had lied about his sex life. The public was duly shocked, offended and fascinated by these little lies. The big lie told by their government on May Day was given a pass.

Lunatics and sociopaths often understand the workings of Neptune better than anybody. Consider the twisted insights of a guy who wrote the book on big lies:

> In the big lie there is always a certain force of credibility; because the broad masses of a nation are always more easily corrupted… and thus in the primitive simplicity of their minds they more readily fall victims to the big lie than the small lie…. It would never come into their heads to fabricate colossal untruths, and they would not believe that others could have the impudence to distort the truth so infamously…even though the facts which prove this to be so may be brought clearly to their minds…
> - A. Hitler, *Mein Kampf,* vol. 1, ch. X

---

[3] The fine print of the pact between Obama and Afghanistan President Hamid Karzai allows for troops and bases to remain in Afghanistan for decades to come.

Refusing to Ignore

(originally published in *Skywatch*,
July 2012)

Just after the lunar eclipse on June 4th, the sky was shimmering with transits. Neptune was stationary and the solstice was right around the corner, with the first exactitude of the Uranus-Pluto square on its heels. As if hearing the signal, two significant reports were released about global warming.[1] For the astrologically inclined, the language used in one of the papers was especially striking. The scientists said Earth was approaching a "tipping point."

This phrase is sometimes used by astrologers to refer to the period between 2008 and 2023, a critical threshold in time over which humanity is now hovering. The scientists' paper went into detail about unchecked population growth, fossil fuels and the conversion of almost half of the planet's land to farms or cities. The news held no surprises for people who care about these things.

This got me wondering: what does it mean to not care about these things?

Limited Scope

I think it must be true that most of the people living on the Earth focus their attention pretty much exclusively on their own personal lives, within the scope of their domestic unit, tribe, village or locality. For the massive numbers of souls who live hand to mouth – almost half the global population[2] – the reasons for this limited focus are self-evident.

For the other half, however, whose day-to-day survival is not in question and

---

[1] The National Oceanic and Atmospheric Administration's National Climatic Data Center claimed that this spring 2012 in the USA has been the warmest since record-keeping began in 1895. The report published in the journal *Nature*, by a group of 22 scientists from five countries, updated the idea of the planet being a point of no return as regards human-caused climate change.

[2] Roughly three billion people globally live on less than $2.50 a day.

whose access to information is just about infinite, the question does seem to cry out for explanation. Why is our scope so limited?

Why is there so much ignoring going on?

Many of us in the privileged sector might explain our lack of interest by saying we are just too overwhelmed. This overwhelm seems to be partly intellectual: there is too damn much information, nonstop and ubiquitous. Harder still to deal with is the emotional overwhelm. We erect boundaries against the things we allow ourselves to care about. Maybe we see ourselves as having only a certain amount of compassion to go around, and if we let in everything there is to care about, our reservoir would get used up.

I believe we suffer from a kind of moral paucity, too, in the dis-ensouled industrialized world. In place of the moral certainties that earlier epochs received from their shaman, guru or priestess, all secular Westerners have are the opinions of talking heads on TV. There seems to be a hole where ethical guidance used to be.

Spiritual Cohesion

Yet we do have all the pieces. We don't lack for the various ingredients that could provide a sense of psychological, moral, and spiritual cohesion. We have access to the knowledge that could help us cope with the world. Among those moderns who have rejected established religion, many have access to a moral compass through other wisdom paths. They may have tried yoga and meditation, subscribe to the philosophy of holistic health and are familiar with the idea of karma and we–create–our-own-reality. They may have even taken classes on Marxism, Buddhist thought and ecology in college. They have heard the great truths reframed.

Still, there seems to be a big difference between hearing these things and applying them to the here- and-now. Whence this gap between theory and practice, and between ideal and feeling?

We may declare ourselves in full agreement, for example, with the spiritual truism that Everything is Connected, yet feel utterly uninterested in the international scene; estranged even from what's happening in countries that share a border with our own. We may consider the Butterfly Effect unarguably true – with respect to bee colonies and ice caps, but not with respect to human societies in turmoil.

I think we must account it a curious inconsistency that many people have no problem believing that the tiniest shift in animal behavior anywhere on Earth has impact on the whole global ecosystem *except* where the human animal is concerned. Once the conversation turns to the decline of drinking water in war-ravaged East Africa, suddenly the boundaries go up and the speaker declares himself "apolitical."[3]

Psychic Pick-Up

But this information cannot be kept out. If one believes that all beings are connected, one must also believe that what happens in one corner of the world is felt in every other corner. We are all privy to it, on some level of consciousness. Whether we read the newspaper or soak up world events psychically, we are all swimming together in the soup of what's happening in the human family. The question is: What we do with the information?

When we shut down to it, we inadvertently shut down other of our psychic mechanisms, too. During the tipping point years, when shutting down will become increasingly hard to do, the effort to close ourselves off will require that we clamp down more and more parts of ourselves. This will make the choice to ignore more and more unhealthy.

The fact that it will get harder and harder to ignore the world may at first strike us as a downer. But it is clearly in the best interests of the rebirth of Earth, which can only heal if humanity has its eyes wide open.

It is also in the interests of our own personal evolution. Ignoring is not only bad for our overall health, but shuts us off from our creative potential.

Creative Blast

When we start to open up fully to the world, we notice that we can let in even the most distressing realities, and engage with them. This happens through a

---

[3] This oft-heard apologia, with its strange use of the word pair *political/apolitical*, bears looking into. On the face of it, the speaker is declaring a lack of interest in the world of elections and governmental systems; and his word choice may gain purchase from the assumption that the listener agrees that these systems are venal and untrustworthy, thus rightfully ignored. But the connotation of "political" in this context encompasses much more than the machinations of politicians. Its usage here seems to refer to any and all arenas beyond the speaker's personal domain (as in: "What do you think of global warming?" "Oh, I'm not political.") The speaker seems to be conflating the activities of politicians with just about everything that happens in the outside world.

profound creative process that feels not so much willed as driven.

Have you ever had an idea or feeling burn away inside your brain, worming its way into your attention even though you didn't know what to do with it – until, finally, maybe you jump out of bed in the middle of the night and grab a paper and write it out, or maybe you dance it out, or call someone and verbally hash it out? All that pent-up, frustrated disquiet is transformed into creative energy.

This is what happens when an idea whose time has come uses us as a crucible. In this spirit, we can allow even the most horrible scenarios into our consciousness, inviting them to mix together with the raw material of our being. When we surrender to this process, a kind of transmutation happens. An initially disturbing obsession (Pluto) suddenly explodes (Uranus) in a creative blast.

Beauty from Garbage

I imagine this is what happened to Brazilian artist Vik Muniz, who makes artworks from the trash piled up at Jardim Gramacho, the immense landfill outside Rio de Janeiro. Instead of shutting down to the desperately poor scavengers who live there, he engaged with them, employing them to pick out materials with him from the mountains of refuse, with which he creates huge portrait mosaics that are now famous throughout the world.

By refusing to ignore the garbage dump, Muniz made it harder for the rest of the world to ignore it. For many of us, he changed the energy around the very idea of it.

A critically acclaimed film has been now been made about Muniz and his helpers: *Wasteland*, by Lucy Walker and Karen Harley. Like Muniz, the documentarians do not shut down in horror from their subject. Quite the opposite: their point of view inspires and touches the heart. They have made of it something beautiful. The film functions to extend even further the transformation process that began when Vik Muiz refused to ignore.

The reality of the Brazilian landfill has now entered further into the world's consciousness. As the information spreads about this community, Vik Muniz, a working class lad from Sao Paulo, is selling his work at expensive art galleries in New York. The garbage pickers have benefitted from improved living conditions. And we who hear about this story are invited to open up to a little bit more to the world of which we are a part, and to the epoch to which we belong.

CHAPTER 6

THE YEARS AHEAD

As 2008 was about to dawn, astrologer Ted Denmark summed up the period to come. "2007," he said, "was the last normal year." Uranus and Pluto were getting ready to force wave after wave of tumultuous change (Uranus) upon a global collective in critical need of transformation (Pluto).

Phases Two and Three

As I write, in early June of 2012, we have begun Phase Two of the Cardinal Cross.

Phase 1, 2008-12, began when Pluto entered Capricorn and the fissures of the world's financial foundations opened into ruptures. Uranus and Pluto started to position themselves a quarter of the sky away from each other.

In Phase Two, 2012-15, Uranus and Pluto form an exact 90° angle to the minute of arc. The sense of global urgency is likely to be unmistakable and actively polarized.

Phase Three, 2016-23, is the assimilation phase, ending with the year Pluto leaves Capricorn and enters Aquarius. As it had a long on-ramp, the Uranus-Pluto square will have a long off-ramp. Humanity will be integrating its effects for a long time to come.

We Already Know

If everything in the cosmos is inextricably interconnected, it follows that every being alive is already cognizant, on some level of consciousness, of what's going on in our shared world. The question that remains is how we make sense of it.

The fact that this is a truly extraordinary epoch is news to no one. Relative to the usual slow slob of collective consciousness, the shifts that have occurred since the onset of the Cardinal Cross have been sudden and jarring. At the same time, none of it was out of the blue. Each of us had access to all the information we needed to know which way the wind was blowing.

For example, around 2008 it started to dawn on masses of people that Wall Street was guilty of an immense con game; but the state of affairs that led up to this recognition was a long time in the making. The financial industry had been gaming the system for years. Similarly, the BP disaster in the Gulf of Mexico in the spring of 2010 was not a shock to anyone who had been watching how the oil companies operate. To such observers the rig explosion seemed a more or less inevitable occurrence, part of a well-established *modus operandi*. Neither did the near-meltdown of those reactors in Japan in 2011 tell the world anything it didn't already know about the dangers of nuclear energy.

The Pluto ingress that coincided with the Wall Street meltdown signified a lurch forward in the consciousness of something that had been long building. The Cardinal Climax that coincided with the rig explosion in the Gulf of Mexico signified a sudden recognition among the public about destructive policies that had been in effect for decades. The conjunction of Uranus onto the hot-button Aries Point the very day of the Japanese earthquake translated to a loud, insistent wake-up call about a danger already amply documented.

It would not be accurate to say that these planetary transits "caused" these events. More precisely, the transits were timing devices. In the case of Uranus and Pluto, we're dealing with alarm clocks with extra loud buzzers. Each peak of their square marks an appointment humanity has with a new level of awareness.

Those observers who are alert to the world moment will not be surprised by any of the events astrologers see as probable in the years to come. The only feature that is new here is our arrival at a threshold of decision.

Threshold of Decision

When we are making our way down a road and come to an intersection, we have to slow down or stop. An element of tension is introduced; our momentum is broken and we have to make a decision. This necessitates a wakefulness that wasn't there before. It is for this reason that in astrology square angles are associated with consciousness raising.[1]

---

[1] Square aspects, formed when planets are a quarter of the sky away from each other, as Pluto and Uranus are during these years, get their tension from the symbolism of the Pythagorean *tetrad*. Spatial relationships based on the four pattern, like a T-square or a Grand Cross, signify blockage or crisis; energies working at *cross*-purposes.

n the symbolism of myth, crossroads have always represented magical choice
points, where multiple potential fates are laid before the traveler. Oedipus made
his patricidal decision where three roads came together; it was at a crossroads
that blues legend Robert Johnson was said to have received his genius; and there
s magic inherent in the crossroads in time that humanity stands at now. We are
choosing between potential futures: the direction we will take upcoming is being
et now.

Underlying this idea is an essentially spiritual premise: that human beings are on
this Earth to learn. Astrology presumes that individuals possess an identity that
predates and outlasts their conscious ego identity – let us call it the soul – and
that this soul has a growth plan: our natal chart and the transits to it. Moreover,
his plan is inextricably connected to the growth plan of the whole of humanity.
Whatever the daunting lessons implicit in tumultuous historical periods like this
one, they are part and parcel of our own individual soul intentions. We chose to
be here, right now. There is power in this understanding.

Conversely, looking at the future deterministically has little power in it. It allows
us barely any role; our choices play no part in what the future is about. The
question "What will happen in the future" implies a scenario where events are
lined up in some cosmic waiting room – in a dimension different from the one we
occupy. They are waiting to happen "to" us. This view puts us in the role of
passive recipient-victim. To view the years ahead this way is to see ourselves as
consumers of the future, rather than creators of it.

Cultural Obstacles

It is not surprising that this approach has become the normative one, given that
contemporary culture encourages us to consume experience rather than
participate in it. The most obvious expression of this skewed mindset is the
economic model used by the First World. Under capitalism, we are trained to see
ourselves as consumers first and citizens second, if at all.

The primary enforcer of this state of affairs is the corporate media – television
and, in the USA, right-wing radio – which seem designed to make mincemeat of
human intelligence. An information stream this compromised cannot help us
understand what is unfolding. We must stay in touch with what's in the
headlines, but we must learn to read between the lines.

We need to be careful of taking on the amoral priorities implied by the
presentation of news (it is not that they are *im*moral; it is simply that they are

profit-driven). In 1989, when the Exxon Valdez spilled hundreds of thousands of barrels of oil into the pristine waters of Prince William Sound, Alaska, the news agencies hopped on it as big news. It was the largest spill in US waters up to that point, and millions of people were appropriately appalled – for a short time; until the headlines moved on to the next big event. Now, in spring 2012, there seems to be little relationship in most Americans' minds between that horrific spill and the fact that Exxon is pumping billions of dollars into the coffers of US Congressmen committed to killing environmental protections. The TV reporters have moved on, so for most viewers the issue has lost its buzz.

Similarly, the near-meltdown of Japan's nuclear reactors on the day Uranus hit the Aries point in March 2011 consumed the attention of the global media for a few very tense months. But, a year later, when radiation from those reactors is being found in kelp off the California coast, there is no similar coverage, and among the public few seem to be connecting the dots.

Increasingly, the New Media, for all of its importance as a democratizer of information, has become another obstacle to the kind of reflective thinking that helps us confer meaning to our lives. In the digital world, information is ubiquitous, fragmented and continuous. The internet has raised up-to-the-minuteness to an art form, but it has undermined our ability to think deeply. With its overwhelming emphasis upon data-collecting and its prioritization of quantity over quality of information, the wired approach to world events does not lend itself to musing and pondering.

The media in all its forms is both friend and foe. Our goal during Phase Two and Three of the Cardinal Cross years should be to use the various channels of information-dissemination at our disposal to keep abreast of the events unfurling in our world, as well as to keep our finger on the pulse of the collective mentality – without letting what we're seeing and hearing undermine our own common sense and innate spiritual knowing.

The USA

The USA has been a bellwether for the industrialized world, and its role in the coming changes will continue to be significant. The Uranus-Pluto square's provocation of the US (Sibly) chart's Sun-Saturn square, peaking in 2014-15, suggests a concentrated period of clashes between conflicting segments of this putatively classless society, as the haves and have-nots take off the gloves. There may be waves of superficially unifying patriotic feeling (for example during the Jupiter conjunction to the US Sun cluster in early 2014), but domestic agitation will be the rule. We know from looking at history that wrenching cultural battles are the crucible from which deep-structure change arises.

During its Pluto Return of 2022, discussed in several of the essays in this book, the USA will confront its karma as a hyper-power. We can anticipate a closure to the process that began when Pluto entered Capricorn in 2008, at which point the economic crisis exposed how the skewed inequities of the system have been increasing over the several generations. The cat is now out of the bag: there has been a steady transfer of wealth upwards to a small number of financial players, supported by the corruption of the political system and expressed in a cycle of bubbles and bailouts.

Student loan debt may make headlines as the big economic crisis during these years. Of the millions of young graduates worldwide trying to enter the work force in a depressed economy while shouldering crippling debt, Americans in particular seem likely to raise this issue to a *cause célèbre*; given that the implicit promises of the American Dream led them to expect a much easier ride. When these young people start to communicate, *en masse,* about the disproportionate burden imposed by their education, and the inaccessibility of the comfortable lifestyle their parents enjoyed, we may see an explosive new generation gap.

At the opposite end of the spectrum, the Baby Boomers' aging *en masse* represents a ticking time bomb for, among other things, the country's irredeemably broken health care system. The corrupt linkage between the drug and insurance industries and the political establishment will continue to be exposed, as the sheer numbers of the geriatric demographic squeeze it to the fore.

Beginning its transit through the US second house (money) in 2011, Pluto (exposure) signifies a breakdown of the system of cover-ups that have hidden the role of investment bankers (Capricorn) in the creation of crises ranging from global food shortages to burgeoning world debt.[2] Financial systems in their current form will continue to be revealed as incapable of managing the world economy. The Fed, the IMF and the World Bank will be subject to increased critical scrutiny as the trajectory of the old financial paradigm makes its way towards breakdown or breakthrough.

China and Russia

The role of China as a rival to Uncle Sam will take shape over these years,

---

[2] See Matt Taibbi, *Griftopia: Bubble Machines, Vampire Squids, and the Long Con That Is Breaking America* (Spiegel & Grau 2010).

geopolitically,[3] in science and supercomputing, alternative energy, perhaps higher education, and certainly as a consumer market. But China's burgeoning environmental and political crises will serve as a counterpoint to its no-holds-barred industrialization. When laid against China's chart, the Cardinal Cross suggests increasing conflict between the clique of aging despots in control of the government (Pluto) and the unpredictable force of two tiers lower down but rising: first, the upstart power of a middle class, ambitious and increasingly wired (Uranus), and second, a teeming rural class displaced by the country's breakneck race to develop and urbanize.

Economic, political or geological shake-ups seem particularly likely during the Uranus-Pluto square's peak on China's natal Sun-square-Uranus[4] in 2012-13. Power plays and financial scandals will continue to rock the government, and the populace will continue to be rocked by crises of sociological instability.

The natal chart of modern Russia, too, is hit hard by the Uranus-Pluto square, all though Phase 2 of the Cross.[5] Personified by its strongman prime minister, Vladimir Putin (about whom a flurry of revealing video and print documentaries came out[6] as Pluto began its T-square to Russia's chart in early 2012), post-millennial Russia is an astrological hotbed of instability, agitated by power struggles at the top and seething with grievance in the general population. A preview of what's in store took place on June 12th 2012 under the third quarter Moon. On what is a national holiday in Russia, with the Pluto-Uranus square about to peak, T-square to Russia's nodal axis, some fifty thousand protesters marched through Moscow in defiance of a police crackdown that had landed their leaders in jail.

Income Disparity

Income equality, whose sudden emergence as a rallying cry is a textbook manifestation of the square between Uranus (individual enterprise) and Pluto

---

[3] A case in point is the jockeying to get a toehold in Afghanistan once Western forces lower their profile. China, along with Iran and India, has been watching and waiting to gain access to Afghanistan's vast natural resources after the NATO occupation reconfigures

[4] Oct 1, 1949 3:15 pm CCT, Beijing

[5] Modern Russia, Dec 8, 1991; 7:45 pm EET; Moskva

[6] See Masha Gessen, *The Man Without a Face* (Riverhead 2012).

(plutocracy), will doubtless intensify in China,[7] the USA and elsewhere over the years of the transit's exactitude. As Pluto (makeovers) makes its way through Capricorn (political and economic stratification), an understanding of the relationship between (political) autocracy and (financial) plutocracy is deepening in the general population. Masses of people in the more stratified societies will continue to push against entrenched interests. A very old, established leadership model is dying: that of patriarchal authority. 2008-15 is the threshold for this process to announce itself as irrevocable.

It will not die gracefully. The one-percent, identified at the end of Phase One by the Occupy Wall Street movement as holding onto the vast majority of the world's wealth, will hunker down and resist, using the media outlets, the police, the militaries and legislative bodies to counter the swelling tide.

As with the other issues facing us in this era, the acrimony over political and economic justice should not surprise us, nor strike us as cause for pessimism. This is the kind of tension by means of which enormous change is squeezed out of the group mind.

As the heat builds, forces on each side of the divide will become regroup and experiment. For example, we can expect artists who identify with the 99% to come out with more works such as Jennifer Baichal's *Payback*, a 2012 documentary about the theories of visionary economist (Capricorn)-activist (Aries) Raj Patel.

The Internet

As became apparent in the Jasmine Revolutions of 2011, the role of the internet in popular uprisings is a wild card. Democracy movements worldwide have taken to cyberspace to circumvent government crackdowns, but the powers-that-be are finding new ways to repress cyber dissent; for example, through the international treaty ACTA and the notorious US bills SOPA and CISPA, which would expand the government access to user information in the name of internet security.

As the age of information sharing ripens, pressure is building between people's desire for the freedom (Uranus) to share unlimited information and the ramifications of ceding control of that information to unselected persons or outside agencies (Pluto). Phases 2 and 3 will intensify the debate over data-

---

[7] The gap between rich and poor in China has become so inflammatory that in the spring of 2012 the government stopped releasing its regular reports about the distribution of the country's wealth.

mining, surveillance and other kinds of tracking by corporations, governments and law enforcement agencies around the world (as detailed, for example, in the American Civil Liberties Union report of April 2012 on the routine and warrantless tracking of cell phones).

In other ways, too, this is a moment of truth for the information revolution. During the years between 2012-23 the world will be grappling with the myriad social and intellectual implications of how life has changed in the age of computers. There will be efforts to come to terms with the fact that technology has careened ahead far faster than humanity has been able to assimilate it psychologically, psychically or spiritually. Like a genie released from a bottle, an onslaught of digital machines is forcing humanity to play a game of catch-up.

In ways that will be apparent by Phase Three, social networks of every kind are being affected by the increasing speed and accessibility of data. The rhythms of daily life are being transformed (Pluto) by portable technology (Uranus) in much of the world, and personal self-expression is changing with them.

These influences portend fundamental changes not only in our communicative patterns, but also in our underlying understanding of the whys and wherefores of interpersonal relationship. The years ahead will offer us a chance to rebalance the psycho-sociological disconnect that has developed between our technical capacity to exchange messages and our human need to convey meaning through them.

Global Population

As a crusade for reformers, overpopulation lay dormant for a few decades. But this issue is experiencing a consciousness surge, as expressed by the recent publicity about the number of human beings on Earth having reached the seven billion mark, and the speculation about what the physical ramifications of these numbers would be if not moderated. The mass mind is waking up to an essential vortex of global crisis.

At the same time, judging by the resurgence of resistance to contraception in even a society as modern as the USA[8] – not to mention in the world's more traditional cultures, where misogyny is a cultural and religious institution - the struggle to control overpopulation triggers deep-seated fears of sexuality and gender politics. These reactive forces will continue to go head-to-head with the

---

[8] For example, in the spring of 2012 GOP Congressmen introduced legislation that would allow any employer to deny access to free birth control to their employees.

scendant forces of human rights and feminism, which, since its activist phase in he 1970s and 80s, has manifested in a slow but steady worldwide recognition of he rights of women.

Moreover, the idea of curbing the global population also threatens the theoretical underpinnings of capitalism, which relies on an ever-increasing demand for growth. In order to accommodate the reality that the Earth cannot support an nfinite amount of human beings, several long-unquestioned and obsolete models of human organization will be under the gun. Understanding the connections between these models is part of the surge of consciousness underway.

Systems Collapse

As the Cardinal Cross progresses, systems collapse, already acute in much of the Third World, will increasingly impress upon the First World the need for profound attitude shifts as a precursor to immense policy reforms. We will continue to see an age-old pattern acted out: that of the most destitute of the world's peoples being hit soonest and hardest by these global problems, playing he role of canary in the mine for the more affluent societies.

As threats to a society's basic functioning, such as governmental collapse, bank failure or food shortages, reach crisis proportions, they undergo a meaning shift. As they spread, they start to be seen by more and more people as not merely a regional problem but as a global emergency; and not merely as an inevitable companion of poverty, unchanged through the ages (a perspective often voiced by those who have enough to eat), but as a function of a decisive moment in history.

Extreme Weather

As discussed in the essays, extreme weather patterns have long been associated with this epoch. Whether these manifest literally or figuratively, a series of ruptures and quakes within the consciousness of humanity is inevitable.

For example, sociological tsunamis will occur as millions of global denizens move from their homes in unprecedented numbers, as a result of global warming, telluric events and storms (in 2010 and 2011, national disasters drove 42 million people from their homes in the Asia-Pacific region[9]). The displacement of this many human beings will have not only physical impact but tremendous psycho-

---

According to the Internal Displacement Monitoring Centre.

sociological ramifications. As their numbers rise, these refugees will force changes in the old thinking about immigration, raising questions about everything from public health to the whole concept of nationalism.

As suggested in several of the essays in this book, on a spiritual level this human flux will bring home the key teaching of Neptune in Pisces (2012-25): that humanity is a united whole. We can expect many strident encounters between exclusionary xenophobes living in the still-functional regions of the world, who loudly proclaim the differences between themselves and those seeking sanctuary (e.g., Sheriff Arpaio in Arizona, Marie Le Pen in France); but the lesson of the transit is more powerful than the forces of reaction. The realization will occur to more and more people that the differences between human beings are dwarfed by the similarities.

Water

The transit of Neptune in Pisces (2012-25) that forms a companion to the Cardinal square highlights the importance of water in a number of ways.

On the literal level, global warming is provoking evaporation, while population increases create rising demand for water, and pollution threatens supplies. These issues will become increasingly difficult to ignore; especially when residents of the still-functioning countries experience an influx of people fleeing their low-lying, flood-prone homelands. During Phase 2 and 3 we are likely to see the nations as-yet-unaffected by coastline flooding reach a tipping point of awareness. When the four million Americans, for example, who live within a few feet of high tide realize the risk posed by flooding (first up: Florida), the awareness of global warming could spike virtually overnight.

Until this tipping point is reached, we may continue to see the impoverished countries of the world playing guinea pig for the recalcitrant West. As of spring 2012, about one in six people worldwide lack the clean water they need; it is believed that by 2025, as Neptune finishes up its tenure in Pisces, the number will grow to half the global population. North Africa, the Middle East and South Asia are teetering on the brink of complete systems collapse around the issue. The U.N. is fully aware of the disaster; it is their own studies that gather statistics about it. But it may not be until the lack of water starts destabilizing governments that the issue's profile gets raised to the point of provoking action among the superpowers.

Neptune also represents the muse that inspires art. It may end up being the artists, not the statisticians, who play the greater role in waking humanity up to this and other burgeoning crises. Two powerful documentaries, 2011's award-winning

"The Island President" and 2012's "Last Call at the Oasis" by Jessica Yu are examples of pictures that say a thousand words. The Neptune in Pisces years are likely to see a general acceptance of the fact that if access to clean water were universally assured, fifty percent of the disease in the world could be eradicated.[10] In this regard, a rising number of clear-sighted scientists and engineers are starting to emerge; for example, the inventor Dean Kamen, who invented a box that creates a thousand liters of pure water a day, usable without major instruction, chemicals or filters.

Where there is need, there will arise human ingenuity. We will doubtless see the formation of more groups like the Women's Earth Alliance in Berkeley, whose training sessions in Africa[11] are meant "not to come in with all the answers, but to connect the dots." This group is a good example of the heart-centered approach to profound social change. Their co-director Amira Diamond understands "how fragile life is, but how possible it is to nurture [it]."

Food

Another building crisis is the degradation of farmland from chemical fertilizers, the monopolization of land for growing bio-fuels and other unsustainable agricultural practices. It is evident already that in Phase 2 and 3 the world will see more and more ecologically-sophisticated young people, trained both formally (in the environmental departments now burgeoning on college campuses) and informally in back-to-the-land lifestyles, implementing sustainable land-use techniques.

A sign of the times in this regard is the offshoot of the Occupy movement that has begun taking over vacant trash-strewn lots and planting vegetable gardens, inspired by the Brazilian Landless Workers Movement. On Earth Day 2012, the Oakland group broke into a locked and gated empty lot, roto-tilled the soil and planted turnips, carrots and broccoli. As food-related issues become more pressing globally, agriculture and political disenfranchisement will continue to be seen as linked, and their relationship to profit-driven enterprises will become clearer to more and more people.

---

[10] Yu's film maintains that half the world's hospital beds are occupied by patients with water-borne diseases.

[11] Diamond's group reports that women in sub-Saharan Africa spend 40 billion hours a year walking to fetch water.

Another example of the power of art to call attention to such issues is the 2011 award-winning documentary "Bitter Seeds." The film highlights the recent epidemic of farmer suicides in India, where traditional ways of growing cotton have been supplanted by genetically engineered methods pushed by companies like Monsanto.[12]

A sure sign of consciousness shift is when a crisis is given a name. As Phase 2 begins, social scientists have identified "suicide by economic crisis" as a global phenomenon. Awareness will continue to rise about the phenomenon of distressed small-business owners taking their own lives in the more fragile economies of Europe.

Ocean of the Mind

On the psycho-spiritual level, the Neptune-in-Pisces transit suggests the opening up of whole new vistas to the exploration of altered states of consciousness. The undersea expedition undertaken by filmmaker James Cameron – just after Neptune's ingress in February 2012 – to the very deepest spot under the ocean provides an apt metaphor for the discoveries ahead in the oceans of the mind.

Cameron described the terrain as so unfamiliar that it was like being in a whole other world. His description calls to mind an earlier such discovery that took place the last time Neptune entered Pisces, in 1847. This was when Europe was enthralled with spiritualism and other trans-physical phenomena, paving the way for Freud's discovery (that is, he recognized it and gave it a name) of the unconscious mind.

In the years between now and 2025 the conditions are ripe to take conventional psychology to its next step: to break through into more sophisticated, post-millennial understandings of the most intangible, inner dimensions of human experience. Collectively and individually we will be diving down to deeper recesses than have ever been explored.

Conclusion

If we believe that our lifetime on Earth is an educational sojourn – that we signed up for this handful of decades in the school of Terra – it follows that the future of

---

[12] As of May 2012 more than a million people had signed a petition to the US Food and Drug Administration to require labeling of genetically engineered food; twice the number who have ever commented on any food petition in the history of the FDA.

Earth cannot be understood as apart from our own growth arc. We grow, as individuals, right along with the collective of which we are a member. To believe this is to recognize the essential folly of trying to deny or avoid the challenges upon the Earth during the years upcoming.

Humanity is a sluggish creature, painfully slow to learn what it needs to learn. The essays in this book have made the case that the crises it faces right now are occurring in order to speed up this learning. To live *through our charts* is to realize that avoiding a confrontation with the world moment isn't possible. If we accept the idea that we had something to do with the decision to be alive right now, we must also accept that the crises upon the world during our lifetimes are *our* crises. They are here for us to experience. They are invitations from the cosmos to develop consciousness. That is their purpose. How can we give them less than our full awareness?

On a personal level, too, we are being provided with events that challenge us to leap boldly into a new level of mindfulness in the areas of life that really count. We must be truer to our charts than to any external ideology or socially mandated goal. Individuals whose natal charts are singled out by the Uranus-Pluto square will be feeling this challenge especially strongly; but everyone alive right now knows, on some level of awareness, that this period is the time of our lives. Let us partake in the great game afoot without getting lost in the melodrama.

Each of us has an intimate relationship with the future. The years ahead can't exist without us. I mean this not in the sense of solipsism, but in the sense that when we are fully showing up, honoring and using the unique energies that we alone personify, whatever the future blossoms into will depend upon our level of awareness as individuals. What's next is generated from what's happening Now. And Now is really all there is.

Knowing this is where our power lies.

CPSIA information can be obtained at www.ICGtesting.com
Printed in the USA
BVOW031055050713

325147BV00001B/92/P